Solveig Marie Wang
Decolonising Medieval Fennoscandia

Religious Minorities in the North: History, Politics, and Culture

Edited by
Jonathan Adams
Cordelia Heß
Christhard Hoffmann

Volume 5

Solveig Marie Wang

Decolonising Medieval Fennoscandia

An Interdisciplinary Study of Norse-Saami Relations in the Medieval Period

DE GRUYTER

We acknowledge support for the open access publication from the University of Greifswald.

ISBN 978-3-11-162477-8
e-ISBN (PDF) 978-3-11-078430-5
e-ISBN (EPUB) 978-3-11-078435-0
ISSN 2627-440X
DOI https://doi.org/10.1515/9783110784305

This work is licensed under the Creative Commons Attribution-NonCommercial-NoDerivatives 4.0 International License. For details go to https://creativecommons.org/licenses/by-nc-nd/4.0/. Creative Commons license terms for re-use do not apply to any content (such as graphs, figures, photos, excerpts, etc.) not original to the Open Access publication and further permission may be required from the rights holder. The obligation to research and clear permission lies solely with the party re-using the material.

Library of Congress Control Number: 2022950628

Bibliographic information published by the Deutsche Nationalbibliothek
The Deutsche Nationalbibliothek lists this publication in the Deutsche Nationalbibliografie; detailed bibliographic data are available on the Internet at http://dnb.dnb.de.

© 2024 with the author(s), published by Walter de Gruyter GmbH, Berlin/Boston.
This volume is text- and page-identical with the hardback published in 2023.
This book is published with open access at www.degruyter.com.

Cover image: © Museum of Cultural History, University of Oslo, Norway: C26831 Runebommehammer av horn, Photo: Johnsen, Erik Irgens. Creative Commons License CC BY-SA 4.0.

www.degruyter.com

Preface

This book investigates the relationship between Norse and Saami peoples in the medieval period and focuses on the multifaceted portrayal of Saami peoples in medieval texts. It is a result of my three years of research on Norse-Saami relations at the brilliant Centre for Scandinavian Studies at the University of Aberdeen, from 2018 to 2021. Through a systematic analysis of the source material, influenced by postcolonial methodologies rooted in interpretations of archaeological material, it demonstrates the many possibilities for reading and including Saami peoples in our narration of medieval Fennoscandian history. I first became interested in the representation of Saami history during my undergraduate studies, when I conducted an analysis of the film *Sameblod* (2016) by Amanda Kernell. While writing my undergraduate thesis on the role of women in the feud narratives of medieval Norse texts, I came across the abundant source material describing Saami characters or culture(s) and was confronted with what I felt was a misrepresentation, or lack of representation altogether, of this material. This confrontation of the material in turn led to bigger confrontations, both personally and professionally, of representation, historiography, identity, and presence.

The book consists of seven chapters, all related to the themes above. Presenting the historiographic and political background of research into Norse-Saami relations in the medieval period, chapter 1 emphasises the need for employing postcolonial methodologies in such research and its current significance. Chapter 2 considers the various sources referring to the Saami from the classical period to the late fifteenth century and provides an overview of the development of the textual motifs associated with the Saami in this textual tradition. In chapter 3, I undertake a structural analysis of how these motifs specifically allude, directly or indirectly, to the Saami. Here, I also problematise the scholarly assumptions often inherent in the discussion of these particular motifs. Chapter 4 discusses spatial relations and geopolitics, primarily focusing on northern Fennoscandia and the portrayal of different northeastern groups. In chapter 5, I cover Norse-Saami trading affairs and employ decolonising tools to provide alternative readings of the source material and again emphasise the many possibilities for interpreting this material. The opportunities for reading Saami characters are further elaborated in chapter 6, which explores personal relationships between Norse and Saami peoples as expressed in the source material. Chapter 7 combines the decolonising tools employed throughout and here I challenge the often-assumed exclusive connection between the Saami and the far north by analysing the multitude of sources pointing to medieval Saami presence in the south.

Primarily, the study demonstrates the normalised, longstanding, spatially wide-ranging, varied, and significant presence of Saami people in medieval Fennoscandia. Overall, the book is both a personal and professional confrontation of the misrepresentation of Saami history in majority history writing and the historiography of the nation state. By writing the thesis and publishing this book, I hope to be able to contribute to a growing field of scholars who are readjusting the colonial episteme and reasserting Indigenous narratives in historiography.

Contents

List of Figures —— XI

List of Abbreviations —— XIII

Acknowledgements —— XVII

Conventions —— XIX

Chapter 1:
Introduction —— 1
1.1 An Introduction to Saami-Norse Relations in the Medieval Period —— 1
1.1.1 Terminology and Chronology —— 2
1.1.2 Saami Pasts and Presents —— 8
 Historical Research, Past and Present, and Prejudice —— 13
1.2 Historiography —— 18
1.3 Postcolonialism, Archaeology, and Theoretical Framework —— 27
1.4 Summary —— 33

Chapter 2:
Classical and Medieval Written Sources on the Saami —— 34
2.1 Introduction —— 34
2.2 Classical and Early Medieval Mediterranean Sources —— 35
2.3 North European Narratives —— 36
2.3.1 Ohthere's Account —— 36
2.3.2 Adam of Bremen —— 37
2.3.3 Passio Olavi —— 39
2.3.4 Saxo Grammaticus —— 40
2.4 Legal Texts —— 41
2.4.1 Eastern Norway —— 41
2.4.2 Western Norway and Iceland —— 42
2.5 Landnámabók —— 44
2.6 Saga Literature —— 47
2.6.1 Íslendingasögur —— 50
2.6.2 Konungasögur —— 55
2.6.3 Fornaldarsögur —— 58
2.7 Other sources —— 62
2.7.1 Eddic Poetry —— 62

2.7.2 Skaldic Poetry —— 65
2.7.3 Official Documentation —— 68
2.7.4 Novgorod, Norway, and the Church —— 68
2.8 Conclusion —— 71

Chapter 3:
The Saami Motif-Cluster —— 73
3.1 Introduction —— 73
3.2 Saami Textual Images —— 74
3.2.1 Fjǫlkynngi Finna —— 74
  Saami Ritual Performance and the "Problem" with Shamanism —— 90
3.2.2 *Finnr skríðr:* Winter Weather and Skiing Deities —— 96
3.2.3 *Finns rauð gjǫld:* Archery and Hunting —— 99
3.2.4 *Sinbundit skip:* Saami Boatbuilding and Fishing Economies —— 107
3.2.5 Appearance and Accommodation —— 110
3.3 Conclusion —— 118

Chapter 4:
Northern Fennoscandian Politics and Spatial Belonging —— 119
4.1 Introduction —— 119
4.2 Northern Nóregi: Within and Without —— 120
4.2.1 Finnmǫrk —— 120
4.2.2 Hálogaland —— 130
4.3 The Extreme North? —— 135
4.3.1 Bjarmaland, Kirjálaland, and Kvenland —— 135
4.3.2 The Finnland "Paradox" and the Lappland(s) Confusion —— 143
4.4 Saami Presence in the South —— 149
4.5 Conclusion —— 149

Chapter 5:
The Saami Trade —— 151
5.1 Introduction —— 151
5.2 Finnkaup and Finnferð —— 152
5.2.1 Finnkaup: From Inheritance to Royal Privilege —— 152
5.2.2 Conflict —— 159
5.2.3 Taxation of the Saami —— 163
5.3 Western Trading Networks and Saami Perspectives —— 167
5.3.1 *Englandsfar:* Saami Exchange in England —— 168

5.3.2   Icelandic *finnkaup* —— 170
5.3.3   Saami Perspectives? —— 173
5.4   Conclusion —— 176

Chapter 6:
Liminal Identities and Fluid Spaces? Norse-Saami Personal Relationships —— 178
6.1   Introduction —— 178
6.2   Norse-Saami Personal Relationships in Literature —— 179
6.2.1   Kinship and Intimate Family Relationships —— 179
6.2.2   Business Partners, Cohabitation, and Saami Soldiers —— 190
6.2.3   "Fiðrenn svarar": Communication, Language Barriers, and Bilingualism —— 194
6.3   Both, and: Liminal Identities and the Archaeological "Inbetweeners" —— 198
6.3.1   Blended Archaeology and Blended Social Milieux? —— 199
6.3.2   Common Ground: Religion, Ritual, and Reorganisation of Identities —— 205
6.4   Conclusion —— 211

Chapter 7:
Saami in the South: Sources and Societies —— 212
7.1   Introduction —— 212
7.2   Politics, Pre-History, and the South Saami —— 213
7.3   A South Saami Archaeology? —— 218
7.4   Saami Characters in Southern Contexts —— 225
7.4.1   Fínmarkr and Saami Dwelling Spaces in the South —— 226
7.4.2   Saami Characters in the South —— 231
7.4.3   Fluidity and Saaminess —— 241
7.5   Conclusion —— 245

Reassessing Norse-Saami Relations in the Medieval Period: Conclusion —— 247

List of References —— 253
         Primary Sources —— 253
         Secondary Sources —— 257

Index —— 273

List of Figures

Figure 1 Sápmi today, by Anders Suneson. "Sápmi," Samiskt Informationscentrum, http://www.samer.se/1002 —— 3

Figure 2 Core Saami Language Location, by Veli-Pekka Lehtola. Printed in Ojala, *Prehistories*, 73, after Veli-Pekka Lehtola, *The Sámi People: Traditions in Transition* (Inari: Kustannus-Puntsi, 2004), 11. —— 10

Figure 3 Important locations referred to in this book, d-maps.com. Compiled by author. —— 120

Figure 4 Finnmǫrk and the surrounding landscapes, according to Egils saga Skallagrímssonar, d-maps.com. Compiled by author. —— 125

Figure 5 Schematic picture of the distribution of Saami (vertical) and Norse (horizontal) archaeological culture, c. 1000 by Inger Zachrisson, from *Möten i gränsland: Samer och germaner i Mellanskandinavien*, Monographs 4 (Stockholm: Statens Historiska Museum, 1997), 219. —— 201

Figure 6 Map of the South Saami area by Carl-Gösta Ojala and Karin Bengtsson, in Carl-Gösta Ojala, *Sámi Prehistories: The Politics of Archaeology and Identity in Northernmost Europe*, Occasional Papers in Archaeology 47 (Västerås: Edita Västra Aros, 2009), 142. —— 214

Figure 7 Vietjere from Rendalen, by Erik Iregren, "C26831: runebommehammer," KHM (CC BY-SA 4.02). —— 222

List of Abbreviations

Ágr	*Ágrip af Noregskonunga sǫgum* Edition: Matthew James Driscoll, ed. and trans., *Ágrip af Noregskonunga sǫgum* (London: Viking Society for Northern Research, 2008)
Án	*Áns saga bogsveigis* Edition: Carl Christian Rafn, ed. *Fornaldar sögur nordrlanda eptir gömlum handritum*, vol. 2 (Copenhagen: Ennu Popsku, 1829)
Bárð	*Bárðar saga Snæfellsáss* Edition: Þórhallur Vilmundarson and Bjarni Vilhjálmursson, eds., *Harðar saga*, Íslenzk fornrit 13 (Reykjavík: Hið íslenzka fornritafélag, 1991)
DN	*Diplomatarium Norvegicum*
Eb	*Eyrbyggja saga* Edition: Einar Ól. Sveinsson, Matthías Þorðarson, and Ólafur Halldórsson, eds., *Eyrbyggja saga*, Íslenzk fornrit 4 (Reykjavík: Hið íslenzka fornritafélag, 1985)
Eddukvæði	*Eddukvæði 1* Edition: Jónas Kristjánsson and Vésteinn Ólasson, eds., *Eddukvæði 1*, Íslenzk fornrit 36 (Reykjavík: Hið íslenzka fornritafélag, 2014)
Eg	*Egils saga Skallagrímssonar* Edition: Sigurður Nordal, ed. *Egils saga Skallagrímssonar*, Íslenzk fornrit 2 (Reykjavík: Hið íslenzka fornritafélag, 1933)
Finnb	*Finnboga saga ramma* Edition: Jóhannes Halldórsson, ed. *Kjalnesinga saga*, Íslenzk fornrit 14 (Reykjavík: Hið íslenzka fornritafélag, 1959)
Fsk	*Fagrskinna* Edition: Bjarni Einarsson, ed. *Fagrskinna*, Íslenzk fornrit 29 (Reykjavík: Hið íslenzka fornritafélag, 1985)
Fær	*Færeyinga saga* Edition: Ólafur Halldórsson, ed. *Færeyinga saga – Óláfs saga Odds*, Íslenzk fornrit 25 (Reykjavík: Hið íslenzka fornritafélag, 2006)
Gautr	*Gautreks saga* Edition: Carl Christian Rafn, ed. *Fornaldar sögur nordrlanda eptir gömlum handritum*, vol. 3 (Copenhagen: Ennu Popsku, 1830)
GHr	*Göngu-Hrólfs saga* Edition: Carl Christian Rafn, ed. *Fornaldar sögur nordrlanda eptir gömlum handritum*, vol. 3 (Copenhagen: Ennu Popsku, 1830)
Gr	*Grettis saga Ásmundarsonar* Edition: Guðni Jónsson, ed. *Grettis saga Ásmundarsonar*, Íslenzk fornrit 7 (Reykjavík: Hið íslenzka fornritafélag, 1936)
GrL	*Gríms saga loðinkinna* Edition: Carl Christian Rafn, ed. *Fornaldar sögur nordrlanda eptir gömlum handritum*, vol. 2 (Copenhagen: Ennu Popsku, 1829)
HálfdEyst	*Hálfdanar saga Eysteinssonar* Edition: Carl Christian Rafn, ed. *Fornaldar sögur nordrlanda eptir gömlum handritum*, vol. 3 (Copenhagen: Ennu Popsku, 1830)

HálfdSv Hálfdanar þáttr svarta
Edition: Peter Andreas Munch, ed. *Fornmannasögur eptir gömlum handritum*, vol. 10 (Copenhagen: Kongelige Nordiske oldsskriftselskab, 1835)

Hamburg-Bremen History of the Archbishops of Hamburg-Bremen
Edition: Adam of Bremen, *History of the Archbishops of Hamburg-Bremen*, trans., Francis Joseph Tschan (New York: Columbia University Press, 2002) [English translation]

Hammaburgensis Gesta Hammaburgensis Ecclesiae Pontificum
Edition: Adam Bremensis, *Gesta Hammaburgensis Ecclesiae Pontificum*, ed. Martin Lappenbergh (Hannover: Impensis Bibliopolii Hahniani, 1876)

Hkr 1–3 Heimskringla
Edition: Bjarni Aðalbjarnarson, ed., *Heimskringla 1–3*, Íslenzk fornrit 26–28 (Reykjavík: Hið íslenzka fornritafélag, 1941–50)

Helgisaga Helgisaga Óláfs konungs Haraldssonar
Edition: Rudolf Keyser and Carl Richard Unger, eds., *Olafs saga hins helga: En kort saga om Kong Olav den Hellige fra anden halvdeel af det tolfte aarhundrede* (Christiania: Feilberg and Landmarks Forlag, 1849)

HHábr Hauks þáttr hábrókar
Edition: Peter Andreas Munch, ed. *Fornmannasögur eptir gömlum handritum*, vol. 10 (Copenhagen: Kongelige Nordiske oldsskriftselskab, 1835)

HN Historia Norwegie
Edition: Inger Ekrem and Lars Boje Mortensen, eds., Peter Fisher, trans., *Historia Norwegie* (Copenhagen: Musueum Tusculanum Press, 2006)

Hrólf Hrólfs saga kraka
Edition: Carl Christian Rafn, ed. *Fornaldar sögur nordrlanda eptir gömlum handritum*, vol. 1 (Copenhagen: Ennu Popsku, 1829)

Hák 1–2 Hákonar saga Hákonarsonar
Edition: Þorleifur Hauksson, ed. *Hákonar saga 1–2*, Íslenzk fornrit 31–32 (Reykjavík: Hið íslenzka fornritafélag, 2013)

IA Islandske Annaler indtil 1578 (Icelandic Annals)
Edition: Gustav Storm, ed. *Islandske Annaler indtil 1578* (Kristiania: Grøndahl & Søns Bogtrykkeri, 1888)

IllGr Illuga saga Gríðarfóstra
Edition: Carl Christian Rafn, ed. *Fornaldar sögur nordrlanda eptir gömlum handritum*, vol. 3 (Copenhagen: Ennu Popsku, 1830)

Ket Ketils saga hœngs
Edition: Carl Christian Rafn, ed. *Fornaldar sögur nordrlanda eptir gömlum handritum*, vol. 2 (Copenhagen: Ennu Popsku, 1829)

Kjaln Kjalnesinga saga
Edition: Jóhannes Halldórsson, ed. *Kjalnesinga saga*, Íslenzk fornrit 14 (Reykjavík: Hið íslenzka fornritafélag, 1959)

Landnáma The Book of Settlements: Landnámabók (English translation)
Edition: Hermann Pálsson and Paul Edwards, eds., *The Book og Settlements: Landnámabók* (Manitoba: University of Manitoba Press, 2006)

Ldn Landnámabók (Old Norse version)
Edition: Jakob Benediktsson, ed. *Íslendingabók – Landnámabók*, Íslenzk fornrit 1 (Reykjavík: Hið íslenxka fornritafélag, 1968)

Ljós	Ljósvetninga saga
	Edition: Björn Sigfússon, ed. *Ljósvetninga saga*, Íslenzk fornrit 10 (Reykjavík: Hið Íslenzka fornritafélag, 1940)
Mesta 1–2	Óláfs saga Tryggvasonar en mesta
	Edition: Peter Andreas Munch, ed. *Fornmannasögur eptir gömlum handritum*, 2 vols (Copenhagen: Kongelige Nordiske oldskriftselskab, 1825–26)
Mork 1–2	Morkinskinna
	Edition: Þórður Ingi Guðjónsson, ed. *Morkinskinna 1–2*, Íslenzk fornrit 23–24 (Reykjavík: Hið Íslenzka fornritafélag, 2011)
NGL 1–3	Norges Gamle Love
	Edition: Rudolf Keyser and Peter Andreas Munch, eds., *Norges Gamle Love*, 3 vols (Christiania: Chr. Gröndahl, 1836–49)
Odds	Óláfs saga Odds
	Edition: Ólafur Halldórsson, ed. *Færeyinga saga – Óláfs saga Odds*, Íslenzk fornrit 25 (Reykjavík: Hið Íslenzka fornritafélag, 2006)
OEH	The Old English History of the World: An Anglo-Saxon Rewriting of Orosius (Ohthere)
	Edition: Malcolm R. Godden, ed. *The Old English History of the World: An Anglo-Saxon Rewriting of Orosius*, Dumbarton Oaks Medieval Library 44 (Harvard: Harvard University Press, 2016)
Orkn	Orkneyinga saga
	Edition: Hermann Pálsson and Paul Edwards, eds., *Orkneyinga saga: The History of the Earls of Orkney* (London: Penguin Classics, 1981)
Ǫrv	Ǫrvar-Odds saga
	Edition: Carl Christian Rafn, ed. *Fornaldar sögur nordrlanda eptir gömlum handritum*, vol. 2 (Copenhagen: Ennu Popsku, 1829)
Passio	A History of Norway & The Passion and Miracles of the Blessed Óláfr (Passio et miracula beati Olavi)
	Edition: Carl Phelpstead, ed. and Devra Kunin, trans., *A History of Norway & The Passion and Miracles of the Blessed Óláfr* (London: Viking Society for Northern Research, 2001)
Reyk	Reykdœla saga ok Víga-Skútu
	Edition: Björn Sigfússon, ed. *Ljósvetninga saga*, Íslenzk fornrit 10 (Reykjavík: Hið Íslenzka fornritafélag, 1940)
RN	Regesta Norvegica
Saxo	Gesta Danorum: The History of the Danes (Saxo Grammaticus)
	Edition: Saxo Grammaticus, *Gesta Danorum: The History of the Danes*, ed. Karsten Friis-Jensen, trans., Peter Fisher, vol. 1 (Oxford: Oxford University Press, 2015)
Skáldskaparmál	Edda: Skáldskaparmál
	Edition: Snorri Sturluson, *Edda: Skáldskaparmál*, ed. Anthony Faulkes, vol. 1. London (Viking Society for Northern Research, 1998)
Sv	Sverris saga
	Edition: Þorleifur Hauksson, ed. *Sverris saga*, Íslenzk fornrit 30 (Reykjavík: Hið Íslenzka fornritafélag, 2007)
StSt	Sturlaugs saga Starfsama
	Edition: Carl Christian Rafn, ed. *Fornaldar sögur nordrlanda eptir gömlum handritum*, vol. 3 (Copenhagen: Ennu Popsku, 1830)

SǫrlaSt   Sǫrla saga Sterka
          Edition: Carl Christian Rafn, ed. *Fornaldar sögur nordrlanda eptir gömlum handritum*, vol. 3 (Copenhagen: Ennu Popsku, 1830)
Vatn   *Vatnsdœla saga*
          Edition: Einar Ól. Sveinsson, ed. *Vatnsdœla saga*, Íslenzk fornrit 8 (Reykjavík: Hið íslenzka fornritafélag, 1939)

Acknowledgements

I wrote this thesis during the final years of my PhD program at the Centre for Scandinavian Studies at the University of Aberdeen and submitted and defended it in the summer of 2021. The years at the Centre were an absolute privilege and I am forever grateful. First and foremost, I extend my gratitude towards my two wonderful supervisors. I am beyond grateful for your valuable feedback and support. Hannah, thank you for supporting me from the very start (struggling with Old Norse cases and whatnot…) and for encouraging me to do the jump from being an undergraduate to a PhD candidate. Your patience, enthusiasm, expertise, and advice have been priceless, and I am incredibly thankful (hand heart!). Charlotta, thank you for the incredibly useful archaeological and postcolonial resources you have introduced me to along the way. A big thank you for all the pep talks and encouragement, and of course, the countless Kilau coffees. Tack så mycket! I truly appreciate all the effort you have both put into my project and all the kindness you have shown me, and I look forward to the next time we get to catch up. I also extend my sincere thanks to my viva examiners, Prof. Ralph O'Connor and Dr Carl-Gösta Ojala, whose input and insightful discussion during and after the viva has been incredibly valuable for the thesis itself and for myself as a researcher.

The research trips I have undertaken during my thesis would not have been possible without financial support. I extend my thanks towards the University of Aberdeen Development Trust, DHP postgraduate funding and the Centre for Scandinavian Studies. Additional thanks go to the Creating the New North research group at the University of Tromsø, who not only hosted me twice but also contributed with very productive feedback and vital input during our many discussions. I am grateful to Svenska Institutet for financing my planned research stay in Sweden, which was unfortunately cancelled due to COVID-19. To CG, thank you for offering to supervise my research in Uppsala and the enthusiasm you showed (and continue to show) for my project and research.

Furthermore, I am incredibly grateful to the Open Access pilot program for monographs at the University of Greifswald (where I find myself incredibly grateful to be employed) for receiving funding for this publication. I extend my gratitude towards my department, the Chair of Nordic History, from which parts of the funding for this publication comes from. I am very thankful, especially for all the encouragement from good colleagues. A major thanks go out to Prof. Dr Cordelia Heß for all her help with getting this process of publication going and for always encouraging me in my research (and for teaching me about feierabend and likewise, for joining in on the utepils). And cheers to my office mates! I also extend my gratitude to Henriette Hellinger, the brilliant student assistant at the Chair, who has helped out with several versions of this manuscript.

A very humble thank you goes out to the editorial team at De Gruyter, particularly Robert Forke and Dominika Herbst. I greatly appreciate your time and patience (!) and I am very much looking forward to being able to thank you in person. It has been a real pleasure working with you! Likewise, I am thankful to the editors of the series. It is a great privilege and incredibly humbling to have my work published among such wonderful company.

I extend my sincerest thanks to my supportive family, friends, and co-workers around the world, without whom this journey would have been so much harder (not to mention uneventful!). To my friends and co-workers, past and present, at the Centre for Scandinavian Studies: thank you for your academic support, but even more so, for the pints, potlucks, and the pandemic calls. To my close and wonderfully brilliant and absolutely outrageous friends Heidi, Ingrid, and Jennifer, thank you for being there for me, for everything (literally!), throughout. Y'all run the world! A special thank you goes out to my extended family up north, who very kindly accommodated "søringen" during my research trips to Troms, and to my uncle for his genuine interest in my project. To my family in Oslo: you rock (*kgid!*). Lastly, I am beyond grateful for my amazing mum (*the* Marianne). For supporting me in everything, for being a voice of reason, for always being there, and for, quite frankly, being my person. Being compared to you is the best compliment.

You all deserve a big drink, and so do I. Skål!

Conventions

This thesis does not anglicise Old Norse names, places, beings, or concepts, unless quoting from scholarly translations that employ other conventions. On first occurrence, individual Old Norse words are marked by double quotation marks, followed by an English translation in square brackets: "ǫndurdís" [skiing (female) deity]. Following its first instance, the word will be italicised and not translated (*ǫndurdís*). Placenames from the source material are maintained in their original form when specific texts or past landscape concepts are referred to (Þrǿndalǫg), but when referring to more general landscapes or contemporary places and regions, the modernised and most contemporary placename is listed (Trøndelag).

The English translations employed in the study correspond to standard scholarly editions. When no edition is referred to, translations are my own. In some modern translations of the source material, the translators have employed the term "Lapp" when translating medieval terms describing Saami peoples. As the term is considered derogatory to Saami peoples today, I have actively avoided using the term myself and the translations have therefore been altered like so: "[Saami]." The term has also been altered in direct quotations, and I have to the best of my ability employed the term "Saami" for Saami peoples throughout (see footnote 1, section 1.1). The term "Finnar" (or similar) has been altered to [Saami] in translations and when employed in direct quotations, the term appears in its first instance but is followed by [Saami]. This is partly because employing the self-designating term Saami is more in line with the suggested episteme, but also because "Finn" is used as a deliberately pejorative term for Saami peoples today. When this change from "*Finnar*" to [Saami] in direct quotations of secondary sources is made, the scholars cited have unquestionably referred to the Saami in their original quotation. The medieval term "Finnar" is not uncomplicated and may sometimes refer to other Fennoscandian groups than the Saami, such as Finnish people (see section 4.3.2), potentially also the Kvenir (see section 4.3.1) and possibly other groups, as I discuss in more detail in sections 1.1.1, 2.2, 2.3, and 4.3.2. In this thesis, as I detail further in the aforementioned sections, the term "Finnar" is primarily treated as denoting Saami peoples (with some exceptions; see section 4.3.2).

In order to avoid confusion, the present study has not adopted the new division of Norwegian counties (11 counties from 1 January 2020), and instead refers to the previous division (consisting of 19 counties). However, Trøndelag is here treated as one region for ease, rather than locating instances into the previous two counties of Nord-Trøndelag and Sør-Trøndelag. When I use the term "Finnmark" in this thesis, I refer to the Norwegian county (pre-2020), and not the medieval landscape which is referred to as Finnmǫrk, fínmarkr or Finnmarkar. Some translations, however, translate Finnmǫrk or similar to "Finnmark," and these translations have not been amended.

The thesis that this book is based on was presented for the degree of Doctor of Philosophy in Scandinavian Studies at the University of Aberdeen, School of Divinity, History and Philosophy in June 2021, and successfully defended in August 2021.

Chapter 1: Introduction

1.1 An Introduction to Saami-Norse Relations in the Medieval Period

Saami[1] people and groups were significant social and political players in medieval Fennoscandian societies.[2] Written sources from as early as the classical period and throughout the medieval period describe the Saami as expert hunters, skilled skiers, and able fishermen, distinct from, but nevertheless part of, Norse society. Sources like *Ágrip af Noregs konungasǫgum* refer to Saami settlements in the medieval period reaching far south into Norway, even incorporating Hadeland and the adjacent Swedish areas.[3] Saami presence in Iceland and in England is alluded to in a handful of sources, which alongside the Saami fur trade monopoly in eastern trading networks demonstrates the far-reaching influence of Saami societies in the medieval period. Archaeological material also supports a wide-spanning Saami settlement area,[4] beyond the current cultural and political borders of Sápmi (see section 1.1.2). Close contact between Saami and Norse groups is therefore not surprising, and trade, personal relationships like marriage and childrearing, alliances, shared ritual performance, and magic, are common themes connected to the Saami across medieval texts, particularly in the Norse sagas. Recent archaeological research focusing on liminal identities and cultural fluidity as significant factors in Norse-Saami interactions has contributed to an understanding of medieval Fennoscandia as less monocultural than previously assumed.[5] While scholarship is gradually moving away from colonial strategies treating Indigenous people as irrelevant to the study of medieval Fennoscandia in general, the rise of Far Right views and ethnocentrism has contributed to the re-emergence of formerly debunked myths like racial superiority, and strengthened monocultural inter-

---

1 For the usage of *Saami* in English, rather than the more commonly used *Sámi*, see Marte Spangen et al., eds., *Currents of Saami Pasts: Recent Advances in Saami Archaeology*, Monographs of the Archaeological Society of Finland 9 (Helsinki: Archaeological Society of Finland, 2020), 3.
2 Fennoscandia refers to the Scandinavian and Kola Peninsulas, mainland Finland, and Karelia.
3 *Ágr*, 4–6.
4 Jostein Bergstøl and Gaute Reitan, "Samer på Dovrefjell i vikingtiden: et bidrag til debatten omkring samenes sørgrense i forhistorisk tid," *Historisk tidsskrift* 87 (2008): 9–27.
5 Marte Spangen, "Silver Hoards in Sámi Areas," in *Recent Perspectives on Sámi Archaeology in Fennoscandia and North-West Russia*, ed. Petri Halinen et al. (Helsinki: Finnish Antiquarian Society, 2009), 94–106 (103).

pretations of past societies.⁶ The return of these harmful concepts represents alarming developments, and is crucial to the motivations behind this thesis. Focusing on an interdisciplinary approach through the comparative analysis of Norse texts, and relevant archaeological material from the medieval period, I demonstrate the multifaceted and cross-cultural reality of medieval Fennoscandia, and highlight the momentous role that Saami people played within this reality. By employing an archaeological framework based on postcolonial methodologies in my analysis of the textual presence and appearance of Saami characters across medieval texts, I emphasise concepts like cultural fluidity and liminality to challenge lingering colonial structures or assumptions about the role of the Saami within Norse society. In emphasising the portrayal of what can be read as Saami people, or people with Saami ties, in the source material, I explore cross-cultural relations, power relations, sociocultural and geopolitical developments, regional variation, borderlands, diversity and less defined cultural identities.

1.1.1 Terminology and Chronology

Throughout this thesis I refer to several contested terms. Ethnicity, for example, is a controversial concept and a notoriously difficult term to define.⁷ I have approached ethnic identity with Siân Jones's definition in mind: "that aspect of a person's self-conceptualisation which results from identification with a broader group in opposition to others on the basis of perceived cultural differentiation and/or common descent."⁸ Several different people inhabited Fennoscandia in the medieval period, including the Saami and the Norse. The Saami and the Norse are described in different terms, have distinctive languages and different cultural expressions, and can therefore be defined as two different ethnicities. Cultural fluidity is nevertheless apparent in several sources, and at times, defining a character or assigning archaeological material using either Norse or Saami ethnicity proves unhelpful. I have actively employed the term "cultural affiliation" rather than ethnicity in my analysis to emphasise this fluidity. By cultural affiliation, I mean the extent to which a character, or the archaeological material, is described with or

---

6 Christoffer Kølvraa, "Embodying 'the Nordic Race': Imaginaries of Viking Heritage in the Online Communications of the Nordic Resistance Movement," *Patterns of Prejudice* 53, no. 3 (2019): 270–84.
7 Carl-Gösta Ojala, *Sámi Prehistories: The Politics of Archaeology and Identity in Northernmost Europe*, Occasional Papers in Archaeology 47 (Västerås: Edita Västra Aros, 2009), 25.
8 Siân Jones, *The Archaeology of Ethnicity: Constructing Identities in the Past and Present* (London: Routledge, 1997), xiii.

1.1 An Introduction to Saami-Norse Relations in the Medieval Period — 3

Figure 1: Sápmi today, by Anders Suneson, "Sápmi," Samiskt Informationscentrum, http://www.samer.se/1002.

assigned cultural markers associated with one or both groups. For the purposes of the thesis, cultural affiliation is therefore to be understood as comparable to the concept of ethnicity and ethnic identity, but without the polarising connotations associated with ethnicity (see section 6.3). Indeed, employing the term cultural affiliation reinforces the idea that commonality is often more apparent than contrasts in the source material, perhaps demonstrating why strictly talking about ethnicity as one or the other, in certain cases, can be unproductive. It should be noted that ethnic identity does play a significant role in both past and present lives, and will have been a crucial factor also in Norse-Saami relations.[9] It does not, however, always have to have been the defining factor for these relations and this fluidity is what I aim to highlight when using the term cultural affiliation. Significantly, it should be emphasised that neither of these concepts should be understood as static, and that these concepts were and are dynamic.

---

[9] Richard Cole, "Racial Thinking in Old Norse Literature," *Saga-Book* 39 (2015): 21–40 (38). See also Basil Arnould Price, "Búi and the *blámaðr:* Comprehending Racial Others in *Kjalnesinga saga*," *Viator* 11, no. 4 (2020): 442–50.

In this thesis I employ postcolonial concepts like "liminality," "fluidity," and "decolonisation." Liminality indicates so-called "in-between" spaces and refers to a kind of intermediate space or transition.[10] When it is employed here, it is used with the meaning of identity formation in the intermediary stages between Norse and Saami cultures. Through the portrayal of characters with both Saami and Norse descent that are not assigned any specific ethnic or cultural affiliation in the texts, liminal identities appear as a kind of in-between space between Norse and Saami identities and cultures. Fluidity is a concept I have employed to contextualise the societies and identities forming as a consequence of Norse-Saami meetings, through the "mixing" of Saami and Norse cultural features and traditions, and creating a new "third room." Hybridity and creolisation are commonly used postcolonial terms referring to similar processes of ethnic or cultural "mixing." Both terms have been debated previously due to their problematic connotations with race and notions of "cross-breeding" (hybridity is originally a botanical term).[11] Generally, the terms refer to the coming together of two distinct entities and the subsequent creation of a third, distinct entity through the mixing of both. By employing the term fluidity, I refer to similar concepts, but avoid problematic connotations with race. The concept of decolonisation is further explained in section 1.3, but in short, it indicates acknowledging a majority culture's presentation of history and actively employing tools to deconstruct colonial notions embedded in this presentation of history.[12] As such, decolonising methodologies acknowledge that "research is not an innocent or distant academic exercise but an activity that has something at stake and that occurs in a set of political and social conditions."[13] The background of these conditions regarding research on Saami history is discussed in detail in section 1.1.2, but it should be emphasised here that decolonisation is an ongoing process and that the current research contributes to this ongoing process.

When employed here, the term "Indigenous" should be understood in a political context as defined in UN's ILO Convention 169 (ILO 169):

> peoples in independent countries who are regarded as Indigenous on account of their descent from the populations which inhabited the country, or a geographical region to which the country belongs, at the time of conquest or colonisation or the establishment of present

---

10 Pramod K. Nayar, *The Postcolonial Studies Dictionary* (Chichester: Wiley Blackwell, 2015), 98–99.
11 Nayar, *Postcolonial Studies*, 91, 39.
12 Walter D. Mignolo, *The Darker Side of Western Modernity: Global Futures, Decolonial Options* (Durham: Duke University Press, 2011), 10.
13 Linda Tuhiwai Smith, *Decolonizing Methodologies: Research and Indigenous Peoples*, 2nd edition (London: Zed Books, 2012), 8.

state boundaries and who, irrespective of their legal status, retain some or all of their own social, cultural and political institutions.[14]

One misunderstanding occasionally arriving in the debate about Indigeneity concerns the commonly accepted view that by being defined as "Indigenous" implies that the group in question must have been the first inhabitants of a given area. This view is incorrect, and in accordance with ILO 169, Indigeneity is not determined by being the first inhabitants of an area, but specifically the affiliation and belonging to a place at the time when present state boundaries were established by others than themselves (i.e., the "coloniser"), and that have retained some or all of their own sociocultural and political institutions. Therefore, the terms native and Indigenous are not synonymous in this thesis, as both Saami and Norwegian people, for example, are native to Norway, but only Saami people are defined as Indigenous according to ILO 169. Nevertheless, these matters are far from simple, and the connections between historical belonging or even "authenticity" prior to the "establishment of present state boundaries" and legal rights are further discussed in sections 1.3. and 7.2. These terms are not uncomplicated, and it should be mentioned that, with the above example in mind, Saami people can identify as Norwegian and Saami, and vice versa. Furthermore, it should also be noted that Indigeneity is difficult to define, and that the above definition is not meant to exclude those Indigenous groups or individuals that do not define themselves according to ILO 169.

Throughout this thesis I refer to what I call the Saami Motif-Cluster. I contextualise the term fully in chapter 3, but it should be defined in brief here. Throughout the textual tradition, Saami characters are portrayed in patterns associated with Othering,[15] primarily connotations with magic and supernatural beings,[16]

---

14 International Labour Organization, "ILO 169: Indigenous and Tribal Peoples Convention, 1989 (NO. 169)," ILO.org, http://www.ilo.org/dyn/normlex/en/f?p=NORMLEXPUB:12100:0::NO::P12100_ILO_CODE:ILO 169.
15 See section 1.2.
16 The term "supernatural" and its place in Norse studies has been debated on several occasions, but it is nevertheless a useful term when used in the broad sense. See Daniel Sävborg and Karen Bek-Pedersen, eds., *Supernatural Encounters in Old Norse Literature and Tradition* (Turnhout: Brepols, 2018), 6–8. In this book, "supernatural" incorporates portrayals involving the paranormal and magical phenomena considered to belong to the real world as well as "fantastic" phenomena belonging to stories "where the question of truth is not relevant," 8. For the term "magic" itself and understandings of the typology of magic in medieval Scandinavia, see Stephen A. Mitchell, "Scandinavia," in *The Routledge History of Medieval Scandinavia*, ed. Sophie Page and Catherine Rider (London: Routledge, 2019), 136–50. I employ Mitchell's working definition of magic as "that part of religious and social life believed to allow those with special knowledge to communicate with

hunting and archery, forest animals, and references to winter weather and skiing. These associations become stereotypes about the Saami in the textual tradition and form part of the Saami Motif-Cluster.[17] Saami characters are often, but not exclusively associated with the north, and to describe this association I employ the designation "far north." Here, the designation refers to the Fennoscandian areas above the polar circle. As I elaborate in chapter 2, the Norse terms *finn* (singular) and *finnar* (plural) are today generally understood as exonyms denoting the Saami people. While there has been some debate regarding the exonym, descriptions of livelihoods, spatial belonging, language and culture, as well as the longlasting usage of the term, particularly in Norway, strengthen the postulation that the term "finn" refers to Saami people.[18] With minor exceptions, accounted for in chapter 4, the term is here treated as denoting Saami people. The designation Fennoscandia includes Norway, Sweden, Finland, the Kola peninsula of Russia, and Russian Karelia.

Regarding chronology, I have chosen to interpret the material analysed in the thesis as belonging to either early in the medieval period, which I count from around the 800s to the 1100s (including the Viking-Age), and later in the medieval period, which I count from the 1200s to the end of the fifteenth century. This chronology is comparable to the approach taken by Judith Jesch in *The Viking Diaspora*, where she argues for the usefulness of considering the "long Viking Age" as a concept stretching from the 750s to c. 1500 based on overall continuities especially visible in the archaeological material as well as in textual sources.[19] Keith Ruiter emphasises the benefits of considering this broad timeframe of continuity in the conceptual analysis of interdisciplinary evidence-sets,[20] such as in the present thesis. While I do not treat the whole timeframe employed in the thesis as the "Viking Age," but rather refer to it as medieval (early or late), I do agree that the evidence for continuity and overall processes of continuity evident in the material, especially the texts, occurring throughout this long period should be emphasised. Most of the archaeological material employed here originates from early in the medieval

---

and acquire the supernatural assistance of otherworldly powers." I have avoided using the terms "sorcerer"/"sorcery," although I have not changed its appearance in translations.

17 As noted in section 3.1, the usage of the term "textual" is not intended to exclude the likelihood that many of the same motifs were also present in oral tradition.

18 Carl-Gösta Ojala, *Prehistories*, 32. Else Mundal, "The Perception of the Saamis and Their Religion in Old Norse Sources," in *Shamanism and Northern Ecology*, ed. Juha Pentikäinen (Berlin: De Gruyter, 1996), 97–116 (98). See section 2.2.

19 Judith Jesch, *The Viking Diaspora* (New York: Routledge, 2015), 10, 55.

20 Keith Ruiter, *Mannjafnaðr: A Study of Normativity, Transgression, and Social Pragmatism in Medieval Scandinavia* (PhD thesis, University of Aberdeen, 2018), 19–20.

period, with the majority of the textual sources originating later in the medieval period. This twofold periodisation has enabled the analysis of overall tendencies in the source material, but when appropriate and when the sources allow, I specify the century/centuries. The chronology of the archaeological material is specified when discussed, as best possible, and the chronology of the textual material is contextualised in chapter 2 as well as throughout.

The starting point of research was a methodological approach where I conducted close readings of a set list of medieval texts focusing on Fennoscandian relations, investigating whether and how Saami characters were described. Each instance was then inserted into a database (Excel), where aspects like context, characters, Saami descent, trade, magic, personal relationships, or alliances, characteristics, and attributes, features of Othering, and locations were noted. This systematic approach enabled the overall analysis of the different appearances and allowed identification of the general tendencies associated with Saami characters in these texts, as well as more detailed analysis of individual characters and specific occurrences. In turn, this approach allowed for the inclusive reading of characters or people that were otherwise not described as Saami, as possible Saami representations in the texts. This approach takes its inspiration from Lars Ivar Hansen's report from 1984 ("Skal en bare bruke kilder som omtaler samer i rekonstruksjonen av samisk fortid?"), which advocates employing historical source material that initially does not mention the Saami specifically, but can highlight Saami presence when reading between the lines.[21] The methodology of actively searching for Saami characters across these texts is admittedly subjective since I rely on my own expectations of how Saami characters are described and use similar descriptions to identify non-specified characters as affiliated with the Saami. As Sirpa Aalto and Veli-Pekka Lehtola say, "our own subjectivity and possible bias may affect the ways we think that the Saami should be represented."[22] It should therefore be stressed that while the Saami Motif-Cluster does consist of repeated textual motifs connected to Saami characters, these are never exclusive, and as will become clear, there are many different ways of reading Saami characters in the source material and Saami portrayals are both multifaceted and diverse.

The textual sources span from early in the medieval period, with Ohthere's account from the 890s being the earliest, and the *fornaldarsögur* from the later medieval period being the most recent, the youngest of which derives from the late

---

[21] Lars Ivar Hansen, "Skal en bare bruke kilder som omtaler samer i rekonstruksjonen av samisk fortid?," in *Viester-Alas: Rapport fra et seminar på Vesterålens bygdemuseum og kultursentrum*, ed. Lars Slettejord and Helge Guttormsen (Melbu [n. p.], 1984), 140–74.
[22] Sirpa Aalto and Veli-Pekka Lehtola, "The Sami Representations Reflecting the Multi-Ethnic North of the Saga Literature," *Journal of Northern Studies* 11, no. 2 (2017): 7–30 (10).

fifteenth century.[23] The texts I have employed in my main analysis include saga material, Ohthere's account, *Gesta Hammaburgensis ecclesiae pontificum*, *Passio Olavi*, *Historia Norwegie*,[24] *Gesta Danorum*, the *Borgarþingslǫg*, *Eiðsivaþingslǫg*, and *Gulaþingslǫg*, *Landnámabók*, both the Poetic and Prose Edda, and official state documents as listed in section 2.7.4 and 7.4.1. This thesis leans most heavily on saga material, as this is the most abundant in portrayals of Saami characters. The saga material covered in this thesis is divided into three commonly accepted genres, being the *Íslendingasögur*, the *konungasögur*, and the *fornaldarsögur*.[25] The relevant texts belonging to each respective genre are further contextualised in section 2.6. A starting point in recent interpretations of archaeological material from the medieval period emphasising the widespread distribution of Saami material culture and the prevalence of Norse-Saami fluid identity markers in this material has been crucial in my reading of the textual material. This starting point is further elaborated in section 1.3 and is grounded in a postcolonial framework, but in short, indicates that I employ these interpretations of the archaeological material to legitimise my own reading of the textual sources.

1.1.2 Saami Pasts and Presents

The Saami are the Indigenous people of Fennoscandia. The traditional Saami settlement area is called Sápmi, and is located within the nation states of Norway, Sweden, Finland, and in the Kola peninsula of Russia, but many Saami people live outside of this region. The borders of Sápmi have been contested throughout history, particularly in the southern areas of Norway and Sweden, and along the Bothnian coast.[26] As I emphasise throughout and discuss more closely in chapter 7, there is considerable evidence indicating that the Saami area was significantly larger in the medieval period. The fight for Saami cultural and social "revival,"

---

23 As discussed in chapter 2.
24 *Historia Norwegie* is a short Latin history of Norway, presumed to have been written in Norway sometime in the mid-to-late twelfth century (see section 3.2.1). The chronicle itself is not a saga, but it is listed among the *konungasögur* in chapter 2, for ease. See *HN*, 8–46, for an overview and discussion of the contents and structure, suggested dating and place of writing, educational background and transmission history.
25 Massimiliano Bampi, "Genre," in *The Routledge Research Companion to the Medieval Icelandic Sagas*, ed. Ármann Jakobsson and Sverrir Jakobsson (London: Routledge, 2017), 4–14 (4–5).
26 Ojala, *Prehistories*, 72.

self-determination, and legal rights has been a long process, and is still relevant.[27] In this section, I will briefly summarise this process and explain why it is relevant for historical research today.

The Saami languages belong to the Finno-Ugric language family and are structurally and etymologically different from the Nordic languages.[28] Traditionally, there are ten "living" Saami languages (figure 2), with North Saami being the most common and spoken by about 90% of the people that speak Saami on a daily basis. The languages are traditionally divided into Western Saami and Eastern Saami, and include North Saami, South Saami, Ume Saami, Pite Saami, Lule Saami, Inari Saami, Skolt Saami, Akkala Saami (the language is considered moribund), Kildin Saami, and Ter Saami.[29] The variation in Saami languages is "an important reminder that 'the Saami' is not a homogenous entity, neither in the present nor in the past."[30] This recognition is significant for our understanding of Saami societies in the medieval period as regionally varied and linguistically diverse. It should also be emphasised that past and present Saami livelihoods and subsistence strategies have been diverse and regionally varied, and include but are not limited to whaling, fishing, forestry, reindeer herding, farming, and hunting.

While the Saami are, for the most part, officially recognised as Indigenous people today, with variable legal and cultural rights across Sápmi, this has not always been the case. With increasing expansion into Saami settlement areas throughout the medieval period, as discussed in chapters 4 and 5, the emerging states of Norway and Sweden and the Novgorod Republic gradually colonised Saami areas by implementing official institutions in order to gain access to natural resources and the Saami trade, in a political power play manifested in geopolitical expansion. These developments meant that Saami people were increasingly incorporated, to some extent, into the nation states as royal subjects. Although severe colonial practices were administered as a result of these developments in the following early modern period, such as mission work and destruction of Saami religious items, the nineteenth century witnessed a marked shift in colonial strategies. With the slogan "lapp ska vara lapp" [the Saami shall remain Saami], the Swedish state initiated segregationist policies directed at the reindeer herding Saami in the nineteenth century "for them to survive as nomads in the modern world" and be protected against "civilisation."[31] These reindeer herders were not permitted to build permanent settlements and so-called "nomad schools" were established

---

27 Ojala, *Prehistories*, 98.
28 Store norske leksikon, "Samisk," snl.no, 12.12.20 https://snl.no/samisk.
29 "Samisk."
30 Ojala, *Prehistories*, 73.
31 Ojala, *Prehistories*, 94.

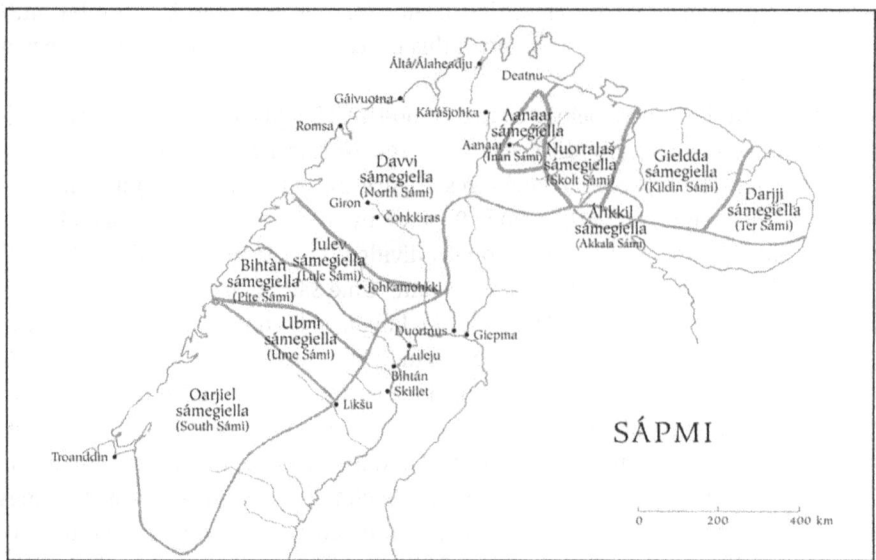

Figure 2: Core Saami Language Location, by Veli-Pekka Lehtola. Printed in Ojala, *Prehistories*, 73, after Veli-Pekka Lehtola, *The Sámi People: Traditions in Transition* (Inari: Kustannus-Puntsi, 2004), 11.

for their children.[32] Another policy employed by the Swedish state was assimilative and directed at non-reindeer-herding Saami. According to the Swedish government, these people were not "authentic Saami people" and were forcibly assimilated into Swedish society through active interventions like forced schooling and relocation.[33] These policies have very clearly affected the Saami population in Sweden today, who prior to 1992 had to be reindeer herders and live in so-called Saami villages in order to gain legal rights as Indigenous people in Sweden. In Norway, the main political strategy from the 1850s onwards was the "fornorskningspolitikk" [Norwegianisation policy], which was built on the assumption that "a Norwegian Norway is a better Norway" and was directed towards the Saami, Kven, and Forest Finn populations.[34] The policy was manifested through forced Christianisation of the Saami population which involved the destruction of ritual objects, forced relocation and assimilation into Norwegian society and obligatory school-

---

[32] The South Saami-Swedish film *Sameblod* revolves around the emotional turmoil of these nomad-schools. *Sameblod*, directed by Amanda Kernell (Nordisk Film, 2016).
[33] Ojala, *Prehistories*, 94.
[34] Ketil Zachariassen, "Fornorskningspolitkken overfor samar og kvenar," Norgeshistorie, 02.02. 2020 https://www.norgeshistorie.no/industrialisering-og-demokrati/1554-fornorskingspolitikken-overfor-samar-og-kvenar.html.

ing. The forced Norwegian schooling, where Saami languages were altogether forbidden to be used in the classroom, is still a very sensitive topic for many, since the policy was only partially repealed in the 1950s and has therefore had detrimental effects on people alive today. A particularly damaging result of the policy was the communication gap it created between children and their own parents, and thereby the gap it created between Saami people and their cultural heritage and kin.[35] Simultaneously, Saami people were increasingly removed from the legal arena and lost hunting, herding, land and fishing rights. Strict policies of segregation and assimilation were also in place in the Kola Saami areas in Russia.[36]

At the beginning of their implementation, the policies were primarily grounded in territorial disputes between three nations wishing to consolidate notions of identity and historical belonging, necessitating clear-cut border agreements. With the growth of Social Darwinism, eugenics and race-biological research in the late nineteenth century, Saami people were increasingly viewed as "static nature people that would not survive the meeting with or benefit from a modern 'civilised' and industrialised life."[37] These theories sought to "separate humans into racial categories and place them on an evolutionary scale from the most 'primitive' to the most 'civilised' based on physioanthropological features."[38] Social Darwinism is here understood as the scientific theory and popular belief that mentality and behavioural patterns were "'inscribed' in people as the result of biological origins."[39] Ethnographic research on the Saami developed and became a popular academic field in the late nineteenth century in an attempt to figure out the "mystery" of the static "Stone Age" people and to create a systematic categorisation of Saami and Nordic racial characteristics in order to fully distance the superior "Nordic race" from the inferior Saami.[40] This dehumanising research was conducted through skull measurements from living Saami individuals as well as from skeletal material from Christian and pre-Christian burials. As Lars Ivar Hansen and

---

35 Zachariassen, "Fornorskningspolitkk."
36 See Anna Afanasyeva, *Forced Relocations of the Kola Sámi People: Background and Consequences* (MA diss., University of Tromsø, 2013), and Mikkel Berg-Nordlie, "Two Centuries of Russian Sámi Policy: Arrangements for Autonomy and Participation Seen in Light of Imperial, Soviet and Federal Indigenous Minority Policy," *Acta Borealia* 33, no. 1 (2015): 40–67.
37 Marte Spangen, *Circling Concepts: A Critical Archaeological Analysis of the Notion of Stone Circles as Sami Offering Sites*, Stockholm Studies in Archaeology 70 (Malmö: Holmbergs, 2016), 109.
38 Norwegian National Human Rights Institution Reports, "A Human-Rights Based Approach to Sámi Statistics in Norway," NHRI, 26.08.2020 https://www.nhri.no/en/2020/a-human-rights-based-approach-to-sami-statistics-in-norway/.
39 Lars Ivar Hansen and Bjørnar Olsen, *Hunters in Transition: An Outline of Early Sámi History*, The Northern World 63 (Leiden: Brill, 2014), 10.
40 Hansen and Olsen, *Hunters*, 12–14 (19).

Bjørnar Olsen assert, "the investigations were frequently done in such a way that the Saami found them offensive and degrading."[41]

An organised Saami ethnopolitical movement emerged at the start of the twentieth century.[42] A particularly important voice in this movement was Elsa Laula-Renberg, who published the book *Inför Lif eller Död? Sanningsord i de Lappska förhallandena* [Facing Life or Death? Words of Truth Regarding the Saami Situation] in 1904. Dealing with issues like harmful stereotypes, problems connected to land ownership, and educational and political rights, the book was a political response to the government policies of assimilation and the increasing popularity of Social Darwinism.[43] Laula-Renberg also organised the first Saami National Assembly, held in Tråante (Trondheim) in 1917. Other significant factors of the ethnopolitical movement were the publications of literary and poetic works written by Saami people, which contributed to the visibility of the Saami struggle and Saami culture.[44] Following the Second World War, Social Darwinism and other theories based on claims of racial supremacy were increasingly discredited. However, the assumption that the Saami people look a certain way is still prevalent,[45] and skull measurements were used by academics as recently as the 1980s to differentiate between "Norse" and "Saami" archaeological remains.[46] The 1970s witnessed the so-called Saami "renaissance," with a new generation of Saami artists reinterpreting and reviving Saami identities and cultural expressions in a modern framework.[47] The Alta-controversy of the late 1970s and early 1980s introduced national and international attention to the Saami case. While the protests and acts of civil obedience against the creation of a hydroelectric power plant in the Alta river were unsuccessful and the station was completed in 1987, it is widely acknowledged that the protests directly resulted in better legal and social terms for Saami people

---

41 Hansen and Olsen, *Hunters*, 19.
42 Ojala, *Prehistories*, 98.
43 Elsa Laula-Renberg, *Inför Lif eller Död? Sanningsord i de Lappska förhallandena* (Stockholm: Wilhemssons Boktryckeri, 1904).
44 Ojala, *Prehistories*, 98–99.
45 See for example Nils Johan Eira, *Negative Discourse in Social Medias: An Analysis of Hate Speech in the Saami Context* (Kautokeino: Sámi allaskuvla, 2019).
46 Lars Fredrik Stenvik, "Samer og nordmenn: Sett i lys av et uvanlig gravfunn fra Saltenområdet," in *Viking*, ed. Sverre Marstrander and Arne Skjølsvold, Norsk arkeologisk årbok, vol. 43 (Oslo: Norsk Arkeologiske Selskap, 1980), 127–39. Stenvik writes: "this is an extreme short skull [kortskalle], obviously Saami," 129 (my translation). While this description is problematic, Stenvik questions assumptions about cultural belonging as based on ethnic categorisation of archaeological material and emphasises that the Saami played a bigger role in the medieval period than previously assumed.
47 Ojala, *Prehistories*, 99.

in Norway. The last couple of decades have seen a further reinvention of Saami identities through increased presence on the public scene. Significant contributors to this reinvention include but are not limited to NRK Sápmi, the bands Keiino, Biru Baby, and Ísak, artists like Nils-Aslak Valkeapää, Mari Boine, Jon Henrik Fjällgren, Maxida Märak, and Sofia Jannok, films like *Ofelaš* (1987), *Sameblod* (2016), and even *Frozen 2* (2019), and youth organisations like *Samiske veivisere* [Saami Pathfinders], online resources like the Saami dictionary (https://sanit.oahpa.no/about/), and the NRK-podcast *Tett På*, among many other contributions.

Historical Research, Past and Present, and Prejudice
The processes mentioned above are essential to emphasise since they occurred recently and are still relevant for the majority of Saami people today. The processes are also significant to emphasise as historical research has been complicit in discrimination against the Saami, and in some ways still contributes to colonial strategies that undermine the notion that the Saami have a historical presence in Fennoscandia (here termed Saami historicity).[48] For example, I would argue that historian Andreas M. Hansen's bigoted statement about the Saami from 1907 can help demonstrate the extent to which colonial strategies continue to pervade historical research on the Saami. Within Hansen's racism lies the supposition that the *finnar* of medieval texts could not be portrayals of the Saami precisely because these *finnar* were positively described:

> While the dwarfish Lapps[49] [Saami] with their frail limbs, and their conspicuous inferiority, must always have stood out, as now, simply as an object of the Norwegians' contempt, the respect with which the Norsemen speak of the ancient Finns is understandable enough... they were not feeble dwarves but of medium height, strong and healthy hunters, unlike the Aryan farmers... They caught whales and walrus from small boats – of which the [Saami], who to this day are poor seamen, are unlikely to have been capable of [. . .]. The fact that the hunting

---

48 See Carl-Gösta Ojala, "Discussion: Colonialism Past and Present: Archaeological Engagements and Entanglements," in *The Sound of Silence: Indigenous Perspectives on the Historical Archaeology of Colonialism*, ed. Tiina Äikäs and Anna-Kaisa Salmi (New York: Berghahn Books, 2019), 182–201. For a recent debate, see Ánde Somby and Øyvind Ravna, "Problematisk perspektiv om det samiske fra NRK," Khrono, 18.12.2021 https://khrono.no/problematisk-perspektiv-om-det-samiske-fra-nrk/642798; Ketil Zachariassen, "Samisk historie – historiefagets oppgåve og funksjon," Nordnorsk debatt, 21.12.2021 https://www.nordnorskdebatt.no/samisk-historie-historiefagets-oppgave-og-funksjon/o/5-124-156793; Steinar Pedersen, "Opptaket som aldri ble sendt," Nordnorsk debatt, 22.12.2021 https://www.nordnorskdebatt.no/opptaket-som-aldri-ble-sendt/o/5-124-157086.
49 The exonym "Lapp" is considered a derogatory term by the Saami today, and I am therefore avoiding its usage from this point onwards. The usage of the term in recent translations of Norse texts like Alison Finlay and Anthony Faulkes' *Heimskringla* clearly demonstrate the need for postcolonial frameworks in Norse studies.

and trapping Finns seem chiefly to have chosen to reside at the very edge of the open sea clearly does not harmonize with the natural inclinations of the [Saami].⁵⁰

Hansen here acknowledges that the *finnar* are ascribed positive attributes across Norse texts.⁵¹ However, while scholars today generally agree that the *finnar* represent the Saami, the understanding of medieval portrayals of Saami people in present day scholarship is in my view stereotypically negative.⁵² Jeremy DeAngelo, for example, writes:

> the great majority of them [the Saami] are depicted negatively, if not outwardly hostile to the Norse then otherwise foreboding ill through their presence. Moreover, there is no admirable individual among them in the corpus of sagas who counterbalances the prevailing stereotypical portrayal.⁵³

Both DeAngelo and Phil Cardew argue that this perceived "negative" portrayal of Saami characters is founded in the need of medieval Icelanders to portray "someone worse off than themselves."⁵⁴ Sirpa Aalto claims that in Heimskringla, the Saami appear as an "outsider-group" that "invariably represent a negative aspect and [...] they seem to have a position as a marginal-group."⁵⁵ In my opinion, the statements above represent a paradox in historical research on the medieval Saami. This paradox is manifested in the fact that, while Hansen could not read the *finnar* as Saami because they were given positive attributes, scholars today

---

50 Andreas Martin Hansen, *Oldtidens Nordmænd: Ophav og Bosætning* (Kristiania: Cammermeyer, 1907), 134. Translated in Hansen and Olsen, *Hunters*, 17.
51 Notably, Hansen also completely disregards the long history of Saami people living by the coast and the Sea Saami communities. This is a result of the forceful policies of assimilation of Sea Saami communities. See Cathrine Baglo, "The Disappearance of the Sea Sámi as a Cultural Display Category: Assimilation Policies and the Role of Industrial Expositions," *The Journal of Nordic Museology* [special issue: From Lappology to Sámi Museology] 27, no. 3 (2019): 25–44, and Steinar Pedersen, "The Coastal Sámi of Norway and Their rights to Traditional Marine Livelihood," *Arctic Review on Law and Politics* 3, no. 1 (2012): 51–80.
52 See Thomas DuBois, "Encounters: Sámi," in *The Pre-Christian Religions of the North: History and Structures*, ed. Jens Peter Schjødt, John Lindow, and Anders Andrén (Turnhout: Brepols, 2020), 353–72 (359–64).
53 Jeremy DeAngelo, "The North and the Depiction of the 'Finnar' in the Icelandic Sagas," *Scandinavian Studies* 83, no. 3 (2010): 257–86 (264–65).
54 DeAngelo, "North." Phil Cardew, "'Mannfögnuður er oss at smjöri þessu': Representations of the Finns within the Icelandic Sagas," in *Text and Nation: Essays on Post-Colonial Cultural Politics*, ed. Andrew Blake and Jopi Nyman (Joensuu: Joensuun Yliopisto, 2001), 146–58.
55 Sirpa Aalto, "Alienness in *Heimskringla*: Special Emphasis on the Finnar," in *Scandinavia and Christian Europe in the Middle Ages: Papers of the 12ᵗʰ International Saga Conference, Bonn/Germany, 28th July 2003*, ed. Rudolf Simek and Judith Meurer (Bonn: Universität Bonn, 2003), 1–7 (2, 6).

read the *finnar* as Saami but predominantly argue that these are ascribed negative attributes in medieval texts. This paradox, I would argue, is to some extent based on lingering remnants of colonial strategies that pervade historiography on the Saami, and as I emphasise throughout, I do not agree with the reading that Saami characters are exclusively negatively portrayed in medieval texts. These aspects are further contextualised in section 1.3. Johan Höglund and Linda Andersson Burnett state that "scholars tied to the field of Scandinavian Studies appear to have been particularly reluctant to engage with the notion of Nordic colonialism."[56] Carl-Gösta Ojala addresses this reluctancy and writes that archaeologists (and by extent historians) working with Indigenous (and Saami) contexts

> must never forget that we are dealing with histories of conquest, violence, oppression, exploitation, relocation, assimilation, discrimination, racism, appropriation and erasure of culture, language, history and heritage – histories with very real consequences and effects on the social, cultural, and economic lives and the well-being and health of Indigenous communities today.[57]

Simultaneously, he adds, as scholars we also need to acknowledge another dimension of these histories, namely "Indigenous agency and Indigenous strategies for resistance and survival through times of great pressure and change."[58] It is therefore important to emphasise that there is an active positive change taking place in historical and archaeological research, where the role of Saami characters as active agents of their own is being emphasised and colonial assumptions are increasingly debunked in current academic research. These positive developments are direct results of the growth of Indigenous Studies as an independent field, and the contributions of Sámi and Indigenous scholars that have actively sought to decolonise historical narratives.[59] As I will elaborate in section 1.2, this change is mainly taking place in smaller fields of historical and archaeological research, and more inclusion in general and large-scale historical compilations is necessary. This inclu-

---

56 Johan Höglund and Linda Andersson Burnett, "Introduction: Nordic Colonialisms and Scandinavian Studies," *Scandinavian Studies* [special issue: Nordic Colonialisms] 91, nos 1–2 (2019): 1–12 (2).
57 Ojala, "Colonialism Past and Present," 182.
58 Ojala, "Colonialism Past and Present," 182.
59 For an overview of this development, see Pirjo Kristiina Virtanen, Pigga Keskitalo and Torjer Olsen, "Contemporary Indigenous Research Within Sámi and Global Indigenous Studies Contexts," in *Indigenous Research Methodologies in Sámi and Global Contexts*, Pirjo Kristiina Virtanen, Pigga Keskitalo, and Torjer Olsen, ed. New Research – New Voices 2 (Leiden: Brill, 2021), 7–23. See also Tarren Andrews, "Indigenous Futures and Medieval Pasts. An Introduction," *English Language Notes* 58, no. 2 (2020): 1–17.

sion is essential since Saami historicity or sources for Saami history (or a lack thereof) are used by certain groups to disadvantage Saami peoples today.[60]

It is precisely because Saami rights to land and water, questions of Indigeneity, and perceived "privileges" are still disputed and heavily debated across the nation states that historicity is a sensitive and challenged topic in the public and political debate.[61] Historical research is intricately interwoven in these debates, and historicity, or lack thereof, has been employed in legal cases to either argue for or against Saami rights to land, water or privileges within an area.[62] In early 2020, the Swedish Supreme Court ruled in favour of the Girjas Saami village's claims for exclusive hunting and fishing rights within their area in Gällivare.[63] The ruling was based on the Saami presence and management of the area "from time immemorial" and is likely to positively affect similar court rulings in the future. Sadly, the court case has provoked hostilities between the Saami and the non-Saami locals, with online harassments, direct threats and the mutilation and killing of reindeer.[64] Nevertheless, cases like that of the continued plans for the iron ore in Gállok (Swedish Sápmi) and the Fosen verdict (Norwegian Sápmi), industrial projects initiated by the nation states on Saami land, demonstrate the continued complexities of land rights within Sápmi.

The everyday discrimination against Saami peoples received increased interest in late 2020, following the harassment of a young Saami woman on a bus in Tromsø. In addition to increased public awareness and a social media campaign ("#doarváidál"), a joint research project between the Equality and Anti-Discrimination Ombud and the Saami Parliament of Norway was initiated as a result, with the goal of documenting harassment of young Saami people and to establish a national framework for dealing with matters relating to the discrimination against Saami

---

60 Trond Gabrielsen and Finnmark Forlag are good examples of this active opposition to Saami historicity.
61 Criticism has been directed towards the nation states for employing stereotypical Saami motifs to promote national tourism; Dan Robert Larsen, "Bruker reinsdyr og joik i markedsføring – men samisk navn vil ikke kommunen ha," NRK Sápmi, 10.10.2020 https://www.nrk.no/sapmi/narvik-kommune-bruker-samiske-elementer-i-markedsforing-av-vm-_vil-ikke-ha-samisk-navn-pa-kommunen-1.15180866, and Eilís Quinn, "How Not To Promote Arctic Tourism: Why Finland's Indigenous Sami Say Marketing Their Region Needs To Change," Eye on the Arctic, 03.02.2020 https://www.rcinet.ca/eye-on-the-arctic-special-reports/how-not-to-promote-arctic-tourism-why-finlands-Indigenous-sami-say-marketing-their-region-needs-to-change/.
62 See section 7.2.
63 Sveriges Domstolar, "Mål: T 853–18, Girjasdomen," Domstol.se, 01.01.2020 https://www.domstol.se/hogsta-domstolen/avgoranden/2020/47294/, 43–50.
64 Spangen et al., *Saami Pasts*, 9.

people in Norway.⁶⁵ The establishment of the Truth and Reconciliation Commission by the Norwegian Parliament in 2018 (with an official report due in 2022) is another positive development. The commission, consisting of twelve professionals, including historians, seeks to 1) survey the Norwegian government's politics and treatment of the Saami, Kven, and Forest Finns both locally, regionally and nationally, 2) examine the effects and consequences of the Norwegianisation policies, and 3) suggest measures contributing to further reconciliation.⁶⁶ A similar commission was initiated in Finland in October 2021, with the purposes stated as 1) identify and assess historical and current discrimination, including state assimilation policy, and violations of rights, 2) find out how these injustices affect the Saami people and their communities today, 3) propose ways to promote links between the Saami and the state of Finland among the Saami people, and 4) to raise awareness about the Saami as the Indigenous people of Finland.⁶⁷ In November 2021, the Swedish Government announced the initiation of the Truth Commission to investigate the abuses of the Saami peoples by the Swedish state. Reconciliation is a complicated theme, and Rauna Kuokkanen has recently problematised aspects of reconciliation and settler colonial policy making in Finland from a Saami perspective.⁶⁸

Continued outrage among the majority of people and a sustained debunking of problematic views based on historical falsehoods means that those questioning Saami presence or historicity are increasingly being challenged and their voices decreasing in power.⁶⁹ In order for the positive developments to continue and take root, also in academia, we need to repeatedly emphasise the responsibility in-

---

65 Mette Ballovara and Dan Robert Larsen, "Vil forske på samehets," NRK Sápmi, 18.12.20 https://www.nrk.no/sapmi/likestillings-og-diskrimineringsombud-tar-abid-raja-pa-ordet-_-vil-forske-pa-samehets-1.15291942.
66 UiT, "Sannhets- og forsoningskommisjonen," https://uit.no/kommisjonen.
67 SDTSK, "Truth and Reconciliation Commission Concerning the Sámi People," SDTSK.fi, https://sdtsk.fi/en/home/.
68 Rauna Kuokkanen, "Reconciliation as a Threat or Structural Change? The Truth and Reconciliation Process and Settler Colonial Policy Making in Finland," *Human Rights Review* 21, no. 3 (2020): 293–312.
69 See for example Jarl Hellesvik, "Er samene i Norge urfolk?," Utrop, 01.11.2020 https://www.utrop.no/plenum/ytringer/232630/. Hellesvik is the leader of the independent interest organisation EDL which works to promote what they believe is unjust treatment of Norwegian people on the basis of preferential treatment of the Saami as Indigenous peoples. Saami politician Runar Myrnes Balto responded with an article claiming that EDL were spreading harmful conspiracy theories about Saami people. Both articles received massive attention in late 2020; Runar Myrnes Balto, "Organisasjonen EDL sprer farlige konspirasjonsteorier om samer," Utrop, 09.11.2020 https://www.utrop.no/plenum/ytringer/234081/?fbclid=IwAR31b7U4dtiOs3j2a_Hj-OeKZ-KKlJD4E4o5SDF_zgd3WZ5ps_JKw5lNNJs.

herent in how we interpret and disseminate our research. Within this emphasis lies the acknowledgement that active work to dismantle colonial structures pervading the fields of Viking-Age and Medieval Studies is needed in order to arrive at fairer and more inclusive presentations of history. The present thesis aims to conduct this active work through readjusting the current episteme (present in scholarship) by using a set methodology influenced by postcolonial frameworks and to contribute to the decolonisation of the field. The following sections discuss the current episteme associated with the Saami in the field of Medieval and Norse Studies and elaborate on the necessity to readjust this (1.2), after which I clarify the research backgrounds of the postcolonial frameworks that have influenced the present study (1.3).

1.2 Historiography

The standard narrative presented in older historical and archaeological research focused on the Saami was founded on a dualistic understanding of medieval Scandinavia, portraying Saami hunting societies as inferior subjects of exploitation by Scandinavian chieftains.[70] Reinforced by deep-rooted colonial structures and the assumptions mentioned above, the Saami of the medieval texts were often treated as static and thereby, as ethnographic rather than historical actors. Following the wider postcolonial discourse introduced in the late 1970s,[71] researchers concentrating on interdisciplinary methods challenged the dualist model throughout the 1980s, claiming that Saami and Norse societies mostly interacted in mutually beneficial ways during the medieval period.[72] A significant factor that led to this development was the discussion of Saami prehistory, particularly in the south, between Knut Bergsland and Jørn Sandnes in the Norwegian historical journal *Historisk Tidsskrift* in the early 1970s.[73] Historiography on the Saami and their re-

---

[70] Bjørnar Olsen, "Belligerent Chieftains and Oppressed Hunters?: Changing Conceptions of Inter-Ethnic Relationships in Northern Norway During the Iron Age and Early Medieval Period," in *Identities and Cultural Contacts in the Arctic: Proceedings from a Conference at the Danish National Museum Copenhagen, November 30 to December 2 1999*, ed. Martin Appelt, Joel Berglund, and Hans Christian Gulløv (Copenhagen: Danish National Museum and Danish Polar Center, 2000), 28–42 (28).
[71] See section 1.3.
[72] Olsen, "Oppressed Hunters?," 29. Audhild Schanche, *Nordnorsk jernalderarkeologi: Et sosialgeografisk perspektiv* (MA diss., University of Tromsø, 1986).
[73] Knut Bergsland, "Om middelalderens Finnmarker," *Historisk tidsskrift* 49, no. 4 (1970): 365–409. Jørn Sandnes, "Om samenes utbredelse mot sør i eldre tid," *Historisk tidsskrift* 52, no. 3 (1972):

lationships with Norse people has slowly expanded since the 1980s, with writers such as Inger Zachrisson, Lars Ivar Hansen, Else Mundal, Håkan Rydving, Sirpa Aalto, Thomas DuBois, and Neil Price investigating the Saami presence in the medieval period and their corresponding portrayal in Norse texts.[74] The emergence of postcolonial scholarship and the associated growth into Indigenous Studies has fostered enthusiasm about Saami presence in the Norse world as well as Saami influence on Norse society (and vice versa).[75] An increasing corpus of work focusing on Saami influence on Norse society is appearing in different disciplines and in public history presentations,[76] demonstrating the importance of interdisciplinarity in the study of Norse-Saami relations.[77] This importance was stressed as early as 1964 during a conference organised by the Institute for Comparative Research in Human Culture at the University of Oslo.[78] Despite the growing awareness of more neutral and liminal relationships between the Saami and the Norse in the medieval period, in addition to the abundance of medieval sources referring to the Saami, historical research committed to investigating the multifaceted relationship between the groups has to date remained small-scale. Thomas DuBois notes: "Often, it is as if the presence of the [...] Saami of mainland Scandinavia [...] is simply a given, taken notice of only when these peoples directly intrude into the

---

113–37. Knut Bergsland, "Synsvinkler i samisk historie," *Historisk tidsskrift* 53 (1974): 1–36 (25). Jørn Sandnes, "Sørsamenes eldre historie igjen," *Historisk tidsskrift* 53 (1974): 415–21.

74 Mundal, "Perception." Håkan Rydving, "Scandinavian-Saami Religious Connections in the History of Research," *Scripta Instituti Donneriani Aboensis* 13 (1990): 358–73. Sirpa Aalto, "Finnar in Old Norse Sources," in *Viking Age in Åland: Insight into Identity and Remnants of Culture*, ed. Joonas Ahola, Frog, and Jenni Lucenius (Helsinki: Finnish Academy of Science and Letters, 2015), 199–226. DuBois, "Encounters." Neil Price, "Drum-Time and Viking Age: Sámi-Norse Identities in Early Medieval Scandinavia," in *Identities and Cultural Contacts in the Arctic: Proceedings from a Conference at the Danish National Museum Copenhagen, November 30 to December 2 1999*, ed. Martin Appelt, Joel Berglund, and Hans Christian Gulløv (Copenhagen: Danish National Museum and Danish Polar Center, 2000), 12–27.

75 See Pirjo Kristiina Virtanen, Pigga Keskitalo, and Torjer Olsen, eds., *Indigenous Research Methodologies in Sámi and Global Contexts*, New Research – New Voices 2 (Leiden: Brill, 2021).

76 Elin Myhre, "Sørreisa: en del av jarledømmet Hålogaland og Namdalen?," in *Årbok for Dyrøy og Sørreisa*, ed. Elin Myhre, Årbok for Dyrøy og Sørreisa, vol. 18 (Lierskogen: RennessanseMedia AS, 2019), 13–25.

77 Language: Ante Aikio, "On Germanic-Saami Contacts and Saami Prehistory," *Suomalais-Ugrilaisen Seuran Aikakauskirja* 91 (2006): 9–55. Archaeology: Ingela Bergman et al., "Stones in the Snow: A Norse Fur Traders' Road into Sami Country," *Antiquity* 81, no. 312 (2007): 397–408. Literature: Aalto and Lehtola, "Representations."

78 *Lapps and Norsemen in Olden Times*, Instituttet for Sammenlignende Kulturforskning Serie A: Forelesninger XXVI (Oslo: Universitetsforlaget, 1967).

events of the saga."⁷⁹ While Saami archaeology has become more or less an established field, the role of the Saami in medieval texts is still, I would argue, considered niche in Medieval Studies. By this I mean that outside certain scholarly environments, and in the general field of Medieval Studies, the Saami are, and have been, underrepresented.

In the past couple of years, there has been an increased emphasis on incorporating postcolonial frameworks into the field of medieval history and to recognise the need for the dismantlement of the oppressive and racist systems in which Norse (and Medieval) Studies unavoidably contributes to given the nature of its subject matter.[80] This need has been drastically aggravated by the rise of movements that "obsess over the myth of a monolithic White Middle Ages and use it to justify their violence."[81] This call to distance the field from and actively confront the misappropriation of the medieval source material by these damaging movements are important factors for the continuation of the field as relevant and valuable for modern day society.[82] At the same time, the need to expressively confront the deeply rooted racist, colonialist, and Eurocentric structures of our field itself have also been called for.[83] As I detail further below, I would argue that the upholding of these structures from within the field is crucial for understanding the historiographic portrayal of the Saami as the "Other." Postcolonial frameworks have been increasingly adopted into other aspects of medieval history and Norse studies,[84] explicitly introduced by Fredrik Svanberg's influential but controversial archaeological study of Viking Age burials from South Scandinavian provinces.[85] For example, decolonising methods have been increasingly incorporated into the study of the so-called Vínland narrative, where new interpretations of the Indige-

---

79 Thomas DuBois, *Nordic Religions in the Viking Age* (Pennsylvania: University of Pennsylvania Press, 1999), 12.
80 Sierra Lomuto, "Becoming Postmedieval: The Stakes of the Global Middle Ages," *postmedieval: a journal of medieval cultural studies* 11, no. 4 (2020): 503–12.
81 Eduardo Ramos, "Confronting Whiteness: Antiracism in Medieval Studies," *postmedieval: a journal of medieval cultural studies* 11, no. 4 (2020): 493–502 (493).
82 Mary Rambaran-Olm, M. Breann Leake, and Mica James Goodrich, "Editor's Introduction. Medieval Studies: The Stakes of the Field," *postmedieval: a journal of medieval cultural studies* 11, no. 4 (2020): 356–70. Adam Miyashiro, "Our Deeper Past: Race, Settler Colonialism, and Medieval Heritage Politics," *Literature Compass* 16 (2019): 1–11.
83 Lomuto, "Becoming Postmedieval," 305–6.
84 Christopher Crocker, "What We Talk About When We Talk About Vínland: History, Whiteness, Indigenous Erasure, and the Early Norse Presence in Newfoundland," *Canadian Journal of History/Annales Canadiennes D'Histoire* 55, nos 1–2 (2020): 91–122.
85 Fredrik Svanberg, *Decolonizing the Viking Age*, Acta archaeologica Lundensia 8, 43, vol. 1 (Uppsala: Almqvist & Wiksell, 2006).

nous characters portrayed as inhabitants of Vínland (North America) in medieval texts, as well as archaeolgical excavations at the alleged Norse settlement site at L'Anse aux Meadows on Newfoundland, have been called for.[86] Despite these developments, postcolonial frameworks have, to my knowledge, yet to be employed when dealing with Saami characters in Norse texts. It should therefore be noted that postcolonial approaches to the medieval Fennoscandian past and Saami (pre)histories have been driven by archaeological analysis such as Carl-Gösta Ojala's examination of the politics of archaeology and identity in northernmost Scandinavia (2009).[87] The role of Saami archaeology and the employment of postcolonial frameworks are more closely discussed in section 1.3 and form significant foundations for sections 6.3 and 7.3. In the following, I briefly present some of the historical scholarship focusing on the Saami in the medieval period.

Else Mundal is the most significant contributor to historical scholarship on Norse-Saami relations and has written about perceptions of the Saami and their belief systems in Old Norse sources, the potential links between Norse and Saami rituals, relationships between Norse and Saami peoples as expressed in family terms and in Norse myths, the role of Saami women in Norse society, Norse-Saami royal marriages, the role of Saami people in Norwegian nation building, and the Christianisation of the Saami and their legal rights in the medieval period.[88] Mundal's work is invaluable and laid the foundation for the following his-

---

86 Crocker, "Vínland." Paul M. Ledger, Linus Girdland-Flink, and Véronique Forbes, "New Horizons at L'Anse aux Meadows," *PANS* 116, no. 31 (2019): 15341–43. Shannon Lewis-Simpson, "Vinland Revisited, Again: On 'Theories, Scuttlebutt, Crossed Fingers', and Next Steps," in *Viking Encounters: Proceedings of the Eighteenth Viking Congress*, ed. Anne Pedersen and Søren Michael Sindbæk (Aarhus: Aarhus University Press, 2020), 565–83. Sverrir Jakobsson's "'Black Men and Malignant-Looking': The Place of the Indigenous Peoples of North America in the Icelandic World-View," in *Approaches to Vínland. A Conference on the Written and Archaeologial Sources for the Norse Settlements in the North Atlantic Region and Exploration of America. The Nordic House, Reykjavík 9–11 August 1999*, ed. Andrew Warn and Þórunn Sigurðardóttir, Sigurður Nordal Institute Studies 4 (Reykjavík, 2001), 88–104, from 2001 demonstrates how research on the Vínland narrative has developed with the "postcolonial wave." Nevertheless, a recent analysis offered by Pernille Hermann focuses on the colonial assumptions of the authors of the Vínland sagas, see "The Horror of Vínland: Topographies and Otherness in the Vínland Sagas," *Scandinavian Studies* 93, no. 1 (2021): 1–22.
87 Ojala, *Prehistories*.
88 "Perception"; "Sami Sieidis in a Nordic Context?," *Journal of Northern Studies* 12, no. 1 (2018): 11–20; "The Relationship Between Sami and Nordic Peoples Expressed in Terms of Family Associations," *Journal of Northern Studies* 2 (2009): 25–37; "Coexistence of Saami and Norse Culture: Reflected in and Interpreted by Old Norse Myths," in *Old Norse Myths, Literature and Society: The Proceedings of the 11th International Saga Conference, 2–7 July 2000, University of Sydney*, ed. Geraldine Barnes and Margaret Clunies Ross (Sydney: University of Sydney, 2000), 346–55; "Samekvinner i norrøne kjelder," in *Åarjel-saemieh. Samer i sør*, Saemien Sijte Årbok, vol. 9 (Snåsa: Saemien

torical research on the appearance of Saami characters in Norse texts. Hermann Pálsson has also commented on the portrayal of the Saami in Norse texts, focusing on Icelandic perspectives.[89] Primarily concentrating on the different ways the Saami are Othered in Norse texts, he writes that Saami people were "ruthlessly exploited by Norwegian traders" and that they are treated in the text as if they "were inferior to Norwegians."[90] I argue against this interpretation throughout this thesis, specifically regarding trade in chapter 5, as I find this reading too simplistic. Other scholars like John Lindow, Sirpa Aalto and Lyonel Perabo also focus on textual tropes of Otherness and how these are associated with the Saami in medieval texts.[91] In *The Viking Way*, Neil Price advocates for an understanding of Norse and Saami interactions during the Viking Age as formed by dynamic processes, with his focus primarily lying on Norse borrowings from what he refers to as "Saami shamanism."[92] Other significant contributors to the topic include but are not limited to Jurij Kusmenko, Sirpa Aalto, Veli-Pekka Lehtola, Triin Laidoner, and Eleanor Rosamund Barraclough.[93] The interdisciplinary work *Hunters in Transition: An Out-*

Sijte, 2007), 110–25; "Kong Harald Hårfagre og samejenta Snøfrid: Samefolket sin plass i den norske rikssamlingsmyten," *Nordica Bergensiana* 14 (1997): 39–53; "Kong Håkon Magnussons rettarbot for Hålogaland av 1313 og andre kjelder til kristninga av samene i mellomalderen," in *Sápmi Y1K: Livet i samernas bösättningsområde för ett tusen år sedan*, ed. Andrea Amft and Mikael Svonni (Umeå: Samiska Studier, 2006), 97–114.

[89] Hermann Pálsson, *Úr landnorðri: Samar og ystu rætur íslenskrar menningar* (Reykjavík: Bókmenntafræðistofnun Háskóla Íslands, 1997); "Searching for the Sámi in Early Icelandic Sources," *Revision* 21, no. 1 (1998): 40–46; "The Sami People in Old Norse Literature," *Nordlit* 5 (1999): 29–53.

[90] Hermann Pálsson, "Sami," 29.

[91] John Lindow, "Supernatural Others and Ethnic Others: A Millennium of World View," *Scandinavian Studies* 67, no. 1 (1995): 8–31. Sirpa Aalto, *Categorizing Otherness in the Kings' Sagas*, Dissertations in Social Sciences and Business Studies 10 (Joensuu: University of Eastern Finland Publications, 2010). Lyonel Perabo, *Here Be Heathens: The Supernatural Image of Northern Fenno-Scandinavia in Pre-Modern Literature* (MA diss., Háskoli Íslands, 2016).

[92] Neil Price, *The Viking Way: Magic and Mind in Late Iron Age Scandinavia*, 2nd edition (Oxford: Oxbow Books, 2019), 196–210. Price's work argues for the significant role of the Saami throughout mainland Fennoscandia in the early medieval period; however it can be criticised for leaning too heavily on early modern ethnographic accounts about Saami ritual performance, among other Indigenous circumpolar groups, as true reflections of Saami ritual performance in the Viking Age.

[93] Jurij Kusmenko, "Sámi and Scandinavians in the Viking Age," *Scandinavistica Vilnensis* 2 (2009): 65–94. Sirpa Aalto, "Hyväksikäyttöä vai kumppanuutta? Saamelaisten ja skandinaavien kohtaamiset islantilaisissa saagoissa," in *The Barents and Baltic Sea Region: Contacts, Influences and Social Change*, ed. Kari Alenius and Matti Enbuske (Rovaniemi: Pohjois-Suomen Historiallinen Yhdistys, 2017), 17–37. Aalto and Lehtola, "Representations," 7–30. Triin Laidoner, "The Flying *Noaidi* of the North: Sámi Tradition Reflected in the Figure Loki Laufeyjarson in Old Norse Mythology," *Scripta Islandica* 63 (2012): 59–93. Eleanor Rosamund Barraclough, "Arctic Frontiers: Rethinking Norse-Sámi Relations in the Old Norse Sagas," *Viator* 48, no. 3 (2017): 27–51.

line of Early Sámi History by Lars Ivar Hansen and Bjørnar Olsen has been particularly influential to this thesis, since the authors emphasise the value of interdisciplinarity when researching Saami pasts.[94]

Together, these works, among others, have led to a shift whereby Saami history is increasingly being accepted as part of general Norse or Nordic history, rather than as a marginal discipline.[95] This scholarship is extremely valuable and significant, and contributes to the inclusion and helps emphasise the relevance of Saami peoples in Norse society. It is, nevertheless, in my view often founded on the idea that Saami characters function as literary tools to emphasise the Other in Norse society or as representations of the foreign northern periphery. Lyonel Perabo, for example, states that the Saami were "the most obvious 'others' in Norse society."[96] On this "Otherness," Keith Ruiter writes:

> Otherness arises from the individual and societal impulse to categorise the world. Fundamentally, otherness is defined in opposition to the known, the experienced, and the self, making it unknowable as, once it is known, it is no longer other.[97]

Ruiter's definition, adopted here, indicates that Otherness is the structured opposition between "Us" and "Them" and that once "Them" are known to "Us," "They" no longer function as Others. Othering is the literary tool whereby the compilers of a text accentuate the Otherness of a given character or group in order to emphasise the perceived distance from this group. In sections 3.2.1 and 4.2.1, I question the assumptions that the Saami are portrayed as the uncivilised and peripheral far northern Others by medieval authors and suggest that these assumptions may be grounded in lingering colonial structures.[98] With this in mind it should be noted that Othering is a postcolonial term, and denotes the often-internalised colonialist discourse in which the Other, in this context Indigenous people, appear as

---

94 Hansen and Olsen, *Hunters*.
95 Bjørnar Olsen, "Samenes fortid som arkeologisk forskningsfelt: virkningshistoriske utfordringer," in *Historisk rätt? Kultur, politik och juridik i norr*, ed. Inga Lundström (Stockholm: Riksantikvarieämbetet, 2007), 209–24.
96 Perabo, *Heathens*, 69.
97 Ruiter, *Mannjafnaðr*, 15.
98 This Othering is also sometimes present in the cultural heritage sector; see Hege Skalleberg Gjerde, "En gjøgler blant guder? Om det samiske i vikingtidsutstillingen," in *Om vikinger og virkninger: Festskrift til Ellen Høigård Hofseths vikingtidsutstilling*, ed. Hege Skalleberg Gjerde and Gro B. Ween (Oslo: Primitive Tider Special Edition, 2016), 103–15.

an inverted and distanced image of the Western self.[99] I argue that in overly focusing on the "grand narratives" Saami characters represent in literature, rather than reading Saami characters as reflections of actual social interactions at the time, or perceptions of past interactions, scholars contribute to the mystification of the Saami as something entirely Other to Norse, and subsequently Scandinavian, society. For example, Troy Storfjell argues, regarding the Saami in medieval texts, that:

> Their geographic proximity to and paradigmatic connection with the *jötnar* [...] served to strengthen the association of both with an existence in the chaotic, wild periphery (*útgarðr*) beyond the boundaries of civilization [...].[100]

I maintain throughout that a result of this emphasised focus on the exclusive Othering of Saami characters is the neglect by scholars to recognise Saami characters as representations of real-life Saami people and individuals. The effects of Othering have been noted in postcolonial works on several occasions, and Nick Shepherd lists consequences such as the de-authentication of Indigenous self-conceptualisation and the perception that Indigenous peoples exist outside history.[101] Colonialist discourses of Othering therefore result in the articulation and acceptance of the assumption that the Other, in this context the Saami, is radically homogenous both in past and present contexts. The portrayal of medieval Saami people is therefore a product of a "particular episteme, Western knowledge, as a way of naming alterity/difference from within the logic of that episteme."[102]

One aspect of the decolonising approach I take in this study therefore involves the reading of Saami characters across the medieval texts discussed in chapter 2 as characters founded on actual observations or interactions rather than as literary tools representing mystery or something entirely Other. This reading also coincides with Ruiter's definition of Otherness, since, I would argue, the evidence suggests that Saami people or people with Saami ties were "insiders" in Norse societies (and vice versa). Although typical "Norse" characters across the textual material are overall not automatically understood as "true reflections" of actual individuals or people, Norse characters are only rarely interpreted as representing "grand nar-

---

99 Nick Shepherd, "Naming the Indigenous," in *Archaeologies of "Us" and "Them": Debating History, Heritage and Indigeneity*, ed. Charlotta Hillerdal, Anna Karlström, and Carl-Gösta Ojala (London: Routledge, 2017), 33–37 (34).
100 Troy Storfjell, "The Ambivalence of the Wild: Figuring Sápmi and the Sámi in Pre-Colonial and Colonial Discourse to the Eighteenth Century," in *L'Image du Sápmi: études comparées, volum 2*, ed. Kajsa Andersson, Humanistica Oerebroensia. Artes et lingua 16 (Örebro: Örebro University Press, 2009), 112–47. See sections 3.2.1 and 4.2.1 for a problematisation of these terms.
101 Shepherd, "Naming," 35.
102 Shepherd, "Naming," 35.

ratives" or as literary tools in the narrative. Furthermore, with some caution, most scholars now agree that the medieval textual material, while not necessarily reflecting truthful depictions of historical events or people, can to some extent reflect society at the time of writing or the perceptions of past societies at the time of writing.[103] In only associating the Saami with these notions of Othering, agency is unintentionally (but effectively) removed from the Saami characters. While I do not disagree that the Saami Motif-Cluster may have occasionally been employed by the compiler of a given text as a means of emphasising the Other or the periphery, I entirely disagree with a classification of Saami characters in these texts as exclusively functioning as textual representations of the far northern periphery. On the contrary, I argue throughout that such an overarching interpretation is a simplification of the role Saami people play, particularly in Norse, but also more generally, in medieval, literature, and subsequently of the role Saami people played in medieval Fennoscandian society. Charlotte Damm summarises the problems connected to this simplification of the Indigenous as Other:

> Half a century ago the majority of historians and archaeologists were not concerned with the past of "Others," relegating them to extras/supernumeraries, at best secondary in our stories. Now we have taken one step up, in wishing to investigate their history, but maybe the most fundamental problem is that we often portray groups such as the San, the Saami, or the Inuit as essentially different. Through such a perspective we may be perpetuating colonial dichotomies constructed in and for the West. To uphold dominance the powerful needs an opposite, a powerless "other." For centuries Indigenous groups across the world have been conveniently amongst these "others," as they have continued to have no access to the authoritative discourse.[104]

The unquestioned or unproblematised assumption postulated by scholars that the Saami are textual representatives of Others of the "uncivilised" world can be directly harmful and contribute to the strengthening of colonial notions portraying the Saami as a static people that were and are inferior to the non-Indigenous population.[105]

Sophie Scheen Jahnsen has analysed the discourse related to national identity in Norwegian Viking-Age research, devoting a chapter to the historiographical dichotomy between the "Norwegian Viking" and the "Saami."[106] Her research dem-

---

103 Aalto and Lehtola, "Representations," 8–9.
104 Charlotte Damm, "Archaeology, Ethno-history and Oral Traditions: Approaches to the Indigenous past," *Norwegian Archaeological Review* 38, no. 2 (2005): 73–87 (84).
105 Crocker, "Vínland," 95.
106 Sofie Scheen Jahnsen, *The Social Construction of the Norwegian Viking: An Analysis of the National Identity Discourse in Norwegian Viking Age Research* (MA diss., University of Oslo, 2015).

onstrates that the term "Viking" is used by scholars to mean "Norwegian," resulting in the term "Saami" (or other words denoting Saami people) being read as "non-Norwegian." Through this discourse, the Saami are removed from both Viking-Age and Norwegian history.[107] In their article "Sámi Vikings?," Hege Skalleberg Gjerde and Jostein Bergstøl also analyse representations of Saami culture in Viking-Age research and note that:

> They [Saami people] are seemingly, however, almost always presented as an exceptional case, and an outlier we should consider, again demonstrating that the world of the Vikings and Viking history is primarily about bona fide Norse culture.[108]

In questioning the ethnic and cultural assumptions made in recent general publications on the Viking Age, Gjerde and Bergstøl note that "Saami prehistory still suffers from the scholarly 'double burden of proof' mentality that has prevailed since the early 1980s."[109] Audhild Schanche and Bjørnar Olsen questioned this mentality in 1985, and highlighted that Norwegian archaeological material was continuously considered to be of Norse origin, unless it had been proven to be undeniably Saami.[110]

In this thesis, I advocate a less rigid understanding of representations of Saami, culturally fluid and/or Norse identities across the textual source material. In deconstructing the colonial notions forming the foundation behind assumptions about ethnic identities and cultural belonging, alternative histories and portrayals of Saami characters emerge. For example, the way I see it, the multifaceted and dynamic portrayal of Saami characters across texts, times, and places demonstrates that we cannot talk about one specific portrayal of Saami characters as exclusively representing the Other or uncivilised in Norse society. Rather, I would assert, these Saami characters should be understood as reflecting actual geopolitical and sociocultural interactions at the time of writing, or minimally, the perceptions of the past portrayed in this writing. This interpretation indicates that the prevalence and significance of Saami characters in the textual material reflects the prevalence and significance of Saami people in and to Norse society, and directly shows

---

107 Jahnsen, *Construction*, 62.
108 Hege Skalleberg Gjerde and Jostein Bergstøl, "Sámi Vikings?," in *Vikings Across Boundaries*, ed. Hanne Lovise Aannestad et al., Viking-Age Transformations 2 (London: Routledge, 2020), 166–78.
109 Bergstøl and Gjerde, "Vikings?," 173. The double burden of proof refers to archaeologists first having to disprove that an object is Norse, before having to prove that the object is undeniably Saami.
110 Audhild Schanche and Bjørnar Olsen, "Var de alle nordmenn? En etnopolitisk kritikk av norsk arkeologi," in *Arkeologi og etnisitet*, ed. Jenny-Rita Næss, AmS-Varia 15 (Stavanger: Arkeologisk Museum UiS, 1983), 87–99.

the value in dismantling colonial structures. Carl-Gösta Ojala stresses the importance of dismantling the colonial structures that are entangled in Saami history and historiography, to avoid static and homogenous representations of Saami pasts, and acknowledge that there are "many Saami histories and prehistories."[111] Scholars of medieval and Viking-Age history have a clear-cut responsibility in creating space for Saami historical narratives since "history is important for understanding the present and reclaiming history is a critical and essential aspect of decolonisation."[112]

1.3 Postcolonialism, Archaeology, and Theoretical Framework

After its introduction in the late 1970s with literary historian Edward Said's book *Orientalism*, which helped identify the discursive strategies of debasement, domination, and power/knowledge relationships through which imperialism worked,[113] postcolonialism quickly became an established theory in an academic-driven focus on majority-culture assumptions and constructions. The main goal of postcolonialism is not the celebration of the end of colonialism, as the term implies, but rather to "identify and explore alternative histories."[114] In this context, a postcolonial approach becomes particularly relevant for the present study, since the main goal of postcolonial methodologies lies in acknowledging the majority culture's presentation of history whilst actively endeavouring to decolonise the narrative. Employing more inclusive frameworks in our readings of medieval texts (and archaeological material) confronts the deeply rooted colonial idea that Indigenous peoples are static historical actors, which enforces the narrative whereby Indigenous peoples of the past (and therefore the present and the future) are "never awarded full humanity."[115] Active confrontation of this narrative is crucial, and as Martin Nakata

---

111 Carl-Gösta Ojala, "Contested Colonial History and Heritage in Sápmi: Archaeology, Indigeneity and Local Communities in Northern Sweden," in *Archaeologies of "Us" and "Them": Debating History, Heritage and Indigeneity*, ed. Charlotta Hillerdal, Anna Karlström, and Carl-Gösta Ojala (London: Routledge, 2017), 258–71 (267).
112 Tuhiwai Smith, *Decolonizing*, 29–30.
113 Edward Said, *Orientalism* (New York: Pantheon Books, 1978). Tariq Jazeel, "Postcolonialism," in *The Wiley-Blackwell Companion to Cultural Geography*, ed. Nuala C. Johnson, Richard H. Schein and Jamie Winders (Oxford: Wiley-Blackwell, 2013), 41–48 (41).
114 Marte Spangen, Anna-Kaisa Salmi, and Tiina Äikäs, "Sámi Archaeology and Postcolonial Theory: An Introduction," *Arctic Anthropology* 52, no. 2 (2015): 1–5 (3).
115 Vine Deloria Jr., "Indians, Archaeologists and the Future," *American Antiquity* 57, no. 4 (1992): 595–98 (597).

asserts, it is not simply enough to rewrite earlier racial discourses into cultural discourses as this only creates a change that says:

> Oops, sorry, we were wrong but we've rethought this and, here, we think this is a better explanation for you and your predicament.[116]

The place of postcolonial methodologies in archaeology became clearer in the 1980s with the emergence of the post-processual movement in archaeological theory, where attention was directed to the subjective nature of interpretations of the past and its material cultures. This growth coincided with the establishment and subsequent progression of the University of Tromsø, where terms such as "Saami archaeology" and "Saami history" were coined whilst the hegemony of Norse and Norwegian historical and archaeological issues was challenged.[117] The development of Saami history and archaeology as an academic field corresponded with the aforementioned crucial Alta-conflict in northern Norway in the late 1970s/early 1980s, which introduced Saami narratives and struggles to national political and public audiences. Growing Saami political and cultural activism, especially in northern Norway, resulted in an increasing awareness of the need for Saami self-determination and a growing appreciation for Saami culture. Simultaneously, and quite significantly, Saami research as a field of study grew from the late 1970s onwards with the "Saami movement" and can be understood as "research with Saami contents from a Saami standpoint and with the aim of producing knowledge about Saami people using their own premises [...]."[118] Saami scholars like Louise Bäckman and Alf Isak Keskitalo, among others, institutionalised Saami research from this period onwards and challenged the so-called "outsider paradigm" prevailing in research on minorities.[119] For example, Keskitalo argued that the Saami themselves should be at the forefront of Saami research, and that the research methodologies should be changed in favour of the Saami rather than the majority society.[120] Today, Saami Studies is an established field of its own.[121] The increasing

---

[116] Martin Nakata, *Disciplining the Savages: Savaging the Disciplines* (Canberra: Aboriginal Studies Press, 2007), 361.
[117] Spangen, Salmi, and Äikäs, "Introduction," 2.
[118] Virtanen, Keskitalo, and Olsen, "Contemporary Indigenous Research," 8, 14–17.
[119] Jelena Porsanger and Irja Seurujärvi-Kari, "*Sámi dutkama máttut:* The forerunners of Sámi Methodological Thinking," in Pirjo Kristiina Virtanen, Pigga Keskitalo, and Torjer Olsen, eds., *Indigenous Research Methodologies in Sámi and Global Contexts*, New Research – New Voices 2 (Leiden: Brill, 2021), 33–64 (52–55).
[120] Alf Isak Keskitalo, "Research as an Inter-Ethnic Relation," *Diedut* 7, Arctic Centre Reports 11 (1994): 7–31 [Republished article based on a speech held in Tromsø in 1974, and an article published in 1976]. Keskitalo also argued for the productivity of employing English (to begin with)

focus on Saami self-determination resulted in the establishment of the Saami Parliament in October 1989, which functions as the representative body for people of Saami heritage in Norway and acts as an institution of cultural autonomy. Similar Saami Parliaments were founded in Sweden (1993), Finland (1996),[122] and the Kola Saami Assembly (2010).[123] Since Norway is the only Fennoscandian nation state to ratify ILO 169, the major international convention concerning the rights of Indigenous people, the Saami Parliament of Norway has substantially more autonomy and cultural standing than the other parliaments. This also indicates that the debate concerning Saami rights and claims, also concerning Saami identity, is manifested differently across the nation statess.[124]

There is still an ongoing debate concerning the historical presence of Saami people across Fennoscandia, particularly in southern contexts. A particularly resilient assumption concerning the place and presence of Saami people in the historical and archaeological record is a consequence of the prevalence of the *framrykningsteori*. The theory, put forth by the Norwegian historian Yngvar Nielsen in 1889, claimed that Saami people were early modern settlers in regions south of Nordland and that the Saami people inhabiting these regions should have no legal rights regarding reindeer herding, land and water resources, among other

---

as the research language of Saami studies, since it was more neutral and less hostile than the Nordic nation-state languages, but more inclusive than using only Saami languages.

121 For processes of decolonisation within Saami research, see Harald Gaski, "Indigenism and Cosmopolitanism: A Pan-Sami View of the Indigenous Perspective in Sami Culture and Research," *AlterNative: An International Journal of Indigenous Peoples* 3, vol. 2 (2013): 113–24 (114). Jelena Porsanger, "The Problematisation of the Dichotomy of Modernity and Tradition in Indigenous and Sámi Contexts," in *Working with Traditional Knowledge: Communities, Institutions, Information Systems, Law and Ethics*, ed. Jelena Porsanger and Gunvor Guttorm (Kautokeino: Sámi allaskuvla, 2011), 225–52. Laura Junka-Aikio, "Institutionalization, Neo-Politicization and the Politics of Defining Sámi Research," *Acta Borealia* 36, no. 1 (2019): 1–22.
122 A "Saami Assembly" was founded in 1979 and served as inspiration for the later parliaments.
123 The Kola Saami Parliament is not recognised by the Russian federal or the local Murmansk oblast governments but is supported by the other Saami parliaments and participate in the Saami council.
124 See Bjørnar Olsen, "Sámi Archaeology, Postcolonial Theory and Criticism," *Fennoscandia archaeologica* 32 (2016): 215–29. Charina Knutson, *Conducting Archaeology in Swedish Sápmi: Policies, Implementations and Challenges in a Postcolonial Context*, Lnu Licentiate 33 (Växjö: Linnaeus University Press, 2021). Carl-Gösta Ojala and Jonas Monié Nordin, "Sámi Archaeology in a Global Perspective: Heritage, Indigeneity and Politics," *Fennoscandia archaeologica*, vol. 34 (2017): 122–26. Eeva-Kristiina Harlin, "Sámi Archaeology and the Fear of Political Involvement: Finnish Archaeologists' Perspectives on Ethnicity and the Repatriation of Sámi Cultural Heritage," *Archaeologies* 15 (2019): 254–84. Spangen et al., *Saami Pasts*, 9. Ojala, *Prehistories*, 215.

things.¹²⁵ Prior to the developments that led to the large-scale support of the *framrykningsteori* in the late nineteenth century, the Saami had generally been viewed as Fennoscandia's original population.¹²⁶ With the emergence of Social Darwinism and race-biological research, the Saami were increasingly treated as a low-standing people from the east that had only very recently settled in Norway and Sweden. These assumptions were quickly adopted by the majority population, particularly in Norway during the national romantic movement, where the need for an independent national history was strong following independence from Denmark.¹²⁷ Although debunked by historians and archaeologists on several occasions, the association between the Saami and the far north is still prevalent across the fields. As I discuss in more detail in section 7.2, this association has increasingly been challenged in archaeological research but is still predominant in general historical research on medieval Fennoscandia (including the Viking Age). It is unfortunately also prominent in certain aspects of popular culture and in the public debate, as documented by the private Facebook group "Duođaš Sámecielaheami" (Document discrimination against the Saami).

The goal of any postcolonial approach is, among other things, to contribute to the deconstruction of historical assumptions built on colonial notions.[128] Helge Salvesen writes that the narration of Saami history should have the same value as the history of the nation state has for the majority population, in that it matters both on societal and individual levels and contributes to the strengthening of Saami self-designation.[129] Salvesen also demonstrates the power in acknowledging the value systems, predestined opinions, and stereotypes within the historiographical accounts of the nation state.[130] Similarly, Spangen, Salmi, Aïkäs, and Fjellström write that one of the many aims for research directed at Saami pasts "should be to maintain and reinforce a position for Saami cultural history as an obvious integrated part of our common pasts in northern Fennoscandia and northern Europe."[131] Narrating the history of Saami people of the past, and especially the question of who has the "right" to perform this narration, is not uncomplicated. This

---

125 Hansen and Olsen, *Hunters*, 16.
126 Hansen and Olsen, *Hunters*, 11.
127 Arnfrid Opedal, "A.W Brøgger and the Norwegianisation of the Prehistory of Norway," *Acta Borealia* 13, no. 1 (1996): 36–46 (36–37).
128 Margaret M. Bruchac, "Decolonization in Archaeological Theory," in *Encyclopedia of Global Archaeology* (New York: Springer, 2014), 2069–77.
129 Helge Salvesen, "Tendenser i den historiske sameforskning: med særlig vekt på politikk og forskning," *Scandia* 46, no. 1 (1980): 21–52 (42).
130 Salvesen, "Tendenser," 42.
131 Spangen, Salmi, and Äikäs, "Introduction," 9.

factor is further complicated by the fact that the majority of the historical sources on the Saami are written by others than the Saami for others than the Saami. However, as Siv Rasmussen argues, by going deeper into the material and analysing what the Saami characters themselves express, a more neutral image can be accessed from sources than what might be apparent on the surface.[132] Similarly, Håkan Rydving has analysed early modern sources (most often written by missionaries) that discuss Saami religion and advocates taking the accounts related by Saami peoples in these sources seriously.[133] Both these approaches have been adopted in the present study, in order to further contribute to the decolonisation of the source material.

The unbiased employment of postcolonial frameworks for studying Indigenous pasts has been criticised for its tendency to focus the critical inquiry on the "imperial gaze," which can result in studies that remain "engaged and enmeshed in colonialism [...] even if from a critical perspective."[134] Elizabeth Edwards and Brenna Duperron rather advocate for what Tarren Andrews has coined the "Indigenous Turn" of Medieval Studies,[135] a turn that demands an epistemic shift within the field itself, but also care, and continuing contentious discussions about how we speak about, write for, and practise an Indigenous Medieval Studies.[136] While the field of Saami history and/or archaeology might be seen as "postcolonial critique,"[137] it has been criticised for lacking explicit mention or coherent use of the theoretical complex.[138] Despite not always being an explicit part of research into Saami relations, postcolonialism often forms an important methodological backdrop or as a source of inspiration in several studies.[139] Because postcolonial-

---

132 Siv Rasmussen, "Å skrive om fortidens samiske mennesker," *DIN: Religionsvitenskapelig tidsskrift* 2 (2018): 7–11 (10).
133 Håkan Rydving, *Tracing Sami Traditions: In Search of the Indigenous Religion Among the Western Sami During the 17th and 18th centuries* (Oslo: Novus, 2010).
134 Brenna Duperron and Elizabeth Edwards, "Thinking Indigeneity: A Challenge to Medieval Studies," *Exemplaria* 33, no. 1 (2021): 94–107 (95).
135 Andrews, "Indigenous Futures," 12.
136 Andrews, "Indigenous Futures," 15.
137 Peter van Dommelen, "Colonial Matters: Material Culture and Postcolonial Theory in Colonial Situations," in *Handbook of Material Culture*, ed. Chris Tilley et al. (London: SAGE Publications, 2006), 104–25 (108). Dommelen divides postcolonial-inspired archaeological texts into three approaches: a) writing alternative histories from the perspective of the colonised (postcolonial critique), b) awareness that colonial situations cannot be treated from a homogenous or dualistic perspective, and c) recognizing that hybrid cultures are a given due to continuous interaction between people and cultures. In this book I combine these approaches.
138 Spangen, Salmi and Äikäs, "Introduction," 3.
139 Jostein Bergstøl, *Samer i Østerdalen? En studie av etnisitet i jernalderen og middelalderen i det nordøstre Hedmark*, Acta Humaniora 325 (Oslo: Unipub, 2008), 28. Ojala, *Prehistories*, 19. Marte

ism is a power-laden and criticised concept, it has been proposed that viewing it as a method for opposing the ongoing aftermath (and continuation) of colonialism is more helpful than treating it exclusively as a body of theory.[140] Allowing for the inclusion of historical and archaeological work employing postcolonial critique rather than an explicit postcolonial theoretical framework, this approach in turn enables the continued discussion of the decolonisation of Saami history and includes room for this history in the overarching nation state histories. Using this methodology, I approach medieval texts with the direct goal of identifying Saami histories and exploring, with grounding in archaeological material, the multifaceted realities offered by emphasising these stories. By this, I mean that I have employed interpretations of some of the archaeological material, influenced by postcolonial methodologies, as expressions of culturally fluid Norse-Saami identities and the widespread Saami settlement area in the medieval period, to legitimise my reading of the texts. This approach seeks to contribute to the decolonisation of Medieval Fennoscandia and the field of Medieval and Norse studies, and the historiography related to the Saami within these fields. A significant implication of the employment of decolonisation as an important framework for this study is the acknowledgement that the field is indeed biased regarding the role of Saami people or characters in the medieval Fennoscandian past, and that there is a clear necessity to actively confront this bias. As Duperron and Edwards state:

> Decolonizing requires a rigorous investigation of the colonizing gaze within Medieval [and Norse] Studies, and its complicity with racist ideologies.[141]

When I use the term "decolonising tools" throughout the present study, this acknowledgement, confrontation, and Duperron and Edwards's rigorous investigation of the colonising gaze, is what I refer to.

Spangen, "Sámi Myths and Medieval Heritage," in *Myths and Magic in the Medieval Far North*, ed. Stefan Figenschow, Richard Holt and Miriam Tveit (Turnhout: Brepols, 2020), 119–42.
140 Jazeel, "Postcolonialism," 44. Marianne Skandfer, "Ethics in the Landscape: Prehistoric Archaeology and Local Sámi Knowledge in Interior Finnmark, Northern Norway," *Arctic Anthropology* 46 (2009): 89–102 (89).
141 Duperron and Edwards, "Thinking Indigeneity," 101.

1.4 Summary

In this chapter, I have presented the historiographic background of the research into Norse-Saami relations in the medieval period, in addition to emphasising the need for employing postcolonial methodologies in such research. In chapter 2, I consider the various sources referring to the Saami from the classical period to the late fifteenth century and provide an overview of the development of the Saami Motif-Cluster in the pre-modern textual tradition. Chapter 3 explores the textual motifs associated with Saami characters across the aforementioned texts and contextualises how these motifs specifically allude, directly or indirectly, to the Saami. Chapter 3 also problematises assumptions about the portrayal of Saami characters in medieval texts that, in my opinion, do not reflect the source material. In chapter 4, I discuss medieval spatial relations and focus on northern Fennoscandia. In concentrating on the portrayed relationships between Saami characters and north-eastern groups like the Bjarmar, I highlight how the texts demonstrate a multifaceted and spatially diverse Fennoscandia. The chapter also analyses the geopolitical developments initiated by the growing nation state(s). Chapter 5 considers how Norse-Saami trading affairs are presented in the textual material, and questions established academic assumptions about the medieval taxation of the Saami. This is achieved by utilising postcolonial methods in the reading of the textual material, which challenge accepted historical dogmas favouring the majority culture. Lesser-discussed trading links to England and Iceland are also emphasised, alongside Saami independent agency in the trade. In chapter 6, I demonstrate the many opportunities for identity negotiation in medieval Fennoscandian societies by analysing Norse-Saami personal relationships as they appear across the texts. In order to achieve this, I apply existing archaeological interpretations of certain finds as identity expressions of Norse-Saami cultural fluidity and develop a similar framework appropriate for the textual material. This framework is continued in chapter 7, where the commonly perceived "exclusive" association between the Saami and the far north is challenged by analysing the textual evidence for medieval Saami presence in southern contexts. Overall, the present study demonstrates the benefits of adopting archaeological frameworks based on postcolonial theory in the reading of medieval literature, and how this reading contributes to the decolonisation of medieval, and thereby modern, Fennoscandia. It is in this context that this research particularly contributes to the advancement of scholarship.

Chapter 2: Classical and Medieval Written Sources on the Saami

2.1 Introduction

The oldest written sources about a people generally identifiable with the Saami appear in Mediterranean works from late antiquity and continue into the Middle Ages and beyond, primarily as part of geographical and historical compilations.[1] North European narratives describing the Saami appear from the late ninth century onwards, introduced by Ohthere's account related at the court of King Alfred in 890. From the mid-eleventh century, the papacy preoccupies itself with the conversion of the Nordic peoples, including the Saami, a tradition maintained later in the medieval period with the equation of Christian Hálogalanders to crusaders defending their territory from the "heathen" Saami.[2] Danish narratives are introduced in the same period with the visit of Adam of Bremen to the Danish court in the 1060s. Mainland Scandinavian accounts are rooted in the 1100s with the advent of the composition of law codes, accompanied by the large-scale saga tradition in the centuries following. Beginning in the late twelfth century but becoming increasingly visible from the thirteenth century onwards, Norse written sources about the Saami increase noticeably, and writers of these texts lean heavily on portrayals of the Saami and their relationship with the Norse. However, possibly older sources such as Eddic and skaldic poetry indicate that the cultural perception of the Saami, reflected in the texts, and their relevance for society in general, was an important and popular topic before the composition of the sagas.

It is important to note that these texts mostly relate external portrayals of Saami life, with varying degrees of credibility and distance from real-life encounters and experiences with the Saami. Nevertheless, Saami voices sometimes shine through in the source material, such as in the self-designating act of the *semsveinar* of *Vatnsdœla saga*,[3] and in the descriptions of different Saami actors, and this autonomy is crucial to emphasise. By discussing some of the texts referring to the Saami from the classical period to the late fifteenth century, I provide an overview of the Saami Motif-Cluster in the pre-modern textual tradition.[4]

---

1 Hans Lindkjølen, *Nordisk saga: Samer i litteraturen* (Oslo: Tyri, 1993).
2 Hálogaland is a medieval term for the region in Norway stretching from northern Trøndelag to Troms, see section 4.2.2.
3 *Vatn*, 34–35.
4 The Saami Motif-Cluster is elaborated further in chapter 3.

2.2 Classical and Early Medieval Mediterranean Sources

The oldest known written source mentioning a group generally agreed to be identifiable with the modern-day Saami is the first-century work *Germania*, written by the Roman senator and historian Publius Cornelius Tacitus. Writing about the well-organised societies of the Germanic peoples as a critique of the "over-civilised" Romans, Tacitus mentions a people called the *Fenni*. The *Fenni* are described as having neither horses, weapons nor homes, as living off the earth and dressing in animal-skins. Both men and women are described as hunting with bone-tipped arrows, and apparently sheltered their children and elderly in studworks made from twigs.[5] In the Alexandrian geographer Claudius Ptolemy's gazetteer *Geographia* from around 150, the *fenni* are mentioned as the northernmost of seven peoples inhabiting the island of Scandia, but the work does not elaborate on their lifestyle.[6]

While the traditional interpretation sees the identification of the *Fenni* people with early Saami groups,[7] Lars Ivar Hansen and Bjørnar Olsen suggests that the classical writers were referring to the hunter-gatherer inhabitants of Southern Finland, the predecessors of Saami and Finnish people.[8] They support their interpretation by referring to the change in the term for the people occurring around the sixth century, when the precursor "skiing" is added. In the Byzantine historian Procopius's book *De Bello Gothico* from approximately 550, the *skrithifinoi* are described as one of thirteen peoples on the island of Thule, following much the same lifestyle as Tacitus's *Fenni*, except they also built sinew-bound boats.[9] Similarly, the hunter-gatherer group *scretefennae* are mentioned in the 551 history *Getica* by the eastern Roman bureaucrat and historian Jordanes, alongside other inhabitants of Skandza. These include the *adogit* [*alogit = "háleygir"?] who lived in the land of the midnight sun and polar nights, the *finnaithae* who lived like animals in caves but were agriculturalists, and the *finni mitisimmi*, who were small.[10]

---

5 Tacitus, *Agricola and Germania*, ed. James Rives, trans. Harold Mattingly (London: Penguin Classics, 2010), 70.
6 J. Lennart Berggren and Alexanders Jones, trans., *Ptolemy's Geography: An Annotated Translation of the Theoretical Chapters*, (Princeton: Princeton University Press, 2000).
7 Inger Zachrisson et al., eds., *Möten i gränsland: Samer och germaner i Mellanskandinavien*, Monographs 4 (Stockholm: Statens Historiska Museum, 1997), 158–61.
8 Lars Ivar Hansen and Bjørnar Olsen, *Hunters in Transition: An Outline of Early Sámi History*, The Northern World 63 (Leiden: Brill, 2014), 37.
9 David Westberg, "Research on Procopius of Caesarea in the Scandinavian Languages," *Histos* 9 (2019): 8–1.0.
10 Charles Christopher Mierow, trans., *The Gothic History of Jordanes*, (Princeton: Princeton University Press, 1915), 54–57.

Around the 700s, an anonymous Ravennese cleric created a work listing placenames from India to Ireland, including a short section on the *skridefinni*, who lived by the coastal mountains in a cold country, where both women and men hunted.[11] The Benedictine monk Paulus Diaconus (Warnefridus) writes in his 780 *Historia gentis Langobardorum* that the *scritobini* lived in the land of the midnight sun where snow fell even in the summers, wild animals were hunted with bows, and that they kept with them an animal similar to the deer whose skin they used for clothing.[12]

While these sources, spanning over nearly seven centuries, present noticeably similar descriptions of the *fenni* peoples, the sources themselves sometimes portray knowledge that cannot have been obtained through the reading of older works. Ptolemy mentions seven peoples on the island of Skandia, several of which are not mentioned by Tacitus, indicating that the geographer did not obtain that information by reading the *Germania*. Procopius, Jordanes, the Ravennese cleric, and Paulus Diaconus introduce unique information about the *fenni* in their works, respectively sinew-bound boats, the three *finni*-groups of *Getica*, residences by the coastal mountains, as well as the keeping of what is most likely reindeer. This concurs that while certain elements appear archaic in these works, specifically the distinctiveness of the *fenni* people from the Mediterranean milieu, new knowledge about the Saami was relevant to these writers. Together, these sources indicate an early medieval interest and acceptance of Saami groups as part of the cultural environment of the north.

2.3 North European Narratives

2.3.1 Ohthere's Account

The foremost written evidence about Norse-Saami trading and Fennoscandian relations from early in the medieval period comes from the possible first-hand account of the ninth century chieftain Ohthere.[13] Reportedly presented at the court of King Alfred of Wessex in approximately 890, the chieftain's account was included as an addendum in the Old English translation of Orosius's classical encyclopaedic work from the fifth century, which had not covered northern Europe-

---

11 Moritz Pinder and Gustav Parthey, eds., *Ravennatis Anonymi Cosmographia* (Berlin, 1860), 201.
12 Paul the Deacon, *History of the Lombards*, ed. Edward Peters, trans. William Dudley Foulke (Philadelphia: University of Pennsylvania Press, 2003), 7–8.
13 Ohthere and his account are further discussed in sections 5.2 and 5.3.

an conditions.¹⁴ Prior to Ohthere's account, the text lists the known peoples of Europe and their locations, placing the *Scridefinne* north of the *Svear* (Swedes; Swedish-settled land), between the Norwegian-settled land in the west and the land of the Kvens in the east.¹⁵

Following this, it is stated that Ohthere lived northernmost of all Norwegians, in Hálogaland, and that only the *Finnas* lived further north from him, in his close vicinity. Ohthere's account and King Alfred's list of peoples use different ethnonyms (*Scridefinne* and *Finnas*), for what are undoubtedly the same group. This difference indicates that while foreign writers preferred the precursor, speakers of Old Norse mostly maintained the *finnar* tradition.¹⁶ It is also important to remember that while Ohthere's account is invaluable as the voice of a Hálogalander who was in contact with Saami people(s), his voice has been mediated into a different language, a different culture and through a different contextual lens.¹⁷ The text therefore carries some uncertainties, but is nevertheless the closest medieval source portraying actual lived and experienced relations with the Saami. Discussing landscape relations and cultural meeting spaces in northern Fennoscandia, language, typical Saami lifestyles such as whaling and reindeer herding as well as the debated tribute paid by the Saami, Ohthere's account is invaluable to our understanding of Norse-Saami relations in the early medieval period.

2.3.2 Adam of Bremen

In 1053, Pope Leo X confirmed the authority of the archbishops of Hamburg-Bremen over the Nordic countries, including the land of the *Scrideuinnum*.¹⁸ In the late 1060s, the German magister Adam was invited to Hamburg-Bremen by its archbishop, Adalbert. Soon after, the magister commenced the writing of the history of the archdiocese, including the Nordic peoples. Adam gathered most of the information about the Nordic regions for his *Gesta Hammaburgensis ecclesiae pontificum*

---

14 Hansen and Olsen, *Hunters*, 54.
15 *OEH*, 36–37.
16 *OEH*, 36–44. The tradition of using *Finnar* as an ethnonym for the Saami is maintained in saga narration and in later Norwegian dialects (up until the mid-twentieth century and beyond, but viewed as derogatory today).
17 Eleanor Rosamund Barraclough, "Arctic Frontiers: Rethinking Norse-Sámi Relations in the Old Norse Sagas," *Viator* 48, no. 3 (2017): 27–51 (37).
18 *Diplomatarium Norvegicum*, vol. 17, no. 849, https://www.dokpro.uio.no/cgi-bin/middelalder/diplom_vise_tekst.cgi?b=14931&s=n&str=. This authority is confirmed by Pope Victor II in 1055 and Pope Innocent II in 1133.

during his stay at the court of King Sveinn Ástríðarson of Denmark. Whether based on first-hand accounts of the Saami lifestyle or Danish perceptions of it, Adam informs that the people could not live without the winter and that they outran wild animals in the deep snow.[19] Stating that Helgeland (Hálogaland) was the most remote part of Norway and the landscape closest to the *scritefini*, Adam adds that:

> Inter Nordmanniam et Sueoniam Wermilani et Finnédi degunt, et alii; qui nunc omnes sunt christiani [...] In confinio Sueonum vel Nortmannorum contra boream habitant Scritefini, quos aiunt cursu feras praeterire. Civitas eorum maxima Halsingland, ad quam primus ab archiepiscopo designatus est Stenphi episcopus [...]. Qui etiam multos carundem gentium sua praeducatione lucratus est. Praeterea sunt alii numero carentes copimus solos Gothos, Wermilanos et partem Scritefinorum, vel qui illis vicini sunt.[20]
>
> Between Norway and Sweden dwell the Wärmilani and [Finnedi] and others; who are now all Christian [...] On the confines of the Swedes and Norwegians toward the north live the Skritefengi, who, they say, outstrip wild beasts at running. Their largest city is Hälsingland, to which the archbishop designated Stenphi as the first bishop [...]. By his preaching he won many of those heathen [...] There are besides countless other Swedish peoples, of whom we have learned that only the Goths, the Wärmilani, and a part of the Skritefingi, and those in their vicinity, have been converted to Christianity.[21]

According to Adam, and most likely the Danish court, the Saami lived in the areas stretching from the coast of Hálogaland across the Scandean mountain range to the West-Bothnian coast of Hälsingland, residing in the north with the *Wermilani*.[22] The ethnonym *Finnedi* is also curious, since it introduces the confusion expressed by later medieval chroniclers when discussing the Saami in the southern areas of Fennoscandia.[23] Rooted in the difficulties in distinguishing the Saami, most often called *finnar* by medieval Scandinavians, and people from Finland (Finnish people), this confusion pertains throughout the medieval period. However, in *Gesta Hammaburgensis*, I would suggest that the *Finnedi* people might represent an early Saami group increasingly associating themselves with the agriculturalist tradition of Adam's Christian *Wermilani*, rather than the hunter-gatherer tradition of the *scritefini*. Adam also relates the conversion to Christianity of certain Saami

---

19 *Hamburg-Bremen*, 213.
20 *Hammaburgensis*, 172–73.
21 *Hamburg-Bremen*, 205–6.
22 *Hammaburgensis*, 173: "a borea Wermilanos cum Scritefinnis" [on the north, the Wärmilani with the Scritefengi], *Hamburg-Bremen*, 206.
23 See Jordanes' *scritefengi* and *finni*-groups, the difference in the ethnonym used for Saami groups by Ohthere and King Alfred in the same text, and Saxo below.

groups in the areas of Hälsingland. If this is the case, Saami groups in the area must have been familiar with Christianity.

Gesta Hammaburgensis maintains the previous scholarly tradition of associating the Saami with winter weather and hunting in areas north of the Norwegian and Swedish peoples, but also introduces the possibility of early Christianisation of the Saami in southern areas and links the Saami to the Värmland area of western Central Sweden.

2.3.3 Passio Olavi

Passio Olavi, originally *Passio et miracula beati Olavi*, is a late twelfth-century compilation of legends and stories narrating the early eleventh century life and miracles of King Óláfr inn helgi Haraldsson of Norway. The account survives in two thirteenth-century Latin versions, and was possibly compiled by the Archbishop of Niðarós, Eysteinn Erlendsson (1161–88), who also supervised the shrine and liturgy of the saintly king.[24] In addition to recounting the *vita* and miracles of Óláfr, the text repeatedly reinforces a Christian narrative by emphasising the benefits of conversion to the "true faith." In one such incident, the fishing luck, or lack thereof, of non-Christian Saami fishermen is juxtaposed with the success of Christian Norwegian fishermen, demonstrating the virtues of Christianity and prayers, and the poverty faced by non-believers.[25] This is in opposition to more stereotypical medieval views of the Saami that traditionally emphasise Saami fishing expertise.[26] More interestingly, however, the incident points to shared fishing economies somewhere presumably in Finnmǫrk (although no place-name is listed; see section 4.2), where the groups fished together on the "borders of the pagan lands."[27] Such a shared fishing economy indicates close sociocultural and economic relations between the Saami and the Norse in northern Norway, or minimally, the late twelfth-century perceptions of such a possibility, which in itself is important.

---

24 *Passio*, xxv–xxxx.
25 *Passio*, 70–71.
26 Saxo, 17–19. See also sections 2.5, 3.2.3, and 3.2.4.
27 *Passio*, 71.

2.3.4 Saxo Grammaticus

On the invitation of Archbishop Absalon of Roskilde, Danish historian and theologian Saxo Grammaticus compiled the history of Denmark, *Gesta Danorum*, in the twelfth or early thirteenth century. Despite its Danish location, Saxo is surprisingly preoccupied with northern Fennoscandian and Saami relations. Depicting the Saami like the chroniclers before him, Saxo describes the *scritefenni* as passionate hunters, good pathfinders and expert skiers, who used animal skins instead of money when trading with their neighbours.[28] In addition, Saxo locates the *scritefenni* in the eastern parts of Norway and Sweden, building on Adam of Bremen's tradition.

Most of the instances involving the Saami are stories relating the ancient past, often connected to meetings between legendary Danish kings and Saami royalty. In one story, the Danish King Gram travels to Finnland to fight King Sumbli ("Phinnorum regem"), but ends up falling in love with his daughter, Signe.[29] However, the Saami king sends his daughter to Saxony to marry King Henry, who is killed by Gram at their wedding. Because of the associations with the Saami Motif-Cluster (discussed below in chapter 3), I would argue that Saxo follows the Nordic tradition of using the ethnonym "Finn" to describe Saami people. A slightly happier wedding is related later when the marriage between King Helgi of Hálogaland and Þora, daughter of the prince of the Saami and the Biarmians ("Finnorum Byarmorumque pricipis"), is celebrated.[30] In addition to describing the social stratification of Saami society, the text also conveys the stereotypes of the Saami as practitioners of magic, expert hunters and skiers, and skilful archers.[31]

Saxo mentions three different peoples or landscapes associated with the Saami: the aforementioned *scritefenni* of the eastern midlands of Norway and Sweden, the *finnar* of the north belonging to the northern geopolitical landscape of Finnmǫrk, and the *Lappia* peoples of both Lapplands.[32] Saxo is the first and only to mention these three different areas together, which I would argue might point to a medieval familiarity or awareness of the stratification of Saami society, since these groups are not portrayed as a homogenous entity but rather as consisting of similar but dynamic groups. Furthermore, Saxo's interest in the Saami demonstrates their relevance to medieval society, even in Denmark, a country that the Saami do not have traditional or Indigenous ties to. Saami characters are impor-

---

28 Saxo, 17–19.
29 Saxo, 39.
30 Saxo, 151. In chapter IX: 4.24, we meet another Saami royal (Matul), 651.
31 Saxo, 17, 163, 343, 461–63, 649, 651, 699.
32 Saxo, 17–19, 39, 331.

tant to the narrative, and *Gesta Danorum* adds a more detailed portrayal of Saami characters than previous chroniclers. Since one of the main objectives behind the writing of *Gesta Danorum* was the glorification of Danish history,[33] the fact that the Saami appear so often demonstrates their relevance to Saxo's expected audience. I believe that this indicates either an actual historical connection between the Saami and Denmark, or that such a connection was crucial to portray due to the familiarity of the Saami as an important group in the political Danish or North-European climate at the time of writing.

2.4 Legal Texts

2.4.1 Eastern Norway

During the consolidation of Norway in the late ninth to early tenth centuries, or perhaps earlier, the traditional landscapes of *Nóregi* were divided into bigger legal areas.[34] Covering the Viken region in the areas around the Oslofjord from [Sarps]Borg to Bohuslän, the *Borgarþingslǫg* was founded prior to 1164 and was most likely based on an older oral tradition of lawspeaking in the area.[35] Only the *cristins doms bolk* (Christian [ecclesiastical] law section) and a short section on village-held *þings* survive, revised in the new *landslov* of King Magnús lagabœtir from approximately 1274.[36] The Christian laws cover the organisation of the church, regulation of the relationship between the Church and secular society, as well as the consequences of the violation of the moral commandments which were equated with criminal offence. One such violation was to seek out the Saami to receive divination: "þet er ok vbota værk. er maðr fær a fínmarkr at spyria spadom" [It is unlawful for persons to travel to the Saami to ask for divination].[37] Similarly, in the law code covering the legal assembly of the *Eiðsivaþing*, enforceable in the Oppland area, it is stated that:

---

[33] Saxo, xli.
[34] Kjersti Selberg, *Eldre norske rettskilder: en oversikt*, Juridisk biblioteks skriftserie, vol. 20 (Oslo: Universitetsbiblioteket, 2013), 12.
[35] Store norske leksikon, "Borgarting," snl.no, 10.11.2017 https://snl.no/Borgarting.
[36] Store norske leksikon, "Magnus Lagabøters Landslov," snl.no, 11.11.2020 https://snl.no/Magnus_Lagab%C3%B8ters_landslov. The oldest surviving manuscript of this law code dates from the last quarter of the thirteenth century and was recorded by the scribe Eiríkr Þróndarson.
[37] *NGL 1*, 372.

> Engi maðr a at trua. a finna. eða fordæðor. eða vit. eða blot. eða rot. eða þat. er til siðar hœyrir. eða leita ser þar bota. En ef maðr fær til finna. oc uærðr hann sannr at þui. þa er hann utlægr. oc ubota maðr.³⁸
>
> No person should believe in [the power of] the Saami, or sorcery, or [their] drum, or sacrifice, or root, or in that which belongs to heathendom, or seek help there. And if a person seeks out the Saami, he is an outlaw and an unlawful person.³⁹

Along with a short section of secular laws, only the Christian section of the *Eiðsivaþingslǫg* survives, possibly first compiled between 1150 and 1160.⁴⁰ The two south-eastern law codes forbid travelling to Finnmǫrk and seeking out the Saami for their magic. Since the legal texts both have jurisdiction in the south-eastern area of Norway, it is most likely that the *finmarkr* referred to was located within the legislative areas of the two law codes and not in the traditional landscape of northern Fennoscandia, as discussed in chapters 4 and 7. Furthermore, the prohibition is not present in the *Gulaþingslǫg*, the legislation relevant for both western and northern Norway where journeys to the (commonly) understood northern landscape of Finnmǫrk would have been more practical and feasible. It is therefore very likely that the *finmarkr* mentioned in the *Borgarþingslǫg* refers to actual dwelling spaces associated with Saami people within the legislative area of the *Borgarþingi* (but possibly also that of the *Eiðsivaþingi* given the prohibition on seeking out the Saami for magical purposes). In addition, the nature of the prohibition to seek out the Saami in these areas indicates that contact between Christians and the Saami occurred on a regular basis and was viewed by the Church as problematic. It is important to note, however, that the problem expressed by the laws is not necessarily the Saami affiliation of the people living in these areas, but rather, their non-Christian behaviour, and the fact that Christian people sought them out.

2.4.2 Western Norway and Iceland

The *Gulaþingslǫg* was the legal code related to the legal assembly covering the traditional areas of the Norwegian west coast, primarily Firðafylki (Nordfjord and

---

38 *NGL 1*, 389–90.
39 Else Mundal, "Sami Sieidis in a Nordic Context?," *Journal of Northern Studies* 12, no. 1 (2018): 11–20 (12). Most scholars only include the first section, however Mundal argues that the surrounding context of the prohibition makes it reasonable to assume that the succeeding bans were also connected to Saami culture, especially considering that "vit" can mean drum. See section 3.2.1 for a discussion on the usage of drums in the medieval portrayal of Saami ritual performance.
40 Store norske leksikon, "Eidsivatingsloven," snl.no, 11.11.2017 https://snl.no/Eidsivatingsloven.

Sunnfjord), Sygnafylki (roughly Sogn), and Horðafylki (roughly Hordaland), with Sunnmørafylki (roughly Sunnmøre), Rygjafylki (roughly Rogaland), and Egðafylki (roughly Agder) incorporated from the 1100s.[41] The *Gulaþingslǫg* may have already been well-established prior to 930, since the Icelandic chronicler Ari fróði claims that the first laws of Iceland were patterned on it. While not explicitly mentioning the Saami, a fragment of the oath *trygðamál* is preserved in the law code.[42] Although only a fragment survives, the oath has survived elsewhere, including in the *Íslendingasögur Grettis saga Ásmundarsonar* (ch. 72) and *Heiðarvíga saga* (ch. 33), and in the pre-1264 Icelandic legal text *Grágás*:

> En sa yckar er gengr a gørvar sáttir eða vegr aveíttar trygðir. þa skal hann sva viða vargr rækr oc rekin sem menn vipðazt varga reka. cristnir menn kirkior søkia. heiðnir menn hof blóta. elldr upp brenr. iorð grør. mögr moðor callar. oc moþir mög föðir. alldir ellda kynda. scip scriðr. scildir blícia. sol scín snæ legr. fiðr scríðr fura vex. valr flygr várlangan dag. stendr honom byr bein vndir báða vængi. himin huerfr heimr er bygðr. vindr þytr. vötn til sævar falla. karlar korne sá.[43]

> But the one of you who tramples on treaties made or smites at sureties given, he shall be an outcast despised and driven off as far and wide as ever men drive outcasts off, Christians come to church, heathens hallow temples, fire flames, ground grows, son calls mother, mother bears son, men make fires, ship glides, shields flash, sun shines, snow drifts, [the Saami] ski, fir tree grows, falcon flies a spring-long day with a fair wind beneath both wings, heavens revolve, world is inhabited, wind whistles, waters flow to the sea, men sow seed.[44]

Due to its archaic language and survival in different sources, Else Mundal claims that the oath must date from pre-Christian times.[45] The fact that it is preserved so well, particularly in the Icelandic sources, indicates a strong tradition of continuity. Listing all things expected and normal, the skiing Saami is portrayed as a normalised motif both in Norway and Iceland, across several centuries.

As is discussed further in section 7.4.2, I find it quite striking that not more sources refer to Saami presence in the area of Þrøndalǫg. While the Eastern Nor-

---

41 Store norske leksikon, "Gulating," snl.no, 10.11.20 https://snl.no/Gulating.
42 *NGL 1*, 110.
43 Vilhjálmur Finsen, ed. *Grágás 1852: Konungsbók*, (Odense: Odense Universitetsforlag, 1974), 206–7. The surviving manuscripts are from the second half of the late thirteenth century, and although codification began in 1117–18, not all laws were written at the time, and the text(s) underwent revisions throughout. Store norske leksikon, "Grågås," 10.11.2021 https://snl.no/Gr%C3%A5g%C3%A5s.
44 Andrew Dennis, Peter Foote, and Richard Perkins, trans., *Laws of Early Iceland: Grágás 1*, vol. 1, University of Manitoba Icelandic Studies 3 (Manitoba: University of Manitoba Press, 2012), 184–85.
45 Else Mundal, "The Perception of the Saamis and Their Religion in Old Norse Sources," in *Shamanism and Northern Ecology*, ed. Juha Pentikäinen (Berlin: De Gruyter, 1996), 97–116 (103).

wegian law codes refer to the Saami, the *Frostuþingslǫg*, the law code relevant for the Þróndalǫg region and which according to Heimskringla was first written in the mid-1000s during King Hákon góði's reign, does not specifically mention Saami peoples.[46] However, by analysing the legal text and using the same approach as here and by Lars Ivar Hansen in his 1984-article,[47] Knut Bergsland theorised that the Saami are referred to by the term *reksþegn* in the *Frostuþingslǫg*.[48] The term, only appearing in Old Norwegian wergild lists, is generally accepted as denoting the social class between the rank of freeborn man and son of a freedman.[49] Because the term is differentiated from the term "búþegn" (same as *búmaðr:* see discussion in section 4.2.1), meaning landowner/farmer (or even householder), Bergsland argues that *reksþegn* should be understood as meaning "nomadic free man," and thereby denoting Saami people in the region covered by the *Frostaþingslǫg* that were not landowners or farmers.[50] On a final note, it should be stressed that the approach of actively searching for Saami people or characters, "between the lines," is particularly productive in the reading of medieval Nordic legal texts, since it has been argued that Saami people are often only mentioned in these texts in contexts relating taxation and Christianity.[51] A thorough reading of the medieval Norwegian law codes not specifically mentioning the Saami would therefore be a fruitful direction to take in future research and has not been undertaken in the present book.

2.5 Landnámabók

Landnámabók, the *Book of Settlements*, is the principal source covering the settlement of Iceland from approximately 870 to 910, concluding with the establishment of the *Alþingi* and the adoption of the common law in 930.[52] It has been suggested that the book was originally compiled by the Icelandic chronicler Ari fróði Þorgils-

---

46 Store norske leksikon, "Frostatingslova," snl.no, 05.03.2020 https://snl.no/Frostatingslova. *Hkr 1*, 163.
47 Lars Ivar Hansen, "Skal en bare bruke kilder som omtaler samer i rekonstruksjonen av samisk fortid?," in *Viester-Alas: Rapport fra et seminar på Vesterålens bygdemuseum og kultursentrum*, ed. Lars Slettjord and Helge Guttormsen (Melbu [n. p.], 1984), 140–74.
48 Knut Bergsland, "Om middelalderens Finnmarker," *Historisk tidsskrift* 49, no. 4 (1970): 365–409 (408).
49 A Lexicon of Medieval Nordic Law, "Reksþegn," https://www.dhi.ac.uk/lmnl/nordicheadword/displayPage/4311.
50 Knut Bergsland, "Synsvinkler i samisk historie," *Historisk tidsskrift* 53 (1974): 1–36 (24).
51 Bergsland, "Synsvinkler," 25.
52 *Landnáma*, 1.

son before 1148, in what is now a lost version, but survives in five extant sources dating from the thirteenth to the seventeenth centuries.[53] The main goal of the work seems to have been to facilitate the Icelandic wish to endorse its own national myth and history, and to tackle foreign misconceptions of past Icelanders. While listing the first settlers of Iceland and their ancestry, the text alludes to the Saami descent of several settlers.

In his work on the *landnám* from the north of Norway, Alf Ragnar Nielssen points out that there are no concrete examples of settlers directly characterised as Saami.[54] However, indirectly through allusions to and associations with the Saami Motif-Cluster, he lists at least 8 of the 37 families settling Iceland from the north of Norway as plausibly having Saami descent.[55] These families, according to Nielssen, are referred to by direct links to Saami royalty, via personal names and nicknames relating to characteristics associated with the Saami, such as skiing and hunting (archery) and supernatural beings like *rísar* and *þursar*,[56] via connections to the Hálogaland power elite and their alliances, and via trading relations and direct meetings with Saami characters in Norway. As I discuss further in section 3.2.1, we need to be cautious not to draw unquestioned parallels between the Saami and supernatural beings, especially when other features of the Saami Motif-Cluster are not present. Nielssen's interpretation, notably treated with some caution, is nevertheless significant since it establishes the likelihood that people from Saami milieux settled in Iceland. If these people identified as Saami, it is noteworthy that the text does not explicitly identify them as such (*finnar*). If not among the first settlers, the fact that Icelanders are portrayed as trading with the Saami in Finnmǫrk[57] introduces the possibility of personal relationships leading to the move of Saami people to Iceland. The possible archaeological remains of Saami presence in Iceland have been discussed in two Master's theses from 2013, both emphasising the presence of archaeological material from the medieval period in Iceland conforming to Saami tradition.[58]

---

53 *Landnáma*, 3, 7. The translation used in this work is based on *Sturlubók* by Sturla Þórðarson from approximately 1275–80. Sturla also wrote the sagas of and for the Norwegian kings Hákon Hákonarson and Magnús lagabœtir.
54 Alf Ragnar Nielssen, *Landnåm fra nord: Utvandringa fra det nordlige Norge til Island i vikingtid* (Stamsund: Orkana Akademisk forlag, 2012), 87.
55 Nielssen, *Landnåm*, 91.
56 *Rísar* and *þursar* are ambiguous terms associated with supernatural beings from Norse mythology, often contrasted with more positive entities such as gods and elves. See section 3.2.1.
57 See section 5.3.2.
58 Einar Ísaksson, *To Die into the Mountain: A Study of a Northwestern Icelandic Burial Mound and the Sámi Cultural Influences in Viking Age Iceland* (MA diss., Stockholm University, 2013). Dennis Moos, *Finnar á Íslandi: Samiske spor i det islandske arkeologiske materialet fra landnåmstid* (MA

The only stated Saami characters in *Landnáma* are the two Saami men visiting the chieftain Ingimundr on Hefni island (unknown location) in Hálogaland, a story also related in *Vatnsdœla saga*.[59] The closest expressed link to actual Saami characters settled in Iceland in *Landnámabók* is related in the account of the marriage between a descendant of the semi-legendary Saami characters Lopthœnu and Erp, and the granddaughter of Mǫttul Finnakonungr (king of the Saami), Jóreiðr Ǫlvisdóttir.[60] Interestingly, most of their listed descendants have names associated with the Saami Motif-Cluster: Finnvarðr (Finnr [Saami] + varðr [guard or mountain cairn]), Tindr (mountain peak), Gríma (mask or helmet), and Kólfinna (Kól [coal] + finnr).[61] I would argue that this indicates that a) the compiler of *Landnáma* thought it important to accentuate their Saami ancestry, and/or b) that Saami descent and its associated "inherited" abilities and associations functioned as an important basis in the naming of children (at least for the writers of these texts). Additionally, while it might have been based on other foundations, the marriage between two characters with expressed Saami descent introduces the possibilities of alliances based on earlier cultural affiliation and belonging in the new settlement. Stressing high-status descent might have been an important tool in the assertion of power in the newly settled society, where hierarchisation was developing. This accentuation of possible Saami descent in the naming of characters is relied upon several times in the text, particularly clear in the accounts relating Finngeir (Finn + geir [spear]), son of the Hálogalandier Þorsteinn ǫndurr (ski), the dream-interpreter Finni whose foreign mother Lekný is depicted as Saami elsewhere, and Finnr enn skjálgi from Vefsn in Hálogaland, whose son Eyvindr skáldaspillir was a famous skald who refers to Saami culture in his poetry.[62]

---

diss., University of Tromsø, 2013). See also Kendra Willson, "A Putative Sámi Charm on a 12th c. Icelandic Spade: Runic Reception, Magic and Contact," in *Finno-Ugric Folklore, Myth and Cultural identity*, ed. Cornelius Hasselblatt and Adriaan Van der Hoeven (Groeningen: University of Groeningen, 2011), 267–81.

59 *Ldn*, 217–18. *Vatn*, 33–35. Earlier in both texts, a female knowledgeable in magic predicts Ingimundr's future, but it is only in the latter she is identified as Saami.

60 *Ldn*, 82–83. Mǫttul Finnakonungr is said to be the foster-father of Gunnhildr konungamóðir in Fagrskinna: *Fsk*, 79.

61 *Ldn*, 82–83, 95. See chapter 3 for an overview of how some of these features fit into the so-called Saami Motif-Cluster.

62 *Ldn*, 127, 275: In both *Finnboga saga ramma* and *Ljósvetninga saga*, Lekný is nicknamed "finnska" [the Saami], reflected in the personal name and abilities of her son; *Finnb*, 268; *Ljós*, 7–9. For Eyvindr, see section 2.7.2.

According to Hermann Pálsson, Saami affiliation may be underlined by referencing supernatural ancestry or abilities.[63] In *Landnáma*, the blacksmith Ljótólfr is said to be "risaættur at móðerni" [descended from giants on his mother's side],[64] and we also read about the hermit Þorði þurs á Þursstǫðum (Þórir the *þurs* at Þurs-place)[65] and the Naumdœla (Namdalen) native Þráinn svartaþurs (black *þurs*).[66] Since neither of these examples contain any supporting context to demonstrate Saami associations (see chapter 3), I believe that Saami affiliation based simply on the nickname *þurs* is unlikely. The discussion of the Saami and supernatural association is continued in section 3.1.

Mostly pre-occupied with the Saami descent of its settlers expressed in inherited abilities, associations, or nicknames, *Landnáma* introduces the possibility that people from Saami milieux were among the first settlers of Iceland. The work concludes with a reminder to its readers that not all relations between the Saami and the Norse were conflict-free: "Gunnstein var síðan skotinn með ǫru finnskrí ór skógi á skipi sínu norðr í Hefni" [Gunnsteinn was then shot onboard his ship north on Hefni by a Saami arrow from the forest.][67]

2.6 Saga Literature

As already noted, I have analysed particular texts from the saga literature that fall into three commonly accepted genres, being the *Íslendingasögur*, the *konungasögur*, and the *fornaldarsögur*,[68] each contextualised in more detail in the sections below. On the development of saga literature, Ármann Jakobsson writes that:

> As far as we can presently assert, saga writing began in the early twelfth century, gaining much momentum in the thirteenth and fourteenth century and surviving well into the fifteenth century.[69]

---

63 Hermann Pálsson, "The Sami People in Old Norse Literature," *Nordlit* 5 (1999): 29–53 (31–33). See section 3.2.1 for a problematisation of these terms.
64 *Ldn*, 147.
65 *Ldn*, 91.
66 *Ldn*, 252.
67 *Ldn*, 366.
68 There are also other saga genres, but these have not been included in my analysis.
69 Ármann Jakobsson, "Introduction," in *The Routledge Research Companion to the Medieval Icelandic Sagas*, ed. Ármann Jakobsson and Sverrir Jakobsson (New York: Routledge, 2017), 1–3.

Unsurprisingly, the relationship between the sagas and the past they allegedly portray is a complicated one.[70] The historical validity of the saga literature is heavily debated, since the texts fail to "depict historical events or persons objectively" and are "narrative interpretations of past events."[71] In recent decades, research has shifted from reading saga literature as historical evidence of the past the texts portray, to becoming increasingly regarded as reflections of society at the time of writing and as historiographic accounts, potentially founded in oral storytelling from earlier in the medieval period.[72] These elements are never objective and both Ármann Jakobsson and Ralph O'Connor, among many others, have summarised the various issues of history and fiction in the different saga genres.[73] On the general understanding of saga material, O'Connor writes that:

> Modern scholars agree that the Norse-Icelandic sagas emerged as a form of historiography, that its authors mixed historical with fictional or imaginative material, and that fictional tendencies become more frequent and sustained in later sagas as the genre developed.[74]

Since the present analysis takes a general approach to medieval texts and the focus lies on the overall portrayal of Saami characters in these texts, the chronology or specific dating (of sagas in particular) will not be dealt with in detail here, although it is elaborated in some places. I have therefore taken a general approach to the dating of the different saga texts and stick to the generally accepted date of writing, as suggested by *Store norske leksikon* and/or the *Dictionary of Old Norse Prose*. As Ármann Jakobsson points out, it is "meaningless to categorize the matter in their [medieval saga authors] texts as either exclusively fictional, on the one hand, or real, on the other."[75] It should rather be read as a mix of historiographic tradition and creative input, and generally, the approach taken here regarding the saga material is based on what Sirpa Aalto and Veli-Pekka Lehtola concurs in their conclusion, namely that:

---

70 Ármann Jakobsson, "King Arthur and the Kennedy Assassination: The Allure and Absence of Truth in the Icelandic Sagas," *Scandinavian-Canadian Studies* 22 (2015): 12–22 (14–17).
71 Sirpa Aalto and Veli-Pekka Lehtola, "The Sami Representations Reflecting the Multi-Ethnic North of the Saga Literature," *Journal of Northern Studies* 11, no. 2 (2017): 7–30 (8).
72 Aalto and Lehtola, "Representations," 8–9.
73 Ármann Jakobsson, "King Arthur," 21–22. Ralph O'Connor, "History and Fiction," in *The Routledge Research Companion to the Medieval Icelandic Sagas*, ed. Ármann Jakobsson and Sverrir Jakobsson (New York: Routledge, 2017), 88–110.
74 O'Connor, "History and Fiction," 88.
75 Ármann Jakobsson, "King Arthur," 21.

> The varied image of the Sami in the sagas seem to reflect the complex interaction between the Sami and [Norse people] in the Middle Ages. Their depictions reflect the different textual levels that the sagas contain [...]. On the one hand, the equal relationship is conveyed through *topos* concerning the marriage between a Norse king and a Sami woman, which may stem from earlier, oral tradition. On the other hand, we see reflections of medieval Christian prejudice in passages in which the Sami way of life, sorcery and paganism are described. Instead of one-lined interpretations, the Sami representations in sagas reveal many kinds of relations and attitudes which emphasize the polyphonic nature of both the saga literature and the Middle Age society. Even if the stereotypes tell us more about the society that created them [...] behind them lie very mundane phenomena.[76]

I have treated the *konungasögur* and *Íslendingasögur* as equally historiographic accounts (i.e., perceptions of past societies, and with quite a lot of caution, as remnants of certain orally transmitted historical accounts from earlier in the medieval period) and reflections of social processes and mentalities at the time of writing. This approach aligns with my interpretation of the long "medieval period" established in section 1.1.1. since, while the overall saga material employed here chronologically spans from the late twelfth to the late fifteenth century, the texts demonstrate clear continuity in their portrayal of Saami characters, also due to the clear intertextuality between certain texts.[77] I would therefore argue that it is possible to draw an image of the general view of Saami people throughout the medieval period, understood through the perceptions of Norse and Icelandic saga-writers and their view of history. I have treated this image as a reflection of society at the time of writing, in addition to also being a perception of the past that has potentially survived through oral transmission.

Due to the fantastical nature of the *fornaldarsögur*, I have treated their portrayal of Saami characters with more caution, although I maintain that aspects like spatial belonging and certain portrayals of lifestyles most likely have foundations in real-life observations. Again, it is the narration of Saami and culturally fluid characters in the texts that is key in my analysis. As will become clear below, the different saga texts also show particular affinities with the texts discussed in sections 2.3, 2.4, 2.5, and 2.7, all dating from the late ninth to the early fifteenth century. This continuity and resemblance should in my opinion be understood as indicative of a long-standing medieval reality where Saami people were present. Additionally, the archaeological material employed in my analysis also span from early to later in the medieval period. While we should be cautious of making uncontextualised comparisons to the texts, interpretations of the archaeological material can to some extent legitimise, or minimally suppose, that the sagas

---

76 Aalto and Lehtola, "Representations," 22–23.
77 Aalto and Lehtola, "Representations," 10.

reflected the long medieval reality in which Saami people were present and significant actors.[78]

2.6.1 Íslendingasögur

The *Íslendingasögur*, also called family sagas, are Icelandic prose narratives relating the settlement of Iceland and the development of its society from the ninth to the eleventh centuries.[79] Written in the period between the early 1200s to the 1300s and later, the genre relies heavily on genealogy and focuses on the stories of newly settled families, their alliances and the different types of conflicts that arose in the young society. The genre comprises approximately 41 sagas, of which nearly half of these (17) either include Saami characters, allude to Saami culture and society, or emphasise Saami descent.[80] Of these 17, seven sagas explicitly mention direct contact with the Saami, both in Iceland and on the Fennoscandian mainland.[81]

Descent is the most common recurring theme connected to the Saami, often expressed by Othering through abilities and features associated with the Saami Motif-Cluster. As seen previously, personal names and nicknames with the component *-finn* can also function as indications of Saami descent. The dream-interpreter Drauma-Finni is introduced as very knowledgeable and "maðr skyggn" [something of a seer/psychic] in *Finnboga saga ramma* and *Ljósvetninga saga*.[82] In addition to his name and his skills, the texts contextualise his abilities by introducing his Saami mother, Leikny finnska, to the narrative. In *Reykdæla saga ok Víga-Skútu*, the character Steinfinnr performs weather magic whilst sitting still and looking into the ground in a near trance-like state.[83] Although not explicitly claimed to be Saami in the text, his name and abilities invite Saami associations for the readers or listeners. In *Egils saga Skallagrímssonar*, believed to have been written in its

---

78 See chapters 4–7 for discussions of the archaeological material.
79 Viðar Hreinsson, ed. *The Complete Sagas of Icelanders Including 49 Tales*, vol. 1 (Reykjavík: Leifur Eiriksson Publishing, 1997), xxx.
80 *Bárðar saga Snæfellsáss, Brennu-Njáls saga, Egils saga Skallagrímssonar, Eyrbyggja saga, Finnboga saga ramma, Fljótsdæla saga, Fóstbræðra saga, Gísla saga Súrssonar, Grettis saga Ásmundarsonar, Gull-Þóris saga, Harðar saga ok Hólmverja, Kjalnesinga saga, Kormáks saga, Ljósvetninga saga, Reykdæla saga ok Víga-Skútu, Vatnsdæla saga, Víga-Glúms saga.* For primary source citations, the original reference (i.e., the primary source itself) will be italicised (e.g., *Eg*) and references to the translations will be cited in quotation marks (e.g., "Eg").
81 *Bárðar saga Snæfellsáss, Brennu-Njáls saga, Egils saga Skallagrímssonar, Finnboga saga ramma, Grettis saga Ásmundarsonar, Reykdæla saga ok Víga-Skútu, Vatnsdæla saga.*
82 *Finnb*, 268. *Ljós*, 7–9.
83 *Reyk*, 192–93.

extant form prior to or in the 1240s,⁸⁴ the Hálogalanders Hallbjǫrn hálftrǫll and Bjǫrgólfr hálfbergrisi are introduced.⁸⁵ Their nicknames, meaning half-troll and half-hill-giant respectively, are often assumed to indicate Saami parentage due to the association between the Saami and the supernatural in certain texts.⁸⁶ This assumed association will be problematised in chapter 3.2.1 since it is in my opinion not as straightforward as often claimed.⁸⁷

Within the genre, *Egils saga Skallagrímssonar* is the work dealing most extensively and in most detail with the Saami. Paramount in the narrative is the portrayal of the Norse-Saami fur trade, the privileges associated with it, the conflicts surrounding it, and the relationship developed between participants in the trade. The introductory passage about the landholder Bjǫrgólfr hálfbergrisi from Torgar (Torget) in southern Hálogaland, relates that he "hǫfðu lengi haft finnferð ok finnskatt" [had long had the right to travel to Finnmǫrk and trade with the Saami.]⁸⁸ This tradition is kept up by Þórólfr Kveld-Úlfsson, whose several trading journeys are described in great detail, unlike anything else found in medieval sources dealing with the Saami, perhaps with the exception of Ohthere. On his first journey after inheriting the rights to *finnferð* and *finnkaup*, Þórólfr brings with him 90 men, 60 more than his predecessors normally brought, along with a great quantity of goods to sell.⁸⁹ The good relations between Þórólfr and the Saami are accentuated in the text, and the groups even collaborate against a common enemy, the north-eastern European group called the Kylfingar.⁹⁰

Finnskatt is also mentioned in *Finnboga saga ramma*, believed to have been written in its extant form in the early fourteenth century,⁹¹ during the meeting between the protagonist Finnbogi and the traveller Álfr Aptrkemba in Hálogaland. A relative to the earls of Hlaðir (Lade) through marriage, Álfr explains he was journeying to Finnmǫrk to collect tax.⁹² While the journey is not elaborated, the text demonstrates how the privilege, even after becoming a royal prerogative, was maintained within a kin-group, as Finnbogi later inherits the right from Álfr after marrying his daughter.⁹³ In *Gull-Þóris saga*, as also related in *Landnáma*,

---

84 Store norske leksikon, "Egils saga," snl.no, 01.04.2014 https://snl.no/Egils_saga.
85 *Eg*, 3, 16–18.
86 Hermann Pálsson, "Sami," 29–31.
87 Aalto and Lehtola, "Representations," 15.
88 *Eg*, 18.
89 *Eg*, 27.
90 *Eg*, 27–28. See section 4.3.1.
91 Store norske leksikon, "Finnboga saga ramma," snl.no, 01.04.2019 https://snl.no/Finnboga_saga_ramma.
92 *Finnb*, 277.
93 *Finnb*, 290.

Þórir Oddsson makes a similar journey, retrieving large quantities of gold somewhere in Finnmǫrk.[94] While the section describing the trip contains a number of fantastical elements like fire-breathing dragons, piles of gold, and far northern giants,[95] the journey might be rooted in reality and oral traditions narrating journeys to Finnmǫrk from Iceland.

In *Vatnsdœla saga*, most likely first written in the second half of the 1200s,[96] the roles are reversed, and Ingimundr is visited by four Saami characters on his farm in Hálogaland. First, he invites "Finna ein fjǫlkunnig" [a Saami woman knowledgeable in magic] to a feast in what seems to be a stunt to impress his southern guests.[97] Preoccupied with the Othering of the woman, the text describes her as foretelling the future of the guests, all while dressed in splendid attire on a raised platform in the middle of the hall.[98] Interestingly, no language barrier between the Saami woman and the (assumed) Norse crowd is recorded, articulated directly in Ingimundr's angry response to her prophecy about him settling in Iceland:

> Ingimundr segir hana þar illu heilli hafa komit. Hon kvað nú svá búit vera mundu, hvár er honum þœtti vel eða illa.[99]
>
> Ingimundr said that ill fortune had brough her there. She said that things would turn out as she had stated, whether he liked it or not.[100]

Hidden by the woman's skills, Ingimundr's cherished amulet is nowhere to be found the morning after the feast, leading him to call for three Saami men. In exchange for butter and tin they agree to undertake a journey to Iceland to search for the item and report back about the lay of the land:

> Þeir svara: "Semsveinum er þat forsending at fara, en fyrir þína áskorun vilju vér prófa. Nú skal oss byrgja eina saman í húsi, ok nefni oss engi maðr," ok svá var gǫrt. Ok er liðnar váru þrjár nætr, kom Ingimundr til þeira. Þeir risu þá upp ok vǫrpuðu fast ǫndinni ok mæltu: "Semsveinum er erfitt, ok mikit starf hǫfu vér haft, en þó munu vér með þeim jarteinum

---

94 Þórhallur Vilmundarson and Bjarni Vilhjálmsson, eds., *Harðar saga*, Íslenzk fornrit 13 (Reykjavík: Hið íslenzka fornritafélag, 1991), 186–89.
95 The story has been reworked several times, with the youngest, employed here, likely deriving from an early fifteenth-century manuscript, but since the story is also related in *Landnámabók* (here called *Þorskfirðinga saga*), it must have been known from the late twelfth century.
96 Store norske leksikon, "Vatnsdœla saga," snl.no, 04.04.2019 https://snl.no/Vatnsd%C5%93la_saga.
97 *Vatn*, 29–30.
98 *Vatn*, 29–30.
99 *Vatn*, 30. See section 6.2.3 for a discussion of the linguistic aspects of Norse-Saami relations.
100 Andrew Wawn, trans., "Vatnsdœla saga," in *The Complete Sagas of Icelanders*, ed. Viðar Hreinsson, 4 (Reykjavík: Leifur Eiriksson Publishing, 1997), 1–66 (15).

fara, at þú munt kenna land, ef þú kemr, af várri frásǫgn, en torvelt varð oss eptir at leita hlutinum, ok mega mikit atkvæði Finnunnar, því at vér hǫfu lagt oss í mikla ánauð [...] ok þar í hǫltinu ǫðru var hlutrinn, ok er vér ætluðum at taka hann, þá skauzk hann í annat holtit, ok svá sem vér sóttum eptir, hljóp hann æ undan, ok nǫkkur hulða lá ávallt yfir, svá at vér náðum eigi, ok muntu sjálfr fara verða."[101]

They answered, "This is a hazardous mission for [Saami] messengers to undertake, but in response to your request we want to make an attempt. You must now shut us up together in a shed and our names must not be revealed." This was duly done. And when three nights had passed, Ingimund went to them. They stood up and sighed deeply and said, "We [Saami] messengers are exhausted and have had much toil and trouble, but nevertheless we have returned with these tokens so that you may recognise the land from our account, if you go there; but it was very difficult for us to search for the amulet, and the spell of the [Saami woman knowledgeable in magic] was a powerful one [as] we placed ourselves in great jeopardy. [...] and there in one of the woods was the amulet, but when we tried to pick it up, it flew off into another wood, and as we pursued it, it always flew away, and some sort of cover always lay over it, so that we could not get hold of it; and so it is that you yourself must go there."[102]

After their journey, which sees them locked up in a house in a trance-like state for three days, the exhausted men relate their difficult out-of-body expedition to Ingimundr, describing the location of his amulet. The emphasis on their tiredness in the text, and the fact that they lie down for three days, is interesting, as it mirrors the aftermath of similar events occurring elsewhere and demonstrates knowledge of (perceived) Saami ritualistic performance.[103] It takes magic performed by the reluctant Saami men to "beat," with limited success, the Saami woman's spell. However, the Saami men, working in favour of the protagonist, are not as extensively Othered as the Saami woman or other magical agents in the text,[104] and the text accentuates the good treatment received by the *semsveinar* after their task is completed.[105] In addition to the anecdotes above, the extract concerning the Saami men is particularly fascinating, as it might include the first known recorded Saami endonym, expressed in the Old Norse as *semsveinar.*

Only appearing in the Old Norse corpus in this extract, the term is used twice by the men, in addition to the exonym *Finnar.* The first component of the word, *sem-*, is used by the Saami men for themselves to describe themselves and is most likely related to the contemporary endonym "Saami," denoting the Saami

---

101 *Vatn*, 34–35.
102 "Vatn," 17.
103 Like the "shamanism" episode in *Historia Norwegie*, discussed in section 3.2.1.
104 See for example the demonisation of Ljótr kerling, *Vatn*, 68–70.
105 *Vatn*, 36: "Vel gerði hann við Finna, ok fóru þeir braut" [He looked after the (Saami) well, and then they left], "Vatn," 17.

people.[106] This interpretation was initially suggested by Magnus Olsen in 1920,[107] with later scholars mostly agreeing that *sem-* derives from the Saami endonym.[108] The second component of the word is the Old Norse word for "boy" or "lad." Mundal explains that although the term *semsveinar* consists of two compounds from two distinct languages, the probable inclusion of the Saami endonym indicates that "the word the Saami used for themselves was known to their neighbours."[109] While I agree that *sem* should be interpreted as "Saami," the two-compound term itself is not as straightforward since the second component "sveinn" is often negatively charged in Old Norse.[110] Saami men elsewhere are also called *sveinn* by Norse addressers, and the term's dismissive associations connected to boyishness and service should be emphasised.[111] It should be noted that the Saami men are accommodating their audience by speaking Old Norse, which strengthens the possibility of the term being a Norse coinage, albeit one that adopts a Saami term. Despite this, given the likelihood that the first compound of the word derives from the Saami endonym, its recording in the saga is crucial as possibly being the earliest recorded self-designating act of the Saami. Furthermore, it is also indicative of Saami bilingual usage when expressing themselves during interaction with Norse people, suggesting that language loans occurred on levels not isolated to majority influence alone and that words could consist of components from both languages.

---

106 Hansen and Olsen, *Hunters*, 36. The term itself is generally agreed by Finno-Ugric linguists to descend from the common Saami-Finnic word "šämä," which is related to the Baltic word "zeme," meaning country/land.
107 Magnus Olsen, "Semsveinar i Vatnsdœla saga: Et sproglig og literaturhistorisk bidrag," *Maal og Minne* 12 (1920): 46–54 (50–53).
108 Jurij Kusmenko, "Sámi and Scandinavians in the Viking Age," *Scandinavistica Vilnensis* 2 (2009): 65–94 (69). Inger Zachrisson, "The Sámi and Their Interactions with Nordic Peoples," in *The Viking World*, ed. Stefan Brink and Neil Price (London: Routledge, 2012), 32–39 (32). Mundal, "Perception," 98. Sirpa Aalto, "Växelverkan mellan samer och skandinaver i medeltiden," in *Uppsala midt i Sápmi – Sábme – Saepmie: En supradisciplinär antologi härrörande från vårsymposium organiserat av Uppsam – Föreningen for samiskrelaterad forskning i Uppsala, Uppsala universitet, 28–29 april 2014*, ed. May-Britt Öhman, Cecilia Hedlund, and Gunilla Larsson, Uppsam skriftsserie 2 (Uppsala: Vulkanmedia, 2017), 114–20 (114). Hansen and Olsen, *Hunters*, 36.
109 Mundal, "Perception," 98.
110 The dictionary lists the following for *sveinn:* boy (child), lad, servant, free man in service, follower, retainer and attendant. These connotations should be kept in mind when discussing the term "semsveinar" and are not necessarily positively coded. Leiv Heggestad, Finn Hødnebø, and Erik Simensen, eds., *Norrøn Ordbok*, 5th edition (Oslo: Samlaget, 2012), 614.
111 See for example *Mork 2*, 32. In the Eddic poem *Hárbarðsljóð*, Þórr initiates the verbal contest when he refers to the ferryman, often assumed to be Óðinn in disguise, as he would a youthful servant: "sveinn sveina" [lad of lads], and later "kǫgur-sveini" [infant]. *Eddukvæði*, 389, 391.

2.6.2 Konungasögur

The *konungasögur*, also known as kings' sagas, are Norwegian and Icelandic historiographic accounts predominantly occupied with the royal biographies of Norwegian kings from the ninth to the thirteenth centuries.[112] Composed from the late twelfth century to the fourteenth, the genre's main focus concerns stories about the kings as well as external and internal governmental and political affairs relevant during their rule. Most of the texts belonging to the genre refer to the Saami directly or indirectly at least once.[113] Portrayed as acting agents in the narrative, Saami actors are involved in affairs of state and foreign affairs, positively, neutrally and negatively, concerning taxation and trade, alliances, and ecclesiastical matters, in addition to personal relations.

While the *Íslendingasögur* traditionally focus more on the Saami Motif-Cluster portrayed through genealogy and northern descent, I have found that the *konungasögur* are slightly more focused on actual Norse-Saami relations grounded in trading and personal affairs, as well as relying heavily on Norse perceptions of the Saami lifestyle. The genre is in no way shy of magical and fantastical allusions associated with Saami agents. The majority of the instances where Saami actors are directly involved are based on the assumption that they offer magical expertise or aid to Norse actors. This is expressed by Gunnhildr konungamóðir somewhere in Finnmǫrk, in *Haralds saga hárfagra* as it is related in Heimskringla, a collection often attributed to Snorri Sturluson and believed to have been compiled in the 1230s:

> Þá er hann kom aptr á Finnmǫrk, þá fundu menn hans í gamma einum konu þá, er þeir hǫfðu enga sét jafnvæna. Hon nefndisk fyrir þeim Gunnhildr ok sagði, at faðir hennar bjó á Hálogalandi, er hét Ǫzurr toti. "Ek hefi hér verit til þess," segir hon, "at nema kunnosto at Finnum tveim, er hér fróðastir á mǫrkini."[114]

---

112 Theodore M. Andersson and Kari Ellen Gade, eds., *Morkinskinna: The Earliest Icelandic Chronicle of the Norwegian Kings (1030–1157)* (London: Cornell University Press, 2000), 291.
113 *Ágrip af Nóregskonungasǫgum, Fagrskinna, Færeyinga saga, Hákonar saga Hákonarsonar, Heimskringla* (of which *Ynglinga saga, Hálfdanar saga svarta, Haralds saga hárfagra, Hákonar saga góða, Haralds saga gráfeldar, Óláfs saga Tryggvasonar, Óláfs saga helga, Magnúss saga ins góða, Haralds saga Sigurðarssonar, Magnúss saga Berfœtts, Magnússona saga, Haraldssona saga,* and *Magnúss saga Erlingssonar* are relevant), *Helgisaga Óláfs konungs Haraldssonar, Historia Norwegie* (counted as a *konungasaga* here), *Jómsvíkinga saga, Morkinskinna, Óláfs saga Tryggvasonar en mesta, Óláfs saga Tryggvasonar eptir Odd munkr Snorrason, Orkneyinga saga,* and *Sverris saga*.
114 *Hkr 1*, 135.

When he came back to Finnmǫrk, his men found in a [Saami] hut a woman whose equal in beauty they had never seen. She told them that her name was Gunnhildr and said that her father lived in Hálogaland and was called Ǫzurr toti. "I have been staying here," she said, "in order to learn witchcraft from two [Saami men] who are the wisest in these forests."[115]

Heimskringla also depicts the Hálogaland chieftains Þórir hundr and Rauðr inn rammi as having Saami associates that help them defeat their enemies by magic,[116] and in a story related in both Heimskringla and the late twelfth-century *Ólafs saga Tryggvasonar* by Oddr Snorrason, Saami people reportedly perform a ritual that helps a Norse couple conceive.[117] In the same texts, King Óláfr Haraldsson is depicted as encountering Saami weather magic on a harrying expedition to Finnland (Finland) and curses such paganism, but is later depicted as seeking the help of a Saami seer in Þrǿndalǫg (Trøndelag).[118]

Trade with and taxation of the Saami is referred to extensively throughout the genre, with repeated patterns across the different texts. Most of the references discuss the bestowal of the trading privilege, demonstrating its political importance in the narrative, as discussed in section 5.2.2.[119] Generally, the texts narrate Hálogalanders as the main Norse participants in Norse-Saami trading affairs.[120] There are even several indications that the Hálogaland trading adventure with the Saami was rooted in international exchange networks across the sea.[121] Trade was in no way isolated to northern Norway, with several pseudo-historical references to Dofri (Dovre mountain range), and harrying expeditions to both Bjarmaland (see section 4.3.1) and Finnland.[122] In the compilation Morkinskinna, likely put together in the 1220s,[123] a man discussing border politics in Gautelfr (Göta älv) expresses "'Snæliga snuggir, sveinar', kvæðu Finnar, áttu andra fala" ["There's a whiff of snow" said the Saami. They had snowshoes for sale],[124] pointing to the sociocultural relevance and knowledge of the Saami trade, even in south-western Sweden.

---

115 Snorri Sturluson, *Heimskringla*, trans. Alison Finlay and Anthony Faulkes, 3 vols (London: Viking Society for Northern Research, 2014), "Hkr 2," 78.
116 Þórir hundr has his Saami associates make him a cloak that indirectly leads to the fall of King Óláfr at the Battle of Stiklastaðir (Stiklestad), *Hkr 2*, 344–45. Similarly, Rauðr inn rammi's paganism is reinforced by his Saami entourage, see *Hkr 1*, 324–26.
117 See the stories about Eyvindr kinnrifa: *Odds*, 257. Condensed in *Hkr 1*, 323.
118 *Hkr 2*, 11 and *Odds*, 187–90.
119 See for example: *Hkr 2*, 175, 344–45; *Sv*, 114.
120 *HN*, 56–57. While the text clearly differentiates the Hálogalanders and the Saami, it is worth noting the Latin "cohabitant," suggesting Norse-Saami cohabitation.
121 See section 5.3.1.
122 *Ágr*, 5–6. *Hkr 1*, 125. *Hkr 2*, 227–34. *Hkr 3*, 10, 115.
123 Store norske leksikon, "Morkinskinna," snl.no, 04.12.2020 https://snl.no/Morkinskinna.
124 *Mork 2*, 32.

In fact, texts of the genre assert that Icelanders were involved in trading with the Saami.[125] Conflict associated with trade is related across the texts, between individuals,[126] based on issues with the distribution of the privilege,[127] between royal brothers on a national level,[128] and even expanding internationally between "nations."[129] These conflicts are further discussed in section 5.2.2.

In order to validate and justify certain privileges, the consolidation of [Norse] power in the exchange network was dependent on the formation of alliances with Saami business partners. These alliances were founded on the establishment of kin-relations such as marriage and fostering, which occur often across the *konungasögur* (not unlike Norse-Norse relations), as will be discussed further in chapter 6. The account of the marriage between King Haraldr hárfagri and Saami royalty Snæfríðr, echoed in Heimskringla's *Haralds saga hárfagra* but first related in *Ágrip* around 1190,[130] is probably the most famous example of such an establishment. Here, King Haraldr is interrupted at a feast in Þoptyn (Toftemo, Dovre) in central Norway by the Saami man Svási, who persuades the king to marry his daughter.[131] King Haraldr's personal relationship with the Saami is repeated in several other *konungasögur* and he is sometimes even described as the "foster-son" of the Saami.[132] Norse-Saami fostering arrangements also appear in Fagrskinna, considered to have been first compiled in the 1220s,[133] with the fostering of the Hálogalandier Gunnhildr by the Saami king Mǫttul in Finnmǫrk representing a similar pattern.[134] Personal relationships are also founded on friendship, and in a story related in Heimskringla's *Haraldssona saga*, Morkinskinna, and Fagrskinna, Sigurðr Slembidjákn, a pretender to the Norwegian throne in the early twelfth century and alleged son of King Magnús berfœttr, receives help and accommodation from the local Saami communities after fleeing northwards, and they celebrate feasts together.[135]

---

125 *Mork 2*, 279, 293–99. See section 5.3.2.
126 *Sv*, 114–15; *Hák 1*, 242.
127 *Mork 2*, 279.
128 *Mork 2*, 117–30.
129 *Hák 2*, 154–55.
130 Store norske leksikon, "Ågrip," snl.no, 20.01.2021 https://snl.no/%C3%85grip.
131 *Ágr*, 5–6.
132 Else Mundal, "The Relationship Between Sami and Nordic Peoples Expressed in Terms of Family Associations," *Journal of Northern Studies* 2 (2009): 25–37 (32). See section 6.2.1.
133 Store norske leksikon, "Fagrskinna," snl.no, 26.09.2019 https://snl.no/Fagrskinna.
134 *Fsk*, 79. In the other sources about Gunnhildr she is depicted as staying with Saami men in Finnmǫrk to learn magic, see sections 3.2.1 and 6.2.
135 *Hkr 3*, 311. *Mork 2*, 193, *Fsk*, 333.

Norse-Saami meetings are not an isolated northern phenomenon, and meetings are related in a variety of places across the genre. Meetings with Saami people in the central inland area of Upplǫnd (Oppland) is a repeated pattern across the saga genres, with King Haraldr hárfagri meeting his Saami wife in Þoptyn, and King Hálfdanr svarti summoning a Saami seer further south in Haðaland (Hadeland).[136] In addition, several instances allude to Saami presence in the eastern inland regions of Norway and on the border to (modern-day) Sweden.[137] This presence is further emphasised by the eastern-Norwegian law codes criminalising seeking out the Saami for magical aid in these areas and is elaborated in chapter 7.

The *konungasögur* reflect the consequences of cross-cultural interaction and shared landscapes. Magic is a re-occurring theme, but trade with the Saami and the privileges associated with it dominate the narrative, probably a result of its relevance during the time of composition. The texts mentioning the Saami visualise meetings across Norway and demonstrate the normalised presence of the Saami even in southern areas such as Haðaland and the eastern inland regions bordering Sweden. This is significant since it challenges the scholarly assumption of locating the Saami exclusively in the north.[138]

2.6.3 Fornaldarsögur

The *fornaldarsögur*, also called legendary sagas, are Scandinavian prose narratives narrating the stories of presumably ancient Germanic and Nordic heroes and tales.[139] The genre's geographical and chronological setting distinguishes it from the other saga genres, as the main action is set in the period before the unification of Norway by King Haraldr hárfagri. Based on a tradition of heroic narrative and affected by continental romance, the texts of the genre narrate legendary history and fiction set in the ancient past, first written during the thirteenth and fourteenth centuries and later.[140] Stories belonging to the genre must at least have been known from the late twelfth and early thirteenth century, since the thirteenth-century writer of *Egils saga* seems to have known both *Ketils saga hœngs*

---

136 *Ágr*, 5–6. *Hkr 1*, 91–92.
137 *Hkr 2*, 298, 259, 149. See section 7.4.3.
138 Neil Price, *The Viking Way: Magic and Mind in Late Iron Age Scandinavia*, 2nd edition (Oxford: Oxbow Books, 2019), 193.
139 Torfi H. Tulinius, "Sagas of Icelandic Prehistory," in *A Companion to Old-Norse Icelandic Literature and Culture*, ed. Rory McTurk (Oxford: Blackwell Publishing, 2005), 447–61 (447).
140 For a more in-depth discussion of the genre, see Torfi H. Tulinius, "Icelandic Prehistory," 449–52.

and *Hervarar saga ok Heiðreks*.[141] The genre was exceedingly popular in the late medieval period, demonstrated by the surplus of manuscript traditions and redactions of the different individual sagas. Of the approximately 25 sagas belonging to the genre, almost half of these mention or allude to the Saami.[142] As a result of the fantastical nature of the genre, the Saami Motif-Cluster is often over-exaggerated and Saami characters stand out as heavily Othered throughout the *fornaldarsögur*. As noted in the introduction to section 2.6, despite the fantastical nature of the genre I have read these instances as sometimes reflecting actual perceptions of Saami spatial belonging and portrayals of lifestyles. By this, I mean that while we should treat the stories of the *fornaldarsögur* with caution, as we should any saga genre due to their subjectivity, there is value in reading these stories as reflections of reality.[143]

Magic is a key theme associated with the Saami in the *fornaldarsögur*, and during a duel between two berserkers in Heðmark (Hedmark) as related in *Sturlaugs saga Starfsama*, probably first composed in the fourteenth century, the Saami contestant shapeshifts.[144] Later in the same saga, the Saami "princess" Mjǫll is burned to death with Sturlaugr's sworn brother Frosti, as a consequence of her practise of magic.[145] In *Hrólfs saga kraka*, in its present form composed around 1400,[146] King Hringr marries Hvít, the daughter of a *Finnakonungr*. After ignoring her sexual advances, Hvít strikes her stepson with her magical wolfskin gloves, cursing him into

---

141 Torfi H. Tulinius, "Icelandic Prehistory," 452.
142 Twelve sagas including *Hrólfs saga kraka, Ǫrvar-Odds saga, Gautreks saga, Hervarar saga ok Heiðreks, Ketils saga hœngs, Gríms saga lóðinkinna, Áns saga bogsveigis, Göngu-Hrólfs saga, Hálfdanar saga Eysteinssonar, Sturlaugs saga Starfsama, Sǫrla saga sterka, Illuga saga Gríðarfostra*, in addition to the *þættir Hálfdanar þáttr svarta* and *Hauks þáttr hábrókar*. All further references to these texts except *Hálfdanar þáttr svarta* and *Hauks þáttr hábrókar* are found in Carl Christian Rafn, ed. *Fornaldar sögur nordrlanda eptir gömlum handritum*, 3 vols (Copenhagen: Ennu Poppsku, 1829–30), Volume I: *Hrólf*, Volume II: *Hrafnistamannasögur*, Volume III: *IllGr, Gautr, GHr, StSt, HálfdEyst, SǫrlaSt*, Volume III also include *Bósa saga ok Herrauðs*, which I refer to in section 3.2.5.
143 The discussions of history or historiography versus fiction (as we understand the term today), alongside the question of whether the stories themselves were actually viewed as credible at the time(s) of transmission, are not something I wish to explore further here; however, these discussions have been excellently covered elsewhere: Annette Lassen, Agneta Ney, and Ármann Jakobsson, eds., *The Legendary Sagas: Origins and Development* (Reykjavík: University of Iceland Press, 2012) and Ralph O'Connor, "History or Fiction? Truth-Claims and Defensive Narrators in Icelandic Romance-Sagas," *Mediaeval Scandinavia* 14 (2005): 1–69.
144 *Stst*, 613.
145 *Stst*, 638. For my usage of the term "princess" here, see section 3.2.1, footnote 23.
146 Jesse Byock, trans., *The Saga of King Hrolf kraki* (London: Penguin, 1998), viii.

becoming a bear.¹⁴⁷ Several Saami men are also portrayed as performers of magic across the genre. In *Halfdánar saga Eysteinssonar*, possibly written in the 1300s but in any case surviving from the 1400s, the Saami kings Finnr and Flóki use their magic fighting against King Eysteinn in the Karelian bay.¹⁴⁸ In *Hálfdanar þáttr svarta* and *Hauks þáttr hábrókar*, both preserved in the late fourteenth-century manuscript Flateyjarbók and both most likely having older roots, Saami characters are able to delude their audiences using magic, leading to the disturbance of both feasts and national governance.¹⁴⁹ Nevertheless, the Saami are not just associated with negatively charged magic, and as in the other genres, Saami characters sometimes offer magical aid to the main protagonists, as emphasised in section 3.2.1.

Within the genre, a group of sagas called the *Hrafnistumannasögur* is perhaps the most occupied with the Saami. The group relates the life and descendants of Ketill hœngr, the son of the aforementioned farmer Hallbjǫrn hálftrǫll. Set for the most part in Hrafnista, a power-complex in northern Trøndelag equated to modern-day Ramstad, the group consists of four texts: *Ketils saga hœngs*, *Gríms saga lóðinkinna*, *Ǫrvar-Odds saga*, and *Áns saga bogsveigis*.¹⁵⁰ These texts were frequently reworked later in the medieval period, especially *Ǫrvar-Odds saga*, but Ben Waggoner nevertheless argues for a fourteenth-century composition with direct roots in earlier texts like *Egils saga* and older oral dissemination of the stories about the men of Hrafnista.¹⁵¹ The *Hrafnistumannasögur* narrate an abundance of magical incidents involving the Saami, including shapeshifting (*Ket*, ch. III), weather magic (*Ket*, ch. 3, *GrL*, ch. 1, *Ǫrv*, ch. 5), trolls (*Ket*, chs. 4–5), staff-riding (*Ket*, ch. 5), bewitching (*GrL*, ch. 1, *Ǫrv*, ch. 18), the ability to shoot targeted arrows from each finger (*Ǫrv*, ch. 29), magical arrows (*Ǫrv*, ch. 1), magical clothing (*Ǫrv*, ch. 12), and the alternance of appearance as a result of Saami presence (*Ket*, ch. 4, *Ǫrv*, ch. 1). It is also relevant to stress the emphasis by the saga writers on Norse-Saami personal relations and its consequences. Possibly portraying such notions from the very beginning with the introduction of Hallbjǫrn hálftrǫll (who is often assumed to have Saami descent), Ketill hœngr travels to Finnmǫrk and initiates a relationship with the Saami woman Hrafnhildr with whom he has a son.¹⁵² After learning archery from Hrafnhildr's father Brúni, Ketill is caught in

---

147 *Hrólf*, 48, 50. The bear-motif is particularly interesting with the Saami Motif-Cluster in mind, as elaborated in Clive Tolley, "*Hrólfs saga kraka* and Sámi Bear Rites," *Saga-Book* 31 (2007): 5–21. See section 3.2.3.
148 *HálfdEyst*, 540–41. See introduction to text.
149 *HálfdSv*, 170–71; *HHábr*, 207–8.
150 Ben Waggoner, ed. *The Hrafnista Sagas* (New Haven: Troth Publications, 2012).
151 Waggoner, xxii–xxviii.
152 *Ket*, 123.

the middle of a power struggle between his father- and uncle-in-law, concluding with the coronation of Brúni as *Finnakonungr*.[153] The narration of the strife demonstrates Norse knowledge or perceptions of social stratification in (late) medieval Saami society. Cross-cultural marriages are strikingly common across the texts, demonstrated for example in *Gríms saga loðinkinna*, where a Víkr-based (Viken) *hersir* marries the Saami woman Grímhildr Jǫsursdóttir.[154] In the succeeding *Ǫrvar-Odds saga*, Grímhildr's Saami ties are further accentuated when her son, Ǫgmundr, is sent to Finnmǫrk to learn magic, presumably from his own kin-group.[155]

Unlike the other genres, the *fornaldarsögur* depict severe hostilities with the Saami, and the main protagonists and heroes sometimes express negative views of the group.[156] Such views are particularly evident in chapter four of *Ǫrvar-Odds saga*, where Oddr, alongside his brother Guðmundr and nephew Sigurðr, stop in Finnmǫrk on their way to Bjarmaland. Guðmundr brings his crew onshore and raids a Saami settlement. However, the raiding does not go unnoticed by Oddr, who condemns Guðmundr's actions and refuses, on behalf of his own crew, to take part in his brother's favourite activity: "at græta Finnunarnar" [to make the Saami women weep.][157] The brothers sail onwards to Bjarmaland, where the Bjarmians also suffer at the hands of the crew, in fights described by Eleanor Rosamund Barraclough as "bloody acts of premeditated violence."[158] Oddr was right in condemning the attacks, as the Saami and Bjarmians co-operate in their vengeance, and the Saami reclaim some of the stolen goods.[159] This co-operation between the Saami and the Bjarmians, further discussed in chapter 4, is in my opinion indicative of the active agency of both groups in medieval Fennoscandia, independent of Norse involvement.

Despite the clear and explicit Othering of several Saami characters across the genre, the *fornaldarsögur* also, somewhat contradictorily, consistently focus on actual Norse-Saami relations. This is especially clear in the *Hrafnistumannasögur*. While several of the main protagonists across the texts actively fight against the Saami, they often have stated Saami descent and partake in more neutral contact

---

153 *Ket*, 120–22.
154 *GrL*, 144. In *Ǫrvar-Odds saga*, Grímhildr's husband is the Bjarmian King Hárek.
155 *Ǫrv*, 241. Although the Saami presence is clear throughout, it is particularly well-articulated in Ǫrvar's death-poem, which refers to Saami groups (*terfinnar*), traditional Saami living spaces (*gammi*), archery, and the bear-hunt, 301–21.
156 *StSt*, 638: the burning of Mjǫll, *Ket*, 123: Hallbjǫrn's disapproval of Hrafnhildr, *GrL*, 144–45: Saami women are punished, *Hrólf*, 50: Queen Hvít, *HálfdEyst*, 540–41: Saami antagonists.
157 *Ǫrv*, 174.
158 Barraclough, "Frontiers," 44.
159 *Ǫrv*, 180–84.

with the Saami on other occasions. Furthermore, the fact that the writers of the texts keep underlining relations with the Saami, predominantly through personal alliances such as marriage, indicates that such relations were relevant and feasible (in the past) for the receivers of the stories. The nature of the *fornaldarsögur* as medieval texts depicting the distant past sometimes enabled the authors or compilers of these texts to portray the past by using images from the present.[160] I would also like to stress that the over-exaggeration of the Saami Motif-Cluster follows the fantastical trope surrounding the genre in general, and that the distinctly Othered portrayal might equally be a result of this.

2.7 Other sources

2.7.1 Eddic Poetry

Eddic poems have been described as representing "a Viking Age cultural practice, without necessarily being Viking-Age texts in their current form."[161] While Eddic poetry only survives in textual form from the thirteenth century onwards, it has been suggested that the heroic and mythical stories, the ideologies and the conceptual vocabulary stem from earlier in the medieval period.[162] However, Eddic poems are both anonymous and portray "timeless" events, and have most likely been subject to alterations over time as well as increased Christian influence by the writer of the texts.

There are several references to the Saami Motif-Cluster throughout the *Poetic Edda*, a collection of anonymous poems primarily found in the Codex Regius (Reykjavík, Arnastófnun, GKS 2365 4to), a manuscript dated to the 1270s.[163] These references are chiefly found in *Hávamál*, where they are connected to Óðinnic magic

---

160 The transmission history of the *fornaldarsögur* (the later ones in particular) show they were rewritten several times during transmission: Martin Arnold, "*Við þik sættumsk ek aldri*: Qrvar-Odds saga and the meanings of Qgmundr Eyþjófsbani," in *Making History: Essays on the Fornaldarsögur*, ed. Martin Arnold and Alison Finlay (London: Viking Society for Northern Research, 2010), 85–104 (85–86). In the first chapter of the same book, Elizabeth Ashman Rowe contextualises how certain stories of the past were adapted to fit the context of the time they were recorded, see "*Sǫgubrot af fornkonungum*: Mythologised History for Late Thirteenth-Century Iceland," 1–16.
161 Judith Jesch, "Poetry in the Viking Age," in *The Viking World*, ed. Stefan Brink and Neil Price (London: Routledge, 2008), 295.
162 Jesch, "Poetry," 295.
163 Paul Acker and Carolyne Larrington, *Revisiting the Poetic Edda: Essays on Old Norse Heroic Legend* (London: Routledge, 2013), 1.

which resembles the stereotypical perception of Saami ritualistic behaviour,[164] as well as in Vǫluspá, but the references are hard to separate from a general mythological topos.[165] The poem Vǫlundarkviða, however, relates the myth of Vǫlundr, who is portrayed as an expert skier, hunter, and smith, and is associated with the bear-hunt.[166] In the prose introduction to the poem, Vǫlundr and his brothers are claimed to be "synir Finnakonungs" [sons of the King of the Saami],[167] which alongside the Saami allusions in the poem itself strengthens the Saami portrayal of Vǫlundr. However, Ármann Jakobsson has argued that since Saami descent (when Vǫlundr and his brothers are described as "synir finnakonungr") is only mentioned in the prose introduction and not in the poem itself, it forms part of a later poetic inclusion:

> Whereas it is possible that the author of the prose introduction had reasons unknown to us for assuming that Vǫlundr was a Sámi hunter and prince, it should also be kept in mind that the prose introduction is often regarded as an interpretation rather than an integral part of the poem.[168]

He therefore does not treat the allusions to the Saami Motif-Cluster in the poem itself as representing Vǫlundr's Saami affiliation, but rather, as textual motifs representing the "supernatural Other."[169] In contrast, both John McKinnell and Ursula Dronke interpret the inclusion of the Saami descent in the prose introduction alongside the Saami allusions in the poem itself, as forming part of an older textual tradition based on skaldic poetry connecting the Saami to skiing, hunting, smithery, and the bear-hunt.[170] I would therefore suggest that the prose introduction may have been used as a way of emphasising the Saami narrative in the poem itself, and that the compiler took the Saami "cues" from the poem and made them explicit.

The so-called *Prose Edda* is a textbook on skaldic poetry and Norse mythology, usually assumed to have been written or at least compiled by Snorri Sturluson

---

164 *Eddukvæði*, 352–55: including chants, shapeshifting, weather magic, poison, and impenetrable garments. See section 3.2.1.
165 *Eddukvæði*, 299–95, 10.
166 *Eddukvæði*, 428–37. See section 3.2.3 for a discussion of the bear-hunt.
167 *Eddukvæði*, 428.
168 Ármann Jakobsson, "The Extreme Emotional Life of Vǫlundr the Elf," *Scandinavian Studies* 78, no. 3 (2006): 227–54 (230).
169 Ármann Jakobsson, "Vǫlundr," 250.
170 John McKinnell, "The Context of Vǫlundarkviða," *Saga-Book* 23 (1993): 1–27 (9–10). Ursula Dronke, ed., *The Poetic Edda: Mythological Poems*, vol. 2 (Oxford: Clarendon Press, 1997), 287–89.

around 1220.¹⁷¹ In my opinion, the portrayal of the "ǫndurdís" [skiing (female) deity] Skaði is the strongest allusion to the Saami Motif-Cluster in the *Prose Edda*, which is reinforced by other sources such as *Ynglinga saga* (a part of *Heimskringla*). In *Ynglinga saga*, Skaði is briefly mentioned as the wife of the Norse god Óðinn, with whom she had a son named Sæmingr.¹⁷² Although discussed in more detail in section 7.4.2, the name Sæmingr has been connected to the endonym for Saami people and some scholars therefore read Sæmingr as a representation for Saami people.¹⁷³ The portrayal of Skaði has led scholars to assume she was meant to be perceived as Saami by the audience. Her Saaminess is supported by her supernatural descent and the associations she bears to archery, hunting, skiing, and the mountains in *Skáldskaparmál*, a part of the *Prose Edda*.¹⁷⁴

Jurij Kusmenko has even gone as far as to argue that Skaði's father, the giant Þjazi, is a Norse re-interpretation of the Saami fishing and water deity Tjaetsiolmai.¹⁷⁵ This connection was initially drawn by the linguist Rasmus Rask in the nineteenth century, emphasising the similarities between the name Þjazi and the North Saami word for water *tjaetsi* [čáhci].¹⁷⁶ Rask's etymology was supported by the linguist Hjalmar Lindroth in 1919, who linked Þjazi with the early modern/ modern Saami deity Tjaetsiolmai, although Lindroth later rejected the idea because of the negative attitudes towards the Saami in the academic world at the time.¹⁷⁷ Kusmenko, however, has furthered their theory by looking at the similarities between Þjazi and Tjaetsiolmai in the mythological narratives, presenting the story related in *Skáldskaparmál* where Þjazi is found rowing at sea after the abduction of the goddess Iðunn.¹⁷⁸ He then connects the story of Þjazi in *Skáldskaparmál* to ethnographic accounts from the early twentieth century describing sacrificial stones by lakes related to the worship of the Saami deity Tjaetsiolmai. These stones, and religious imagery of the deity, were reportedly often naturally shaped or

---

171 Snorri Sturluson, *Edda: Prologue and Gylfaginning*, ed. Anthony Faulkes (London: Viking Society for Northern Research, 1988), xi–xvii.
172 *Hkr 1*, 21–22.
173 Mundal, "Family," 28.
174 Mundal, "Family," 27.
175 Kusmenko, "Sámi and Scandinavians," 76–77.
176 Rasmus Rask, "En Afhandling om Sprogkyndigheden (Lingvistikken), især de finniske Folkeslags Inddeling," in *Ausgewählte Abhandlungen*, ed. Louis Hjelmeslev, vol. 2 (Copenhagen: Levin & Munksgaard, 1932–33), 285–320 (305–6). "Tjaetsi" is a Danish simplification of the word. See Neahttadigisánit, "Čáhci," sanit.oahpha.no, https://sanit.oahpa.no/detail/sme/nob/%C4%8D%C3%A1hci.html?no_compounds=true&lemma_match=true.
177 Kusmenko, "Sámi and Scandinavians," 76.
178 *Skáldskaparmál*, 2.

drawn as resembling a bird or a bird's foot.¹⁷⁹ Because of the connection between Þjazi's rowing over the sea, his transformation into an eagle and the sacrifice he receives (the ox meat) in *Skáldskaparmál*, with Tjaetsiolmai's nature as a water and fishing deity that received sacrifices (by the aforementioned stones) and association with birds, Kusmenko assumes a development where the Saami deity was re-interpreted by the Norse as the giant Þjazi.¹⁸⁰ While Kusmenko's hypothesis is interesting, I find it difficult to support since the sources on Tjaetsiolmai are from the modern period and are therefore problematic to connect to Norse sources. However, given the etymological similarities and the fact that there is no overarching agreement on the etymology behind Þjazi, a connection is plausible. The references to the Saami Motif-Cluster in the depiction of both Þjazi and Skaði promotes such a possibility.

Later in *Skáldskaparmál*, a stanza by an anonymous skald states that with the mountains to their east, the poet was leaving the land the Saami crossed on their skis.¹⁸¹ Beyond this, Saami references in the text are scarce and the compiler never directly focuses on the Saami.

2.7.2 Skaldic Poetry

Unlike Eddic poetry, skaldic poetry is usually attributed to a specific poet and composed for a specific patron, often to commemorate a specific event.¹⁸² As such, while the dating of skaldic poetry is complicated since it mostly survives in texts that are later than when the poem was reportedly composed, scholars can nevertheless date the poems with some accuracy on the basis of this information and expected minor alterations in verse content.¹⁸³ The Saami and associations with them are frequently used in skaldic poetry, appearing across skalds, stanzas, and in different contexts.¹⁸⁴ Most often the skalds use images of the Saami and

---

179 *Skáldskaparmál*, 1. Kusmenko, "Sámi and Scandinavians," 78. Jurij Kusmenko, "Jätten Thjazi och det samiska elementet i nordisk mytologi," in *Sápmi Y1K: Livet i samernas bösättningsområde för ett tusen år sedan*, ed. Andrea Amft and Mikael Svonni (Umeå: Samiska Studier, 2006), 11–28.
180 Kusmenko, "Sámi and Scandinavians," 77.
181 *Skáldskaparmál*, 93.
182 Margaret Clunies Ross, *A History of Old Norse Poetry and Poetics* (Cambridge: D.S. Brewer, 2005) 69–82.
183 Jesch, "Poetry," 295.
184 See Tarrin Wills, ed., "Finnr," Lexicon Poeticum, https://lexiconpoeticum.org/m.php?p=lemma&i=20183, for a list of the recorded times "finnr" [Saami] is referred to in skaldic poetry.

the Saami cultural world in kennings referring to the Saami Motif-Cluster. In Halldórr skvaldri's *Útfarardrápa 10*, King Sigurðr Jórsalafari's exploits in the Mediterranean are related:

> Knátti enn en átta
> oddhríð vakit síðan
> (Finns rauð gjǫld) á grœnni
> (grams ferð) Manork verða.
>
> Then the eight point-storm [BATTLE] was again awakened in green Minorca; the ruler's company reddened the [Saami's] compensation [ARROWS].[185]

Reportedly recited by the skald Máni at the court of Sigurðr's grandson, King Magnús Erlingsson, in 1184, Halldórr relies on familiarity with *finnskatt* in linking it to the Saami's reputed skills in archery. In Þjóðolfr Arnórsson's *Sexstefja*, relating the exploits of King Haraldr harðráði Sigurðarsson in southern Europe, the same familiarity is deployed:

> Alm dró upplenzkr hilmir
> alla nôtt inn snjalli;
> hremsur lét á hvítar
> hlífr landreki drífa.
> Brynmǫnnum smó benjar
> blóðugr oddr, þars stóðu
> — flugr óx †fannings† vigra —
> Finna gjǫld í skjǫldum.
>
> The valiant Oppland king drew his elm-bow all night long; the land-ruler made shafts pelt onto white shields. The bloody point pierced the wounds on the byrnie-men, where (the tribute of the [Saami]) [ARROWS] penetrated the shields; the flight of †fannigs's† spears increased.[186]

John McKinnell argues that the usage of the Saami Motif-Cluster in skaldic poetry forms part of a traditional poetic motif, rather than being based on personal knowledge about Saami lifestyles and cultures.[187] While the archaic portrayal of

---

[185] Kari Ellen Gade, "Halldórr skvaldri, *Útfarardrápa* 10" in *Poetry from the Kings' Sagas 2: From c. 1035 to c. 1300*, ed. Kari Ellen Gade, Skaldic Poetry of the Scandinavian Middle Ages 2 (Turnhout: Brepols, 2009), 491.
[186] Diana Whaley, "Þjóðólfr Arnórsson, *Sexstefja* 15," in *Poetry from the Kings' Sagas 2: From c. 1035 to c. 1300*, ed. Kari Ellen Gade, Skaldic Poetry of the Scandinavian Middle Ages 2 (Turnhout: Brepols, 2009), 127–28. The crosses around *fannigst* indicate that it is not a known Old Norse word, and that there is no obvious emendation to make it one (it is a garbled word).
[187] McKinnell, "Vǫlundarkviða," 9–10.

the Saami in skaldic poetry could be based on such a poetic image referring to magic,[188] hunting (archery), and skiing, it is not unlikely that skalds had personal knowledge of or received first-hand accounts about the Saami way(s) of life. I would argue that this knowledge is particularly clear in Eyvindr skáldaspillir Finnson's *lausavísa* 12, which uses a traditional image from Saami life to display the severity of a famine in Hálogaland:

> Snýr á Svǫlnis vǫru
> — svá hǫfum inn sem Finnar
> birkihind of bundit
> brums – at miðju sumri.
>
> It is snowing on (the spouse of Svǫlnir <= Óðinn>) [= Jǫrð (*jǫrð* 'EARTH')] in the middle of summer; we have tied up (the bark-stripping hind of the bud) [GOAT] inside just like the [Saami].[189]

Growing up in Vefsn in Hálogaland, Eyvindr was the son of Finnr enn skjálgi, whose name might refer to their family's important role in the *finnkaup*.[190] Since Eyvindr's son Hárekr ór Þjǫtta (Tjøtta) also trades with the Saami, it seems unlikely that Eyvindr had no personal knowledge of actual Saami lifestyles. His observation that the Saami keep their goats inside during the summer indicates that he, and his audience, associated the Saami with animal husbandry.[191]

Skaldic poetry frequently uses images from the Saami Motif-Cluster by linking different tropes associated with the Saami, formed from Norse perceptions of Saami lifestyles. Building a traditional poetic image based on Norse stereotypes about the Saami, these tropes are important tools for understanding how the

---

188 "Fjǫlkunnigra Finna" [the Saami woman knowledgeable in magic]: Judith Jesch, "Sigvatr Þórðarson, Erfidrápa Óláfs helga 16," in *Poetry from the Kings' Sagas 1: From Mythical Times to c. 1035*, ed. Diana Whaley, Skaldic Poetry of the Scandinavian Middle Ages 1 (Turnhout: Brepols, 2012), 683.
189 Russell Poole, "Eyvindr skáldaspillir Finnsson, *Lausavísur* 12," in *Poetry from the Kings' Sagas 1: From Mythical Times to c. 1035*, ed. Diana Whaley, Skaldic Poetry of the Scandinavian Middle Ages 1 (Turnhout: Brepols, 2012), 231.
190 *Eg*, 25–27.
191 On the debate concerning the historical roots of (Saami) reindeer herding, see, amongst others, Jostein Bergstøl, "Hunting Native Reindeer, While Herding Imported Ones? Some Thoughts on the Development of Saami Pastoralism," in *Currents of Saami Pasts: Recent Advances in Saami Archaeology*, ed. Marte Spangen et al., Monographs of the Archaeological Society of Finland 9 (Helsinki: Archaeological Society of Finland, 2020), 34–45. Anna-Kaisa Salmi et al., "Earliest Archaeological Evidence for Domesticated Reindeer Economy Among the Sámi of Northeastern Fennoscandia AD 1300 onwards," *Journal of Anthropological Archaeology* 6 (2021): 1–15.

Norse viewed and interpreted Saami lifestyles, especially the high-standing elite, since skalds often entertained at courts. Overall, these observations are especially significant since they help establish cross-cultural personal relationships between the groups.

2.7.3 Official Documentation

A letter by an unknown author dated between 1216 and 1237 printed in the book series *Diplomatarium Norvegicum* relates the rights of Danes and Norwegians in London, and mentions several Nordic peoples also subject to these rights, including the *Lappa*.[192] This *Lappa* people may be comparable to Saxo's two *Lappia* peoples,[193] and may indicate the English awareness of the stratification of Saami societies. The letter also points to the change in terminology when describing Saami peoples, since the late ninth century Old English rewriting of Orosius's work employed the term *Finnas*, as discussed previously. If we accept that the *Lappa* of the letter are identifiable with Saami people, it indicates that Saami people sometimes travelled to England, potentially maintaining the trading tradition mentioned by Ohthere. This is significant and is further discussed in section 5.3.1.

2.7.4 Novgorod, Norway, and the Church

In the chronological inventory of Norwegian medieval documents *Regesta Norvegica*, an entry from 1251 narrates the peace-treaty between King Hákon Hákonarson and Prince Aleksander Nevskij of Novgorod. Also related in *Hákonar saga Hákonarsonar*, most likely written in the 1260s, the entry states that peace should be made between the Norwegian subjects, the Saami, and the Novgorod subjects, the Karelians.[194] Following the peace-treaty between Norway and Novgorod in 1251, it seems as if the relationship between the Norwegians and the Saami grew more tense, especially in northern areas, than previously. An entry in the Icelandic Annals from 1258 relates the return of two women to Norway, 16 years after their entourage was murdered in Finnmǫrk.[195]

---

[192] *Diplomatarium Norvegicum*, vol. 19, no. 112," https://www.dokpro.uio.no/cgi-bin/middelalder/diplom_vise_tekst.cgi?b=16086&s=n&str=.
[193] Saxo, 17–19, 39, 331.
[194] *Regesta Norvegica*, vol. 1, no. 849, https://www.dokpro.uio.no/cgi-bin/middelalder/regest_vise_tekst_2020.cgi?b=851&s=n&str=. *Hák 1*, 242.
[195] *IA*, 133–34.

The tension between the Saami and the Norwegians seemingly continues into the fourteenth century, and an entry from 1310 in the annals preserved in the *Flateyjarbók* manuscript stresses that tax had stood uncollected from Finnmǫrk for several years.[196] A royal *sýslumaðr* (see section 5.2.2) is therefore sent northwards to collect the tax, returning the next year. Perhaps this is the reasoning behind *Finnakonungr* Marteinn's visit to the court of King Hákon Magnússon in 1313, related in the Flateyjar-annals: "þetta sumar kom Marteinn (finna kongr) til Hakonar kongs" [this summer Marteinn King of the Saami visited King Hákon.][197] While there are few details surrounding the high-status political visit, King Hákon makes a law that same year criminalising frightening the Saami when collecting tax, in addition to amending the law to make life easier for newly converted Saami in Hálogaland.[198]

Similarly, the religion of the Saami in Hálogaland also concerned the Avignon Pope John XXII, who in 1323 equated the salvation of those fighting the "pagani dicti Finnar" [heathen Saami] to that of crusaders falling in battle.[199] The "fight" against the "heathen Saami" continue into the 1320s, with Bishop Audfinnr of Bergen writing to the archbishop in 1326, requesting help in the Hálogaland defence against the Saami, Russians, and Karelians.[200] A Norwegian-Russian agreement from the same year confirmed a common taxation area between the realms with outer limits to the east and the west, which an extant report from circa 1330 helps to clarify:

> Þessor endða merke ero millim Noregs kononghs ok Ruza konunghs effir þui sem gamler men hafua sagt ok en fœghia [j ðagh gamler bumenn ok finnar. [Eigha Ruzar At taka skat með sio til Ly(n)ghesþufuu. En Aa fialle till Mœleaar ok liggr hon beinsta [upp af Ly(n)gesþufuu ok austr mote Kili. En konoghr af Noreghe [tœkar skatta austr till Triancema ok inn effir Ganduik till Veleaga huar sem halfkarelar œða halffinnœr ero þeir sem Finzska moðor hafua aat. tœkzt ok ei meira j þeim œðsta œnðamœrkium en [v] graskin af huovim bogha of þa effir Fyrnð er þeir vilia effir [fyrnð gera.[201]

---

196 *IA*, 392.
197 *IA*, 393.
198 *NGL 3*, 106–8. Else Mundal, "Kong Håkon Magnussons rettarbot for Hålogaland av 1313 og andre kjelder til kristninga av samene i mellomalderen," in *Sápmi Y1K: Livet i samernas bösättningsområde för ett tusen år sedan*, ed. Andrea Amft and Mikael Svonni (Umeå: Samiska Studier, 2006), 97–114.
199 *Diplomatarium Norvegicum*, vol. 6, no. 106, https://www.dokpro.uio.no/cgi-bin/middelalder/diplom_vise_tekst.cgi?b=5857&s=n&str=.
200 *Diplomatarium Norvegicum*, vol. 8, no. 79, https://www.dokpro.uio.no/cgi-bin/middelalder/diplom_vise_tekst.cgi?b=7439&s=n&str=.
201 *NGL 3*, 153–54.

> These are the border marks between the realm of the Norwegian king and the Russian king, according to what old men have told and old settled men and Saami still tell to this day: the Russians have the right to demand tax along the sea until Lyngstuva, and in the mountains until Maeleå, which is situated straight up from Lyngstuva and eastward, toward the Keel. But the king of Norway collects tax eastward until Trianaema and along Gandvik until Veleaga, any place where there are half-Karelians or half-Saami who are born of a Saami mother. And on the uttermost borders no more than five squirrel pelts (skins) may be collected from each bow, according to old custom, if they agree.[202]

The 1330-report portrays the common Norwegian-Russian taxation area as stretching from Lyngen, the traditional territorial "border" for Norse/Saami land, to the easternmost point on the Kola Peninsula, probably Ponoy. However, the Norwegian right to taxation stretched further along the Kola Peninsula and the river Veleaga could be identifiable with a branch of the Umba (Finnish: Vieljoki).[203] These territorial delineations help contextualise the relationship with and portrayal of Bjarmaland and its inhabitants, which will be further discussed in section 4.3.1. It also enlightens the ethno-cultural diversity found in northern Fennoscandia and reminds us of the multifaceted and varied reality and possibilities of interactions for medieval Saami people. As discussed in chapter 4, dominance of the northernmost Saami settlement areas became an important geopolitical strategy for the Norwegian central authorities and the Novgorod city-state from the twelfth century onwards. Although the geopolitical situation grew more tense in the early fourteenth century, an extract from 1403 in the Icelandic annals stresses the maintenance of the traditional portrayal of the Saami in the texts:

> Jtem þat sama ar uard sa atburdur nordur Haloga landi j Noregi at einn Finnur. sa er Fedmingur hiet. ia uti j einne bargskorv heil þriu aar. suo sem daudar væri. la þar hia honum bogi hans oc orfva mæli. fiellu huorli a hann dyr ne fvglar alla þessa stund. sidan reis hann upp oc lifdi morg aar.[204]

> Item that same year was that north in Hálogaland in Norway a Saami man named Fedming lay down in a birch forest for three years, as if he was dead. Next to him he had his bow and he spoke with animals and birds in the mountain all this time. He then rose and lived for many years.

The early thirteenth century sees the continuation of official documentation negotiating the rights of the Saami, changing from most letters asserting religious authority to letters stressing political matters. That the political climate changed

---

202 Hansen and Olsen, *Hunters*, 163.
203 Hansen and Olsen, *Hunters*, 164.
204 *IA*, 286–87.

from the 1250s onwards is evident from the growth of documents stressing tension involving the Saami. The 1251 peace-treaty between Norway and Novgorod officially subjected the Saami to the Norwegian crown and demonstrates the dramatic changes following the re-organisation of the north-eastern fur trade. A Saami response to this is expressed in the visit of the *Finnakonungr* Marteinn to the court of King Hákon Magnússon in 1313, which leads to the implementation of Norwegian laws attempting to protect the Saami. The Church continued to preoccupy itself with the religion of the Saami, seeking help against the "heathenism" of the group.[205]

2.8 Conclusion

The classical to early medieval descriptions of the Saami introduce similar yet independent knowledge of the group, establishing associations and stereotypes maintained in the later Norse tradition narrating a unique Saami Motif-Cluster. From the 1100s onwards, the texts balance between discussing the magic of the Saami and its benefits, and equally the lack of Christianity and the dangers associated with what is referred to as paganism and heathenry (with the exception of Adam of Bremen). The increasing focus on the religion of the Saami is nearly parallel to the growth of Christianity in the Nordic world, expressed in law codes and religious *vitas*, in addition to a growing focus from the Church. However, the legal texts from eastern Norway, and other later sources relating Norse people seeking out the Saami for their expertise in magic, demonstrate that the belief systems of the Saami were not necessarily viewed as a problem for everyday Christians. Nordic narratives relate portrayals of the past. This portrayal often heavily relies upon Saami descent, often through allusions to the Saami Motif-Cluster, normalising personal relations across Norse and Saami cultures. Although these events are set in the past, the writers nevertheless thought it important to accentuate. Even though some of the *Íslendingasögur* and *konungasögur* are set in the past, the similarities they share with later sagas demonstrate the importance of Norse-Saami relations

---

[205] Similar processes were also in place in Finland, where conversion was slow. Caroline Wilhelmsson writes that several papal letters seem to suggest Swedish attempts to convert Finnish people from the twelfth century onwards and that the Nordic/Baltic crusades led to the incorporation of Finland into the Swedish realm in the thirteenth century. See Caroline Wilhelmsson, "Crusades, Cities and Castles: Finland as Sweden's Militarised Borderland c. 1150–1300," *Apardjón* 2 (2021): 49–76 (55–58). Notably, because of the confusion in terms for both Saami and Finnish peoples, it is sometimes difficult to differentiate the Saami and Finnish people in medieval sources discussing Finland, see section 4.3.2.

and the relevance to the contemporary socio-political situation at the time of composition. With the growth of the nation state across borders, previous institutions such as trade and taxation, national borders and the relationship between different cultural groups within these borders, become increasingly tense and heavily politicised, as demonstrated in the Icelandic annals. As Barraclough puts it:

> In their various ways, Norse texts with an interest in Norse-*Finnar* [Saami] relations take a dynamic approach in their depiction of the culture and politics of [the Saami] [...], informed not only by historical fact and present reality but also coloured by collective cultural perceptions and social memories of Norse-[Saami] interactions.[206]

The multi-dimensional and dynamic presence in medieval texts mentioning the Saami accentuates their socio-political gravity held as a group, both historically (through genealogies or fantastical background stories), as well as contemporaneously with the time of composition demonstrating interesting aspects of Norse-, and increasingly Norwegian-, Saami relations. These relations span across centuries and are positively, neutrally, and negatively charged.

---

206 Barraclough, "Frontiers", 34.

Chapter 3: The Saami Motif-Cluster

3.1 Introduction

The qualities and attributes ascribed to Saami characters in medieval texts are remarkably consistent.[1] The stability of the textual tradition to purvey these stereotyped textual motifs is the most commonly recurring theme in the academic discussion of the role of the Saami in Norse society.[2] According to Eleanor Rosamund Barraclough, the dominant scholarly tendency to focus on the patterned portrayals of the Saami in Norse narration concentrates on what sets them apart from the Norse, thereby enforcing their Otherness.[3]

The Saami, from the first classical sources to the later medieval texts, tend to be portrayed in manners associated with Othering, primarily through connotations of magic, forest animals such as bears and wolves, supernatural beings, and hunting and archery, in addition to references to winter weather and skiing. These associations form what I call the "Saami Motif-Cluster" and allude to the Saami in the texts. While I assert that it is imperative to look beyond the stereotyped textual motifs associated with the Saami in Norse narration in order to arrive at more deeper understandings of medieval Saami lifestyles, the Saami Motif-Cluster enables the identification of the Saami in the source material and is therefore invaluable to discussion. Although we need to be cautious not to reinforce stereotypes about the Saami, I nevertheless believe that identifying the Saami Motif-Cluster to "trace" Saami characters in the source material can allow for the deconstruction of these stereotypes. Here it should therefore also be emphasised that these attributes are not exclusive to the Saami only, and that other non-Saami characters can

---

[1] Jeremy DeAngelo, "The North and the Depiction of the 'Finnar' in the Icelandic Sagas," *Scandinavian Studies* 83, no. 3 (2010): 257–86 (258). Sirpa Aalto, and Veli-Pekka Lehtola, "The Sami Representations Reflecting the Multi-Ethnic North of the Saga Literature," *Journal of Northern Studies* 11, no. 2 (2017): 7–30 (12–16). Else Mundal, "The Perception of the Saamis and Their Religion in Old Norse Sources," in *Shamanism and Northern Ecology*, ed. Juha Pentikäinen (Berlin: De Gruyter, 1996), 97–116 (98–101).
[2] John Lindow, "Supernatural Others and Ethnic Others: A Millennium of World View," *Scandinavian Studies*, 67, no. 1 (1995): 8–31 (11–12). Thomas DuBois, "Ethnomemory: Ethnographic and Culture-Centered Approaches to the Study of Memory," *Scandinavian Studies* 85, no. 3 (2013): 306–31 (309). Hermann Pálsson, "The Sami People in Old Norse Literature," *Nordlit* 5 (1999): 29–53 (29). Alf Ragnar Nielssen, *Landnåm fra nord: Utvandringa fra det nordlige Norge til Island i vikingtid* (Stamsund: Orkana Akademisk forlag, 2012), 87–89.
[3] Eleanor Rosamund Barraclough, "Arctic Frontiers: Rethinking Norse-Sámi Relations in the Old Norse Sagas," *Viator* 48, no. 3 (2017): 27–51 (28).

be portrayed using images from the Saami Motif-Cluster. It is when several motifs from the Saami Motif-Cluster are employed to describe a given character, and when the overall context points in the direction of such a reading, that we can utilise them to identify characters with Saami affiliation in the texts. It should be noted that the usage of the term "textual" is not intended to exclude the strong likelihood that many of the same motifs were also current in oral tradition, even though we by definition can now only see them in textual sources. In the following sections I will discuss and analyse these motifs and how they specifically allude, directly or indirectly, to the Saami.

3.2 Saami Textual Images

3.2.1 Fjǫlkynngi Finna

Magic is the predominant theme associated with the Saami in Norse texts, and is the theme most commonly discussed by scholars focusing on medieval portrayals of the Saami.[4] Through depictions involving bewitching and spellbinding, supernatural beings, weather magic, divination, shapeshifting, and spirit journeys, ritual performance and healing, as well as the abilities to disappear, hide objects, and shoot targeted arrows, Saami characters materialise as magical experts in the texts.[5] These aspects of portrayed "magical" expertise or performance are the abilities I refer to when employing the term "magic" in this work.[6] Frequently, the Saami appear in the texts as teachers of magic or providers of magical expertise, and Norse actors often seek out the Saami for supernatural help, as discussed below. The association is well established in the saga genres, but it is difficult to confirm the textual origins of the trope. Adam of Bremen's *Gesta Hammaburgensis* from the late 1060s asserts the paganism of the majority of the Saami, which becomes an important factor in later works portraying the Saami.[7] However, given the authenticity of the source, the earliest connection between the Saami and magic may be found in stanza 16 of the court poet Sigvatr Þórðarson's *Erfidrápa*

---

[4] Hermann Pálsson, "Sami," 29. Aalto and Lehtola, "Representations," 13. Mundal, "Perception," 114. Barraclough, "Frontiers," 28.
[5] See for example: *Ágr*, 5–6; *Hrólf*, 48–50; *Ket*, 123; *SǫrlaSt*, 444–46; *Stst*, 613; *Hkr 2*, 11; *Odds*, 96, 187–90; *Vatn*, 30, 34–35; *HN*, 62–63; Saxo, 344.
[6] See Stephen A. Mitchell, "Scandinavia," in *The Routledge History of Medieval Magic*, ed. Sophie Page and Catherine Rider (London: Routledge, 2019), 136–50, and section 1.1.1, footnote 17.
[7] *Hammaburgensis*, 172–73.

Óláfs helga, a memorial poem reportedly dedicated to King Óláfr Haraldsson following his death at the battle of Stiklastaðir in 1030:

> Mildr fann gǫrst, hvé galdrar,
> gramr sjalfr, meginrammir
> fjǫlkunnigra Finna
> fullstórum barg Þóri,
> þás hyrsendir Hundi
> húna golli búnu
> — slætt réð sízt at bíta —
> sverði laust of herðar.
>
> The gracious prince discovered most clearly himself how the mightily strong spells of the magic-skilled [Saami] saved the very powerful Þórir when the sender of the fire of the mast-tops [(lit. "fire-sender of the mast-tops") GOLD > GENEROUS MAN = Óláfr] struck with the sword adorned with gold across the shoulders of Hundr ("Dog"); the blunt one succeeded least in biting.[8]

Presumably recited sometime after the canonisation of the king in 1031, the stanza relates the well-known story of the Hálogaland chieftain Þórir hundr's reported magical protection by his Saami allies during the battle. In later accounts, the protection becomes a magical cloak fashioned by the Saami and is the key catalyst leading to the death of the king.[9] It is difficult to establish whether the association between the Saami and their perceived magical skills became manifested in literary tradition following the poem's composition, or whether it was re-introduced with the composition of the sagas and other texts. It is likely that this link between the Saami and magic became a conventional part of oral tradition concerning the Saami, and that this oral tradition stemmed from discussions about people living in close proximity to the Norse. As such, this tradition reflects constant and repeated cross-cultural interaction between Norse and Saami peoples throughout the medieval period. If the eastern Norwegian law codes prohibiting Christians from visiting the Saami and participating in Saami rituals were implemented prior to their earliest surviving thirteenth-century composition, they might have been relevant from the mid-twelfth century onwards.[10] Unfortunately, the law codes are hard to date since they only survive in later compositions and there is no certain way of establishing whether they were archaic or included at the time of composition.

---

8 Judith Jesch, "Sigvatr Þórðarson, *Erfidrápa Óláfs helga* 16," in *Poetry from the Kings' Sagas 1: From Mythical Times to c. 1035*, ed. Diana Whaley, Skaldic Poetry of the Scandinavian Middle Ages 1 (Turnhout: Brepols, 2012), 663.
9 *Hkr 2*, 344–45. *Helgisaga*, 70.
10 Store norske leksikon, "Borgarting," snl.no, 10.11.2017 https://snl.no/Borgarting. *NGL 1*, 389–90.

Nonetheless, the increasing focus on the paganism of the Saami and their magic coincides with the establishment of Christianity in the Nordic world. The anonymous cleric composing *Historia Norwegie*, for example, strongly opposes the magic performed by the Saami and juxtaposes it with Christianity:

> Horum itaque intollerabilis perfidia uix cuiquam credibilis uidebitur, quantumue diabolice supersitcionis in magica arte exerceant. Sunt namque quidam ex ipsis, qui quasi prophete a stolido uulgo uenerantur, quoniam per immundum spiritum, quem "gandum" uocitant, multis multa presagia, ut eueniunt, quandoque percunctati predicent. Et de longinquis prouinciis res concupiscibiles miro modo sibi alliciunt, nec non absconditos thesauros longe remoti mirifice produnt.[11]

> A person will scarcely believe their unendurable impiety and the extent to which they practise heathen devilry in their magic arts. There are some who are worshipped by the ignorant masses as though they were prophets, since, whenever questioned, they will give many predictions to many folk through the medium of a foul spirit which they call "gand," and these auguries come true. Furthermore they attract themselves desirable objects from distant parts in an astounding fashion and miraculously reveal hidden treasures, even though they are situated a vast distance away.[12]

Lars Boje Mortensen argues, based on statements put forth in the text about Norwegian tax-land nationally and abroad, descriptions about ecclesiastical administration, mention of royals and other high-standing people, and of natural events in Iceland like earthquakes, that the text should be dated between 1165–70.[13] As the text emphasises, the apparent "heathen devilry" practised by the Saami did not stop Norse actors from seeking it out. As established in chapter 2.6.2, a majority of the medieval texts directly involving Saami actors are founded on their magical expertise or aid to Norse actors.[14] The stories relating the first meeting between Eiríkr blóðøx and Gunnhildr exemplify this, explaining Gunnhildr's presence in Finnmǫrk as a result of her apprenticeship with Saami people to learn magic.[15] *Ǫrvar-Odds saga* relates Ǫgmundr's visit to his kin group in Finnmǫrk where he learns "allskyns galdra ok gjörnínga" [all kinds of incantations and magical acts].[16] Requesting the magical aid offered by Saami magical experts becomes a stable trope across the sources, and in the late twelfth/early thirteenth century,

---

11 *HN*, 60.
12 *HN*, 61.
13 *HN*, 24, 11–24.
14 Hermann Pálsson, *Úr landnorðri: Samar og ystu rœtur íslenskrar menningar* (Reykjavík: Bókmenntafræðistofnun Háskola Íslands, 1997), 131–40.
15 *Hkr 1*, 135. *Fsk*, 79. *Mesta 1*, 8–9. Gunnhildr is described as "fjǫlkunning mjǫk" [knowledgeable in magic], but this ability is not associated with the Saami in *Eg*, 94, 113.
16 *Ǫrv*, 241.

Saxo relates that Óðinn required magical expertise only offered by the Saami.[17] As discussed in chapter 2, the motif is appropriated twice in *Vatnsdœla saga*, first with the invitation of "Finna ein fjǫlkunnig" [a Saami woman knowledgeable in magic] to a feast where her prophesying skills are emphasised, followed by the calling for three Saami men offering their magical expertise to retrieve Ingimundr's lost item in exchange for butter and tin.[18]

Despite an academic tradition of associating both King Óláfr Tryggvason and King Óláfr Haraldsson with derogatory views of the Saami,[19] the two kings are also portrayed as seeking help from or depending on Saami actors. In the Icelandic monk Oddr Snorrason's *Óláfs saga Tryggvasonar* from the 1190s, King Óláfr agrees to ask a Saami man dwelling in the mountains of Þjálfahellir (somewhere in Agdenes) in Þróndalǫg for help with troublesome Hálogalanders. Although the king is reluctant to meet "þesskyns men" [men of that kind], the Saami man has foreseen their arrival and advises the king on how to resolve the conflict, and "fór þetta allt eptir því sem Fiðrinn hafði sagt" [everything turned out as the Saami man had said].[20] The Saami man himself also addresses his Otherness by stating "í þínu foruneyti eru bjǫrt guð, en þeira samvistu má ek eigi bra, því at ek hefi annarskonar natúru" [accompanying you are bright spirits, and I cannot endure their presence because I am of a different nature].[21] This expressed Othering is in my opinion likely referring to his paganism and the fact that the king appropriates it by taking his advice when dealing with a royal issue, rather than leaving it in the hands of God as in other stories. Since there are no instances in the extract where the negative expressions are directly connected to the man's cultural affiliation, the negative Othering is likely connected to his lack of Christianity since that is the feature rejected by the king.[22] The fact that the man is portrayed as Saami, however, does emphasise the pagan aspects of the situation. In *Helgisaga Óláfs konungs Haraldssonar*, preserved in a mid-thirteenth century manuscript (possibly based on a late twelfth century text), a Saami man in the saintly king's retinue shares his prophetic vision with the king, with his story later proving true and concluding with victory in battle.[23]

Prophetic abilities are associated with Saami actors on other occasions as well, and Saami prophesiers often form part of an elite or appear in relation to it, indi-

---

17 Saxo, 163.
18 *Vatn*, 30, 34–35.
19 DeAngelo, "North," 260.
20 *Odds*, 187–90.
21 *Odds*, 188.
22 *Odds*, 188–90.
23 *Helgisaga*, IV–VIII, 16. See section 6.2.2.

cating high status. For example, *Ágrip* relates the abilities of Rǫgnvaldr reykill, the reported son of the Saami "princess" Snæfríðr and King Haraldr hárfagri, including the ability to foretell the future.[24] In the scene including the Saami practitioner of magic in *Vatnsdœla saga*, she is portrayed as predicting the future, and Saxo relates that the Saami prophesier Rostiophus Phinnicus's skills help the god Óðinn avenge his kin.[25] As already seen and will be furthered below, *Historia Norwegie* also emphasises the abilities of some Saami to predict the future, in addition to retrieving lost items.[26] However, the latter ability is not mentioned (as far as I am aware), other than in the famous *semsveinar* incident, and in the stories relating Hálfdan svarti's banquet when a Saami man is accused of stealing the banquet food and is then ordered to reconjure it,[27] which will be further discussed later.

The stigmatised magical abilities of the Saami related across Norse texts most often prove very useful for some of the Norse characters and work as catalysts in the narrative. In my opinion, this "usefulness" becomes particularly clear in the events revolving around the Hálogaland chieftains, especially Þórir hundr, whose storyline as an antagonist to the Norwegian king Óláfr Haraldsson is founded on his relationship with Saami groups, with one such perceived group granting him an impenetrable cloak, as related in Heimskringla's *Ólafs saga helga:*

> Þórir hundr hafði Finnferð haft þessa tvða vetr lengi á fjalli ok fengit óf fjár. Hann átti margs konar kaup við Finna. Hann lét þár gera sér tólf hreinbjálba með svá mikill fjǫlkynngi, at ekki vápn festi á ok síðr miklu en á hringabrynju.[28]

> Þórir hundr had been engaged in trading with the [Saami] for these two winters, and both winters he had spent a long time in the mountains and had made a lot of money. He did various kinds of trade with the [Saami]. He had prepared for himself there twelve reindeer-skin

---

24 *Ágr*, 5. Also the case for Drauma-Finni in *Finnboga saga ramma*, 268. I sometimes refer to Snæfríðr as a Saami "princess" to emphasise her high status as the daughter of a *Finnakonungr*. This is also the case for other Saami characters that are described as the daughters of kings. In my opinion, her high status as the daughter of what the Norse referred to as *Finnakonungr* is often neglected by scholars discussing her portrayal, something that I wish to avoid since I believe it reinforces colonial notions of Saami submissiveness to the Norse (see section 6.2.1). However, I have kept the term emphasised with punctuation marks since Snæfríðr is never referred to as being a "princess" in any of the texts and refering to her as such is my invention.
25 *Vatn*, 29–30. Saxo, 163.
26 *HN*, 60–61. See Lyonel Perabo, *Here Be Heathens: The Supernatural Image of Northern Fenno-Scandinavia in Pre-Modern Literature* (MA diss., Háskoli Íslands, 2016), 91–114, for an overview of the Saami diviner motif in pre-modern literature.
27 *Vatn*, 34–35. *Hkr 1*, 92. *HálfdSv*, 170–71.
28 *Hkr 2*, 344–45. In *Ǫrv*, 202, Oddr is given a magical cloak impenetrable to weapons, fashioned by different people knowledgeable in magic, including the Saami.

coats, using such powerful magic that no weapon could penetrate them, and much less than a coat of mail.²⁹

As demonstrated by *Erfidrápa* 16 above, the cloak and its Saami connotations are key catalysts leading to the death of the Norwegian king at the battle of Stiklastaðir in 1030.³⁰ Similarly, in *Helgisaga Óláfs konungs Haraldssonar*, Þórir hundr flees to Finnmǫrk after a disagreement with the king arising from a grain shortage in Hálogaland culminating in the several murders of members of both sides of the conflict, and "træystizc miock fiolkynga Finna" [had much confidence in the magic of the Saami], staying with the group for two winters.³¹ Later, during the battle of Stiklarstaðir, the saga relates that when a soldier from the king's army attempts to stab Þórir, it is as if his sword is nothing but a stick, explained by the fact that Þórir and his entourage wear cloaks the Saami had made with "mikill fjǫlkyngi" [great magic].³²

In several sources dealing with King Óláfr Tryggvason, the motif of Saami magical aid is expanded to include help with the fertility of a childless Norse couple. The couple is depicted as struggling with childbearing and seek the magical assistance of a Saami group outside Niðarós (Nidaros), who call for a spirit eventually incarnated in the couple's offspring, as related in Oddr Snorrason's *Óláfs saga*:

> Faðir minn ok móðir váur saman langa hríð með lǫligum hjúskap ok áttu ekki barn. Ok er þau eldusk, þá hǫrmuðu þau þat mjǫk ef þau dœi erfingjalaus. Fóru þau siðan til Finna með miki fé ok báðu þá gefa sér nǫkkvorn erfingja af fjǫlkynngis íþrótt. Finnar kǫlluðu þá til hǫfðingja þeira anda er loptit byggja, fyrir því at jafnfullt er loptit af óhreinum ǫndum sem jǫrðin. Ok sjá andi sendi einn óhreinan anda í þessa hina døkku myrkvastofu er at sǫnnu má kallask minnar móður kviðr. Ok sá hinn sami andi em ek, ok holdguðumk ek svá með þessum hætti, ok síðan sýndumk ek með mannligri ásjá, ok var ek svá borinn í heim [...] ok fyrir því má ek eigi skírask at ek em eigi maðr.³³
>
> My father and mother spent a long time together in lawful wedlock and had no children. When they grew old, they were much grieved that they might have to die with no heir. They then visited the [Saami] with a great deal of money and asked that they grant them an heir with the exercise of magic. The [Saami] then called on the chief of their spirits, who dwell in the sky, for the sky is as full of unclean spirits as the earth. This spirit sent an unclean spirit into the dark dungeon that in fact may be called my mother's womb. That same spirit am I, and I was incarnated in this way and then appeared in human

---

29 Snorri Sturluson, *Heimskringla*, trans. Alison Finlay and Anthony Faulkes, 3 vols (London: Viking Society for Northern Research, 2014), "Hkr 2," 230.
30 Jesch, "Erfidrápa 16," 683. *Hkr 2*, 344–45.
31 *Helgisaga*, 52.
32 *Helgisaga*, 69.
33 *Odds*, 257. In *Hkr 1*, a later source, the story is shortened but follows the same pattern, 323.

form. That was the manner of my birth [...] I cannot be baptized for the reason that I am not a man.[34]

The couple's offspring, Eyvindr kinnrifa, a friend of the Hálogalandier Hárekr ór Þjótta and a thorn in the king's side, later explains why he must refuse baptism on the grounds that he is not even human (because of his reported magical origins), introducing the difficult conversion narrative of people from Hálogaland in the sagas. The story is echoed and further elaborated in the probably early fourteenth-century compilation *Óláfs saga Tryggvasonar en mesta*, where the Saami performers of magic reluctantly agree to help the struggling couple with their request only if they promise with an oath that "sá maðr skal alt til dauðadags þjóna Þór ok Óðni, ef vér megum öðlast þat barn er líf ok aldr hafi til" [the child shall serve Thor and Odin till the day of its death, and that we may have him when he is old enough].[35] Whether or not the medieval audience understood the Saami character's demand that Eyvindr should return to the group in adolescence as a common request, there is no doubt that the text stresses the importance felt by the Saami that he should stay devoted to the pre-Christian gods. The explicit emphasis on the Norse gods Þórr and Óðinn, instead of simply "heathen beliefs" or Saami deities, is interesting since it demonstrates the contrast between the Christian and the non-believer, rather than Saami beliefs specifically.

Sirpa Aalto asserts that a key feature of the European medieval tradition of historiography is based on the creation of contrast between the Christian and the non-Christian.[36] In this case then, since the text does not elaborate on the condition of Eyvindr returning to Saami society, I argue that it is not the juxtaposition between the Norse-Saami that is important, but rather a lack of Christianity, presented for the audience as the Saami wish for Eyvindr to remain devoted to the pre-Christian Norse gods. Similarly, when unruly Hálogalanders associated with the Saami are demonised in the narrative, the problem posed is never the lines drawn between culturally or ethnically different social groups, but rather fundamental religious differences between the old beliefs and the new. I would also suggest that the emphasis on Eyvindr's Saami "creators" as worshippers of the Norse gods help illuminate the possibilities of different medieval Saami and Norse societies for negotiating belonging and identity discussed in chapter 6.

A similar pattern of conversion is mirrored in the stories concerning the Hálogaland chieftain Rauðr inn rammi, whose large entourage of Saami people accen-

---

[34] Oddr Snorrason, *The Saga of Olaf Tryggvason*, trans. Theodore M. Andersson (Ithaca: Cornell University Press, 2000), 96.
[35] *Mesta 2*, 168.
[36] Sirpa Aalto, "Encountering 'Otherness' in the *Heimskringla*," *Ennen ja Nyt* 4 (2004): 1–10 (6).

tuates his paganism, differentiating him from the Christian population socioculturally and in turn enabling him to perform weather magic obstructing the king.[37] In Heimskringla's Óláfs saga Tryggvasonar, King Óláfr Tryggvason is portrayed as having to make several attempts to sail into the Sálpti fjord (Salten) where Rauðr kept his residence, only succeeding when the bishop and "guð sinn styrk" [the strength of his god] managed to quell the storms allegedly conjured by the farmer.[38] The description of the king's difficulties in reaching the fjord is probably not completely fabricated, as Rauðr's farm is located near Saltstraumen. The maelstrom, just south of Bodø, is located in a small strait with one of the strongest tidal currents in the world. Without any natural explanations at the time, the difficult waters were associated by those unfamiliar with the area with Rauðr's paganism, which is reinforced here by his familiarity with Saami people. It is interesting, and important, to note that it is not necessarily the Saami that are Othered or demonised in the narrative, despite being the ones often ascribed with magical abilities, but rather, the Hálogalanders who associate themselves with and appropriate non-Christian magic.

Weather magic and the ability to manipulate the weather is sometimes associated with Saami actors.[39] As related in chapter 2.6, the magically skilled Steinfinnr carries out weather magic whilst in a near trance-like state in Reykdœla saga ok Víga-Skútu, likely first written in the mid-thirteenth century. Described as sitting still and looking into the ground, he reportedly darkens the sky.[40] In Ketils saga hœngs, Gríms saga loðinkinna, and Ǫrvar-Odds saga, Saami characters are associated with weather magic but are not directly portrayed as the actors behind it.[41] Since the instances where the weather changes drastically as an antagonistic force in the narrative appears in contexts where the Saami function as antagonists, a connection is expressed by the presence of both. The connection is furthered later in Ǫrvar-Odds saga with a direct association between the foul weather and the Saami: "Nú mun ek gefa þeim byr bertu hèðan, jafnt slíkan sem Finnar gáfu þeim híngat" [Now I will give them a favourable wind away

---

[37] See section 6.2. "Hann var ríkr maðr. Fylgði honum mikill fjǫlði Finna, þegar er kunnigr. Hann var vinr mikill ok mjǫk fjǫlkunnigr" [He was a rich man. A large number of (Saami people) attended him when he needed them. Rauðr was a great pagan and very skilled in magic], Hkr 1, 324; "Hkr 1," 202.
[38] Hkr 1, 326.
[39] See Jennifer Hemphill, Weather Magic in the Nordic Middle Ages (forthcoming PhD thesis, University of Aberdeen) for a detailed analysis of weather magic in medieval and early modern Fennoscandia.
[40] Reyk, 192–93.
[41] Ket, ch. 3; GrL, ch. 1; Ǫrv, ch. 5.

from here, just like the one the Saami gave them to send them here].⁴² Following the killing of the Saami men housing Gunnhildr in *Haralds saga hárfagra* in Heimskringla, a terrible thunderstorm hinders the departure of the Norse crew, insinuating that the death of the magically-skilled characters was the catalyst behind the bad weather.⁴³ The association between the Saami and weather magic is clearest in the extracts portraying a harrying trip to Finnland in *Óláfs saga helga*, also from Heimskringla. Here, the young king encounters Saami weather magic in a valley called Herdalar:

> Þeir Finnar gerðu um nóttina œðiveðr með fjǫlkynngi ok storm sjávar. En konungr lét upp taka akkerin ok draga segl ok beittu um nóttina fyrir landit. Mátti þá sem optar meira hamingja konungs en fjǫlkynngi.⁴⁴

> During the night the [Saami] caused horrible weather and stormy seas by magic. But the king had the anchors weighed and the sails lifted and during the night they sailed along the coast. Then again, as on other occasions, the king's good fortune had more power than magic.⁴⁵

The magic conjured by the Saami is used as a contrasting force to the king's Christianity, emphasising the king's sanctity and the relative merit of Christianity. Although initially portrayed as good archers using the thick forest to their advantage, the Saami are ultimately defeated due to the power of Christianity. Such an opposition between the Saami and Christianity is also traceable in the stories relating the marriage between King Haraldr hárfagri and the Saami "princess" Snæfríðr, echoed in Heimskringla's *Haralds saga hárfagra* but first related in *Ágrip*. Here, allusions to the dangers of not conforming to Christianity are represented as foul odours, vermin, and unnatural decomposition following Snæfríðr's death:

> Jólaaptan, er Haraldr sat at mat, þá kom Svási fyrir dyrr ok sendi konungi boð, at hann skyldi út ganga til hans, en konung brásk reiðr við þeim sendiboðum, ok bar inn sami reiði hans út, er boð hans hafði borit inn. En hinn bað hann þá eigi fyrir því at síðr [í] annat sinni ok gaf hónum bjórskinn eitt til ok kvað sik vera þann Finnin, er hann hafði ját at setja famma sinn annan veg brekkunnar á Þoptyn, þar sem þá var konungrinn. En konungrinn gekk út ok varð hónum þess játsi, at hann gekk yfir í gamma hans með áeggjan sumra sinna manna, þó at sumir letti. Stóð þar upp Snjófríðr{r}, dóttir Svása, kvenna vænust, ok byrlaði ker mjaðar fullt konunginum, ok hann tók allt saman ok hǫnd hennar. Ok þegar var sem eldshiti kœmi í hǫrund hans, ok vildi þegar hafa hana á þeiri nótt. En Svási sagði at þat mundi eigi vera, nema hónum nauðfum, nema konungrinn festi hana ok fengi at lǫgum. Ok hann festi ok fekk ok unni svá með [œrslum], at ríki sitt ok allt þat, er hans tígn byrjaði, þá fyrlét

---

42 *Ǫrv*, 184–85.
43 *Hkr 1*, 136.
44 *Hkr 2*, 11. See section 4.3.2.
45 "Hkr 2," 9.

hann ok sat hjá henni nótt ok dag náliga, meðan þau lifðu bæði, ok þrjá vetr síðan hón var dauð. Syrgði hann hana dauða, en landslýðr allr syrgði hann villtan [...] Ok þegar er hón var hrœrð, þá slœri á óþefjani ok ýldu ok hverskyns illum fnyk af líkamanum. Var þá hvatat báli ok hón brennd; blánaði þó aðr allr líkaminn ok ullu ór ormar ok eðlur, froskar ok pǫddur ok allskyns illyrmi.

On the eve of Yule, as Haraldr sat at table, Svási came to the door and sent word in to the king that he should come out to him. This request angered the king, and the same man bore his anger out as had borne the message in. Svási asked him nevertheless a second time and also gave him a beaver skin and said that he was that [Saami] whom the king had allowed to set up his hut on the other side of the hill at Þoptyn, where the king then was. The king went out and he agreed to go to Svási's hut, egged on by some of his men, though others tried to dissuade him. There Snjófríðr stood up, the most beautiful of women and offered the king a cup full of mead. He took it and with it her hand, and suddenly it was as if fiery heat entered into his flesh and he wished to have her that same night. But Svási said that this should not be so – except against his will – unless the king betrothed himself to her and then wedded her according to the law. And he betrothed himself to her and wedded her and loved her so witlessly that he neglected his kingdom and all that beseemed his kingly honour, and he stayed by her almost night and day while they both lived and for three years after she died. He mourned for her, dead, but the people all mourned for him, bewitched [...] And when she was moved there issued from the body a rank and fulsome stench and foul odours of every sort. A pyre was hastily prepared and she was burnt, but before that the body blackened and there bubbled out worms and vipers, frogs and toads and multitudes of vermin.[46]

The context in which this account appears relates the many marriages and children of King Haraldr, and how these marriages offered him kinship relations which granted him control over vast areas of land, with his steadily growing kingdom symbolising his power.[47] The account therefore exemplifies, or glorifies, a medieval attempt to unify the neighbouring groups through the establishment of kinship between Norwegian and Saami elites. Snæfríðr's insinuated bewitchment of the king has led several scholars to interpret the episode as a Norse expression of hostility to, or derogation of, the Saami.[48] However, her "spell" follows the exact same pattern as the conversion narrative of the farmers from Guðbrandsdalr (Gudbrandsdalen) in Heimskringla's *Óláfs saga helga*, where the saintly king destroys a pre-Christian idol leading to the outpouring of mice the size of cats, adders, toads, and snakes.[49] The two instances mirror the Biblical account of Antiochus IV Epiphanes (2 Maccabees 9.8–9), whose death is portrayed using similar imagery of (bodily) worms, rotting flesh, and decay. I would therefore sug-

---

46 *Ágr*, 5–6.
47 Mundal, "Perception," 108.
48 See section 6.2.1.
49 *Hkr 2*, 189.

gest that the authors of *Ágrip* and the stories about the Guðbrandsdalr-farmers used motifs known from the account of the "pagan" King Antiochus to reinforce the heathenism of these situations. This similarity strengthens the notion, in my opinion, that while Snæfríðr's powers might have been perceived as more powerful because of her Saaminess, it is her paganism, via the implied magic, that poses a problem in the text, rather than her cultural affiliation. The Saami, who stereotypically did not convert to the new religion until the early modern period, bore stronger associations with the fears of the old religion(s) than the "forgiven" pagan King Haraldr. It should nevertheless be mentioned that there is evidence that several Saami peoples and groups converted to Christianity, probably as a combination of voluntary and forced conversion as the rest of the population, throughout the medieval period. For example, in King Hákon V's 1313 law amendment for Hálogaland, Saami people converting to Christianity would be granted reduced fines for offences in the first twenty years following conversion.[50] The conversion of Hálogaland and the northern regions of Finnmǫrk is complicated and might have begun earlier than traditionally assumed.[51] While the conversion of Saami peoples is a complicated issue, and while results from archaeological investigations such as at the Rounala churchyard in northern Sweden indicate the prevalence of medieval Christian burial customs in inland Sápmi, large-scale conversion of Saami peoples was instigated in the seventeenth and eighteenth centuries with intensified missionary work.[52]

In addition to the incidents described above, there are several other tropes associated with the magical abilities of the Saami. Enchantment of someone or something is a prevalent theme in connection with Saami magical actors.[53] Similar to Queen Hvít's curse transforming her step-son into a bear in *Hrólfs saga kraka* as discussed previously and below, the Saami woman Grímhildr curses her step-daughter into becoming an ugly troll-woman in *Gríms saga loðinkinna*.[54] As previously mentioned, a Saami man is accused of enchanting away the food during a feast in Haðaland in *Hálfdanar saga svarta* (Heimskringla) and *Hálfdanar þáttr*

---

[50] *NGL 3*, 107
[51] Asgeir Svestad, "Svøpt i myra: Synspunkter på Skjoldehamnfunnets etniske og kulturelle tilknytning," in *Viking*, ed. Herdis Hølleland et al., Norsk arkeologisk årbok, vol. 80 (Oslo: Norsk Arkeologiske Selskap, 2017), 129–56 (136–38).
[52] See Svestad, "Skjoldehamnfunnet," 136–38, and Kjell-Åke Aronsson, "Research on Human Remains of Indigenous People: Reflections from an Archaeological Perspective (With an Example from Rounala)," in *More than Just Bones: Ethics and Research on Human Remains*, ed. Halvard Fossheim (Oslo: Forskningsetiske komiteer, 2012), 65–80. See also the discussion in section 6.3.2.
[53] Saxo, 343.
[54] *GrL*, 151–52.

svarta.⁵⁵ However, it is not necessarily always the Saami characters that do the enchanting, as demonstrated in Heimskringla's *Ynglinga saga*, where the Saami woman Drífa hires the magical performer Huld to bewitch Vanlandi.⁵⁶ Huld is never ascribed with any cultural affiliation in this passage, and is therefore not necessarily Saami. Despite this, it is Saami magic that is demonised in the text:

> En er seiðr var framiðr, var Vanlandi at Uppsǫlum. Þá gerði hann fúsan at fara til Finnland, en vinir hans ok ráðamenn bǫnnuðu honum ok sǫgðu, at vera myndi fjǫlkynngi Finna í fýsi hans.⁵⁷

> And when the spell was cast, Vanlandi was at Uppsalir. Then he became eager to go to [Finnland], but his friends and advisors forbade him and said that his enthusiasm must be caused by [Saami] magic.⁵⁸

As mentioned above, this demonisation of (perceived) Saami magic might be a manifestation of the European medieval tradition of historiography juxtaposing the Christian with the non-Christian. However, the instance from *Ynglinga saga* is curious: depicting the pre-Christian past, it narrates both Saami and, if Huld was perceived as not Saami, Norse magic. Although the Saami woman Drífa hires what is possibly a Norse performer of magic, it is the Saami associations that are emphasised, contrasting with the extracts above where the problem is not necessarily the Saami affiliation of some practitioners of magic, but rather, the lack of Christianity. The portrayal of Saami magic, or lack of Christianity as something inherently Saami, is potentially only elsewhere found in *Historia Norwegie*, mentioned above. However, *Historia Norwegie* also portrays Norse actors actively seeking Saami expertise in magic, thereby demonstrating that while Saami magic was viewed as something Othered and dangerous, it was still a powerful tool for Norse characters. In section 6.2, I argue that seeking out Saami magic might have become more desirable for Norse actors following the conversion, since they in this way could participate in a previously important but now forbidden ritual.

Another common trope associated with the Saami is the ability to shapeshift.⁵⁹ In *Sturlaugs saga Starfsama*, the Saami characters shapeshift into both eagles and

---

55 *Hkr 1*, 92; *HálfSv*, 170–71.
56 *Hkr 1*, 29.
57 *Hkr 1*, 29.
58 "Hkr," 17.
59 Shapeshifting is also a common trope in pre-Christian Norse beliefs, see for example Lotte Hedeager, *Iron Age Myth and Materiality: An Archaeology of Scandinavia AD 400–1000* (London: Routledge, 2011), 82–84.

hounds,⁶⁰ and when Ketill hœngr meets his Saami father-in-law for the first time in *Ketils saga hœngs*, he is a whale.⁶¹ In *Hálfdanar saga Eysteinssonar*, the Saami king Finnr shapeshifts into a whale, and the extract perfectly exemplifies the collective magical stereotypes attributed to the Saami in Norse narration, focusing on shapeshifting, the shooting of targeted arrows from one's fingers and healing.⁶² In the late *Sǫrla saga sterka*, most likely first written in the fourteenth or fifteenth centuries, in addition to having the ability of magically vanishing (into the ground), the Saami characters are portrayed as able to shapeshift and shoot targeted arrows from their fingers and have healing abilities.⁶³

As emphasised by several scholars, Saami characters are sometimes associated with supernatural beings and otherworlds.⁶⁴ Hermann Pálsson argued that certain unqualified mythical terms, such as those denoting giants, elves, dwarves, *trǫll*, and *þursar* were sometimes used for the Saami people.⁶⁵ This connection has been suggested as being manifested in the different portrayals of Svási Finnakonungr, Snæfríðr's father. In the introduction to the Snæfríðr-episode in *Ágrip*, commonly accepted as being composed in Norway around the 1190s, Svási is only described as "finnakonungr."⁶⁶ In Heimskringla, assumed to have been compiled around 1230, he is called a *finnr* (Saami) and, according to Else Mundal and Miriam Horn, a "jǫtunn" [giant].⁶⁷ However, the *jǫtunn*-reference only appears in a chapter title, "Frá Svása jǫtni" [Of the *jǫtunn* Svási], and it is most likely a later addition as titles are often relatively modern. Svási's description as a *jǫtunn* in the chapter title has nevertheless been treated as authentic by Mundal and Horn. In the later *Hauks þáttr hábrókar*, found in the late fourteenth-century manuscript Flateyjarbók, Svási is referred to as "dvergr" [dwarf], in addition to being a *finnr*.⁶⁸ I would therefore argue that the motifs associated with the Saami evolved into incorporating super-

---

60 *Stst*, 613.
61 *Ket*, 116–17.
62 *HálfdEyst*, 584–49.
63 *SǫrlaSt*, 444–46.
64 Else Mundal, "The Relationship Between Sami and Nordic Peoples Expressed in Terms of Family Associations," *Journal of Northern Studies* 2 (2009): 25–37 (29–30). Aalto and Lehtola, "Representations," 14–16. Hermann Pálsson, "Sami," 31. Triin Laidoner, "The Flying *Noaidi* of the North: Sámi Tradition Reflected in the Figure Loki Laufeyjarson in Old Norse Mythology," *Scripta Islandica* 63 (2012): 59–93 (66).
65 Hermann Pálsson, "Sami," 31.
66 *Ágr*, 4.
67 *Hkr 1*, 125–26. Mundal, "Family," 29. Miriam Horn, "Möndull Pattason: A Sami Identity in a Dwarfish Guise," in *Samer som "de andra," samer "om de andra": Identitet och etnicitet i nordiska kulturmöten*, ed. Else Mundal and Håkan Rydving (Umeå: Samiske studier, 2010), 146–50 (151–52).
68 *HHábr*, 207.

natural beings such as giants and dwarves later in the medieval period, and a character like Svási could then therefore be described as a supernatural being in addition to being a Saami. This interpretation aligns with Ralph O'Connor's aforementioned statement that scholars today generally agree "that fictional tendencies become more frequent and sustained in later sagas as the genre developed."[69] This development could just as likely also be suggestive of the fact that Saami and Norse cultures had become more estranged from each other, which I further elaborate on in chapters 4 and 5.

As he interpreted the nicknames *hálftrǫll* and *hálfbergrisi* as alluding to Saami parentage in *Egils saga Skallagrímssonar*, Hermann Pálsson claimed that the whole semantic range of *trǫll* must have included notions of the Saami.[70] There is a twofold problem with this interpretation. Primarily, we cannot accept that the nicknames above undoubtedly refer to Saami descent, despite several scholars often assuming that they do.[71] Neither Hallbjǫrn halftrǫll nor Bjǫrgólfr hálfbergrisi are otherwise described using (other) images from the Saami-Motif-Cluster, and it should also be noted that *Egils saga* portrays the stated Saami characters (the *finnar* encountered during *finnkaup*) in normalised language and that these characters are not significantly Othered or called *trǫll* or *rísar*. I would therefore argue that their nicknames should most likely not be understood as indicating Saami descent, and that new interpretations of these nicknames are called for in future research. Secondly, *trǫll* is also often associated with magic and mythical beings such as monsters and giants,[72] and can therefore be ambiguous and is quite rarely connected to the Saami.[73] In *Ketils saga hœngs*, Hallbjǫrn (halftrǫll) uses the term *trǫll* about his daughter-in-law Hrafnhildr.[74] While this may seem like a direct reference to Hrafnhildr's Saami descent through her father Brúni, especially as she is not portrayed as practising magic herself, the coinage is not as straightforward as

---

69 Ralph O'Connor, "History and Fiction," in *The Routledge Research Companion to the Medieval Icelandic Sagas*, ed. Ármann Jakobsson and Sverrir Jakobsson (New York: Routledge, 2017), 88–110 (88).
70 Hermann Pálsson,"Sami," 31–32. *Eg*, 16. One of Haraldr hárfagri and Snæfríðr's sons is nicknamed *hrísi* (*Hkr 1*, 126), which Else Mundal interprets as a representation of his Saami descent: "Når den 'rette' teksten er rang: Tolkinga av tilnamnet Sigurd rise," *Scandinavian Philology* 15 (2017): 248–60.
71 Hermann Pálsson, "Sami," 29–31; Aalto and Lehtola, "Representations," 15.
72 *Eb*, 28–29. In *Eyrbyggja saga*, the magical performer Geirríðr is called a "trǫll," and the coinage refers to her practise of magic.
73 Martin Arnold, "Hvat er tröll nema þat? The Cultural History of the Troll," in *The Shadow-Walkers: Jacob Grimm's Mythology of the Monstrous*, ed. Tom Shippey (Tempe: Arizona Centre for Medieval and Renaissance Studies, 2005), 111–55.
74 *Ket*, 123.

first assumed. Hallbjǫrn's disapproval of his daughter-in-law may lie in the fact that he suspects that Hrafnhildr had bewitched Ketill into falling in love with her, analogous to the suspicions of Vanlandi and Harald's advisers in Heimskringla's *Ynglinga saga* and *Haralds saga hárfagra*.⁷⁵ As such, Hallbjǫrn's usage of the term strengthens the association between the Saami and magic in the source material, and demonstrates once again that the negative factor, if present, is never Saaminess but almost exclusively always the practise of something inherently non-Christian like magic (or bewitchment). The instance can also be read humorously, since Hallbjǫrn's nickname does indeed contain the term. When associated with the Saami, regardless of its context, supernatural terms such as *þurs* and *trǫll* are not as straightforward as was suggested by Hermann Pálsson. I therefore disagree that the semantic range of *trǫll* unquestionably included Saami people, but rather, as Ármann Jakobsson argues, that it incorporated everyone perceived as having supernatural abilities,⁷⁶ as some Saami characters were. The articulation of association between the Saami and the supernatural should thus be read as a probable result of the suggested Otherness increasingly (with time) accompanying the Saami in Norse literature. As Ármann Jakobsson writes, regardless of what the ambivalent term *trǫll* referred to, it at least meant strange or Other.⁷⁷ Triin Laidoner follows the same logic when discussing the *jǫtnar* (giants), stating that it is:

> impossible to overlook the fact that the Saami characterisation as "different" and "dangerous" is paralleled by that of another set of intimidating "others," namely the *jǫtnar*, something which suggests a connection between the natures and roles of the two groups.⁷⁸

As Jurij Kusmenko has noticed, many common characteristics are shared between the giants and the Saami in Norse narration, such as magical abilities associated with the control of weather, healing, and shapeshifting.⁷⁹ Importantly, these are positive values, and giants also seem to embody attributes like attractiveness and fertility, but also the possession of desirable objects and knowledge.⁸⁰ While not exclusively associated with the Saami, otherworldly and supernatural terms, and portrayals such as *trǫll* and *jǫtnar* are associated with (meeting) the Other,

---

75 *Hkr 1*, 29, 126.
76 Ármann Jakobsson, *The Troll Inside You: Paranormal Activity in the Medieval North* (Santa Barbara: Punctum Books, 2017), 34.
77 Ármann Jakobsson, *Troll*, 58.
78 Laidoner, "Noaidi," 66.
79 Jurij Kusmenko, "Sámi as Giants and Dwarves in Old Scandinavian Literature," *Scandinavian Philology* 11 (2011): 84–95. See section 6.2.1.
80 Mundal, "Family," 30.

which in some contexts encompass the Saami.[81] However, it is important to be constantly aware of the prejudices associated with supernatural connections, especially when they are expressed negatively. Assuming a simple equation between the Saami and, for example, trolls, without questioning the overall contextual framework the association appears in, risks perpetuating a colonial framework disregarding the Saami as people.[82] In clarifying terms such as *trǫll* and problematising the connection between the supernatural Others and the Saami, and demonstrating awareness of the contemporary situation, we avoid unconsciously supporting a colonial framework.

In sum, magic is undoubtedly the most common trope associated with the Saami in Norse narration. Involving an abundance of different aspects and abilities, the repeating themes include Saami actors as teachers of magic or as offering magical aid, shapeshifting, divination, and enchantment. While the paganism of the Saami has been discussed since the establishment of the authority of the archbishop of Hamburg-Bremen over the Nordic countries from the 1060s onwards, the earliest source associating the Saami with magic might predate this by a few decades. In Sigvatr Þórðason's *Erfidrápa Óláfs helga*, performed sometime after the canonisation of King Óláfr Haraldsson following the battle of Stiklastaðir in 1030, the veneration of the king is associated with Saami magic, since it was the reported catalyst for his death. However, while Saami magic is portrayed with ambiguity, it is also necessary and works as a catalyst in different stories. *Historia Norwegie* accentuates this paradoxical view of Saami magic: although strongly opposing it and painting it in a demonic light, the text also normalises the motif of Norse, or more correctly, Christian people seeking out such magic. Simultaneously attractive and intimidating for the stereotyped skill, Saami characters with reported magical abilities are sought by other actors in the texts. The texts rarely problematise the cultural affiliation of the Saami, but rather, their "paganism" and lack of Christianity. This problematisation is reflected in King Hákon Hákonarsonar's aforementioned "réttarbót" [amendment] of the law code relevant for Hálogaland in 1313, which intended to make life easier for newly converted Saami in the region.[83] I therefore assert that it is not necessarily the juxtaposition between the Norse and the Saami that is relevant when discussing the portrayal of Saami

---

81 John McKinnell, *Meeting the Other in Norse Myth and Legend* (Cambridge: D.S. Brewer, 2005), 2–6.
82 See section 1.1.2.
83 See section 2.7.4. *NGL 3*, 106–8. Else Mundal, "Kong Håkon Magnussons rettarbot for Hålogaland av 1313 og andre kjelder til kristninga av samene i mellomalderen," in *Sápmi Y1K: Livet i samernas bösättningsområde för ett tusen år sedan*, ed. Andrea Amft and Mikael Svonni (Umeå: Samiska Studier, 2006), 97–114.

magic, but that these instances should rather be read as textual manifestations of the religious fears associated with non-Christian belief systems. I also find it necessary to stress that the magic associated with the Saami, such as shapeshifting, weather magic, and spirit journeys, also fall within the rules of Norse performances of magic. In turn then, when there is a problem with magic, it is not because of the cultural affiliation of the performer, but due to the practise of something essentially non-Christian. The texts nevertheless portray this magic as productive, and at times, necessary.

Saami Ritual Performance and the "Problem" with Shamanism

Shamanism as a concept is generally agreed to be a religious configuration involving a practitioner or social functionary reaching states of altered consciousness in order to communicate with the perceived supernatural world.[84] As part of a belief system, shamanism consists of an ideology and set of expectations concerning shamans.[85] A feature of shamanism is the all-encompassing view of one's surroundings as animated, including both natural features and phenomena, as well as animals, people, the deceased, gods/goddesses, spirit beings, and various objects. By entering a trance through playing a ceremonial drum, singing chants, and sometimes consuming mind-altering substances, individuals granted special power could in this trance communicate with the animated world surrounding them.[86] In this state, the shamans could visit far-off places and find missing objects, animals, and people, communicate with the spirit world and sometimes raise the dead. Since Norse portrayals of and experiences with Saami ritual performance is so prevalent in the material mentioned above, it is reasonable to assume Norse knowledge of and familiarity with Saami ritual performance. Saami magic is actively sought out, and the Saami are appreciated and acknowledged for their magical skills and expertise, albeit ambiguously.

Until recently, the predominant focus regarding Saami medieval belief systems and shamanism has been on their connections to Óðinnic magic and *seiðr*. *Seiðr* is a notoriously difficult term to define, but in short, has been suggested as an Old Norse (pre-Christian) form of ritual performance used for "gaining knowledge about the future or trying to change the options for events to come."[87] Parallels

---

[84] Juha Pentikäinen, ed., *Shamanism and Northern Ecology* (Berlin: De Gruyter, 1996), 10–12.
[85] Pentikäinen, *Shamanism*, 12.
[86] Marte Spangen, *Circling Concepts: A Critical Archaeological Analysis of the Notion of Stone Circles as Sami Offering Sites*, Stockholm Studies in Archaeology 70 (Malmø: Holmbergs, 2016), 71.
[87] Catharina Raudvere, "*Trolldómr* in Early Medieval Scandinavia," in *Witchcraft and Magic in Europe: The Middle Ages*, ed. Bengt Ankarloo and Stuart Clark, *The Athlone History of Witchcraft and Magic in Europe*, vol. 3 (London: The Athlone Press, 2002), 73–171 (111).

between *seiðr* and Saami ritual performance include spirit journeys and trance-like séances sometimes involving shapeshifting, magically skilled travellers offering their services, World Tree ideologies, and animistic features.⁸⁸ Although interesting, the parallels between *seiðr* and Saami ritual performance have traditionally been discussed in manners where the focus lies on the process of cultural borrowings, resulting in the Saami predominantly becoming the borrowers.⁸⁹

When discussing the portrayal of Saami ritual performance in medieval texts, the focus tends to be on its shamanistic features, with John Lindow concluding that "most Norwegians would have known the rules for a Saami shamanic performance."⁹⁰ In Norse narration, the most famous example of a so-called shamanic performance is related in *Historia Norwegie*, depicting the ritual performance of Saami "magicians":

> Quadam uero uice dum christiani causa comercii apud Finnos ad mensam sedissent, illorum hospita subito inclinata expirauit. Vnde christianis multum | dolentibus non mortuam, sed a gandis emulorum esse depredatam, sese illam cito adepturos ipsi Finni nichil contristati respondent. Tunc quidam magis extenso panno, sub quo se ad profanes ueneficas incantaciones preparet, quoddam uasculum ad modum taratantarorum sursum erectis minibus extulit, cetinis atque ceruinis formulis cum loris et ondriolis nauicula eciam cum remis occupatum, quibus uehiculis per alta niuium et deuexa monciun uel profunda stagnorum ille diabolicus gandus uteretur. Cumque diutissime incantando tali apparatu ibi saltasset, humo tandem prostratus totus niger ut ethiops, spumans ora ut puta freneticus, preruptus uentrem uix aliquando cum maximo {fremore} emisit spiritum. Tum alterum in magica arte peritissimum consuluerunt, quid de utrisque actum sit. Qui simili modo, sed non eodem euentu suum implens officium – namque hospita sana surrexit – et defunctum magum tali euentu interisse eis intimauit: Gandum uidelicet eius in cetinam effigiem inmaginatum ostico gando in preacutas sudes transformato, dum per quoddam stagnum uelocissime prosiliret, malo omine obuiasse, quia in stagni eiusdem profundo sudes latitantes exactu uentrem perforabant. Quod et in mago domi mortuo apparuit.

> Once, when Christians who had come to trade had sat down at table with some [Saami], their hostess fell forward all of a sudden and expired. While the Christians felt serious grief at this calamity, the [Saami] were not in the least saddened, but told them that the woman was not dead, merely pillaged by the *gands* of her adversaries, and that they could quickly restore her.

---

88 Laidoner, "*Noaidi*," 68.
89 Clive Tolley, *Shamanism in Norse Myth and Magic* (Helsinki: Academia Scientarium Fennica, 2009), 587–88.
90 John Lindow, "Myth Read as History: Odin in Snorri Sturluson's *Ynglinga saga*," in *Myth: A New Symposium*, ed. Gregory Schrempp and William Hansen (Indianapolis: University of Indiana Press, 2002), 107–23 (117–18). Dag Strömbäck established the precedent associating the Saami with shamanism in his 1935 thesis on *seiðr*, where he claimed that *seiðr* was not only shamanistic but a direct loan from the Saami: *Sejd: textstudier i nordisk religionshistoria* (Stockholm: Gebers, 1935), 196–206.

> Then a magician, spreading out a cloth under which he might prepare himself for intoning unholy sorcerer's spells, raised aloft in his outstretched hands a small vessel similar to a [sieve], decorated with tiny figures of whales, harnessed reindeer, skis, and even a miniature boat with oars; using these means of transport the demonic spirit was able to travel across tall snowdrifts, mountain-sides and deep lakes. After chanting incantations for a very long time and leaping about there with this paraphernalia, he finally threw himself to the ground, black all over [...] and foaming at the mouth as if he were mad; ripped across his stomach, with a mighty roar he eventually relinquished his life. Next they consulted another specialist in the magic arts as to what had happened in each case. This individual went through all his practises in similar fashion, though with a different outcome: the hostess arose in sound health and then he revealed to them that the sorcerer had died in the following way: his gand, having taken on the likeness of a whale, was shooting rapidly through a lake when it had the misfortune to encounter a hostile gand, which had transformed itself into sharply pointed stakes; these stakes, hidden in the depths of the lake, penetrated the repulsed creature's belly, and this was also manifested by the death of the magician in the house.[91]

The extract is the most detailed medieval source depicting Saami ritual performance. Mirrored by the *semsveinar*-episode in *Vatnsdœla saga*, which also sees a similar "spirit journey" being undertaken through a trance,[92] the extract depicts the séance undertaken by two Saami ritual performers. Several aspects of the performance have been connected to shamanism, particularly the *gandus* of the bereaved woman and the performers, the cloth placed under the initial performer, the chanting, and the usage of the riddle/bowl (drum?) decorated with figures enabling the trance.[93] "Gand" is a Norse term connected to the Saami from the *Historia Norwegie* instance onwards, and is adopted in the Saami languages in the same period, being the mid-to-late twelfth century.[94] In this context, the term denotes a sort of soul or helping spirit sent out by a ritual performer during a trance, and represents the embodiment of the spirit journey, both as a part of and external to the performer.[95]

However, the trend of associating Saami ritual performance exclusively with shamanism has been challenged in recent scholarship, with some scholars doubting whether shamanism is the right term to describe the belief system of the Saami

---

[91] *HN*, 62–63.
[92] *Vatn*, 34–35. The Saami men lie down for three days in a shed without moving or eating, inducing a trance that enables their mind-journey to Iceland.
[93] Hansen and Olsen, *Hunters*, 345.
[94] See Eldar Heide, *Gand, seid og åndevind* (PhD thesis, University of Bergen, 2006), 65–68, 72–82.
[95] Heide, *Gand*, 5.

in the medieval period.⁹⁶ This follows the wave of postcolonial scholarship emphasising the heterogeneity and regional variation of what has previously often been viewed as the traditional and static Saami lifestyle. The recent trend challenging the assumption associated with (medieval) Saami ritual performance and shamanism is founded in the opposition of the static portrayal of "Saami shamanism" as something "naïve" and undeveloped.⁹⁷ The view of "Saami shamanism" as primitive and unevolved is also endorsed by some scholars discussing shamanistic features in the pre-Christian Norse belief systems, who tend to claim that the shamanistic features of *seiðr* should not be confused with "classic shamanism" or the "tundra shamanism of the Saami."⁹⁸ The diversity and sophistication of the Norse belief-system(s) are emphasised at the expense of a diverse and multifaceted discussion of early Saami belief systems, which then, unconsciously but efficiently, fall into a primitive and static category devoid of inner developments and variations. It should nevertheless be mentioned that scholars like Neil Price and Lotte Hedeager emphasise the complexity of what they refer to as Saami (or circumpolar) "shamanism," as judged by early modern and modern sources, and rather push towards Norse belief systems (specifically *seiðr*) having been just as complex.⁹⁹

I suggest that the discussion of Saami shamanism in Norse studies needs to be problematised since it, more often than not, validates a system of progression and juxtaposes the social advancement of the Norse and the Saami, without discussing Saami factors. Instead, we could emphasise that certain features of Saami (medieval) ritual performance were shamanistic in nature and consistent with the shamanism found in circumpolar areas in the modern period, while avoiding the definition of this performance as shamanism (and shamanism alone), due to the limitations and contemporary associations it carries.¹⁰⁰ In its place, it has been suggested to use the Saami terms *noaidi* (ritual performer, sometimes compared to a shaman) and *noaidevuohta* (the conceptualisation of the *noaidi's* function as com-

---

96 Spangen, *Circling Concepts*, 71. Heide, *Gand*, 309. Håkan Rydving, "Shamanistic and Postshamanistic Terminologies in Saami (Lappish)," *Scripta Instituti Donneriani Aboensis* 12 (1987): 185–207 (186).
97 Åke Hultkrantz, "A Definition of Shamanism," *Temenos* 9 (1973): 25–37; "the natural setting for shamanism is the milieu of the *simple* gatherers, hunters and fishermen," (italics mine).
98 Tine Jeanette Bierning, "The Concept of Shamanism in Old Norse Religion from a Sociological Perspective," in *Old Norse Religion in Long-Term Perspectives: Origins, Changes and Interactions: An International Conference in Lund, Sweden, June 3–7 2004*, ed. Anders Andrén, Kristina Jennbert, and Catharina Raudvere, Vägar till Midgård 8 (Lund: Nordic Academic Press, 2006), 171–78 (175).
99 Neil Price, *The Viking Way: Magic and Mind in Late Iron Age Scandinavia*, 2nd edition (Oxford: Oxbow Books, 2019), 268–71. Hedeager, *Myth and Materiality*, 99–134.
100 Spangen, *Circling Concepts*, 71.

municator with the supernatural world).¹⁰¹ These terms were first documented later in the early modern period and I am therefore reluctant to use them as descriptors for the ritual performance described in medieval texts.¹⁰² Rather than using specific terms such as "shaman" or "noaidi" I have therefore decided to use general designations such as "ritual performer" or "performer/agent of magic," in order to avoid the problematic connotations of the former terms.

As seen above, Saami ritual performance is evident throughout Norse narration and the sagas offer fragmented glimpses of Saami belief systems, sometimes portraying what can generally be associated with shamanic practices. When discussing these glimpses, it is important to emphasise and acknowledge the heterogeneity and regional variation involved in the belief systems of the Saami, features that have been increasingly emphasised regarding the Norse belief systems.¹⁰³ I therefore suggest that the starting point for discussion should always be the internalisation of the concept that the Saami historic belief systems and ritual practices were not static entities, but instead exhibited substantial spatial and chronological variation. Marte Spangen for example, has noted that the many variants of Saami religion were observed by scholars from the seventeenth century onwards, but has later been downplayed to more systematic and static images of Saami beliefs.¹⁰⁴

Nevertheless, there are certain features associated with Saami ritual performance (as perceived/assumed by the Norse) that recur in the saga material, including, as discussed above, trance-induced spirit journeys, the ability to manipulate the weather, and natural phenomena, magical clothing, and weapons, enchantment and, potentially, the bear hunt.¹⁰⁵ These mostly fall within the overview of elements of the Saami belief systems that Neil Price considers to go back to "at least as far as the Viking Age," including a) the existence of a thought-world of spirits and natural powers, b) the bear hunt and its ritual foundations, and c) *noaidevuohta* [sic] and the social role of the *noaidi* [sic].¹⁰⁶ However, we need to be careful in linking ethnographic sources (from the seventeenth century at the earliest) with written sources (from the twelfth century at the earliest) depicting the pre-

---

101 Heide, *Gand*, 309. Spangen, *Circling Concepts*, 71. Terms standardised in North Saami.
102 For an overview of medieval to modern textual portrayals of *noaidevuohta* see Konsta Ilari Kaikkonen, *Contextualising Descriptions of Noaidevuohta: Saami Ritual Specialists in Texts Written until 1871* (PhD thesis, University of Bergen, 2019).
103 Stefan Brink, "How Uniform was the Old Norse Religion?," in *Learning and Understanding in the Old Norse World: Essays in Honour of Margaret Clunies Ross*, ed. Judy Quinn, Kate Heslop, and Tarrin Wills (Turnhout: Brepols, 2007), 105–36.
104 Spangen, *Circling Concepts*, 70.
105 See sections 3.2.1 and 3.2.3.
106 Price, *Viking Way*, 198.

ceding centuries. I do nevertheless agree that by comparing the written sources from both the early modern and medieval periods with the archaeological material, certain continuities and overarching features can be traced. These features generally indicate that the medieval Saami worldview was animistic, regionally varied, and included ritual performance.[107]

As already mentioned, the *Eiðsivaþingslǫg* might help illuminate Saami ritual practice, at least in eastern Norway. The law code, possibly in use from the mid-twelfth century, states that no person should seek out or believe in the power and magic of the Saami, their drum, "root," or sacrifice.[108] The drum mentioned in the *Eiðsivaþingslǫg* is comparable to the decorated object described in the mid-to-late twelfth-century text *Historia Norwegie*, and the drum seems to have been used for ritual practices.[109] The ceremonial drum could be used as a tool to enter a trance and for divinatory purposes by interpreting the movement of an item placed on the surface in relation to the symbols painted on it.[110] Unfortunately, during the 1600–1700s and later, many drums were collected and destroyed by missionaries representing the Nordic nation states' ambitions to convert the Saami to Christianity and root out their "devilry."[111] The law code also prohibits the belief in "blót" [sacrifice] and "rót" [root of a tree]. The "rót" may refer to a holy place dedicated to sacrifice in Saami tradition, a so-called *sieidi*, typically an unusually shaped or anthropomorphic rock, but sometimes also a manipulated wooden figure or a tree, in accordance with later historical and ethnographic sources. While the law code is the only written source directly associating the Saami with this type of *sieidi*, a potential link can be found in the conversion narrative of the Guðbrandsdalr farmers in Heimskringla's *Óláfs saga helga* mentioned above.[112] The Guðbrandsdalr area falls under the southern region associated with the Saami in the Norse sources and the similarities to *sieidi* worship is therefore noteworthy. In addition, the conversion narrative directly mirrors that of Snæfríðr's corpse discussed above, relating the destruction of a wooden effigy idolised by the farmers which leads to the outpouring of different unwanted animals.[113] As

---

107 Spangen, *Circling Concepts*, 71. Else Mundal, "Sami Sieidis in a Nordic Context?," *Journal of Northern Studies* 12, no. 1 (2018): 11–20 (14–15).
108 *NGL 1*, 389–90.
109 Mundal notes that the word "vit" was used for any magical remedy but that it in some contexts also meant drum, "Sieidis," 2.
110 Spangen, *Circling Concepts*, 71. Hansen and Olsen, *Hunters*, 222. The terminology for these drums varies within and outside Sápmi.
111 Spangen, *Circling Concepts*, 40–42.
112 *Hkr 2*, 189.
113 *Hkr 2*, 189.

has become increasingly visible in recent scholarship, the Norse (in this instance Norwegians) and the Saami lived in close contact, and it is not unlikely that Saami cult or ritual performance spread amongst or influenced the Norse.[114] Potentially, a shared belief system might have come about in some areas, based on the fluidity and closeness of the cultures and similarities in worldviews.

Sociology theorises that people come to think alike when they find themselves in comparable situations, allowing the possibility of a blending of "religious" fields following meetings of cultures.[115] Symbols do not necessarily represent the same meaning in different cultures or even in parts of the same culture, indicating that while an influence is evident, it forms part of a new contextual framework. Nevertheless, the fact that this "blending" of different ritual aspects may be evident in these texts indicates close contact, specifically through the portrayal of Norse people seeking out Saami "magic." The fact that the Saami reportedly allow visits from the Norse to their ceremonial places or homes, is in my opinion indicative of established bonds of trust. Norse actors repeatedly seek out the Saami, and were presumably welcomed by the Saami ritual performers, meaning that there were expectations associated with these visits. These expectations carry with them both cultural knowledge and stereotypes, which were founded on rumours, observations of, and participation in Saami ritual performances, particularly evident in the *semsveinar*-episode of *Vatnsdæla saga* and the *gandus*-episode in *Historia Norwegie*.[116] Saami ritual practice is expected and well known across the medieval texts, with some archaeological material as well as historical and ethnographic sources from later in the early modern period backing up the texts. This once again points to less rigid sociocultural boundaries between the Norse and the Saami and reflects close connections between the cultures in certain areas. While the source material follows traditional stereotypes associated with the ritual performance of Saami characters, I would also like to emphasise the regional variation that will have been evident and that the above examples are based on the perceptions of the contributors to these texts.

3.2.2 *Finnr skríðr:* Winter Weather and Skiing Deities

Saami expertise in skiing and associations with winter weather appear as general tendencies across Norse texts. According to Hansen and Olsen, these associations

---

114 Mundal, "Sieidis," 18. See section 6.2.
115 Bierning, "Shamanism," 172.
116 *Vatn*, 34–35. *HN*, 60–61.

are "element[s] in Norse people's ethnic stereotyping of the Saami."[117] This stereotyping is particularly clear in the aforementioned Icelandic oath *trygðamál*, which states the expected and normal in Norse society, including the motif "fiðr scríðr" [the Saami skis].[118] This motif appears to have become widespread from the sixth century onwards, with the addition of the precursor "skiing" to the exonym associated with the Saami by European writers.[119] *Historia Norwegie* clarifies the association between the group and skiing, stating that the Saami travelled:

> inponentes leuigatis asseribus pedibus subfixis, quot instrumentum "ondros" appellant, et per condensa niuium ac deuexa moncium agitantibus ceruis cum coniugibus et parulis aue uelocius trasferuntur.
>
> with smooth planks fastened beneath their feet, implements which they call "ondrar," swifter than birds they are conveyed with their wives and little ones, swept forward by their reindeer across the packed snow and down the mountain slopes.[120]

The usage of the word "ondrar" is peculiar, as it is originally a Norse word for a particular type of ski, a word most often associated with the areas of Østerdalen, Trøndelag, and the neighbouring Swedish districts.[121] The apparent Saami usage of the Norse word for a particular type of skiing is noteworthy and indicates that Saami people, at least in the eyes of the learned elite, had adopted Norse words for an activity most commonly associated with themselves, minimally indicating some sort of linguistic contact as well as probabilities of bilingualism. The word is repeated in the description of the *ǫndurdís* Skaði, whose skiing abilities accentuate her "Saami-ness."[122] When Eiríkr blóðøx encounters Gunnhildr in Finnmǫrk, as related in Heimskringla, she explains that the Saami men she stayed with were so able on skis that neither animals nor humans could escape them.[123]

Adam of Bremen even claims that Saami livelihoods depended on the winter since they could outrun wild animals in the snow and thereby provide sustenance

---

117 Hansen and Olsen, *Hunters*, 36.
118 Vilhjálmur Finsen, ed., *Grágás 1852: Konungsbók* (Odense: Odense Universitetsforlag, 1974), 206–7. The oath is also found *in Grettis saga* and *Heiðarvíga saga*. See section 2.4.2.
119 Procopius (550: *skrithifinnoi*), Jordanes (551: *scretefennae*), Ravennese cleric (700s: *skridefenni*), Paulus Diaconus (780: *scritobini*), Alfred (890: *scridefinne*), Adam of Bremen (1060s: *scritefini*), Saxo (1200s: *Skritfinni*). See section 2.2. Norse sources maintain the *finnr*-tradition throughout.
120 *HN*, 58–59. Saxo writes that the *skritfinni* travelled on curved boards that they used to race across the snowfields between mountains, 343.
121 Store norske leksikon, "Andor," snl.no, 12.12.2018 https://snl.no/andor.
122 *Hkr 1*, 22.
123 *Hkr 1*, 135.

throughout the cold season.¹²⁴ The association is furthered by Saxo who relates the defeat of the legendary Swedish-Danish King Ragnarr loðbrók due to the skiing abilities of a Saami group.¹²⁵ As mentioned in chapter 2, a man discussing border politics in Gautelfr expresses "'Snæliga snuggir, sveinar', kvæðu Finnar" ["There's a whiff of snow," said the Saami], maintaining the importance of the snow motif when referring to the Saami.¹²⁶ Eyvindr skáldaspillir's *lausavísa* 12, reportedly recited in the tenth century, enhances the motif by connecting it to the severe famine in Hálogaland which saw its inhabitants keeping their goats inside during the summer due to unpredictable snow, as the Saami did.¹²⁷

References to the Saami in connection with snow and winter weather can be found in the descriptions of semi-mythological characters portrayed as Saami royalty. These characters have names associated with snow such as Snær [snow], Mjǫll [fine, powdery snow], Drífa [snowdrift], Frosti [frost], and Þorri [dry frost], and appear across the saga genres. In Heimskringla's *Ynglinga saga*, the Uppsalian king Vanlandi travels north to the country of the Saami, to marry Drífa, the daughter of Snjár hinum gamli.¹²⁸ In *Sturlaugs saga Starfsama*, King Snær is portrayed as the father of Mjǫll and the characters are directly described as Saami.¹²⁹ The association between the Saami and winter weather is particularly clear in the portrayal of the Saami "princess" Snæfríðr, whose name literally means "beautiful snow."¹³⁰ In *Hrólfs saga kraka*, the Saami queen Hvít ["white"] calls forth similar associations.¹³¹

While some scholars emphasise the associations between dwellers of cold, snowy, and barren areas with forces of destruction and chaos connected to the dangers of wintertime,¹³² Norse descriptions of the Saami rarely portray such a

---

124 *Hamburg-Bremen*, 213.
125 Saxo, 651. Saxo also relates the abilities of the Saami to magically disappear by flinging snow on the ground, 343.
126 *Mork 2*, 32.
127 Russell Poole, "Eyvindr skáldaspillir Finnsson, *Lausavísur* 12," in *Poetry from the Kings' Sagas 1: From Mythical Times to c. 1035*, ed. Diana Whaley, Skaldic Poetry of the Scandinavian Middle Ages 1 (Turnhout: Brepols, 2012), 231.
128 *Hkr 1*, 28–29. Their grandchildren also have names associated with winter: Gísl [ski-staff] and Ǫndur [ski].
129 *Stst*, 638. In *Barðar saga*, these characters also appear but are never directly described as Saami, which raise questions about whether these characters were understood as Saami "by default" in all the stories about them. This is not discussed further here but introduces interesting directions for future research about perceptions of Saaminess; see *Barð*, 102.
130 *Hkr 1*, 126.
131 *Hrólf*, 48–50.
132 Lotte Motz, "Supernatural Beings," in *Medieval Scandinavia: An Encyclopedia*, ed. Phillip Pulsiano, Garland reference library of the humanities, vol. 934 (London: Garland Publishing, 1993), 622.

connection as negative. In fact, the associations between the Saami and winter weather are most often positive. Able to traverse snowy mountainsides and manoeuvre packed snow and steep slopes, the Saami are portrayed as particularly good skiers and masters of the cold weather. As will be discussed in chapter 5, the portrayal of the trade with the Saami most often takes place in the winter season, meaning that direct interactions and/or observations between the Norse and the Saami, at least in certain areas, occurred during the cold season. The motif occurs across the genres and survives from the sixth century onwards, demonstrating a manifested association between the group and winter, and everything it brought with it.

3.2.3 *Finns rauð gjǫld:* Archery and Hunting

The Saami are repeatedly associated with hunting and archery from the classical sources onwards, with both men and women portrayed as hunting with bone-tipped arrows.[133] An extract from *Historia Norwegie* demonstrates that this perception survived into the late twelfth century: "Sunt equidem uenatores peritissimi, soliuagi et instabiles" [They are truly the most skilful of huntsmen, patrolling alone and always on the move].[134] Likewise, when Eiríkr blóðøx meets Gunnhildr in Finnmǫrk, she explains that the Saami men she was staying with to learn magic were away hunting with their bows.[135]

Archery is the sole hunting technique associated with the Saami in Norse narration, with several texts stressing the expertise of Saami archers. In *Ketils saga hœngs,* Ketil overwinters with his Saami family somewhere in Finnmǫrk and takes the opportunity to hunt with and learn archery from his Saami father-in-law.[136] In *Ǫrvar-Odds saga,* the archery motif is further enhanced by Oddr's nickname "Ǫrvar," meaning arrows, from the magical Saami arrows he inherited from his father.[137] The association between the Saami and archery was so predominant it manifested in the Norse name "Finnbogi" [Finnr (Saami) + bogi (bow)].[138] In the

---

133 See section 2.2.
134 *HN*, 58–59.
135 *Hkr 1,* 135.
136 *Ket,* 118. This skill comes in handy later, when his wife's uncle Gúsir challenge him to an archery duel.
137 *Ǫrv,* 173. The archery motif is continued in the nicknaming of Oddr's son, Án, called "bogsveigis" [bow-bender].
138 See for example *Finnboga saga ramma.* Juoksa is the Saami equivalent of the name, meaning "bow."

skaldic poetry mentioned in section 2.7.2, textual motifs directly associated with the Saami are utilised by the skalds to create kennings for arrows.[139] Similarly, the Saami portrayal of the skiing deity Skaði is enhanced by, among other abilities and features, her archery skills. Characters with implicit Saami descent sometimes "inherit" skills in archery,[140] but most clearly, Saami characters in the texts are portrayed as being skilful archers. *Hálfdanar saga Eysteinssonar* portrays the Saami king Flóki as extremely capable with a bow and arrow, shooting three arrows at once, each killing a man.[141] Several portrayals of the "stereotypical" Saami character Finnr litli describes him as skilled in the mixing of potions, quick on his feet, a good skier, but mostly, an excellent archer.[142] Furthermore, when we meet the aforementioned Saami man Fedming in northern Hálogaland, he is lying in a birch forest in a trance-like state, with his bow by his side.[143] In the stories relating the possible Saami huntsman Átti inn dœlski from Vermalandi (Värmland), he is described as an expert huntsman, aided by his skis and his skills in archery.[144]

A story narrated in Heimskringla's *Óláfs saga Tryggvasonar* relating the reported battle of Svǫlðr (somewhere in the Baltic Sea, circa 999/1000) uses the textual motif of Saami skills in archery as one of the catalysts behind King Óláfr's downfall. An archer called Finnr, of whom "sumir segja at hann væri finnskr – sá var inn mesti bogmaðr" [some say he was Saami, he was the greatest archer], shoots an arrow that breaks the bow of the king's own archer.[145] The king asks what the sound made from the bow was, and his own archer replies "Nóregr ór hendi þér, konungr" [Norway snapping out of your hands, King].[146] The king is then defeated. In the aforementioned episode in Heimskringla when King Óláfr Haraldsson goes on a harrying trip to Finnland, *Óláfs saga helga* explains that he was met by hostile Saami people in the forests using weather magic and archery to hinder the advances of the king and his crew.[147] Similarly, in *Landnámabók*, Gunnsteinn is reportedly shot by a Saami arrow.[148]

---

139 See section 2.7.2.
140 See for example *Orms þáttur Stórólfssonar.*
141 *HálfdEyst*, 541.
142 *Hkr 2*, 120.
143 *IA*, 286–7.
144 See section 7.4.3.
145 *Hkr 1*, 362.
146 *Hkr 1*, 363. See also *Mesta 2*, 168, elaborated in section 7.4.1.
147 *Hkr 2*, 11. Finnland will be further discussed in section 4.3.2.
148 *Ldn*, 366.

Sometimes, the texts manipulate the Saami archery trope by associating it with the ability to magically shoot arrows from one's fingers, as related in *Sǫrla saga sterka:* "en svá þótti mǫnnum, sem ör flýgi af hverjum þeirra fíngri, ok fyrir hverri ör maðr til dauða kjörinn" [it appeared to men as if an arrow flew from each of their fingers, and a man was marked for death from each arrow].[149] The local Hálogaland deity Þorgerðr Hǫlgabrúðr, alongside her sister, is also portrayed as exercising this skill, depicted as appearing on the deck of Hákon Hlaðajarl during the reported battle of Hjörungavágr [Hjørungavåg, late tenth century].[150] The ability to shoot arrows from one's fingers might be a textual motif connected to the Norse perception of northeastern peoples, since it is also the case in *Ǫrvar-Odds saga*, which sees the king and priestess of Bjálkaland (literally "Fur land"), as well as the mysterious king of Novgorod, shooting arrows from each finger.[151] However, in *Hrólfs saga kraka*, the motif is transferred to a wild boar, shooting arrows from each bristle.[152]

In Norse texts, Saami expertise in archery is connected to hunting, warfare, and magic. Archery as a textual motif associated with the Saami is most likely based on observations of Saami culture and lifestyles, reflecting the importance of hunting to medieval Saami societies. Archaeological material suggests that hunting was the most important subsistence strategy among early medieval Saami groups.[153] The deposition of arrowheads, primarily of bone (circa AD 0–600), in Saami burial contexts terminates prior to the early medieval period, with the tradition of deposition moving to sacrificial sites early in the medieval period (600– 1050).[154] Audhild Schanche and Inga Malene Bruun interpret the change of tradition as an archaeological expression of the separation of burial rites and the hunting cult as a result of changing cultural factors.[155] Initially being a crucial important subsistence strategy, Saami hunting skills and expertise grew into a large-scale economic industry connected to the Norse demand for fur and participation in the eastern trading network. I would suggest that the change from subsistence strategy

---

149 *SǫrlaSt*, 444.
150 Þorleifur Hauksson, ed., *Jómsvíkinga saga*, Íslenzk fornrit 33 (Reykjavík: Hið íslenzka fornritafélag, 2018), 36–37. See Perabo, *Heathens*, 77–79.
151 *Ǫrv*, 286–7, 296–7.
152 *Hrólf*, 87–88.
153 Audhild Schanche, *Graver i ur og berg: Samisk gravskikk og religion fra forhistorisk til nyere tid* (Karasjok: Davvi Girji, 2000), 321–6.
154 Inga Malene Bruun, *Blandede graver: blandede kulturer? En tolkning av gravskikk og etniske forhold i Nord-Norge gjennom jernalder og tidlig middelalder* (MA diss., University of Tromsø, 2007), 38, 70.
155 Schanche, *samisk gravskikk*, 324–6. Bruun, *Gravskikk*, 70–71.

to economic venture is crucial in the association between the Saami and archery, since archery is connected to hunting, and hunting to the Saami trade.

In the late ninth-century account, Ohthere observes that the Saami were engaged in hunting during the winter season and fished by the sea during the summers. His statement is supported by the several saga texts relating trade journeys into Finnmǫrk during the winter season, in addition to accounts stressing potentially shared fishing industries, presumably taking place in the summer.[156] Throughout the account, the Saami are described as hunters, fishers, whalers, and fowlers, potentially herding reindeer and hunting wild animals for their fur and skins.[157] The text claims that the Saami paid Ohthere and others like him with bird feathers, whale bones, walrus, and seal hide, as well as reindeer, marten, and bear skins. *Historia Norwegie* further elaborates on the animals hunted by the Saami and lists bear, wolf, lynx, fox, sable, otter, badger, beaver, squirrel, and ermine, while also stressing the importance of reindeer.[158] This is reflected in the textual material, which particularly favours reindeer, wolves, and bears.

The Saami are possibly associated with the keeping or herding of reindeer from Paulus Diaconus's late eighth-century text, but at least from the late ninth-century account of Ohthere and onwards.[159] Ohthere's account also adds that the Saami kept with them so-called *stœl*-reindeer, extremely valued by the group who used them to catch wild reindeer.[160] In *Ketils saga hœngs*, the *Finnakonungr* Gúsir is introduced in the narrative engulfed in wind-driven snow, riding a wagon drawn by two reindeer, maintaining the motif from *Historia Norwegie*.[161] A story relating possible Saami ties describes how the mysterious mountain dweller Úlfr rescues the protagonists during a winter storm, attired in a reindeer cloak and carrying a reindeer on his back.[162] The clearest association between the Saami and reindeer in the saga material is narrated in the stories revolving around the Hálogaland chieftain Þórir hundr. Þórir's storyline as an antagonist to the Norwegian King Óláfr Haraldsson is founded on his relationships with different Saami groups, with one such perceived group granting him an impenetrable reindeer cloak as related in Heimskringla's *Óláfs saga helga*.[163] As already mentioned in sec-

---

156 See for example *Eg*, 27, and for fishing, see sections 2.3.3 and 3.2.4.
157 *OEH*, 39–41.
158 *HN*, 59–61.
159 Paul the Deacon, *History of the Lombards*, ed. Edward Peters, trans. William Dudley Foulke (Philadelphia: University of Pennsylvania Press, 2003), 7. *OEH*, 41.
160 *OEH*, 39–41.
161 *Ket*, 118. *HN*, 58–59.
162 *Fær*, 23. See section 7.4.1.
163 *Hkr 2*, 344–5.

tion 2.7.2, the association between the Saami and reindeer, specifically the chronology for the Saami domestication of reindeer, is still a hot topic in contemporary scholarship. Recent archaeological interpretations of medieval Saami dwelling sites in northern Finland suggests the presence of working reindeer in Saami contexts from as early as the fourteenth century onwards.[164] This is the earliest direct evidence for draught reindeer use by the Saami in the archaeological record, as far as I am aware, but it should be noted that the late ninth-century account of Ohthere may point to earlier use of draught reindeer. It should also be noted that the development of reindeer herding was a gradual and regional varied process and may have roots in the period prior to the Middle Ages.[165] Jostein Bergstøl, amongst others, argues that adaptation to reindeer herding among Saami groups was a response to the intensification of contact between Norse and Saami peoples prior to, and early in, the medieval period, due to increased trading (which was focused on Saami fur specialisation).[166] Recent research has also highlighted the presence of early medieval reindeer trapping systems in Hedmark in southern Norway, of which possible Saami origins have been suggested.[167] The cultural affiliation of these trapping systems are nonetheless difficult to determine, and the authors state the importance of further discussion on the relationship of Saami and Norse cultures in the south and the extent to which the groups may have cooperated in hunting activities.[168] The possibility of this cooperation is significant, especially considering the factors that will be discussed in chapter 7.

Although following the same pattern of events as Heimskringla, *Helgisaga* states that the Saami cloaks granted king Óláfr were made from wolfskin, not reindeer skin.[169] In the late fourteenth-century *Hauks þáttr hábrókar*, the Hálogalandier Vígharðr is introduced as he elegantly skis down a steep mountainside dressed

---

[164] Anna-Kaisa Salmi et al., "Earliest Archaeological Evidence for Domesticated Reindeer Economy Among the Sámi of Northeastern Fennoscandia AD 1300 onwards," *Journal of Anthropological Archaeology* 6 (2021): 1–15 (13).
[165] Salmi et al., "Domesticated Reindeer," 13.
[166] Jostein Bergstøl, "Hunting Native Reindeer, While Herding Imported Ones? Some Thoughts on the Development of Saami Pastoralism," in *Currents of Saami Pasts: Recent Advances in Saami Archaeology*, ed. Marte Spangen et al., Monographs of the Archaeological Society of Finland 9 (Helsinki: Archaeological Society of Finland, 2020), 34–45 (43). This is further discussed in chapter 5.
[167] Hilde Rigmor Amundsen and Kristin Os, "Funnel-Shaped Reindeer Trapping Systems in Hedmark: Saami or Norse?," in *Currents of Saami Pasts: Recent Advances in Saami Archaeology*, ed. Marte Spangen et al., Monographs of the Archaeological Society of Finland 9 (Helsinki: Archaeological Society of Finland, 2020), 16–33 (24–26).
[168] Amundsen and Os, "Trapping Systems," 30.
[169] *Helgisaga*, 69–70.

in wolfskin, and in *Hrólfs saga kraka*, the Saami queen Hvít wears wolfskin gloves when she strikes her stepson and thereby curses him to become a bear.[170]

An animal often associated with the Saami in the textual material is the bear. Lyonel Perabo notes that the animal is nearly exclusively associated with the far north and a Saami context in saga literature, particularly if the ursine interaction forms part of a supernatural motif.[171] Rarely, the bear is portrayed as a source of meat, and if it is, its consumers are predominantly Saami.[172] In *Vǫlundarkviða*, one of the mythological poems found in the *Poetic Edda*, Vǫlundr returns from hunting (with a bow) with a bear and prepares the meat, consuming it while lying on the animal's fur.[173] As discussed earlier, Vǫlundr is sometimes interpreted as a Saami character, and the hunt and following consumption of the meat accentuates such an association. In my opinion, the clearest connection between the ursine species and the Saami can be found in *Hrólfs saga kraka*. As mentioned previously, the *fornaldarsaga* relates the curse put on Bjǫrn by his Saami stepmother Hvít, turning him into a bear. After some time as a bear, Bjǫrn is encircled by hunters and killed on the orders of his stepmother, who holds a celebratory bear feast where the meat is served.[174] Bjǫrn's pregnant lover, Bera, is forced by the queen to eat the meat, resulting in her three sons having supernatural features and abilities.[175] Due to this, Bera and Bjǫrn's son Bǫðvarr later reportedly shapeshifts into a bear during the battle of Hleiðargarðr.[176]

In recent years, multiple scholars have emphasised the similarities between the bear hunt and bear-shapeshifting episodes in *Hrólfs saga* with the central place of the bear in early modern and medieval Saami mythology and worldviews.[177] Based on the archaeological material discussed below, Hansen and Olsen state that "the bear was sacred to the Saami, and the hunt, the subsequent bear feast, and the burial of its bones were all associated with various rituals."[178]

---

170 *HHábr*, 121. *Hrólf*, 48–50.
171 Perabo, *Heathens*, 168.
172 *Hrólfs saga Gautrekssonar* is an exception.
173 Ursula Dronke, ed., *The Poetic Edda: Mythological Poems*, vol. 2 (Oxford: Clarendon Press, 1997), 430.
174 *Hrólf*, 52–54. The pun on the name "Bjǫrn" [bear] is also utilised in *Helgisaga*. As Þórir hundr attacks one of King Óláfr's men, Bjǫrn, during the battle of Stiklastaðir, he exclaims: "sva bæitum ver biarnuna a morkenne norðr" [this is how we hunt bears in Finnmǫrk], 70.
175 One half-elk, one with feet like a dog, and one with an ursine nature.
176 These names all mean bear, emphasising the ursine theme.
177 Clive Tolley, "*Hrólfs saga kraka* and Sámi Bear Rites," *Saga-Book* 31 (2007): 5–21 (7, 13–15); Perabo, *Heathens*, 170; Juha Pentikäinen, *Golden King of the Forest: The Lore of the Northern Bear* (Helsinki: Etnika, 2007).
178 Hansen and Olsen, *Hunters*, 120.

Already introduced in the third and fourth century as interpreted by archaeologists, a special ritual practice associated with the bear hunt and bear burials becomes particularly visible and widespread across Saami areas early in the medieval period.[179] Particularly evident in archaeologically expressed border zones between Norse and Saami settlements in northern Norway, the ceremonial burial of bears is believed to represent the symbiotic relationship shared with the species in Saami mythology, where the ultimate goal was the resurrection of the animal and its communication with other members of its species of its well treatment by humans.[180] This was facilitated through a carefully executed hunt, strict performance following the slaying and flaying of the animal, the preparation of the meat, and the subsequent bear feast, before its bones were buried anatomically correctly.

Only documented in written sources from the early seventeenth century onwards, descriptions of the Saami bear hunt are remarkably similar to the bear hunt incident in *Hrólfs saga*. In short, the saga relates that before Bjǫrn is encircled by the hunters, he places a ring under his left arm in order to be identified after his death to expose Hvít's wickedness.[181] Following his death, Bera retrieves the ring before the animal is carefully flayed by the hunters, bringing the meat to Hvít who holds a celebratory bear feast culminating in the consumption of the meat.[182] In the 1755 work *Kort berättelse om Lapparnas björna-fänge* [A short account of the bear hunt of the Saami], Pehr Fjellström relates the aetiological legend of Saami bear rites, based on first hand experience and relations with Saami people in northern Sweden. Here, Fjellström narrates a story where a bear asks his human wife to fasten a piece of brass on his brow in order to distinguish himself from other bears and so that his human son would not kill him during the hunt.[183] During the hunt his wife is unable to watch as her husband is killed but catches a glimpse during the flaying of the animal. Fjellström uses this as an explanation for the restrictions associated with women and the ritual, only allowed to view the bear or its hunters through a brass ring or with their faces hidden.[184] I remain cautious of comparing early modern sources with medieval sources but agree that the

---

179 Hansen and Olsen, *Hunters*, 120–22.
180 Hansen and Olsen, *Hunters*, 121. Ursine tales are often based on the premise that the bear was originally human, and the strict regulation of the ritual associated with the hunt and the succeeding burial was connected to this.
181 *Hrólf*, 52.
182 *Hrólf*, 52.
183 Pehr Fjellström, *Kort berättelse om Lapparnas björne-fänge*, reprinted and ed. Louise Bäckman (Umeå: Två Forläggere, 1981), 14–17.
184 Fjellström, *björne-fange*, 17.

similarities between the incident in *Hrólfs saga* and Fjellström's eighteenth-century description of Saami bear rites are striking.

As expressed literarily and archaeologically, the bear occupied an important role in medieval Saami societies and there were strictly regulated rituals connected to the bear hunt and the succeeding treatment of the bear. Given the close and sometimes intimate relations between different Norse and Saami groups in certain areas, I would argue that it is not unlikely that some or several Norse actors were at least familiar with the ceremonial practice. After time, this might have developed into a textual motif associating the Saami with the bear. In *Finnboga saga ramma*, the protagonist Finnbogi sets off to kill a particularly bothersome bear in Hálogaland. Perabo has emphasised the nearly ceremonial and complex deference directed at the hunting of the bear.[185] As Finnbogi approaches the animal's cave, he carefully walks backwards while talking to the bear, before throwing away his weapons and fighting barehanded, breaking the animal's back on a boulder.[186] Arriving in town with the body of the bear, Finnbogi refuses to relate how he went about the hunt and the killing, leaving the villagers to flay the bear.[187] The motif is extended further in *Ǫrvar-Odds saga*, when Oddr kills a bear in Finnmǫrk, flaying it, and raising the skin on a pole.[188] Later, Oddr uses the raised bearskin to scare off a female troll, by putting burning coals in its mouth and hiding beneath it, before shooting the troll three times with his magical Saami arrows.[189] Considering the recurring textual motif associating the Saami with the bear, this instance, while differing from the other bear hunt episodes, may purvey Norse observations and perceptions of the Saami bear cult.

Following magic, archery is probably the textual motif repeated most often in the narration of the Saami in Norse sources. The repetition allows for the motif to evolve, starting with depictions of adept archers, to magically skilled archers able to hunt big beasts, project arrows from their fingertips, and shoot several arrows at once, each hitting its target. Norse observation of, or participation in, Saami lifestyles reveals that hunting must have been particularly significant to Saami societies in the medieval period. The textual portrayal, with early sources such as *Germania* narrating adept hunting societies to "later" sources such as Ohthere's account and *Historia Norwegie* focusing on the large-scale hunting of big game, coincide with the archaeological material which suggests a change of tradition occur-

---

185 Perabo, *Heathens*, 172.
186 *Finnb*, 274–75.
187 *Finnb*, 275.
188 *Ǫrv*, 181.
189 *Ǫrv*, 181, 306.

ring from the 700s onwards.[190] Hunting, initially primarily expressed as a subsistence strategy, grows into a large-scale industrial organisation connected to the Norse demand for fur and participation in the eastern trading network.[191] The Norse textual tradition particularly emphasises the hunting by the Saami of reindeer (also herding), wolves, and bears, with a certain focus on the bear in association with Saami portrayals. Clive Tolley, amongst others, suggests that this association derives from the Norse knowledge or observation of Saami ceremonial activities connected to the bear hunt in medieval and early modern societies.[192] Potential Saami influence is visible, I would argue, with some caution, in the *fornaldarsaga* relating the legend of King Hrólfr kraki, since the compiler(s) of the text has made the instigator of both the bear hunt and bear-shapeshifting episodes the Saami Hvít. Either rooted in Saami tradition or of the Norse knowledge of or perception of such a tradition, the connection between the Saami and the bear hunt, in addition to other cultural activities such as reindeer herding, fur preparation, and archery, should in my opinion be read as indicative of close social bonds between the groups.

3.2.4 *Sinbundit skip:* Saami Boatbuilding and Fishing Economies

Already from the mid-sixth century with Procopius's *De Bello Gothico*, the Saami are associated with the binding of boats with animal sinew. This image is enhanced in Heimskringla's *Haraldssona saga*, *Morkinskinna*, and *Fagrskinna*, all first compiled in the early thirteenth century. Here, the Norwegian pretender to the throne and alleged son of King Magnús berfœttr, Sigurðr Slembidjákn, seeks Saami boatbuilding expertise in northern Norway, as related in *Haraldssona saga*:

> Þann vetr, er sagt, at Sigurðr léti Finna gera sér skútur tvær inn í fjǫrðum ok váru sini bundnar ok engi saumr í, en viðjar fyrir kné, ok røru tólf menn á borð hvárri. Sigurðr var með Finnum, þá er þeir gerðu skúturnar, ok hǫfðu Finnar þar mungát ok gerðu honum þar veizlu.[193]
>
> That winter, it is said, Sigurðr had the [Saami] build him two light ships deep in the fjord and they were fastened together with sinews and there were no nails in them, and withies instead of knees [under the beams], and they had twelve rowers on each side. Sigurðr stayed with the

---

190 Inga-Marie Mulk, "The Role of the Sámi in Fur-Trading During the Late Iron Age and Nordic Medieval Period in the Light of the Sámi Sacrificial Sites in Lapland," *Acta Borealia* 13, no. 1 (1996): 47–80. See chapters 4 and 5.
191 Mulk, "Fur-Trading," 47–49.
192 Tolley, "*Hrólfs*," 13.
193 *Hkr 3*, 311.

[Saami] while they were building the ships, and the [Saami] had beer there and put on a banquet there for him.¹⁹⁴

The extract emphasises the recognition of Saami boatbuilders in medieval society, perhaps due to the different technique using organic materials such as withies and sinew rather than metal.¹⁹⁵ Sigurðr allegedly composed a poem about the light going "sinbundit skip" [sinew-bound ship], praising its exceptionality.¹⁹⁶ In the archaeological material, sinew-bound (sewn) boats are mostly associated with the Saami, although the construction technique is hard to tie to any specific ethnic group.¹⁹⁷ It should be mentioned that although sewn boats cannot be said to be exclusively Saami, Saami boats are traditionally sewn, not riveted (which is associated with Norse shipbuilding). In some cases, sinew-bound boats found in northern Norway and Sweden have been found to show affiliation to both Saami and Norse cultures, and may be read as expressing culturally fluid identities.¹⁹⁸ The textual tradition, however, seems to exclusively associate sinew-bound boats with the Saami.

Saami fishing economies are also highlighted, first mentioned by Ohthere at the court of King Alfred at the end of the ninth century, stating that the *Finnas* fished during the summer.¹⁹⁹ The section of *Historia Norwegie* concerning "De Finnis" [the Saami] from the mid-to-late twelfth-century, furthers the textual motif associating the Saami with fishing by accentuating nearly magical expertise and shared fishing economies with the Norse:

> Item dum Finni unacum christianis gregem squamigeram hamo carpere attemptassent, quos in casis fidelium pagani perspexerant, sacculis fere plenis unco suo de abysso attractis scapham cum piscibus impleuerunt.²⁰⁰

---

194 "Hkr 3," 191.
195 On the archaeology of sewn boats associated with the Saami, see Gunilla Larsson, *Ship and Society: Maritime Ideology in Late Iron Age Sweden*, AUN 67 (Uppsala: Uppsala Universitet, 2007), 121–25.
196 *Mork 2*, 194.
197 Anja Roth Niemi, "En båtgrav på Hillesøy ved Tromsø," Norark, 01.03.2018 http://www.norark.no/prosjekter/nodvegen-pa-hillesoy/en-batgrav-fra-yngre-jernalder-pa-hillesoy-ved-tromso/. Eva Panagiotakopulu, Paul C. Buckland, and Stephen Wickler, "Is There Anybody in There? Entomological Evidence from a Boat Burial at Øksnes in Vesterålen, Northern Norway," *PloS ONE* 13, no. 7 (2018): 1–18, 11. Larsson, *Ship*, 121–25.
198 Panagiotakopulu, Buckland, and Wickler, "Boat Burial," 11. Larsson, *Ship*, 122–23.
199 Hansen and Olsen, *Hunters*, 55.
200 *HN*, 62.

Again, when the [Saami], together with the Christians, had gone about catching by hook a flock of fish such as these heathens had seen in Christian dwellings, they drew almost full traps out of the deeps with their wand, and so loaded the boats to capacity.[201]

Shared fishing economies are also hinted at in the mid-to-late twelfth-century *Passio Olavi* mentioned in chapter 2.3.3, which sees the contrast between the success of Christian Norwegian fishermen with that of the heathen Saami.[202] Fishing, both in coastal areas and in lakes and watercourses of the interior, must have been an important sustenance activity for medieval Saami groups. Fishing in coastal fjords, as expressed by Ohthere, could have featured prominently in seasonal migratory patterns and formed part of the summer activities.[203] Later in the medieval period and onwards, different Saami groups living along the northern Norwegian coastal zone became increasingly involved with the large-scale Bergen industry and traded both dried and salted fish.[204] It has also been suggested that Saami people living along the coast of what is today northern Norway functioned as the primary suppliers of whale oil and walrus ropes from before the medieval period and onwards.[205]

Norse accounts exclusively associate sinew-bound boats with the Saami. Fishing, on the other hand, is not primarily associated with either the Norse or the Saami. However, the accounts ranging from the late ninth century to later in the medieval period describing fishing as both a subsistence activity and large-scale economy among coastal Saami groups should, according to my way of thinking, be understood as based on real life observations of Saami lifestyles. The portrayal of shared fishing economies between the Norse and the Saami in northern Norway, found in two late twelfth century texts, further this claim and demonstrate close connections between the Christian Norse population and different coastal Saami groups. Overall, these accounts can help illuminate or emphasise the long history of different Sea Saami communities, touched upon in footnote 54 (chapter 1).

---

201 *HN*, 63.
202 *Passio*, 70–71. Stephen Wickler, "The Centrality of Small Islands in Arctic Norway," *Acta Borealia* 11, no. 2 (2016): 171–94.
203 Lars Ivar Hansen, "Sami Fisheries in the Pre-modern Era: Household Sustenance and Market Relations," *Acta Borealia* 23, no. 1 (2006): 56–80 (57).
204 Hansen and Olsen, *Hunters*, 154, 174.
205 Marte Spangen and Johan Eilertsen Arntzen, "Sticky Structures and Opportunistic Builders: The Construction and Social Role of Longhouses in Northern Norway," in *Re-Imagining Periphery: Archaeology and Text in Northern Europe from Iron Age to Viking and Early Medieval Periods*, ed. Charlotta Hillerdal and Kristin Ilves (Oxford: Oxbow Books, 2020), 11–32 (26).

3.2.5 Appearance and Accommodation

There are few defining physical characteristics associated with Saami characters across the textual material. In the following section, I aim to account for these characteristics and the context in which they appear, in addition to discussing the dwelling spaces associated with the Saami across the source material.

Ketils saga hœngs states that Brúni's Saami visitors were "eigi mjóleitir" [not narrow faced] and Hrafnhildr is described as having an "álnarbreitt andlit" [face as broad as an ell].[206] Ketils saga is the only medieval source, as far as I am aware, that describe the Saami in this manner, and it should be noted that these descriptions are most likely tied to a Norse need expressed later in the medieval period to Other Saami characters or characters from the far north. With that in mind, it should be mentioned that being broad or wide in general seems to be a common stereotype associated with far northern or otherwise supernatural characters in the *fornaldarsögur*,[207] and so the above description may be a result of this association given the genre of Ketils saga. Nevertheless, the connection between Saami characters and broad faces specifically should be treated with caution, especially since such a connection was used in the harmful and racist colonial race-biological research on Saami people up until the twentieth century.[208] It should therefore be repeated that there is no expected or recurrent association between, or any medieval stereotype connected to, the Saami and broad faces in the medieval source material, and that Ketils saga is an anomaly. I would therefore argue that the descriptions associated with the Saami visitors and Hrafnhildr, occurring somewhere in Finnmǫrk, should be read as representative of tendencies associated with the *fornaldarsögur* to describe far northern characters as having broad or wide appearances.

In *Ǫrvar-Odds saga*, the presence of Saami characters during the conception of Grímr apparently leads to a change in his own facial features: he is born with a hairy birthmark on his cheek (that no iron could bite), which grants him the nickname *lóðinkinna* [hairy cheek].[209] However, the Saami connection only appears in *Ǫrvar-Odds saga*, and the other texts relating Grímr and his birthmark simply mention he has one.[210]

---

206 *Kjaln*, 31. *Ket*, 118.
207 See for example the descriptions of the supernatural creatures in *Egils saga einhenda ok Ásmundar berserkjabana* and *Hjálmþés saga ok Ölvis*, in Carl Christian Rafn, ed. *Fornaldar sögur nordrlanda eptir gömlum handritum*, vol. 3 (Copenhagen: Ennu Popsku, 1829–30), 372–73, 471–73.
208 See section 1.1.2.
209 *Ǫrv*, 161.
210 *Ket*, 123. *GrL*, 143.

Saami characters are described as both short and tall.[211] In other words, there is no consensus in the textual tradition regarding the heights of Saami characters. Else Mundal nevertheless writes that the Saami "were shorter than their Nordic neighbours," without backing up this statement in any way, and it is unclear whether she refers to descriptions in the texts themselves or assumptions about the actual heights of medieval people.[212] More worryingly, Hilda Radzin compares the portrayal of thralls in the Eddic poem *Rígsþula* to that of (her perceived) physical traits of Saami people:

> The Skald describes the thralls as having black hair, and an unsightly countenance, thick ankles, coarse fingers, and as being of a low and deformed stature; these are physiological traits characteristic of the [Saami], who were probably reduced to a state of vassalage by their Scandinavian conquerors.[213]

Radzin's claim that the Saami are of "deformed stature" is clearly problematic and very vividly reflects common colonial and racist assumptions about the Saami, particularly prior to the postcolonial "reform" in the 1980s. While these assumptions have been largely debunked and are unacceptable in scholarship today, an inherent problem lies in the fact that research concerning the Saami within Norse or Medieval Studies is a small field and that harmful ideas about the Saami may be repeated through uncritical referencing of earlier scholarship.[214]

As discussed in the introduction, racial discrimination against the Saami was based on an amalgamation of nationalism and colonialism backed up by scientific theories like Social Darwinism which had grown in popularity in the late nineteenth century. Together, these views supported the notions of the "Nordic race" as superior and as the evolutionary "peak" in Fennoscandia, whereas the Saami were viewed as inferior and nonevolving.[215] Measurements of the length and width of human skulls was seen as one of the most efficient ways of asserting racial belonging, with "langskaller" [long narrow craniums] equating to Nordic supe-

---

[211] See for example *Hkr 2*, 120 (Finnr litli) and *Ket*, 118 (Hrafnhildr).
[212] Else Mundal, "Coexistence of Saami and Norse Culture: Reflected in and Interpreted by Old Norse Myths," in *Old Norse Myths, Literature and Society: The Proceedings of the 11th International Saga Conference, 2–7 July 2000, University of Sydney*, ed. Geraldine Barnes and Margaret Clunies Ross (Sydney: University of Sydney, 2000), 346–55 (348).
[213] Hilda Radzin, "Names in the Mythological Lay 'Rigsþula'," *Literary Onomastics Studies* 9 (1982): 177–82 (179).
[214] See sections 1.1.2 and 1.2.
[215] Audhild Schanche, "Knoklenes verdi: Om forskning på og forvaltning av skjelettmateriale fra samiske graver," in *Samisk forskning og forskningsetikk*, Forskningsetiske komiteer, vol. 2 (Oslo, 2002), 99–133 (103–5). Schanche, "Knoklenes verdi," 104.

riority and the "kortskaller" [short broad craniums] equating to Saami inferiority.[216] Through the identification and categorisation of "typical" Saami and Nordic characteristics, prevalent until the Second World War, the mistreatment of and discrimination against the Saami was grounded in ideas of the superiority of the "Nordic race." Since the skull measurements and racial discrimination against the Saami people is still a sensitive and relevant topic in contemporary society,[217] scholars cannot simply let descriptions such as the ones conferred upon Hrafnhildr and Brúni's visitors stand unproblematised. A careless focus on the Saami as looking a certain way, regarding height, skin colour, and facial features is unhelpful and endorses colonial and ethnographic approaches supporting the previously strong standing notion of the Saami people as static and inferior. It is particularly important that we actively reject these colonial approaches, since the majority of Saami people today have experienced discrimination based on ideas such as the ones mentioned above.[218] Rather, as scholars, we need to repeatedly emphasise, as I have done here, that there are no clear patterns associated with Saami physical appearance in either the classical or medieval sources. As a matter of fact, the most common descriptive marker associated with Saami characters in terms of physical appearance is beauty, a result of the abundance of incidents involving Saami women, often marrying Norse men.[219]

The clothing of Saami characters is rarely mentioned, and not more than that of "Norse" characters. When it is emphasised, such as for the woman knowledgeable in magic in *Vatnsdœla saga*, it is usually to accentuate grandeur and high status.[220] However, a few common denominators appear. Already from Tacitus's *Germania* from the end of the first century, the Saami are portrayed as dressing in animal skins, something which is reiterated in 780 by Paulus Diaconus.[221] The saga texts sometimes associate the Saami with clothing made from reindeer- or wolfskin.[222] Hermann Pálsson assumes that the nickname and garment *skinnkyrtill* [skin-tunic] is an indication that the person associated with it is portrayed as

---

[216] Schanche, "Knoklenes verdi," 104.
[217] Norsk Teknisk Museum, "Bilder fra raseforskning/Images from Race Science," (Youtube video), 14.06.2018 https://www.youtube.com/watch?v=urcIBW2NrHk.
[218] Marita Melhus and Ann Ragnhild Broderstad, *Folkehelseundersøkelsen i Troms og Finnmark: Tilleggsrapport om samisk og kvensk/norskfinsk befolkning* (Tromsø: Senter for samisk helseforskning, 2020).
[219] See *Hkr 1*, 125–26. *Kjaln*, 29–30. Saxo, 39.
[220] *Vatn*, 30.
[221] Tacitus, *Agricola and Germania*, ed. James Rives, trans. William Dudley Foulke (London: Penguin Classics, 2010), 70. *History of the Lombards*, 7.
[222] *Mesta 2*, 98.

Saami.²²³ These instances never occur when a character is explicitly portrayed as Saami, but during meetings with the "extreme Other" in the far north, often with so-called "trolls."²²⁴ One should therefore be careful with a simple assumption associating *skinnkyrtill*-wearers with the Saami, since they are never exclusively mentioned together. Cloaks, however, are regularly associated with the Saami in Norse texts.²²⁵ The name of the *Finnakonungr* Mǫttul literally means cloak in Old Norse, and Saami characters sometimes fashion magical cloaks impenetrable to weapons.²²⁶ The connection between the cloak and the Saami might lie in the mystery surrounding the "cloaked figure," indicating something hidden and secret: the unknown. Lyonel Perabo has investigated the association between Saami ritual behaviour and the covering of the ritual performer with a cloak or a garment, claiming that "cloak rituals" in Norse society were direct borrowings from participation in, observation or knowledge of, Saami ritual performances.²²⁷ In *Historia Norwegie*, for example, the Saami ritual performer spreads out a cloak before initiating the ritual.²²⁸

Regarding Saami dwelling spaces, the sagas predominantly portray the *gammi* [tent/(turf-)hut(s)].²²⁹ The term itself is exclusively associated with the Saami in Norse narration, with one exception that I am aware of, being the chivalric *Þiðreks saga af Bern* where the traditional Saami dwelling space houses a dwarf.²³⁰ Upon meeting King Haraldr in *Ágrip* and *Haralds saga hárfagra*, Svási introduces himself as "þann Finninn er hann hafði ját at setja gamma sinn annan veg brekkunnar á Þoptyn, þar sem þá var konungrinn" [that Saami whom the king had allowed to set up his hut on the other side of the hill at Þoptyn, where the king then was].²³¹ The king later visits the *gammi*, where he

---

223 Hermann Pálsson, "Sami," 32.
224 See for example *Ket*, 127. *GrL*, 145–47, 149. *Án*, 361. *HHábr*, 204.
225 *Mesta 2*, 98. *Ldn*, 82–83. *Helgisaga*, 70. *HHábr*, 121. *Hrólf*, 48–50. *Fsk*, 79. Aalto and Lehtola, "Representations," 17.
226 *Ldn*, 82–83. *Fsk*, 79. Saxo, 649. Aalto and Lehtola, "Representations," 17. Björn K. Þórólfsson and Guðni Jónsson, ed., *Vestfirðinga sǫgur*, Íslenzk fornrit 6 (Reykjavík: Hið íslenzka fornritafélag, 1943), 16.
227 Perabo, *Heathens*, 107, 111–12. See Jón Hnefill Aðalsteinsson's *Under the Cloak: A Pagan Ritual Turning Point in the Conversion of Iceland* (Reykjavík: Háskolautgafan, 1999), 102, 123.
228 *HN*, 60–61.
229 Mundal, "Perception," 100. The North Saami term is "goahti." As with the term "noaidi," I have decided against using the contemporary Saami term, and rather stick with the descriptive "Saami dwelling spaces" or employ the term sometimes used in the Norse sources (*gammi*).
230 Henrik Bertelsen, ed. *Þiðreks saga af Bern*, vol. 2 (Copenhagen: S. L. Møllers Bogtrykkeri, 1905–11), 34.
231 *Ágr*, 4–5. *Hkr 1*, 125–27.

meets his future wife Snæfríðr. Similarly, when Eiríkr blóðøx first meets Gunnhildr, she is staying with her Saami mentors in a *gammi*.[232] Staying at an anchorage somewhere on the northern coast of Finnmǫrk, Ǫrvar-Oddr and his crew observe Saami people in an abundance of "gamma á landi uppi" [huts on land].[233] In Oddr's *Óláfs saga Tryggvasonar*, the Saami man visited by the king is portrayed as living in a *gammi* in the mountains of Agdenes in Þróndalǫg.[234] The most elaborate portrayal of life in the Saami dwelling spaces is related in the aforementioned accounts about Sigurðr slembidjákn and his stay with Saami people, here from *Morkinskinna:*

Gótt vas í gamma
þars vér glaðir drukkum,
ok glaðr grams sonr
gekk meðal bekkja.
Vasa þar gamans vant
at gamansdrykkju;
þegn gladdi þegn
þar lands sem var.[235]

It was pleasant in the turf-hut where gladly we drank, and the glad-hearted son of the prince passed between the benches; there was no lack of cheer at the cheerful drinking, retainer delighted retainer, there as everywhere.[236]

Allegedly composed in the early twelfth century by Sigurðr himself, the poem does not emphasise any "us" versus "them" differentiation between the Norse protagonist and the Saami actors, indicating close personal relations.

Although the term *gammi* is associated with the Saami in Norse narration, it is problematic to assume that this was the only dwelling structure appropriate and available for Saami actors in the medieval period. This assumption is prevalent in the contemporary majority culture's view of and communication of traditional Saami lifestyles and is connected to majority cultural stereotypes about the "right" way to be Saami.[237] It is therefore crucial to note that there are also exceptions in the saga material, portraying the Saami as living on farms.[238] In *Ketils saga hœngs*,

---

232 *Hkr 1*, 135–36.
233 *Ǫrv*, 174.
234 *Odds*, 187.
235 *Mork 2*, 193.
236 Theodore M. Andersson and Kari Ellen Gade, eds., *Morkinskinna: The Earliest Icelandic Chronicle of the Norwegian Kings (1030–1157)* (London: Cornell University Press, 2000), 374.
237 Mette Ballovara, "Bekymret over kunnskapsmangel," NRK Sápmi, 12.02.2020 https://www.nrk.no/sapmi/vanja-reiste-rundt-til-norske-skoler-_-bekymret-over-kunnskapsmangel-1.14865671.
238 *Ket*, 117. *Mork 2*, 111.

Ketill first meets his Saami father-in-law after finding his farm, somewhere in Finnmǫrk: "fann bæ; þar stóð maðr fyri dyrum ok klauf skíð, hann hét Brúni" [he found a farm and a man stood outside in front of the doors, chopping wood. His name was Brúni].²³⁹ The fact that Saami groups sometimes preferred other dwelling spaces than the *gammi* is also insinuated in *Gull-Ásu-Þórðar þáttr*; here from the version found in Morkinskinna, narrating the hostility between a Saami group and the Bjarkarey (Bjarkøy) chieftain Viðkunnr Jónsson: "Farið nú ok hittið Sigurð Hranason ok biðið hann hér koma, ok ef hann hefir nǫkkura undansfœrslu þá minnið hann á þat hverr honum dugði bezt þá er Finnar tóku bú hans" [Go now and find Sigurðr Hranason, and tell him to come here. If he makes some pretext, remind him who helped him when the [Saami] seized his farm].²⁴⁰ Naturally, there might have been other motivations behind the Saami group's appropriation of Sigurðr's farm than wanting to live on it, but it is important to emphasise nonetheless since it challenges the assumption of the *gammi* as the only acceptable Saami dwelling space in the medieval period.

An interesting term appears in the Flateyjarbók version of *Sneglu-Halla þáttr* (its version in Morkinskinna is summarised in section 5.3.2). The Flateyjarbók manuscript is an Icelandic manuscript compiled in the late fourteenth century.²⁴¹ Here, the term "Bufinna" is used in a context relating the Saami trade, by Einarr fluga, son of the Hálogaland chieftain Hárekr ór Þjǫtta. Einarr reportedly relates to King Haraldr harðráði that the trading he had done with "Bufinna edr fiskimenn" [settled Saami or fishermen] had been peaceful.²⁴² The term *búmaðr*, discussed in more detail in section 4.2.1, is generally agreed to mean settled farmers, and as such, the term "bufinna" could therefore denote Saami people that settled as farmers. Knut Bergsland has identified two initial instances of the term in late fifteenth century legal texts (notably, from the West of Norway), in contexts clearly referring to farms settled by Saami people.²⁴³ Both Bergsland and Else Mundal therefore argue that the term as it appears in *Sneglu-Halla þáttur* should be understood in conjunction with the early modern designation *búfinnar*, which is com-

---

239 *Ket*, 117.
240 *Mork 2*, 111. "Mork," 332. Sigurðr also appears in a Saami context in *Þinga saga*, see section 5.2.2.
241 Torgrim Titlestad et al., eds., *Flatøybok*, vol. 1 (Hafrsfjord: Sagabok, 2015).
242 Guðbrandr Vigfússon and Carl Richard Unger, eds., *Flateyarbok: En samling af Norske Konge-Sagaer med indskudte mindre Fortællinger om Begivenheder i og udenfor Norge samt annaler*, vol. 3 (Christiania: P.T. Mallings Forlagsboghandler, 1868), 422. See *NGL* 2, 491, for a possible legal description from the mid-to-late thirteenth century about a Saami farmer.
243 Knut Bergsland, "Om middelalderens Finnmarker," *Historisk tidsskrift* 49, no. 4 (1970): 365–409 (371).

monly understood as Saami people that had settled in one place, as freeholders and fishermen.[244] It is therefore likely that the appearance of the term in Flateyjarbók reflects the normality of Saami people having settled as farmers and/or being freeholders.

We should also not neglect the nature of cross-cultural societies and possibilities of cross-cultural relations. Marriages, fostering arrangements, and neighbourly visits occur across the saga material, and given the likelihood that these were reflections of the physical society at the time of composition, and cohabitation, whether on the stereotypical "Norse farm" or in a "Saami *gammi*," or in a mix of both, is possible. I therefore argue that it would be a major simplification of medieval Fennoscandian society to maintain a dichotomy where Norse = the farm,[245] and Saami = the *gammi*. Nevertheless, the *gammi* is a recurring textual motif associated with Saami dwelling spaces in Norse texts, and this repetition is most likely a reflection of Norse observations of Saami societies.

The *gammi* may also be mirrored in the archaeological material, which sees the emergence and manifestation of so-called "hearth row sites" in connection with material expressions of Saami identity from circa 800.[246] Sven-Donald Hedman, Bjørnar Olsen, and Maria Vretemark define hearth row sites as "a set of three or more equally oriented and regularly interspaced hearths organized in a linear pattern."[247] The sites become numerous and widespread early in the medieval period, but discontinue abruptly around 1300. Their highly interregional appearance suggest that shared practices and common material features spread rapidly over a vast territory, appearing in northern Norway, Finland, and most likely the Kola peninsula, but are also found as far south as Aursjøen, close to Dovre.[248]

---

244 Bergsland, "Finnmarker," 371. Mundal, "Perception," 99–100.
245 See also Spangen and Arntzen, "Longhouses," 27–28.
246 Hansen and Olsen, *Hunters*, 31, 82. In the centuries just before the medieval period (c. 700–800), archaeologists have witnessed a change in settlement patterns and the arrival of material forms of expressions later interpreted as central to Saami culture, 90. See also Sven-Donald Hedman, *Boplatser och offerplatser: Ekonomisk strategi och boplatsmönster bland skogssamer 700–1600 AD*, Studia Archaeologica Universitatis Umensis 17 (Umeå: University of Umeå, 2003).
247 Sven-Donald Hedman, Bjørnar Olsen, and Maria Vretemark, "Hunters, Herders and Hearths: Interpreting New Results from Hearth Row Sites in Pasvik, Arctic Norway," *Rangifer* 35, no. 1 (2015): 1–24 (2).
248 Hedman et al., 3. Jostein Bergstøl, *Samer i Østerdalen? En studie av etnisitet i jernalderen og middelalderen i det nordøstre Hedmark*, Acta Humaniora 325 (Oslo: Unipub, 2008), 141–42. Hege Skalleberg Gjerde has even suggested that the hearth row sites can be found as far south as Hallingdal; "Samiske tufter i Hallingdal?," in *Viking*, ed. Ellen Høigård Hofseth and Egil Mikkelsen, Norsk arkeologisk årbok, vol. 42 (Oslo: Norsk arkeologiske selskap, 2009), 207. For a general overview of hearth-row sites, see Petri Halinen and Bjørnar Olsen, eds., *In Search of Hearths: A*

This distribution is mirrored in the saga material, which portrays Saami *gammi* in Bjarmaland (most likely the Kola peninsula, see discussion in chapter 4), Finnmǫrk, Hálogaland, and in Dofri.[249] Usually rectangular and consisting of 3–8 hearths, the sites were solidly built by large frame stones and compact stone packing "within" the space, and show traces of intense firing which indicate they were most probably used as dwelling spaces.[250] As there are no evident traces of possible superstructures like post holes and walls, evidence such as the spatial pattern, distribution of finds, cultural layers, and soil chemicals suggest the hearths formed parts of circular dwelling structures, most likely tents.[251] While earlier dwelling sites are usually found along the shores of lakes and larger rivers, the hearth row sites normally appear in forest areas away from or not in relation to large bodies of water, "situated in dry moraine outcrops in marsh areas, on forested terraces or next to small creeks and tarns often surrounded by heathland rich in reindeer lichen."[252] The appearance of the sites is sometimes linked to possible changes in reindeer economy from hunting to herding due to its ideal location for winter pastures,[253] although a blend of strategies has been proposed and seems more likely, particularly when keeping the saga material in mind.[254]

There are no clear patterns associated with Saami physical appearance, with the exception of beauty, in the source material I have analysed. Saami characters are described in various ways, and according to my way of thinking, these diverse descriptions accentuate the normalised presence of Saami people in Norse society. The clothing of Saami characters is also diverse, with cloaks and clothes made from reindeer- and wolfskin being repeatedly emphasised. The *gammi* is the predominant dwelling site associated with the Saami in Norse texts, although there are ex-

---

Book in Memory of Sven-Donald Hedman (Helsinki: The Finnish Antiquarian Society, 2019), 197–210. See chapter 7.
249 *Bós*, 210; *Hkr 1*, 135–36; *Mork 2*, 193; *Ágr*, 4–5.
250 Hedman et al., 3.
251 Hedman et al., 3.
252 Hedman et al., 3.
253 Inger Storli, "Sami Viking Age Pastoralism: Or the Fur Trade Paradigm Reconsidered," *Norwegian Archaeological Review* 26, no. 1 (1993): 1–20. This is also stirred by the appearance of so-called Stallo-sites which are similar spatially organised sites coming into use at the same time in the northern Norwegian and northern Swedish mountain region.
254 Hedman et al. suggest the possibility of the inhabitants of the hearth row sites as being both hunters and herders of reindeer, mixing different strategies, also incorporating farm animals such as sheep, 2–3. In Eyvindr Finnsson's *lausavísa* 12, it is insinuated that the Saami sometimes kept sheep (or goat).

amples of Saami living on farms.²⁵⁵ Overall, the portrayal of the appearance and accommodation of Saami character is multifaceted across Norse texts.

3.3 Conclusion

The Saami Motif-Cluster is formed by associations grounded in real life interactions, experiences, observations, perceptions, expectations, and stereotypes, utilised in the textual tradition to portray the Saami. These allude to the Saami by Othering through connotations with magic, supernatural beings, the winter season, hunting and archery, and forest animals such as bears and wolves. The narrative is consistent across the saga genres and in other medieval texts. I therefore suggest that when overlapping in the right contextual situations, the Saami Motif-Cluster welcomes Saami allusions and therefore sometimes enables the identification of the Saami in the source material. As will be discussed in the following chapters, this can also include the portrayal of characters that are never explicitly described as Saami. While these textual tropes allow the identification of Saami characters in the texts, it is also crucial to emphasise their nature as stereotypes based on perceptions with varying degrees of distance to actual interaction and experiences with Saami peoples. The sources on the Saami are written by others than themselves for others than themselves and depending on the source and the ideology behind it, are sometimes subject to over-exaggeration and fantastical invention, as well as Christian ideals and implicit Othering. Nevertheless, I would also like to highlight that very often, the Saami Motif-Cluster is connected to positive, albeit sometimes ambiguous, associations. The abilities ascribed to Saami characters in the textual tradition such as being knowledgeable in magic, archery, and hunting, boatbuilding, and skiing are often overtly favourable and frequently work as useful catalysts for the protagonists. Even the sometimes negatively charged magical skills of the Saami are valued in the texts and function as a productive tool even for canonised kings.²⁵⁶ Characters with cross-cultural backgrounds are nicknamed accordingly and given specific characteristics and abilities following a pattern associated with magic, shapeshifting, winter weather, archery, and hunting. Finally though, it should be mentioned that while these textual motifs are common, they are never exclusive and Saami characters are portrayed in diverse ways.

---

255 *Ket*, 117. *Mork 2*, 111.
256 *Odds*, 187–90. *Helgisaga*, 16.

Chapter 4: Northern Fennoscandian Politics and Spatial Belonging

4.1 Introduction

Despite sometimes being described as "desolate" and "remote" (especially clear in the *terra nullius* colonialism exercised by the Scandinavian nation states in early modern times), the northernmost parts of the Fennoscandian landscape complex are described as inhabited in several medieval texts.[1] The texts assert that the far north of Fennoscandia was a special and supernatural place.[2] Somewhat paradoxically, these areas are also described with normalcy and depict habitual interactions. This is also the case for landscapes further south, with the Upplǫnd region appearing in the source material as a hub for both normalised Saami encounters and mysterious happenings connected to a group of Others. Medieval Scandinavian writers narrating Norse-Saami affairs view the Saami as both separate to and a part of the "Norse" spatial area and the texts often contradict themselves on the matter. Medieval texts highlight Saami presence in a wide spanning area reaching from as far south as the Oslo region to the Kola peninsula in the northeast, opposing the tendency to exclusively associate the Saami with distant and northern snowscapes.[3] As I will elaborate in section 4.4 and chapter 7, the historical landscape is not always as "northern" in spatial distribution as typically assumed. The emphasis in the saga material and other medieval texts of a spatially diverse and multifaceted Saami presence across Fennoscandia is accounted for below.

---

1 The introduction to this chapter repeats some of the arguments put forth in Solveig Marie Wang, "Conceptualizing the Multicultural 'North' in the *Íslendingasögur:* Peoples, Places and Phenomena," *Nordlit* 46 (2020): 245–62.
2 Nils Oskal, "Political Inclusion of the Saami as Indigenous People in Norway," *International Journal on Minority and Group Rights* 8 (2001): 235–61 (257–58).
3 Jeremy DeAngelo, "The North and the Depiction of the 'Finnar' in the Icelandic Sagas," *Scandinavian Studies*, 83, no. 3 (2010): 257–86 (272–73).

∂ Open Access. © 2023 the author(s), published by De Gruyter. This work is licensed under the Creative Commons Attribution-NonCommercial-NoDerivatives 4.0 International License.
https://doi.org/10.1515/9783110784305-009

Figure 3: *Important locations referred to in this book*, https://d-maps.com/carte.php?num_car=5970&lang=en. *Compiled by author.*

4.2 Northern Nóregi: Within and Without

4.2.1 Finnmǫrk

Finnmǫrk is the landscape most frequently associated with the Saami in medieval texts. Appearing across the saga material in varying contexts, Finnmǫrk materialises as the home of Saami people,[4] a place to visit,[5] harrying grounds,[6] an area of mysticism, and supernatural beings,[7] a pit-stop on the way to Bjarmaland,[8] a source of riches, and as tax-land.[9] It is always associated with the Saami, directly or indirectly. The landscape is traditionally and most often associated with the north (of Norway) and areas east of the Hálogaland coast (into modern day Sweden). This is reflected by the travel descriptions in the text which focus on journeys either "norðr" [north] or "á fjáll upp" [up in the mountains].[10] Since it is rarely demarcated, medieval writers relating Saami affairs view the Saami and Finnmǫrk as both internal and external to the "Norse" spatial area. The texts often contradict themselves on the matter, such as Oddr Snorrason's *Ólafs saga Tryggvasonar* which states that "norðr frá Nóregi er Finnmǫrk" [north of Norway is Finnmǫrk], in addition to "En landit er greint ok kallat þessum heitum: Vík, Hǫrðaland, Upplǫnd, Þróndheimr, Hálogaland, Finnmǫrk" [The land (Nóregi) is divided into the regions called Vík, Hǫrðaland, Upplǫnd, Þróndheimr, Hálogaland, Finnmǫrk].[11] *Historia Norwegie* portrays a similar stance, stating that:

> Es[t terra] nimis sinuosa, innumera protendens promunctoria, III [habita]bilibus zonis per longum cincta: prima, que maxima [et] maritima est, secunda mediterranea, que et montana [dicitur], tertia siluestris, que Finnis inhabitur, sed non aratur.
>
> Full of fjords and creeks, it is a country that pushes out countless headlands, and along its length encompasses three habitable zones: the first and largest is the seaboard; the second is the inland area, also known as the mountain region; the third is wooded and populated by the [Saami], but there is no agriculture there.[12]

The Saami here form part of Norway, which is also the case when the text later discusses Hálogaland as one of four legal districts within the coastal zone, stating that the inhabitants of the area lived with and frequently dealt with the Saami.[13] However, in the following chapter of the text, the immense wilderness bordering Norway is described, dividing the country along its length and only inhabited by

---

4 *Stst*, 638. *Ket*, 120–23.
5 *Hkr 1*, 324–26. *Hkr 2*, 344–45.
6 *Ǫrv*, 174.
7 *Hkr 1*, 325. *Ǫrv*, 161, 241.
8 *Ǫrv*, 174. *Hkr 1*, 135. Saxo, 601.
9 See section 5.2.3.
10 *Sv*, 6. *Eg*, 36.
11 *Odds*, 203.
12 *HN*, 51–52.
13 *HN*, 55–56.

Saami people.[14] Lars Ivar Hansen has examined the somewhat contradictory view offered by the chronicle and argues that the focus on the Saami as living in the wilderness bordering Norway is the author's attempt to convey Germanic notions of the delimitations of political land.[15] According to Hansen, pre-Christian Germanic ideology utilised a "wilderness tactic" which saw the benefits of being surrounded by widespread wilderness that functioned as a border as well as guarded against hostile attacks from outsiders. I would suggest that it is also likely that the descriptions involving notions of wilderness and wasteland reflect diverging sociocultural conceptions of landscape and spatial awareness.

In toponymical terms, Finnmǫrk suggests a defined geographical area, as perceived by the Norse. Consisting of the components "Finn" meaning Saami, and "mǫrkr" denoting a border, forest, border forest, or periphery, the toponym in turn defines the area as ascribed to Saami groups or on the periphery of Norse culture. In *Sverris saga*, first written in parts between the late twelfth and early thirteenth centuries,[16] King Sverrir Sigurðarson relates his dream of becoming a bird so big his beak covered the eastern parts of the country and his tail feathers "norðr í Finnbúin" [north where the Saami live], with the wings covering the whole country.[17] *Helgisaga* supports this view, assuming the traditional area of Finnmǫrk as internal to Norway when describing the length of Norway as reaching from Egðafylki and Gautelfr in the south to Vegistafr, an area possibly referring to contemporary Murmansk, in the north.[18] However, and possibly more in line with the toponym, the Saami are elsewhere perceived as inhabiting a fringe area: bordering Norway.

When King Hákon góði allegedly built beacons of war on the high mountains inland all over Norway, Fagrskinna relates that it took a week for the war summons to reach the northernmost community in Hálogaland.[19] Hálogaland is here therefore perceived as the far end of the country, on the fringe of something else and bordering something other, exemplified by the return of Þórir hundr as related in *Helgisaga*: "kom Þorer hundr norðan af Finnmork til Noregs" [Þórir

---

14 *HN*, 58–59.
15 Lars Ivar Hansen, "Om synet på de 'andre': ute og hjemme: Geografi og folkeslag på nordkalotten i følge Historia Norvegie," in *Olavslegenden og den latinske historieskriving i 1100-tallets Norge*, ed. Lars Boje Mortensen, Karen Skovgaard-Petersen, and Inger Ekrem (Copenhagen: Museum Tusculanum Press, 2000), 54–87 (65).
16 Store norske leksikon, "Sverres saga," snl.no, 04.03.21 https://snl.no/Sverres_saga.
17 *Sv*, 6.
18 *Helgisaga*, 21.
19 *Fsk*, 83.

hundr came from the north from Finnmǫrk to Norway].²⁰ The Icelandic treatise *Rímbegla* from the end of the 1100s notes that "fjörðr er Málángr heitir, hann skilr Finmörk við Búmenn; fyrir sunnan Málangr stendr kirkja er heitir í Lengjuvík" [the fjord called Malangen separates Finnmǫrk from the *búmenn*; south of Malangen stands the church called Lenvik].²¹ The term *búmaðr* has been heavily debated in both scholarship and public debate, but is generally agreed to mean settled farmers.²² It is not an ethnic divider but a cultural one, and delineates traditional Norse and Saami areas on agricultural terms. It does not separate the areas on Saami versus Norse terms but based on the cultivation of land. It has been noted that archaeological finds indicate that there was a farming population farther north than Malangen early in the medieval period, for example on Karlsøy, that several burial monuments on islands in north-Troms conform to Norse tradition, and worth mentioning is the "typical" Norse farm found on Loppa in Finnmark.²³ These factors again point to the cultural fluidity of the region and dynamic processes of identity discussed throughout.

This "fluid spatial awareness" becomes particularly clear in the aforementioned stories relating Sigurðr slembidjákn's refuge with Saami boatbuilders in Northern Norway.²⁴ While the Fagrskinna and Morkinskinna texts locate Sigurðr in Finnmǫrk, with the latter specifying Ægisfjörðr (Øksfjord), the Heimskringla-version quoted above sees the royal pretender in Tjaldasund (Tjeldsund) on Hinnøya (in Hálogaland), after sailing through Ægisfjörðr (Øksfjorden).²⁵ Since the texts state that Magnús, Sigurðr's (perceived) nephew who fled with him, sought refuge with the Norse chieftain Viðkunnr Jónsson to the north on Bjarkarey, I find it more likely that Sigurðr's Saami friends lived on Hinnøya. This indicates that Hinnøya was perceived as an area where both Norse and Saami people lived and were in contact with each other. Based on archaeological interpretations of dwelling

---

20 *Helgisaga*, 52.
21 Arnamagnæanske samling, "AM 727 I 4to," handrit.is, https://handrit.is/en/manuscript/view/is/AM04-0727-I. The text states that the church in Lengjuvík was the northernmost church in Norway, until *Hákonar saga* relates the building of the church in Tromsø around 1250; *Hák 2*, 155.
22 Tarrin Wills, ed. "Búmaðr," Lexicon Poeticum, https://lexiconpoeticum.org/m.php?p=lemma&i=11761.
23 Marte Spangen and Johan Eilertsen Arntzen, "Sticky Structures and Opportunistic Builders: The Construction and Social Role of Longhouses in Northern Norway," in *Re-Imagining Periphery: Archaeology and Text in Northern Europe from Iron Age to Viking and Early Medieval Periods*, ed. Charlotta Hillerdal and Kristin Ilves (Oxford: Oxbow Books, 2020), 11–32 (25). The typical "Norse" traits of the farm include burial cairns, boathouses and longhouses, see section 6.3.1.
24 See section 3.2.4.
25 *Mork 2*, 193. *Fsk*, 333.

sites associated with the different groups,[26] Marte Spangen and Johan Eilertsen Arntzen argue that Saami and Norse settlements existed relatively close to one another, especially on the larger islands, like Hinnøya.[27]

The landscape of Finnmǫrk is sometimes used as the geographical boundary between Norway and Sweden.[28] In my opinion, this portrayal is particularly valuable, since it indicates that Finnmǫrk as a geopolitical area stretched from the traditional associations of Finnmǫrk in the north, down the Scandinavian mountain range. The portrayal of Finnmǫrk as on the border between Norway and Sweden indicates that the Saami were associated with being present also in the more southern areas of the mountain range. *Egils saga* states that:

> Finnmǫrk er stórliga víð; gengr haf fyrir vestan ok þar af firðir stórir, svá ok fyrir norðan ok allt austr um; en fyrir sunnan er Nóregr, ok tekr mǫrkin náliga allt it efra suðr, svá sem Hálogaland it ýtra. En austr frá Naumudal er Jamtaland, ok þá Helsingjaland ok þá Kvenland, þá Finnland, þá Kirjálaland; en Finnmǫrk liggr yfir fyrir ofan þessi ǫll lǫnd, ok eru víða fjallbyggðir upp á mǫrkina, sumt í dali, en sumt með vǫtnum. Á Finnmǫrk eru vǫtn furðuliga stór ok þar með vǫtnunum marklǫnd stór, en há fjǫll liggja eptir endilangri mǫrkinni, ok eru þat kallaðir Kilir.[29]

> [Finnmǫrk] is a vast territory, bordered by the sea to the west and the north, and all the way to the east with great fjords, while Norway lies to the south of it. It extends as far south along the mountains as Halogaland does down the coast. East of [Naumudal] lies [Jamtaland: Jämtland], then [Helsingjaland: Hälsingland], Kvenland, [Finnland] and [Kirjálaland]. [Finnmǫrk] lies beyond all these countries, and there are mountain settlements in many parts, some in valleys and others by the lakes. In Finnmǫrk there are incredibly large lakes with great forests all around, while a high mountain range named [Kilir: Kjølen] extends from one end of the territory to the other.[30]

Describing the area *á fjáll upp* as separated from Norway but stretched to the east of it as far as the Hálogaland coast following the mountain range (the geological border between Norway and Sweden), the text emphasises the large lakes and great forests of the territory, also including the detail that the area is not uninhabited. The inhabitants of these settlements are later described as Saami.[31]

An increasing focus on the establishment of churches and fishing villages in the northernmost "frontier" on the long Finnmark coast was undertaken by

---

26 See section 6.3.1.
27 Spangen and Arntzen, "Longhouses," 29.
28 *Hkr* 2, 79.
29 *Eg*, 36.
30 Bernard Scudder, trans. "Egil's saga," in *The Complete Sagas of Icelanders including 49 Tales*, ed. Viðar Hreinsson, vol. 1 (Reykjavík: Leifur Eiríksson Publishing, 1997), 33–117 (47).
31 *Eg*, 27.

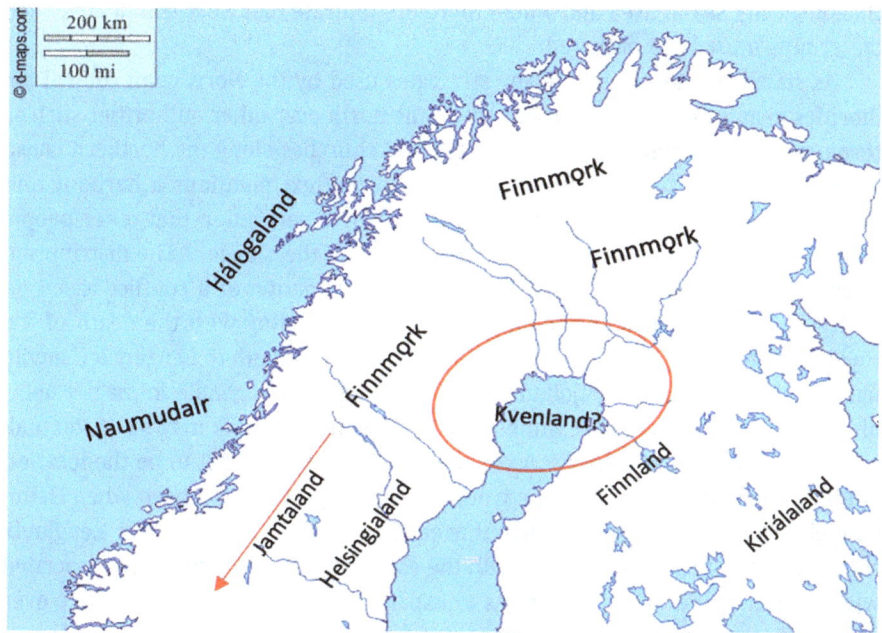

Figure 4: *Finnmǫrk and the surrounding landscapes, according to* Egils saga Skallagrímssonar, https://d-maps.com/carte.php?num_car=5970&lang=en. *Compiled by author.*

both Norwegian central authorities and the Novgorod city-state in attempts to exert power over traditional Saami settlement areas. These attempts were grounded in the prospect of colonisation of the northern areas and the benefits offered by the conversion of the Saami such as papal recognition (from a Norwegian point of view), but more so in the increasing importance of geopolitical dominance over disputed areas in the north.[32] These areas were rich in natural resources such as fish, sea mammals, small and big game, with a population competent in the extraction of these resources. As far as I am aware, the earliest (Norse) placename known from Finnmǫrk is Geirsver (Gjesvær; figure 3) and appears in Heimskringla's *Ólafs saga helga* as the landing stage to or from Bjarmaland (figure 3).[33] Although the placename is most likely Norse and there is no Norse-Saami meeting in the one source that mentions the place, Geirsver is located in an otherwise ar-

---

[32] Lars Ivar Hansen and Bjørnar Olsen, *Hunters in Transition: An Outline of Early Sámi History*, The Northern World 63 (Leiden: Brill, 2014), 158. The establishment of the church in Vardø in 1307 and the building of Vardøhus during King Hákon Magnússon's reign (1299–1319) is connected to these developments.
[33] *Hkr 2*, 155.

chaeologically Saami area and would therefore indicate that close contact between the groups must have occurred.

As stated previously, one of the strategies used by the Norwegian central authorities to gain geopolitical dominance in the north over other authorities such as Novgorod, was to establish fishing villages and churches along the northern coast. Geirsver might be such an establishment, and the text mentions a harbour and that the men "settled in," meaning that there was a perception that other people able to accommodate them were already present in the village.[34] The distribution of goods acquired in Bjarmaland leads to the culmination of a conflict based on diverging loyalties between the two sailing parties, ending with the death of the royal retainer Karli.[35] Karli's kinsman Gunnsteinn flees south to Lengjuvík (Lenvik; figure 3), where a woman "fjölkunnig mjök" [very knowledgeable in magic] helps him hide. Loyal to King Óláfr, Gunnsteinn's refuge in Lengjuvík may be contextualised by the late twelfth-century account of *Rímbegla* claiming it to be the location of the northernmost church in the world (which it also will have been when Heimskringla was compiled in the early thirteenth century). The church in Lengjuvík should also be seen in connection with the establishment of institutions associated with the central and royal ambitions to expand their geopolitical dominance over Saami settlement areas in the north. Since Gunnsteinn, unlike his rival Þórir, was loyal to King Óláfr, seeking refuge in Lengjuvík was a tactical strategy as it most likely was a place with loyalties to the king. However, Gunnsteinn receives help from a woman knowledgeable in magic, and this may perhaps point to the cross-culturalism of the area's inhabitants, also attested by placenames and archaeology which point to varied societies utilising the same landscape.[36]

A silver hoard from around the year 1000 found in Botnhamn, a nearby village on Senja, accentuates the earlier cross-cultural ties of the area. Depositions of silver hoards in northern Norway from early in the medieval period are most often found on the margins of both Norse and Saami settlement areas and have been interpreted as symbolic expressions of liminality at a border or meeting place between Norse and Saami groups.[37] Since these deposits usually contain both Saami and Norse elements, Marte Spangen interprets them as expressions of a dual

---

34 *Hkr* 2, 232.
35 *Hkr* 2, 233.
36 Jon Gunnar Blom, *Mennesker og steder i et nordnorsk landskap: en studie av landskapsforståelse og landskapsbruk fra jernalderen til nyere tid* (MA diss., University of Tromsø, 2012), 83–88 (90). Marte Spangen, "Coast as Meeting Place for Believes [sic] and Traditions: Silver Hoards in North Norway," in *Kystkultur: Aktuel arkæologi i Norden*, ed. Anna Beck et al., Kontaktstencil, vol. 44 (Copenhagen, 2004), 85–93 (86, 91).
37 Hansen and Olsen, *Hunters*, 74–75.

Norse-Saami identity actualised on the margins or border areas between more traditional Norse and Saami settlement areas.[38] Whether or not this is the case, the depositing of these objects indicate the prevalence of a mutual ritual performed by Norse and Saami people together for a joint purpose. Since one of these hoards was found not far from Lengjuvík, it is likely that Norse people were in contact with Saami people in this area. Although not articulated, the Saami presence is also evident in these sources, potentially as the woman knowledgeable in magic helping Gunnsteinn flee from Þórir, but particularly evident in the archaeological material emphasising both Norse and Saami presence.

Although Finnmǫrk as a traditional landscape *á fjall upp* and *norðr* is very much associated with the Saami across the textual material, it is not the only area where the Saami appear. Unlike the common assumption that the Saami "in reality lived (and in most cases still live) in the extreme north of Europe, in settlements in Finnmark and the Kola peninsula into northern Russia along the coast (Bjarmaland), and in the forested interior of Scandinavia,"[39] Finnmǫrk as a sociocultural concept encompassed a larger area than traditionally assumed.[40] As a spatial concept connected to Saami people, it does not stand out as the epitome of the far north but rather, and in line with the toponym, as areas where Saami people lived.[41]

With regard to the discussion in section 2.4.1 and chapter 7, I argue that it is productive to have a twofold understanding of the general term *Finnmǫrk* in order to allow for more dynamic readings of Saami characters associated with the landscape(s). The term "Finnmǫrk" is therefore here understood as the geopolitical landscape associated with the area north of Hálogaland but stretching as far south on the Swedish-Norwegian border forests as Hálogaland does along the coast (and potentially further south), according to *Egils saga*. The term "fínmarkr," on the other hand, appearing in the *Borgarþingslǫg* and in other texts discussed in chapter 7, should be understood as a sociocultural concept associated with Saami belonging in southern contexts. This allows for a more dynamic reading whereby the increasing Norwegian political and governmental presence of the northern landscape Finnmǫrk later in the medieval period is acknowledged. Knut Bergsland has analysed a *réttarbót* [law amendment] found in the *Frostaþingslǫg*, reportedly put forth by King Sigurðr jórsalafari and his brothers in 1115 and directed at "Háleygium öllum" [all of Hálogaland], that supports my suggested two-fold reading of

---

38 Spangen, "Coast," 91–92.
39 DeAngelo, "North," 257.
40 *Eg*, 36. *NGL 1*, 389–90.
41 See section 7.4.1.

the landscape.⁴² The amendment enforces the royal monopoly of *finnkaup* (see section 5.2) and confirms the taxation on the fishing industry in Vágar (Vågan, Lofoten), in addition to providing the Hálogalanders with:

> almenninga alla slíca sem þeir höfðu um hins helga Ólafs daga, bæði hit ytra oc hit øfra, sunnarla oc norðarla. En klórvöru alla fyrir norðan Umeyjarsund, þar á konungr einn caup á.⁴³

> all the "commons"⁴⁴ which they had in the days of Óláfr Haraldsson, both the outer and the upper, to the south and to the north. But only the King has the right to purchase [or collect] the fur-products north of Umeyjarsund.⁴⁵

Umeyarsund has not been properly identified, although Vennesund just south of Brønnøysund (Norway) and the lake Över-Uman on the border between Sweden and Norway have been suggested.⁴⁶ Either way, the law amendment seems to define the sole royal privilege to trade (presumably with the Saami) north (and east) of Rana in Norway. This definition, alongside the granting of common rights to the Hálogalanders in "hit ytra oc hit øfra, sunnarla oc norðarla" [the outer and the upper, to the south and to the north], is especially intriguing since it seems to imply a two-fold understanding of Saami areas. Indeed, Bergsland suggested that this differentiation in the *rettarbót* should be read as indicative of a medieval understanding of two kinds of *Finnmǫrk*, with one being the region north of Rana where the king had monopoly to the Saami fur trade and a southern one, south of Hálogaland, where others could trade with the Saami and where other Saami people lived.⁴⁷ I would therefore argue that the extract above, and Bergsland's interpretation of it, demonstrate the productivity of employing my suggested two-fold understanding of the term Finnmǫrk/fínmarkr, since the spatial designations most likely were understood in this multidimensional way in the medieval period. Understanding the designation "fínmarkr" as being associated with Saami people in southern contexts not (necessarily) connected to the northern geopolitical landscape allows for less constrictive readings of the Saami in southern contexts, as further examined in section 7.4.1. It should nevertheless be mentioned that both terms effectively mean the same thing, and indicates geographical spaces associated with Saami people. Another important factor which should be stressed is that

---

42 Knut Bergsland, "Om middelalderens Finnmarker," *Historisk tidsskrift* 49, no. 4 (1970): 365–409 (377). The amendment was not confirmed until the 1130s; *NGL 1*, 257–58.
43 *NGL 1*, 257.
44 Dictionary of Old Norse Prose, "Almenning," ONP, https://onp.ku.dk/onp/onp.php?o2730.
45 Translation based on Bergsland, "Finnmarker," 373–76.
46 Bergsland, "Finnmarker," 373–76.
47 Bergsland, "Finnmarker," 408.

up until the seventeenth to eighteenth centuries, there were no fixed borders for the area north of what is presently Troms county.[48] This indicates that a significant proportion of the northern Fennoscandian regions discussed here were not incorporated into the Fennoscandian nation states until later in the early modern period, and more importantly, that these regions were understood as, or at least associated with being, Saami land prior to this.

The Saami settlement area encompassed a wide-stretching landscape, from the Kola Peninsula in the east to the coastal area around Lyngen and mid-Troms in the west, down the Scandinavian mountain range and southwards into Upplǫnd and Jamtaland. The landscape of Finnmǫrk was imagined by the Norse and dependent on the sociocultural and geopolitical experiences of the Norse. This is strengthened by the textual material which is written from a Norse perspective, but we should nevertheless not neglect and remove the agency of medieval Saami groups and their ability to negotiate the delineation of areas perceived as "theirs." However, interpreting the place in terms of a border, margin or periphery between the Norse and the Saami can be unhelpful since it introduces the risk of falling back on a simplistic understanding of the area and its inhabitants as something more static than dynamic.[49] Instead, it has been suggested that the term should be perceived as a frontier, a liminal space where colliding worldviews interfere and norms are challenged, in turn dissolving stricter cultural identities and creating space for more culturally fluid identities.[50] I would like to add that the question posed should not necessarily be where Finnmǫrk was but rather where it was when. In my opinion, viewing the area of Finnmǫrk as adjacent to Norse settlement areas proves more helpful, with some places being clearly delineated in the landscape or simply distant, and others as closer, sometimes directly linked to and part of Norse societies (or vice versa), with meeting spaces, shared landscapes, and culturally fluid communities. We also need to determinedly remind ourselves of the regional and chronological variation evident in the medieval written, toponymic, and archaeological sources, that are often absent from discussion.

---

48 Lars Ivar Hansen, "Fra Nöteborgfreden til Lappekodisillen ca. 1300–1751: Folkegrupper og statsdannelse på Nordkalotten med utgangspunkt i Finnmark," in *Grenser og grannelag i Nordens historie*, ed. Steinar Imsen (Oslo: Cappelen Damm Akademisk, 2005), 362–86.
49 Eleanor Rosamund Barraclough, "Arctic Frontiers: Rethinking Norse-Sámi Relations in the Old Norse Sagas," *Viator* 48, no. 3 (2017): 27–51 (30).
50 Barraclough, "Frontiers," 51.

4.2.2 Hálogaland

Hálogaland is the medieval landscape most often associated with the Saami after Finnmǫrk, and generally coincides with the coastal strip north of Þrǿndalǫg (Naumdœla) to a culturally fluid frontier with Finnmǫrk somewhere in the north. Archaeological material also suggests the cultural complexity of the region and so the presence of Saami peoples in Hálogaland in Norse texts is not surprising.[51] The conceptualisation of the region changes throughout the medieval period with Norwegian expansion extending northwards. These changes are reflected in the saga material which gradually moves its focus from conflicts with powerful Hálogaland chieftains, portrayed as occurring in the eleventh century, to the introduction of religious and political institutions of the Norwegian kingdom, portrayed as appearing from the twelfth century onwards.[52] The rise of the Novgorod republic and its increasing appropriation of the eastern fur trade changed the dynamics of Saami societies that had previously almost monopolised the European fur trade, and also affected the Swedish areas of interest.[53]

The saga material portrays Hálogaland as a landscape similar to Finnmǫrk as both within and without *Nóregi*. The stories relating King Haraldr hárfagri's acquisition of land and "unification" of Norway in the late ninth century claim that he also took possession over Hálogaland, described as north of Þrǿndalǫg and the land all the way north to Finnmǫrk.[54] Subsequently, the stories following this narrative always include Hálogaland as a Norwegian province from a geopolitical perspective.[55] However, Hálogaland characters traditionally disagree with this delineation, and are often portrayed as unwilling to associate themselves with the central authorities.[56] Conversion to Christianity is presented as the main issue.[57] In Heimskringla, King Óláfr Tryggvason is portrayed attempting to convert the northern Norwegian province, but the Hálogaland chieftains Hárekr ór Þjótta, Þórir hjǫrt from Vágar, and Eyvindr kinnrifa, with their Saami entourages, gather armies in the fight against him, leading to the king's retreat.[58] Óláfr re-

---

51 Spangen and Arntzen, "Longhouses," 26.
52 *Hkr 1*, 324–26. *NGL 3*, 106–8. See section 5.2.2.
53 Hansen and Olsen, *Hunters*, 147–52.
54 *Fsk*, 74. *Eg*, 7. This is reflected in Ohthere's account which claims that "nan man ne bude be norðan him" [no man lived north of him (Ohthere)]; *OEH*, 42–43.
55 Björn K. Þórólfsson and Guðni Jónsson, eds., *Vestfirðinga sǫgur*, Íslenzk fornrit 6 (Reykjavík: Hið íslenzka fornritafélag, 1943), 17. This instance icludes Finnmǫrk, which is anachronistic.
56 With the exception of the Earls of Hlaðir. It could be noted that Hákon jarl never takes the title of *konungr* and may therefore have been viewed as less of a threat by the Hálogaland chieftains.
57 *Hkr 1*, 302.
58 *Hkr 1*, 308–9. See also *Hkr 2*, 174–75.

plies that: "ek ætla mér i sumar at koma norðr þannug ok vitja yðar Háleygjanna. Skuluð þér vota, hvárt ek kann refsa þeim, er neita kristninni" [I am intending to come there to the north and visit you men of Hálogaland. You will then find out whether I know how to punish those who refuse Christianity].[59] Later in Heimskringla's *Ólafs saga Tryggvasonar*, the Salpti-chieftain Rauðr inn rammi refuses to convert to Christianity, and King Óláfr kills him by forcing a snake down his throat.[60]

In the eleventh century, *Gesta Hammaburgensis* relates that:

> Alii dicunt, Halagland esse partem Nordmanniae postreman, quod sit proxima Scritefengis, aperitate montium et frigoris inaccessibilis.[61]
>
> Others say Helgeland [Hálogaland] is part of farthest Norway, lying very near the Skritefengi and inaccessible by reason of the rugged mountains and the cold.[62]

Hálogaland is here described in relation to the Saami, a notion also supported by the twelfth century *Historia Norwegie*.[63] Eleanor Rosamund Barraclough argues that even though the sociocultural ties between the Norse and the Saami were not always clear-cut, Hálogalanders, given their location, emerge as the principal Norse players on the liminal borderland stage.[64] Others have claimed that their association with the Saami led to the negative portrayal of the Hálogalanders in Norse texts, with Jeremy DeAngelo stating that the Saami were victims of the "detrimental effects" of the colder climate in the north and that:

> The very presence of the *Finnar* [Saami] in Halogaland would reflect negatively on the area, and the fact that they mingled with Norwegians on the frontier placed any Halogalander under suspicion since one never knew what kinds of distasteful foreign habits were picked up while there.[65]

DeAngelo's analysis is based on medieval ideas of mental geography and asserts that Saami characters were purposefully negatively portrayed by medieval Icelandic authors in order to distinguish the Saami as the "northern uncivilised group" and avoid these connotations for Iceland and Norway.[66] I find DeAngelo's state-

---

59 *Hkr 1*, 322.
60 *Hkr 1*, 327–28.
61 *Hammaburgensis*, 185.
62 *Hamburg-Bremen*, 219.
63 *HN*, 55–56.
64 Barraclough, "Frontiers," 33.
65 DeAngelo, "North," 266.
66 DeAngelo, "North," 260.

ment problematic since I disagree that the portrayal of the Saami is specifically negative. With regard to the above statement, I disagree since it fails to acknowledge that the sometimes less favourable portrayal of the Hálogalanders in the saga material is never due to their associations with the Saami. Instead, the portrayal is focused on their defiance connected to the emergence of Christianity and conversion, and their continued devotion to the pre-Christian belief systems. Their "mingling" with the Saami does strengthen this portrayal, but it seems to be rooted above all in their lack of Christianity rather than their association with the Saami. This is reflected in *Hákonar saga Hákonarsonar*, written in the 1260s, which relates King Hákon's appropriation of important geopolitical areas by establishing Christianity in the north: "Hann lét gera kirkju norðr í Trums ok kristnaði alla þá kirkjusókn" [He let a church be built north in Troms and Christianised all these parishes].[67] Although placenames, archaeological, and written sources indicate that northern Troms fell within the traditional Saami settlement area and was a culturally fluid Norse-Saami sociopolitical environment, the Saami presence is not mentioned in *Hákonar saga*.[68] The main emphasis is on the fact that these parishes were Christianised, not the cultural affiliation of those converted.

From the mid-to-late twelfth century, institutions of the Norwegian kingdom were gradually introduced in the northern province and an overall review of the legal system gave Hálogaland equal status in the kingdom to the southern provinces in the 1270s.[69] Due to changing internal and external political factors, the establishments of fishing villages and ecclesiastical institutions such as chapels and churches along the northern coasts became increasingly important geopolitical tools for the Norwegian central authority. This is amongst other texts included in Morkinskinna, which describes King Eysteinn Magnússon's reported establishment of a church in Þrándarnes (Trondenes) and the church and harbour at Vágar in the early twelfth century.[70] The growing success of the fishing villages and market towns in Hálogaland for northern Norwegian and national trade is also emphasised in several of the *Íslendingasögur*, demonstrating the significance of the trade also across the sea.[71] As demonstrated in chapter 3.2.4 and as will be furthered in chapter 5, there is evidence suggesting the heavy involvement of dif-

---

67 *Hák 2*, 155.
68 Inga Malene Bruun, *Blandede graver: blandede kulturer? En tolkning av gravskikk og etniske forhold i Nord-Norge gjennom jernalder og tidlig middelalder* (MA diss., University of Tromsø, 2007), 83. Astrid Mellem Johnsen, *Troms som etnisk sammensatt grenseområde ca 600–1600* (forthcoming PhD thesis, University of Tromsø).
69 Hansen and Olsen, *Hunters*, 143.
70 *Mork 2*, 133.
71 *Eg*, 42. *Finnb*, 276. *Gr*, 73–78. See section 5.3.2.

ferent Saami groups in this trade and Saami participation in shared economic fishing ventures. The large-scale changes to society also affected Saami societies across Fennoscandia, and these stresses resulted in a change in overall geopolitical and sociocultural dynamics, particularly in terms of social stratification and the growth and decline of economic industries. However, these were not necessarily viewed as negative by the people experiencing them.

Later in the medieval period, northern Norwegian coastal Saami groups became intimately involved in the Bergen and Hanseatic League trade and participated in the growing dried fish industry.[72] This industry would become crucial for Norwegian economy from the medieval to the early modern/modern period. In addition, adaption to or intensification of reindeer herding, farming, and participation in the defence of the northeastern border against Novgorod (Russia) and/or Karelians, could either have been conscious strategies taken by some Saami groups or seemingly random developments affecting Saami groups, as a result of the increasingly emerging state powers in the south and east.[73] Changes within Saami societies took place, with regional variation depending on internal responses and processes such as social stratification, and in some cases increased homogenisation. In any case, it is important to stress that these changes were not necessarily viewed as oppressive by Saami populations and that many, both on group and individual levels, may have appropriated the advantages of change. However, we should also keep in mind that with the increased attention to the taxation of the Saami and the colonisation of Saami land, the nation states' appropriation of the Saami settlement areas and discrimination against Saami people now had an ideological basis in the promotion of the nation state's interests.

As has already been established, Hálogaland was a socioculturally diverse region where Norse-Saami interaction was normalised and multifaceted. Through personal, cultural, and economic strategies, with the exotic objects gained from the *finnkaup* boosting both their power and prestige in the Norse market trade, the Hálogaland elite were empowered by their Saami connections.[74] The distancing of the Hálogalanders and their close associations with the Saami were viewed as a conflict of interest and as a direct threat to the interests of the central authorities. In *Egils saga*, this is particularly clear when the antagonists attempt to harm Þórólfr's reputation by spreading false rumours about his relations with the Saami to King Haraldr hárfagri:

---

72 Hansen and Olsen, *Hunters*, 174.
73 Hansen and Olsen, *Hunters*, 124, 202–3.
74 See section 5.2.1.

> Hafði hann kaup ǫll; guldu Finnar honum skatt, en hann bazk í því at sýslumenn yðrir skyldi ekki koma á mǫrkina. Ætlar hann at gerask konungr yfir norðr þar, bæði yfir mǫrkinni ok Hálogalandi, ok er þat undr, er þér látið honum hvetvetna hlýða.⁷⁵
>
> He took all the trade and the [Saami] paid him tribute, and gave them a guarantee that your [the king's] collectors wouldn't enter the territory. He intends to proclaim himself king of the northern territories, both Finnmark and Halogaland, and it is astonishing of you to let him get away with everything he does.⁷⁶

The weighted threat of the unification between the spatial power complexes encompassing the "northern territories" of Hálogaland and Finnmǫrk point to the area's geopolitical and sociocultural importance. Furthermore, the instance demonstrates that, at least in the eyes of the learned elite during the composition of the saga, most likely early in the 1200s, the areas were sometimes understood together. This factor empowered the northern Norwegian elite, who cultivated multifaceted relations with the Saami and increasingly attempted to differentiate themselves from their southern neighbours, as Rauðr inn rammi attempts in Heimskringla's *Óláfs saga Tryggvasonar*. As further discussed in chapter 6, Saami people most likely formed part of this elite, and their involvement in it also worked as an empowering factor for the chiefdoms.

The active endeavour by the Hálogaland elite to differentiate themselves sociopolitically from the central authorities should be seen as an attempt to maintain sociocultural privileges and certain trade relations with the Saami. Saami involvement in the Hálogaland elite enabled extremely rich chieftaincies early in the medieval period, and by refusing conversion to Christianity, the multifaceted relationship, based on political, economic, personal, social, and ritual aspects, could be maintained.⁷⁷ However, through violent persuasion, colonisation of Saami land, conversion to Christianity, manipulation, the bestowment of trading privileges, and the appointment of so-called royal *sýslumenn*, Hálogaland moved away from its individuality, and became fully and legally incorporated into the Norwegian realm in the 1270s.

---

75 *Eg*, 43.
76 "Eg," 50–51.
77 See Marte Spangen, "Silver Hoards in Sámi Areas," in *Recent Perspectives on Sámi Archaeology in Fennoscandia and North-West Russia*, ed. Petri Halinen et al. (Helsinki: Finnish Antiquarian Society, 2009), 94–106 (102–3). See section 6.3.

4.3 The Extreme North?

4.3.1 Bjarmaland, Kirjálaland, and Kvenland

Norse-Saami relations in northern Fennoscandia were also dependent on and influenced by interaction with other peoples in the northeast. *Historia Norwegie* addresses this in its introduction, stating that the areas north in Norway was inhabited by several pagan peoples from the east such as the "Kweni" [Kvens], the "Kyriali" [Karelians], and the two kinds of "Biarmones" [Bjarmians].[78] Throughout the source material, these groups often appear in contexts related either directly or indirectly to the Saami, and are briefly discussed below.

Bjarmaland and its inhabitants (Bjarmar) appear in approximately thirty medieval texts, the majority of which are Norse, a few are Latin and one is Old English, spanning from the ninth century to the thirteenth.[79] As there is no corresponding people or landscape today known as Bjarmaland, its origin has been heavily debated by scholars, particularly since Ohthere reportedly related at the end of the ninth century that the Bjarmians spoke a similar language to the Saami.[80] Due to the travel descriptions following the many Norse expeditions to Bjarmaland, its location is generally agreed by scholars to include the Kola Peninsula, the White Sea, and the lower part of the Dvina river valley.[81] While Saxo and the *fornaldarsögur* portray a distant and Othered Bjarmaland with inhabitants such as giantesses,[82] the remaining sources mainly relate trading and harrying expeditions.[83] These expeditions surprisingly often involve royals and harrying in Bjarmaland seems to have been a journey connected with high status.[84] The journeys usually end with hostilities, however, and the relationship between the Norse and the Bjarmar is portrayed as tense. Before he reportedly trades with them and they share stories, Ohthere is reluctant to go ashore in Bjarmaland due to hostilities.[85] Later, in Heimskringla's *Óláfs saga helga*, Þórir hundr's trading trip to Bjar-

---

78 *HN*, 52–53.
79 Merri Koskela Vasaru, "Bjarmaland and Interaction in the North of Europe from the Viking Age until the Early Middle Ages," *Journal of Northern Studies* 6, 2 (2012): 37–58 (38).
80 Vasaru, "Bjarmaland," 39. Hansen and Olsen, *Hunters*, 149–50.
81 *OEH*, 39.
82 Saxo, 601–3, 649; *IllGr*, ch. 6; *GrL*, ch. 1.
83 *Eg*, ch. 113; *Fsk*, chapters 5, 14, 31, 55; *Gr*, ch. 20; *Hák*, ch. 81; *HHárf*, ch. 32; *ÓH*, chapters 132 and 139.
84 Gormr inn gamli of Denmark and Ragnarr Loðbrók reportedly make the trip, in addition to Haraldr gráfeldr, Eiríkr blóðøx and Hákon Þórisfóstri.
85 Hansen and Olsen, *Hunters*, 54.

maland quickly becomes an attack on the Bjarmar once the "sundr sagt friði við landsmenn" [truce with the people was declared at an end].[86]

In contrast to the treatment of the Saami which tends to be generally positive, Else Mundal observes a code of conduct considered in Bjarmaland, where Norse people were at liberty to kill and rob as they wished.[87] Eleanor Rosamund Barraclough suggests that this was partially due to the lack of frontier territory shared between the Norse and the Bjarmar, in turn denying cross-cultural spaces for the negotiation of identities.[88] Another contrasting feature with the Saami, despite the observation that the Bjarmar and Saami spoke a similar language, is that the Norse are repeatedly depicted as struggling to understand the Bjarmians and need interpreters to communicate.[89] Furthermore, the magic performed by the Bjarmians is often dramatised and fantastical, contrasting with the portrayal of Saami magic which falls under the same categories as that which is performed by the Norse.[90] Despite their re-occurring presence in the saga material, the Bjarmians are portrayed as outside the social horizon and unlike the Saami, they are rarely present as insiders in Norse society. This does not mean that the relationship with the Bjarmar was irrelevant to the writers of the sagas or to Fennoscandian society.

As already emphasised, large-scale rearrangements of different socio-economic processes in the northeast led to marked geopolitical changes in the northern region in the mid-to-late twelfth and particularly thirteenth century onwards. With the increasingly growing central authorities and their overarching organised control of the economy, new directions for the (fur) trade and the emergence of new economies such as dried fish, circumstances in the northeast changed. The expansion of Novgorod led to increased hostilities between the city-state and Norwegian and Swedish state power in the north.[91] Several scholars have suggested that the inhabitants of Bjarmaland became increasingly occupied with the Novgorod trade and worked as their agents, thereby gradually becoming incorporated into the city-state's realm.[92] The first source directly mentioning Norwegian royals' interests in Finnmǫrk can be found in the *Gulaþingslǫg* from the early 1200s, stating

---

86 *Hkr* 2, 229.
87 Else Mundal, "The Perception of the Saamis and Their Religion in Old Norse Sources," in *Shamanism and Northern Ecology*, ed. Juha Pentikäinen (Berlin: De Gruyter, 1996), 97–116 (107).
88 Barraclough, "Frontiers," 50.
89 *Ǫrv*, ch. 4. The language of the Bjarmians could have been similar to modern-day Finnish, since Heimskringla's *Óláfs saga helga* claims the Bjarmians used the word "jómala" for god. "Jumala" is the contemporary term for god in Finnish.
90 Barraclough, "Frontiers," 49–50. See for example *GrL*, ch. 1; *HHábr*, ch. 3; *IllGr*, ch. 6; Saxo, 649; *Hkr* 2, 229–32.
91 Hansen and Olsen, *Hunters*, 157.
92 Vasaru, "Bjarmaland," 47. Hansen and Olsen, *Hunters*, 149–50.

the defence demanded by the Hálogalanders in this area against intruders from the east.[93] These intruders may have been the Bjarmar. A similar observation is made in *Hákonar saga Hákonarsonar* from the 1260s, relating a war between the Hálogalanders and Bjarmians, culminating with the last officially organised Norwegian expedition to Bjarmaland in 1222, that failed.[94] Nevertheless, the relationship between the Norwegians and the Bjarmar was not always antagonistic, as is also emphasised in *Hákonar saga:* "til hans komu ok margir Bjarmar, er flýit höfðu austan fyri ófriði Tattara, ok kristnaði hann þá, ok gaf þeim einn fjörð, er Malángr heitir" [to him came many Bjarmir who had fled from the east and the strife of the Tatars; and he christened them and gave them the fjord called Malangen].[95]

Unlike the predominantly tense relationship with the Norse, the Bjarmar and the Saami are portrayed as enjoying more neutral interactions. While personal relations such as marriage and fostering between the Norse and the Bjarmar are not unheard of in the texts,[96] they appear more frequently between the Saami and the Bjarmar. Saxo recounts the marriage between King Helgi of Hálogaland and Thora, the daughter of the prince of the Saami and the Bjarmar.[97] *Ǫrvar-Odds saga* describes the marriage of the high-standing Saami woman Grímhildr to King Hárek of Bjarmaland.[98] Unlike the Norse experience with the Bjarmar, the Saami did share frontier space with the inhabitants of Bjarmaland, which could have allowed for the negotiation of cross-cultural identities in an overlapping area with fluid borders and societies. Furthermore, since Ohthere claims that the Bjarmar and the Saami spoke a similar language, language similarities introduce shared ideas and values which again would help enable relationships. The possibilities of such neutral relationships offer new perspectives on the diversity of northern Fennoscandian history by emphasising the agency of Saami and Bjarmian groups independent of the Norse.

Ohthere's account relates that prior to entering Bjarmaland, Ohthere ventured through the land of the Terfinnas.[99] Unlike the settled land of the Bjarmar, this land is described as waste except for where the Terfinnas camped for fowling, fishing, and hunting. In the poem *Ævidrápa* from *Ǫrvar-Odds saga*, the "Tyrfifinnar" are

---

93 *NGL 1*, 104.
94 *Hák 1*, 252.
95 *Hák 2*, 266.
96 For Norse-Bjarmar relationships, see Saxo, 67 and *Ldn*, 150.
97 Saxo, 150–51: "Cusonis Finnorum Byarmorumque principis."
98 *Ǫrv*, 241.
99 Hansen and Olsen, *Hunters*, 55.

mentioned in stanza 9 as targets of Oddr's crew before reaching Bjarmaland.[100] The word does not appear anywhere else in Old Norse records. The oldest manuscript containing the term dates to the second half of the fifteenth century (AM 471 4to), with the earliest manuscript of the saga dating from the early fourteenth century (Holm perg 7 4°).[101] It has been argued that the stanzas *Ævidrápa* were originally earlier *lausavísur* about Ǫrvar-Oddr's life. These were then later added into the *Ǫrvar-Odds saga* as a result of the desires of the compiler(s) to fill out the text.[102] The recension of the saga containing the term "Tyrfifinnar" is indeed accepted as a reworking of an earlier version of the saga (notably, it is not present in AM 343a 4to, dated between 1450–75) that does not contain the term (the earliest version is represented by Holm perg 7 4°).[103] Despite the chronological distance from Ohthere's report to the first composition of the term in of *Ǫrvar-Odds saga* (minimally the fifteenth century), the linguistic similarity and proximity to Bjarmaland indicate that the Tyrfifinnar are identifiable with the Terfinnas.[104] The term can therefore be recognised as an ethnonym for Saami people living in proximity to Bjarmaland. This identification is strengthened by present day factors. The easternmost Saami people, living on the Kola Peninsula, are called Ter Saami today, although the language and culture of the group is moribund. Furthermore, the southeast coast of the Kola Peninsula is still called the "Terskiy bereg" [Ter Coast] in Russian, and the eastern Kola Peninsula is called "Tarje" in the Kola Saami languages.[105] Minimally, the fact that Hálogalanders called the inhabitants of the Kola peninsula by a landscape denotation in their language, indicates some levels of communication and contact.

According to *Hákonar saga*, northern Saami groups did not get on with the Kirjálar (Karelians). The Kirjálar were the inhabitants of the landscape Kirjálaland (associated with today's Karelia), stretching from the coast of the White Sea to the Gulf of Finland.[106] This conflict was seemingly rooted in stress caused by taxation and rights to land and trade, with King Hákon reportedly sending men to Novgorod in 1250 to make peace with the Novgorod prince: "settu þeir þá frið at

---

100 *Ǫrv*, 303.
101 Margaret Clunies Ross, "Ǫrvar-Odds saga 79 (Ǫrvar-Oddr, Ævidrápa 9)," in *Poetry in fornaldarsögur*, ed. Margaret Clunies Ross, Skaldic Poetry of the Scandinavian Middle Ages 8 (Turnhout: Brepols, 2017), 894.
102 Ross, "*Ævidrápa.*"
103 Richard Constant Boer, ed., *Ǫrvar-Odds saga* (Leiden: E.J. Brill, 1888), xxxiv.
104 Alan Strode Campbell Ross, *The Terfinnas and Beormas of Ohthere* (London: Viking Society for Northern Research, 1980), 7.
105 Ross, *Terfinnas*, 26–27. Store norske leksikon, "Tersamisk," snl.no, 25.09.2019 https://snl.no/tersamisk.
106 *Hák 1*, 242.

sinni milli skattlanda sinna, svá at hvárigir skyldu öðrum ófrið gera, Kirjálar né Finnar, ok helzk sú sætt eigi lengi síðan" [they made peace at once between their taxlands, so that neither should raise strife against the other, Kirjalar nor (Saami), but the peace was not kept very long after].[107] Several scholars have noticed the disappearance of the Bjarmar from the written sources after the mid-thirteenth century and connect it to the appearance of the Karelians in the area previously associated with Bjarmaland in the same period.[108] An Icelandic *landalýsing* [short description of the world] informs that by the beginning of the thirteenth century, Bjarmaland was under Novgorod rule.[109] The Kirjálar were simultaneously drawn into Novgorod's sphere of interest and Karelian merchants became increasingly involved as representatives of Novgorod's trading interests in the interior of northern Fennoscandia.[110] In addition, the Karelian settlement increasingly expanded its territory and had by the mid-thirteenth century incorporated Bjarmaland and the area around the White Sea into their sphere of interest. The Karelians and the Bjarmar shared several circumstances such as involvement in trade and Novgorod allegiance, and it has been suggested that the Bjarmar were assimilated into the expanding Karelian society.[111] The conflict in *Hákonar saga* between the Saami and the Karelians should in my opinion be interpreted with this assimilation in mind, and again stresses the increasing geopolitical changes in northern Fennoscandia connected with the rise of Novgorod. However, by the early fourteenth century Karelian-Saami interactions reportedly became more neutral, as suggested by a treaty between Norway and Novgorod confirming the common taxation area of the Saami.[112] The treaty is confirmed on the basis of an older agreement stating the rights of the Norwegian king to tax the Saami as far east as the Kola Peninsula where "halfkarelar œða halfinnœr ero, þeir sem finska moðor hafua aat" [there are half-Karelians or half-Saami who had a Saami mother].[113] Heimskringla alleges Swedish dominance over the area from the ninth century, and asserts Swedish claims to Kirjálaland from the thirteenth century.[114] The assertions in early thirteenth-century Heimskringla about the Swedish claim to Kirjálaland demonstrates the interests of the emerging nation states in ex-

---

107 *Hák 2*, 155. See section 5.2.2.
108 Vasaru, "Bjarmaland," 46. Hansen and Olsen, *Hunters*, 150.
109 Arnamagnæanske samling, "AM 736 I 4to," handrit.is, https://handrit.is/en/manuscript/imaging/en/AM04-0736-I#page/1r++(1+of+4)/mode/2up.
110 Hansen and Olsen, *Hunters*, 150.
111 Vasaru, "Bjarmaland," 45.
112 The treaty replaced the older agreement in 1326: *NGL 3*, 151–52.
113 *NGL 3*, 151–52.
114 *Hkr 2*, 115.

pansion of land, and consequently, power. However, by 1323, the peace treaty of Nöteborg/Orekhovec between Sweden and Novgorod formally included Kirjálaland and its (eastern) inhabitants as subjects of Novgorod.[115]

While the emergence of the Kirjálar in northernmost Fennoscandia certainly seems to have caused conflict with the neighbouring peoples, they were not the only eastern people involved with the Saami. In *Egils saga*, the good relationship between Þórólfr Kveld-Úlfsson and a Saami group *á fjáll upp* from Sandnes collaborate against a common enemy, the Kylfingar:

> Þórólfr fór víða um mǫrkina; en er hann sótti austr á fjallit, spurði hann, at Kylfingar váru austan komnir ok fóru þar at finnkaupum, en sumstðar með ránum. Þórólfr setti til Finna at njósna um ferð Kylfinga, en hann fór eptir at leita þeira ok hitti í einu bóli þrjá tigu manna ok drap alla, svá at engi komsk undan, en síðan hitti hann saman fimmtán eða tuttugu. Alls drápu þeir nær hundrað manna ok tóku þar ógrynni fjár ok kómu aptr um várit við svá búit.[116]

> Thorolf travelled at large through the forests, and when he reached the mountains farther east he heard that the Kylfing people had been trading with the [Saami] there, and plundering too. He posted some [Saami] to spy on the Kylfing's movements, then went off to seek them out. In one place he found thirty and killed them all without anyone escaping, then found a group of fifteen or twenty more. In all they killed almost one hundred men and took enormous amounts of booty before returning in the spring.[117]

The origins and locations of the Kylfing people are unknown but it is likely that the group was of Balto-Finnic origin. The extract establishes the importance of collaboration between the Norse and the Saami and also demonstrates the benefits of cooperation and trade. Later in the saga, the news of the collaboration reaches the Kvenir (Kvens), portrayed as seeking out Þórólfr in Finnmǫrk for similar help:

> En er hann sótti langt austr ok þar spurðisk til ferðar hans, þá kómu Kvenir til hans ok sǫgðu, at þeir váru sendir til hans, ok þat hafði gjǫrt Faravið konungr af Kvenlandi; sǫgðu, at Kirjálar herjuðu á land hans, en hann sendi til þess orð at Þórólfr skyldi fara þangat ok veita honum lið; fylgði þat orðsending at Þórólfr skyldi hafa jafnmikit hlutskipti sem konungr, en hverr manna hans sem þrír Kvenir. En þat váru lǫg með Kvenum at konungr skyldi hafa ór hlutskipti þriðjung við liðsmenn ok um fram at afnámi bjórskinn ǫll ok safala ok askraka.[118]

> As he advanced farther east and word about his travel came around, the Kven people came and told him that they had been sent to him by their king, Faravid. They told Thorolf how the

---

115 Hansen and Olsen, *Hunters*, 151.
116 *Eg*, 27–28. Note that Þórólfr and his retinue are portrayed as staying in Saami territories until spring.
117 "Eg," 42–43.
118 *Eg*, 35–36.

Karelians had been raiding their land and gave him a message from the king to go there and give him support. Thorolf was offered an equal share of the spoils with the king, and each of his men the same as three Kven. It was a law among the Kven people that their king received a third of his men's plunder, but reserved all the beaver skins, sables and martens for himself.[119]

As an ethnonym in medieval texts, the designation "Kvenir" only appears in a few sources. The oldest source describing the group derives from the end of the ninth century with Ohthere's account, relating that alongside the northern part of Svealand was the land of the "Cwenas."[120] These people, according to the account, often fought with the Norwegians after entering their land by carrying small boats to lakes in the interior and from there raid villages.[121] *Egils saga* describes Kvenland as located to the east of Norway and sometimes north of Sweden, aligned with Finnland and Kirjálaland, between Helsingjaland (Hälsingland) and Finnland (figure 4). "Kvenir" then, appears as a designation for inhabitants of the coastal area around the northern coastal landscape of the Gulf of Bothnia, which is reflected in the endonym of the people and the place, referring to the low lying marshy fields typical of this area.[122] In *Orkneyinga saga*, a frequently reworked text from the thirteenth century onwards with its reputed first roots in the late twelfth century,[123] this link is directly stated: "Eptir þat fór hann af Kvenlandi ok fyrir innan hafsbotninn, ok kómu þar, er þeir men váru, er Lappir heita" [After that he set out from Kvenland skirting the head of the Gulf, and so reached the land of the (Lappir)].[124]

The incident between Þórólfr and the Kvenir in *Egils saga* demonstrates co-operation and alliances made against a common enemy, but also trading competition since both are described as participating in the Saami fur trade. I would argue that this trading competition may have been the background for the hostilities described by Ohthere between the Norwegians and the Kvenir. Nevertheless, it is paramount to emphasise the friendship portrayed between Þórólfr and Faraviðr, which

---

119 "Eg.," 47.
120 Hansen and Olsen, *Hunters*, 56.
121 Hansen and Olsen, *Hunters*, 56.
122 Irene Andreassen, "Kven og kainu(lainen)," Kainun Institutti, http://www.kvenskinstitutt.no/kvener/kven-og-kainulainen/. From Norse "hvein" meaning lowlying marshy area or thin grass, and independently, the old Finnish designation "Kainuu" for the northernmost parts of the Bothnian bay.
123 Store norske leksikon, "Orkneyinga saga," snl.no, 04.04.2020 https://snl.no/Orkneyinga_saga.
124 *Orkn*, 4. Hermann Pálsson and Paul Edwards, eds., *Orkneyinga saga: The History of the Earls of Orkney* (London: Penguin Classics, 1981), 23–24. The term "Lappir" is discussed further in section 4.3.2.

is never questioned in the text. Unfortunately, the Kvenir are only mentioned a few times in the saga material, the majority of which are associated with the mythological past.[125] The last medieval source, as far as I am aware, to mention the Kvenir is found in an entry in the Icelandic Annals from 1271 stating that "Þá gǫrþv Kereliar ok Kvénir mikit hervirki á Hálogalanndi" [Karelians and Kvens were participating in much plunder in Hálogaland].[126] Some scholars have argued that the emergence of the "birkarlar" in 1328 in the Tälje-stadgan decree indicate that the economic function of the Kvenir had become more important than their ethnic identity and that the *birkarlar* appear as a kind of "redefined" Kvenir, continuing trade with and taxation of the Saami.[127] However, the fact that the Kvenir disappear from the medieval sources does not prevent the term from reappearing through later historical processes as an ethnic identity associated with Balto-Finnish culture and relocation to northern Norway and Sweden in the early modern period.[128]

Across northern Norway and Sweden,[129] the Kola Peninsula and Finland, Saami people were dependent on and influenced by other peoples in the northeast, often independent of the Norse. Saga material, chronicles, geographical records and annals relate complex relationships between the Saami, Bjarmar, the Kirjálar, Kylfingar, the Ter Saami, and the Kvenir in association with the nation states, but also independent of them. Although ethnic terms such as "Kven," "Karelian," and "Kylfingar" are very much still debated in scholarly research, the care attended to distinguishing these groups across the medieval textual material is noteworthy.

---

125 See *Ork*, 3; *Bárð*, 102. These sources portray a far northern snowscape and supernatural creatures such as *jǫtnar, trǫll*, and one *finnálfr* (?).
126 *IA*, 138.
127 Hansen and Olsen, *Hunters*, 154. See section 4.3.
128 Sara Hagström Yamamoto, *I gränslandet mellan svenskt och samisk: Identitetsdirskurser och förhistorien i Norrland från 1870-tal til 2000-tal*, Occasional Papers in Archaeology 52 (Västerås: Edita Västra Aros, 2010). It should be noted that Kvens are a contemporary ethnic group, see section 1.1.2.
129 On northern Sweden in the medieval period, see Inga-Marie Mulk, "The Role of the Sámi in Fur-Trading During the Late Iron Age and Nordic Medieval Period in Light of the Sámi Sacrificial Sites in Lappland," *Acta Borealia* 13, no. 1 (1996): 47–80, and Inger Zachrisson, "The So-called Scandinavian Cultural Boundary in Northern Sweden in Viking Times: Ethnic or Socio-Economic? A Study Based on the Archaeological Material," *Acta Borealia* 5 (1998): 70–97.

4.3.2 The Finnland "Paradox" and the Lappland(s) Confusion

Relating King Óláfr Haraldsson's harrying expedition in the Baltics (Eysýsla), Heimskringla's *Ólafs saga helga* states that on his return "sigldi hann aptr til Finnlands ok herjaði þar ok gekk á land upp" [he sailed back to Finnland and harried there and went ashore].[130] King Óláfr's court poet, Sigvatr Þórðarson, allegedly reports in the eleventh century that:

> Hríð varð stáls í stríðri
> strǫng Herdala gǫngu
> Finnlendinga at fundi
> fylkis niðs en þriðja.
> En austr við lǫ́ leysti
> leið víkinga skeiðar.
> Bálagarðs at barði
> brimskíðum lá síða.[131]

> There on the taxing trip to Herdalar
> took place the third harsh tempest
> of steel [BATTLE] of the king's descendant [Óláfr],
> strong, in meeting the Finnish [the Saami].
> And the sea by the shore unshackled
> ships of vikings in the east;
> Alongside the surf-skis' [SHIPS]
> stems lay Bálagarðssíða.[132]

Due to their descriptions as weather magicians and skilful archers able to traverse thick forests, the *Finnlendingar* in the text are generally identifiable with the Saami, with most scholars agreeing on this.[133] However, due to the infrequency of the placename in the saga material and the geographical description, Sirpa Aalto argues that this instance refers to a meeting between the saintly king and Finnish, not Saami, people.[134] The confusion is heightened by the two placenames

---

130 *Hkr 2*, 11.
131 *Hkr 2*, 12.
132 "Hkr 2," 8.
133 This is particularly clear in recent translations of the text where Finnland is translated to "Lappland" and its inhabitants called "Lapps," see: Snorri Sturluson, *Heimskringla*, trans. Alison Finlay and Anthony Faulkes, 3 vols (London: Viking Society for Northern Research, 2014), "Hkr 1," 7–8.
134 Sirpa Aalto, "Finns in the sagas," in *Footprints in the Snow: The Long History of Arctic Finland*, ed. Maria Lähteenmäki, Prime Minister's Office Publications 12 (Helsinki: Prime Minister's Office, 2017), 24–42 (24).

Herdalar and Bálagarðssíða. Bálagarðssíða is most commonly associated with the Baltic Sea and the southwest coast of modern day Finland, but *Helgisaga Óláfs konungs Haraldssonar* locates it on Zealand in Denmark.[135] Herdalar however, is sometimes associated with the landscape Härjedalen in mid-Sweden, bordering Norway.[136] As discussed in chapter 7, the landscape is associated with Saami people and/or culturally fluid identities. In my opinion, since the Heimskringla version emphasises the king's journey to the Baltic countries, it is geographically more feasible that the meeting occurred on the coast of Finland. Nevertheless, this does not mean that the people encountered were not Saami, since different Saami groups were present and interacted with Finnish people in southern Finland in the medieval period.[137]

Egils saga locates Finnland between Kvenland and Kirjálaland, below Finnmǫrk, but Heimskringla's *Ynglinga saga* portrays it as north of Uppsala.[138] Saxo mentions both "Finnmarchia" and "Phinniam/Finniam" (usually translated as Finland), but does not elaborate on their differences.[139] Already from the sixth century onwards, a continental separation between the Saami and the Finnish people is observable in the change of term for the Saami with the addition of the precursor "skiing."[140] According to Hansen and Olsen, this change reflects the processes of social stratification in Finland between the years 200–600 that effectively disjointed Saami and Finnish cultures.[141] These processes included the consolidation of agricultural society, increased sociocultural affinities with Europe in southern and western Finland, and augmented utilisation of the forests for hunting in the northern interior of Finland which saw growing affinities with other northeastern communities. As in the other cultural groups, these processes eventually solidified Saami and Finno-Norse culture as diverging entities. Nevertheless, the consolida-

---

135 Einar Ól. Sveinsson, ed. *Brennu-Njáls saga*, Íslenzk fornrit 12 (Reykjavík: Hið íslenzka fornritafélag, 1954), 302–3. *Hkr 2*, 12. *Helgisaga*, 6.
136 Inger Zachrisson, ed., *Möten i gränsland: Samer och germaner i Mellanskandinavien*, Monographs 4 (Stockholm: Statens Historiska Museum, 1997), 169. *Sv*, 21.
137 Timo Ylimaunu et al., "Borderlands as Spaces: Creating Third Spaces and Fractured Landscapes in Medieval Northern Finland," *Journal of Social Archaeology* 14, no. 2 (2014): 244–67 (250–51). Hansen and Olsen, *Hunters*, 102, 106–7. Milton Núñez et al., "Animal Remains from Saami Offering Places: Glimpses of Human-Animal Relations from Finnish Lapland AD 1000–1900," in *Currents of Saami Pasts: Recent Advances in Saami Archaeology*, ed. Marte Spangen et al., Monographs of the Archaeological Society of Finland 9 (Helsinki: Archaeological Society of Finland, 2020), 61–78 (64, 70).
138 *Eg*, 36. *Hkr 1*, 28–29.
139 Saxo, 39, 335.
140 See section 2.2.
141 Hansen and Olsen, *Hunters*, 44.

tion of diverging entities enabled the establishment, whether consciously or unconsciously, of cross-cultural relationships and fluid societies. Perhaps then, the confusion in *Óláfs saga helga* in Heimskringla is based on meeting such a culturally fluid group.

Early in the medieval period, six culturally distinct regions had already evolved in Finland: northern Finland, eastern Finland, the Lake Ladoga region, southwestern Finland, Åland, and Ostrobothnia.[142] With the accumulative ambitions for geopolitical dominance over Fennoscandian natural and human resources, the Swedish and central authorities of Novgorod become increasingly interested in Finnish landscapes from the twelfth century onwards. These ambitions are reflected in Heimskringla's *Óláfs saga helga*, which presents Finnland as one of the many eastern landscapes subjugated by the Swedish king.[143] In the 1150s, Swedish armed troops sailed into Turku as "crusaders" and declared the people living in the coastal districts of southwestern Finland as Swedish subjects.[144] This was followed by the gradual establishment of churches and the building of Turku castle on the banks of the Aura river and were manifestations of Swedish geopolitical dominance and administration over Österlanden (the Eastlands).[145] The early fourteenth century sees the Novgorod destruction of Turku castle, and the following treaty of Nöteborg between Sweden and Novgorod in 1323.[146] The peace treaty effectively divided the mixed Finnish-Karelian population on the Karelian isthmus into a Swedish (Catholic) "sphere of influence" and an Eastern (Orthodox) "sphere of belonging" to Novgorod.[147] The peace treaty rendered the majority of the northern Fennoscandian areas as shared zones where peoples from Novgorod, Swedes, and Norwegians could settle and appropriate land, in addition to trading with different Saami communities. This was also the case in the Finnish interior and northern coastal communities. An account from 1346 reflects the cultural diversity in the northern Ostrobothnian area, and describes the baptism of twenty Saami and Karelians by two Swedish bishops in Tornio.[148] In addition, the Christian cemeteries of coastal villages in the same area display great cultural diversity represented by their grave goods, which has been interpreted as indicating cross-cultur-

---

[142] Maria Lähteenmäki, *Footprints in the Snow: The Long History of Arctic Finland*, Prime Minister's Office Publications 12 (Helsinki: Prime Minister's Office, 2017), 22.
[143] *Hkr 2*, 115.
[144] Lähteenmäki, *Footprints*, 22.
[145] Lähteenmäki, *Footprints*, 22–23.
[146] Lähteenmäki, *Footprints*, 22.
[147] Lähteenmäki, *Footprints*, 23.
[148] Ylimaunu et al., "Spaces," 245.

al ties connected to Saami, Karelian, Swedish, and other groups.[149] I find it likely that this diversity was rooted in earlier medieval interaction between several northern peoples. The emergence of the landscape "Lappland" in the thirteenth century is according to my way of thinking reflective of this diversity.

Today, Lappland and Lappi are the northernmost provinces of Sweden and Finland. "Lappmarken" was the later medieval and early modern designation for the areas inhabited by Saami people (in Sweden) and can be compared to the toponym Finnmǫrk. In English, the term Lapland sometimes denotes Sápmi, the self-designating term for the Saami settlement area today. The landscape appears in Saxo Grammaticus's *Gesta Danorum*, describing the Swedish and Baltic landscapes and their inhabitants legally appropriated by the Danish King Frothi, appointing his retainer Dimar in charge of the "Provincias Helsingorum, Jarnberorum et Jamtorum cum utraque Lappia" [the Provinces of the Hälsings, the Jarnbers, the Jämts and both Lapplands].[150] Whether the term "utraque Lappia" refers to the people or the landscape is debated, but the consensus is that it refers to a landscape or people associated with the northwestern and northeastern areas of the Bothnian coast.[151] This link is furthered in the mythological introduction to *Orkneyinga saga*, relating the story of how the eponymous King Nórr founded Norway:

> Eptir þat fór hann af Kvenlandi ok fyrir innan hafsbotninn ok kómu þar, er þeir menn váru, er Lappir heita; þat er á bak Finnmǫrk. En Lappir vildu banna þeim yfirfǫr, ok tóksk þar bardagi, ok sá kraptr ok fjǫlkynngi fylgði þeim Nór, at óvinir þeira urðu at gjalti, þegar þeir heyrðu heróp ok sá vápnum brugðit, ok lǫgðu Lappir á flótta. En Nórr fór þaðan vestr á Kjǫlu ok var lengi úti ok svá, at þeir vissu ekki til manna, ok skutu dýr ok fugla til matar sér, fóru þar til, er vǫtn hnigu til vestrættar af fjǫllum.[152]

> Then [Nor] set out from Kvenland skirting the head of the Gulf, and so reached the land of the [Lappir] on the far side of Finnmark. The [Lappir] tried to bar the way and this led to a clash between them. But so great was the uncanny power and magic of Nor and his men that as soon as the [Lappir] heard their war-cry and saw them drawing their swords, they were scared out of their wits and ran away. From there Nor and his men journeyed on westward to the [Kjølen] mountains. For a long they saw no sign of people, and for food they had to shoot birds and deer [...] they came to the watershed where the rivers start to flow west [of the mountains].[153]

According to *Orkneyinga saga*, the Lappir people inhabited an area west of Kvenland and behind (or beyond) Finnmǫrk, but east of the Keel. This locates the space

---

149 Ylimaunu et al., "Spaces," 252–58.
150 Saxo, 331.
151 Hansen and Olsen, *Hunters*, 38. Saxo, 331, footnote 16.
152 *Ork*, 4.
153 "Ork," 23–24.

associated with the Lappir in the Swedish interior, and/or the northwestern Bothnian coast. The Lappir people are therefore connected to the inner northeastern areas of Sweden by both Saxo and *Orkneyinga saga*, which is reflected in the usage of the term. In historical times, the term "Lapp" for Saami people was primarily used by those on the Swedish and Finnish sides and does not appear to have been used in Norway until later in the early modern period.[154] It should again be emphasised that the exonym "Lapp" is regarded as derogatory by Saami people today. The Lappir people are first mentioned in a Swedish source in 1328, in the Tälje-stadgan decree ordered by the Swedish-Norwegian King Magnus Eriksson. In an attempt to quell the conflict between the inhabitants of Hälsingland and the *Birkarlar*, the decree states that neither *Birkarlar* nor Hälsingar should hinder the:

> homines siluestres et vagos vulgariter dictos Lappa in suis venacionibus nullus debeat impedire, nec eciam prefatos Birkarlaboa ad eosdem Lappa accedentes, apud ipsos commorantes [...].[155]

> forest and nomadic people who are called [Lappa] in the folk dialect in their hunting, nor the earlier mentioned Birkarlaboa, who travel to the aforementioned [Lappa], visit them and return from them with their property.[156]

By the early fourteenth century, the term "Lappir" was associated with the Saami living in the interior of northern Sweden. The "Lappir" people were also associated with peoples living in the northern parts of the Bothnian coast and the modern Lapland landscapes. These areas are archaeologically fluid and present diverse societies on the borderscapes of the growing nation states. The appearance of "Lappir" in thirteenth-century written sources in the interior of Sweden and on the Bothnian coast helps emphasise this diversity.

The landscape Finnland might also point to diversification of medieval Finno-Ugric societies. However, Finnland appears as slightly more confusing, since the primary and secondary sources disagree about whether or not it should be associated with the Saami or the Finnish people.[157] *Egils saga* locates the area more or less in line with the (southwestern) modern day location of Finland and does not mention its Saami inhabitants, but *Ynglinga saga* (Heimskringla) places it to the north of Uppsala and addresses the magically-skilled Saami people living

---

154 Hansen and Olsen, *Hunters*, 38. This was probably a result of Swedish dominance over Norway in the early modern period.
155 Riksarkivet, "SHDK-nr 3558," https://sok.riksarkivet.se/dokument/sdhk/3558.pdf.
156 Hansen and Olsen, *Hunters*, 154.
157 *Hkr 1*, 28–29. *Eg*, 36. Aalto, "Finns," 24.

there, more in line with Saxo's northwestern "Lappia."[158] Since Finnland etymologically can be understood as the "land of the Saami," I would suggest that in *Ynglinga saga*, the "Finnish" landscape has been confused with other landscapes associated with the Saami of interior Sweden. The composer of *Egils saga*, however, differentiates the Saami and the Finnish, associating Finnland with the eastern landscape in between Sweden and the Baltic. Nevertheless, this does not mean that medieval Finland was not inhabited by Saami people, and toponymic, written, and archaeological material emphasise that Finnish and Saami people lived in shared landscapes throughout the medieval period.[159] As mentioned above and briefly in section 2.7.4, differentiating Saami and Finnish people in medieval texts discussing Finland is complicated because of the similar terminology sometimes used for both peoples (i.e., *Finns*). Similarly, archaeological material from Finland in the medieval period, especially its earlier phases, has proved to be difficult to categorise as either "Saami" and "Finnish" because the material is often culturally fluid.[160] It should therefore be repeated that both the textual and archaeological material point to cultural fluidity in medieval Finland.

Despite their ambiguity, the emergence of Finnland and the landscapes associated with the "Lappir" on the northern Bothnian coast in written sources from the thirteenth century onwards demonstrate the complex social processes and cross-cultural interactions taking place in interior and northern Fennoscandia in the medieval period. Contemporary with the emergence of the terms, the Swedish and Norwegian kingdoms as well as the principality of Novgorod increasingly appropriated these landscapes as displays of power connected to the importance of geopolitical dominance over resources linked to Saami fur trade and taxation. These developments had social, political, and economic implications for the inhabitants of the northern areas, which resulted in more pronounced processes of social stratification within Saami societies. Interaction with other Saami people, Finnish peoples, Karelians, Novgorodians, Swedes, and Norwegians, will have coloured the realities of Saami people living in Finnland and the Lapplands, and their loyalties will have also differed.[161] This diversity is important to emphasise and might have been based on internal structures rather than external forces.

---

[158] *Eg*, 36. *Hkr 1*, 28–29.
[159] Ylimaunu et al., "Spaces," 245, 250–58. Hansen and Olsen, *Hunters*, 106–7.
[160] Ville Hakamäki, "Late Iron Age Transculturalism in the Northern 'Periphery': Understanding the Long-Term Prehistoric Occupational Area of Viinivaara E, Finland," *Acta Borealia* 33, no. 1 (2016): 30–51 (33–34).
[161] Núñez et al., "Animal Remains," 64–67.

4.4 Saami Presence in the South

The textual material often alludes to Saami presence south in Fennoscandia. In fact, after Finnmǫrk and Hálogaland, the Upplǫnd region in mid-Norway is the landscape most often associated with the Saami in the texts. The landscape traditionally included the inland districts Valdres, Þótn (Toten), Haðaland, Hringaríki (Ringerike), Dofri, Guðbrandsdalr, Eystridalr (Østerdalen), and sometimes also Heiðmǫrk and Raumaríki (Romerike). The late twelfth-century text *Ágrip* famously relates the meeting between the Saami "princess" Snjófríðr and King Harad hárfagri in Þoptyn (Toftemo: Dovre).[162] Mid-eastern associations with the Saami are also expressed by Saxo early in the thirteenth century, writing that the Saami were the inhabitants of the Norwegian-Swedish border forests.[163] This is mirrored in the saga material, which alludes to Saami presence in the Vermaland, Járnberaland (Dalarna), and Jamtaland areas on the Swedish side, and the Heiðmǫrk landscape on the Norwegian side.[164] Saami presence in the south as suggested by the source material is the main focus of chapter 7 and the discussion will therefore be continued there.

4.5 Conclusion

Medieval texts associate the Saami with a wide area, from the Kola Peninsula in the east to the coastal area around Lyngen and mid-Troms in the west, down the Scandinavian Mountains (i.e., the Keel) and southwards into the Oppland region and Jämtland. The Norse geopolitical landscape Finnmǫrk is always associated with the Saami, and the area is rarely demarcated, leading to its ambiguity and portrayal as both internal and external to the concept of *Nóregi*.

The central authorities of Norway, Sweden, and Novgorod increasingly appropriated traditional Saami landscapes in northern Fennoscandia in displays of power connected to the significance of geopolitical dominance over resources associated with Saami fur trade and taxation. Simultaneously with the negotiation of the northern borders between the growing nation states, an awareness of intricate social processes in northern Fennoscandia is reflected in the written material. Multifaceted relationships with the Bjarmar, the Kirjálar, Kylfingar, Ter Saami, the Lappir people(s), people from "Finnland," and the Kvenir, in relation to the Saami,

---

162 *Ágr*, 4–5.
163 Saxo, 17–19.
164 *Stst*, 613. *Hammaburgensis*, 173.

the Norse, and/or Novgorod, are related across the saga material and other texts. The care attended to distinguishing these different groups indicates an awareness of the intricate social processes taking place at the time of composition. It also demonstrates the sociocultural diversity prevalent in a region where the Saami interacted with several other peoples in normalised and multifaceted ways.

Interpreting Saami spatial belonging as adjacent to Norse spatial belonging becomes a helpful decolonising tool since it allows for both regional and chronological variation and differing ideas of cultural belonging, political loyalties, and personal associations. Simultaneously, it should be emphasised that significant areas of medieval Fennoscandia consisted of both Norse, or Finnish, and Saami peoples, and so therefore, room should be given to shared spatial belonging. The fluid spatial awareness concept suggested in section 4.2.1 therefore becomes particularly useful for our understanding of Fennoscandian landscapes, since it acknowledges liminality. Geopolitically, Finnmǫrk becomes increasingly associated with the north and areas connected to Hálogaland in the texts, as a hub for Saami fur trade and the border with other central authorities such as Novgorod. Socioculturally, however, the textual material relates that the landscape stretched southwards and inwards to the Upplǫnd region and the coinciding Swedish sides.

Chapter 5: The Saami Trade

5.1 Introduction

Finnkaup, Norse-Saami fur trade, has often been treated as the main aspect of Norse-Saami relations or the foundation on which such relations were built.[1] That the Saami and the Norse traded with each other is not contested. However, the ways in which this exchange occurred, its geographical and sociocultural borders, are debated. Previously, the standard understanding of these economic transactions portrayed Saami hunting societies as subjects of exploitation by Scandinavian chieftains.[2] This view originated from Ohthere's account of the Hálogaland chieftains' wealth as based on the annual tribute paid to them by the Saami and the descriptions of the collection of *finnskatt* in various Norse sources.[3] Lars Ivar Hansen and Bjørnar Olsen comment on the paradoxical view that despite the small portion of research explicitly concerned with the Saami prior to the 1980s, their continuous presence is assumed in the "many postulates about taxation and trade with the Saami (finnkaup) as a basis for the chieftains' power."[4] The Saami were viewed as crucial to both the wealth and growth of the Hálogaland chieftains, but were stripped of agency as independent actors by being Norse subjects. The confrontation of the structural portrayal of Norse-Saami relations from the late 1970s onwards led to the acknowledgement that Saami hunting societies and Norse chiefdoms mostly interacted in peaceful and mutually beneficial ways during the early medieval period.[5] Economic transactions between the Norse and the Saami are referred to extensively and constitute a recurring theme associated with the Saami in Norse texts, with repeated patterns across the different sources.[6] In this chapter I focus on the portrayal of *finnkaup* in the textual materi-

---

[1] Inger Storli, "Sami Viking Age Pastoralism: or the Fur Trade Paradigm Reconsidered," *Norwegian Archaeological Review* 26, no. 1 (1993): 1–20 (1).
[2] Bjørnar Olsen, "Belligerent Chieftains and Oppressed Hunters?: Changing Conceptions of Inter-Ethnic Relationships in Northern Norway During the Iron Age and Early Medieval Period," in *Identities and Cultural Contacts in the Arctic: Proceedings from a Conference at the Danish National Museum Copenhagen, November 30 to December 2 1999*, ed. Martin Appelt, Joel Berglund, and Hans Christian Gulløv (Copenhagen: Danish National Museum and Danish Polar Center, 2000), 28–42 (28).
[3] Lars Ivar Hansen and Bjørnar Olsen, *Hunters in Transition: An Outline of Early Sámi History*, The Northern World 63 (Leiden: Brill, 2014), 68. *Hák* 1, 242. *Mork* 2, 117–30.
[4] Hansen and Olsen, *Hunters*, 65.
[5] Olsen, "Oppressed Hunters?," 29.
[6] *Saxo*, 17–19. *Eg*, 16–19. *Ágr*, 5–6.

al, the conflicts associated with it, the taxation of the Saami and the debate around tribute, in addition to the Western trading networks. By emphasising lesser-discussed trading links to England and Iceland in addition to questioning the nature of taxation, I reintroduce often disregarded aspects of the Saami trade. Finally, the chapter points to the possible Saami perspectives offered by the saga material.

5.2 Finnkaup and Finnferð

5.2.1 Finnkaup: From Inheritance to Royal Privilege

The strong associations with hunting and archery found in the Saami Motif-Cluster are clearly reflective of the important role played by the Saami, both in terms of their expertise and direct participation, in the fur trade. While the Saami fur traders exchanged goods in several directions not isolated to the Norse, the textual material predominantly focuses on the Norse participation in the Saami fur trade. In brief terms, the Norse concept *finnkaup* denotes medieval Norse-Saami participation in an exchange network based on a redistributive system founded on Saami specialisation in hunting and fur preparation. Literally meaning "trade with the Saami," the term often appears alongside *finnferð* which denotes the journey taken to Saami areas. In exchange for fur and other Saami products, the Norse are portrayed as reciprocating with butter, metal, and other "luxury goods" portrayed as in demand in Saami medieval communities.[7]

The texts emphasise the mutual obligations for Norse and Saami actors involved in the *finnkaup*, and both parties seek out the other.[8] *Historia Norwegie* addresses these obligations by stating that the Hálogalanders and the Saami lived in close proximity to each other: "et inter se commercia frequentant" [so that there are frequent transactions between them].[9] Although sources from the classical period onwards emphasise Saami expertise in hunting and fur preparation, Ohthere's account from the late ninth century is the first known source actively discussing (Norse) trade with the Saami.[10] As I will return to below, Ohthere's text describes the levy paid by the Saami to the Hálogaland chieftains, including bird

---

7 *Vatn*, 34–35.
8 Else Mundal, "The Perception of the Saamis and Their Religion in Old Norse Sources," in *Shamanism and Northern Ecology*, ed. Juha Pentikäinen (Berlin: De Gruyter, 1996), 97–116 (101).
9 *HN*, 56–57.
10 See section 2.2.

feathers, whale bone (or walrus tusks), seal hide, and animal skin from marten, otter and bear, and most likely wild and domesticated reindeer.[11]

Interestingly, Ohthere's account coincides with the usage of the Adamvalldá stone-slab trail in Arjeplog in northern Sweden, close to the Norwegian border. Archaeological investigations near the trail have revealed what has been interpreted as a large number of Saami settlement sites dating back to the 800s and believed to have been in use until the 1100s. The trail covers a distance of 10 km, from the lake Bieskehávrre to the river Varvekjåkkå, with pairs of trail markers in the form of erected stones, all easily recognisable in the landscape during archaeological surveys, even when covered by snow.[12] Lichenometric data collection from the stones and archival research suggest that the trail was in use early in the medieval period, simultaneously with the Saami settlements recorded in the area.[13] The archaeologists involved in the excavations of the trail assert that the formal structure and organisation of the trail suggests it was facilitated by a society organised at a chiefdom level and therefore interpret the trail as built by a Norse elite facilitating meetings across the mountains with the Saami for trade.[14] Interpreting the trail as representative of Norse traders' road into Saami settlement areas can therefore contextualise the many *finnferð* journeys *á fjáll upp* found in the saga material.[15] Another indicator that strengthens the interpretation of the trail being such a "trading passage" into Saami communities, is that it appears to have been used during winter, evident by the lack of visible strain on the soil around the stones and their visibility under heavy winter snow.[16] As emphasised in sections 3.2.2 and 3.2.3, journeys to visit the Saami across the textual material usually occur in the winter, perhaps with the exception of maritime journeys along the coast, conceivably due to easier overland travel access granted by snow and frozen rivers and lakes.[17] The winter season is also the time when hunting is most ideal since the game will have its winter fur.[18] I therefore find it likely that the trail represents one of the many *á fjáll upp* trading routes into Saami communities, as described across the saga material.

---

11 Hansen and Olsen, *Hunters*, 56.
12 Ingela Bergman et al., "Stones in the Snow: A Norse Fur Traders' Road into Sami Country," *Antiquity* 81, no. 312 (2007): 397–408 (401).
13 Bergman et al., "Stones," 401–3.
14 Bergman et al., "Stones," 406.
15 See for example *Eg*, 17, 36. Archaeological investigations in the high mountain areas of Northern Norway and Sweden may uncover similar trails.
16 Bergman et al., "Stones," 405.
17 *Eg*, 36; *Hkr 2*, 149, 344; *Hkr 3*, 311. Ohthere also states that the Saami hunted in the winter; *OEH*, 37–38.
18 Hansen and Olsen, *Hunters*, 191.

As the medieval text dealing most extensively and in most detail with *finnkaup*, the early thirteenth-century *Egils saga Skallagrímssonar* exemplifies the emphasis on winter journeys *á fjáll upp*. On his first journey after inheriting the rights to *finnferð* and *finnkaup* from his dying companion, Þórólfr Kveld-Úlfsson is portrayed as bringing ninety men and a great quantity of goods to the Saami across the mountain:

> Þórólfr gerði um vetrinn ferð sína á fjall upp ok hafði með sér lið mikit, eigi minna en níu tigu manna; en áðr hafði vanði á verit at sýslumenn hǫfðu haft þrjá tigu manna, en stundum færa; hann hafði með sér kaupskap mikinn. Hann gerði brátt stefnulag við Finna ok tók af þeim skatt ok átti við þá kaupstefnu; fór með þeim allt í makendum ok í vinskap, en sumt með hræzlugœði.[19]

> That winter Thorolf went up to the mountains and took a large band of men with him, no fewer than ninety in number. Previously, the [*sýslumenn*] used to take thirty men with them, or sometimes fewer. He also took a great quantity of goods to sell, soon arranged a meeting with the Saami, collected their taxes and traded with them. All their dealings were cordial and friendly, partly because the [Saami] feared them.[20]

Since the text emphasises that Þórólfr journeyed "up to the mountains" [during the winter], it is probable that the entourage found their way using a trail like the one found in Adamvalldá. Traversing steep mountainsides in the winter season is a dangerous task, and trails like Adamvalldá will have enabled or helped ease the travel to the Saami winter markets for the journeying tradesmen. I would also argue that the fact that Þórólfr brings a great quantity of goods to sell once again demonstrates the mutual exchange between the groups, and that despite the reported collection of tax, less politicised trade took place. However, it is interesting that the text mentions the significant increase in companions, from thirty to ninety. The sudden increase in companions, alongside the usage of the word *sýslumenn*, should in my opinion be read as reflective of current events at the time of composition. I would argue that the expressed *hræzlugœði* experienced by the Saami represents the same, but either way, the portrayed fear is not surprising given that the Hálogaland party was reportedly more than three times its usual size.

Þórólf's journey *á fjáll upp* reportedly takes place in the mid-ninth century, centuries before the implementation of royally appointed statesmen and around 250 years earlier than the proposed earliest composition of the saga in the

---

19 *Eg*, 27.
20 Bernard Scudder, trans., "Egil's saga," in *The Complete Sagas of Icelanders including 49 Tales*, ed. Viðar Hreinsson, vol. 1 (Reykjavík: Leifur Eiríksson Publishing, 1997), 33–117 (43).

1200s.²¹ The active organisation of such statesmen or district governors, the *sýslumenn*, was not introduced until the end of the twelfth century, and royal involvement in the trading and taxation of the Saami can only be traced to the mid-eleventh century.²² This chronology coincides with the last suggested usage of the Adamvalldá-trail in the medieval period, and the restructuring of how *finnkaup* was organised may be a factor behind why the trail seems to have been discontinued in the twelfth century.²³

I believe that the anachronistic features of *Egils saga* are associated with the conflicts following the shift from *finnkaup* as mainly kin-based to a royally or governmentally appointed privilege happening at the time of composition, as discussed in more detail in chapter 5.2.2. *Egils saga* addresses this shift (with another anachronistic feature), claiming that King Haraldr hárfagri implemented the royal privilege by summoning the Hálogaland elite to Þrándheimr where he granted them privileges such as the *finnkaup*.²⁴ According to the saga, prior to King Harald's acquisition of land and the appointment of governance in Naumdœlir and Hálogaland, these areas were self-governed by Hálogaland chieftains.²⁵ The introductory passage on the landholder Bjǫrgólfr hálfbergrisi and his son Brynjólfr, who lived on Torgar island in southern Hálogaland, states that they "hǫfðu lengi haft finnferð ok finnskatt" [long held the right to *finnferð* and *finnkaup*].²⁶ When King Haraldr summons the Hálogaland elite to Þrándheim, he grants Bjǫrgólfr both land and revenues, including "finnferð, konungssýslu á fjálli ok finnkaup" [the right to travel to the Saami, the royal privilege to the mountains, and the trade with the Saami].²⁷ Following the death of Bjǫrgólfr, his son Brynjólfr continues to trade with the Saami, passing on the privilege to his son Bárðr.²⁸ In other words, the right to *finnkaup* is explicitly passed from father to son across several generations, implying that the prerogative to trade with the Saami was inherited from generation to generation in a power arrangement based on kin and spatial belonging. However, as with the conflicts associated with the emergence of the *sýslumenn*, the kin-based system was also a source of conflict. When Bárðr dies, he grants the *finnkaup* privilege, in addition to his farm on Sandnes and his wife Si-

---

21 Hansen and Olsen, *Hunters*, 49.
22 Hansen and Olsen, *Hunters*, 49.
23 Bergman et al., "Stones," 399–400.
24 *Eg*, 16–18.
25 *Eg*, 18.
26 *Eg*, 18.
27 *Eg*, 19.
28 *Eg*, 17–19.

gríðr, to his companion Þórólfr.[29] Prior to his death, Bjǫrgólfr had remarried and fathered two sons with his new wife, Hildiríða, who were the same age as Bárðr. The duo is called *Hildiríðarsynir* in the text and attempt to claim their right to *finnferð* and *finnkaup* by spreading false rumours about Þórólfr to the king and state their paternal right.[30] Consequently, the king seizes Þórólf's possessions on Torgar and the *Hildiríðarsynir* are granted the privilege to *finnkaup*. Unlike Þórólfr, the brothers experience difficulties collecting the goods from the Saami, who are said to have been far less impressed with them.[31] While the Saami expression of disappointment might be a literary tool to paint the brothers as antagonists in the text, it is also important to emphasise that the expression demonstrates Saami agency, at least textually. Þórólfr seems indifferent to the losses and moves his kin group further north to his inherited farm on Sandnes, maintaining the same lifestyle there.[32] His move further north coincides with a general trend maintained by several Hálogaland chieftains across the texts like Þórir hundr, Rauðr inn rammi, and Hárek ór Þjǫtta, who lived (north in present day Nordland) in Hálogaland, opposed and challenged the royal powers and were associated and had contact with the Saami.[33] Despite losing the royal privilege, Þórólfr continues to trade with the Saami and is described as maintaining his big industry in the north. Having sent men to Vágum to fish cod and herring, Þórólfr loads several of his ships with stockfish and clipfish, as well as Saami products, before he journeys south along the Norwegian coast and into England to trade.[34] The emphasis on Þórólf's maintenance of the trade even after losing the royally appointed privilege to it, demonstrates the longstanding significance of trade and exchange with the Saami, both on personal and economic levels.

In the saga material, Hálogalanders are the main Norse participants in the Saami fur trade. Trade with the Saami is portrayed as multifactorial, and relations between the Hálogalanders and the Saami were not isolated to trading alone:

> Þórir hundr hafði Finnferð haft þessa tvá vetr lengi á fjálli ok fengit óf fjár. Hann átti margs konar kaup við Finna.[35]

---

29 *Eg*, 24.
30 *Eg*, 30–31.
31 *Eg*, 37–38, 42–43.
32 *Eg*, 27.
33 See section 4.2.
34 See section 5.3.1.
35 *Hkr 2*, 344–45.

> Þórir hundr had been engaged in trading with the [Saami] for these two winters, and both winters he had spent a long time in the mountains and had made a lot of money. He did various kinds of trade with the [Saami].[36]

As will be emphasised in section 6.2.2, the fact that Þórir is explicitly said to have spent a long time with the Saami is indicative of the portrayal of close personal relations, in addition to trade. The products provided by the Saami were crucial to the wealth of the Hálogaland elite, who built rich chieftaincies founded on their trading and personal relations with the Saami. As discussed in chapter 3.2.3, the products offered by the Saami included fur and skin products from the bear, wolf, lynx, fox, sable, otter, badger, beaver, squirrel, ermine, and reindeer, in addition to fowling products, fish, and whale products like oil and blubber.[37] Reserving the rights to trade with the Saami, *finnkaup* also involved the preservation of geopolitical resources like rights to land, maintenance of familial relationships, and other privileges for the kin group. In the early fourteenth-century *Finnboga saga ramma*,[38] the protagonist Finnbogi meets the traveller Álfur afturkemba, who is described as travelling to Finnmǫrk to collect *finnskatt*. Finnbogi inherits Álfur's *finnskatt*-privilege (notably, after killing Álfur) and marries his daughter,[39] similarly to how Þórólfr acquired the privilege in *Egils saga* (but Þórólfr did not kill Bárðr). By maintaining the rights to *finnkaup*, Hálogaland power elites could maintain both geopolitical and sociocultural power and strengthen "their" space against southern (or governmental) outsiders. Possessing the rights to *finnkaup* therefore demonstrated both geopolitical and sociocultural power in addition to being a source of wealth.

The aforementioned *birkarlar*, external Swedish tradesmen trading with the Saami of the Kemi, Pite, Lule and Torne rivers from the fourteenth century onwards, appropriated the *finnkaup* for economic means.[40] Although slightly different, the tradesmen can be compared to the Norwegian *sýslumenn*, as they received royal protection against competition that granted them monopoly over the Saami trade on the Swedish side, with increasing power and influence on the Norwegian

---

36 Snorri Sturluson, *Heimskringla*, trans. Alison Finlay and Anthony Faulkes, 3 vols (London: Viking Society for Northern Research, 2014), "Hkr 2," 230.
37 *HN*, 59–61.
38 Store norske leksikon, "Finnboga saga ramma," snl.no, 01.04.19 https://snl.no/Finnboga_saga_ramma.
39 *Finnb*, 290. The instance once again highlights the economic motivations behind gaining access to the trading privilege.
40 Ingela Bergman and Lars-Erik Edlund, "*Birkarlar* and Sámi: Inter-Cultural Contacts Beyond State Control: Reconsidering the Standing of External Tradesmen (*birkarlar*) in Medieval Sámi Societies," *Acta Borealia* 33, no. 1 (2016): 52–80 (53–55).

side, from the 1340s to the sixteenth century.[41] Knut Bergsland argued that by the mid-fourteenth century, the *birkarlar* had in reality incorporated most of the Saami fur trade monopoly, with the exception of that which was claimed by Novgorod but including the Norwegian king's old tax land, into their sphere.[42] Despite the poor reputation of the *birkarlar* and their subordination of the Saami, recent research has highlighted that the relationships between the tradesmen and the Saami were founded on mutuality and interdependence.[43] However, as with the *sýslumenn* on the Norwegian side, the increasing involvement of the Swedish Crown from the fourteenth century onwards made the *birkarlar* representatives of royal power, and thus, enforcers of colonial structures. By the mid-1500s, the *birkarlar* had become pioneers of the Swedish state in both [contemporary Swedish] Lappland ("lappmarker")[44] and [contemporary Norwegian] Finnmark.

Ágrip relates the giving of a beaver skin by Svási to King Haraldr, before the text explains that Svási was "Finninn er hann hafði ját at setja gamma sinn annnan veg brekkunnar á Þoptyn, þar sem þá var konungrinn" [the [Saami] whom the king had allowed to set up his hut on the other side of the hill at Þoptyn where the king then was].[45] In Morkinskinna, a man discussing border politics in Gautelfr uses what seems to be an everyday expression related to the Saami: "'Snæliga snuggir, sveinar', kvæðu Finnar, áttu andra fala" ["There's a whiff of snow," said the Saami. They had snowshoes for sale].[46] As I see it, both instances, while minor, can demonstrate the sociocultural relevance and knowledge of the Saami trade, even in southern contexts.

Finnkaup was a significant feature of Norse-Saami relations in the medieval period. Based on Saami specialisation in hunting and fur preparation, the exchange system was founded on a redistributive system that relied on mutual obligations between the trading parties. Trading fur products with metal, butter, and other items portrayed as Saami "luxury goods," Saami actors involved in *finnkaup* empowered the Hálogaland elite both economically and personally.

---

41 Hansen and Olsen, *Hunters*, 155.
42 Knut Bergsland, "Om middelalderens Finnmarker," *Historisk tidsskrift* 49, no. 4 (1970): 365–409, 390.
43 Bergman and Edlund, 74. Risto Nurmi, Jari-Matti Kuusela, and Ville Hakamäki, "Swedenization of the North: The Early Medieval Swedish Northern Expansion and the Emergence of the Birkarls," *Acta Borealia* 37 (2020): 1–26 (18–19).
44 Bergman and Edlund, 58.
45 *Ágr*, 4–5.
46 *Mork 2*, 32. See section 3.2.2.

5.2.2 Conflict

Finnkaup was not without conflict. The intricate politics associated with the fur trade and the valuable goods it rendered is particularly evident in the politically charged murders of royal *sýslumenn* returning to Hálogaland from their *finnferð* in *Sverris saga* and in *Hákonar saga Hákonarsonar. Sverris saga* was written during King Sverrir Sigurðarson's life in the mid-to-late twelfth century and finished after his death in the early thirteenth century.[47] In an episode claimed to have taken place in 1183, King Sverrir's *sýslumaðr* is murdered bringing the goods from the *finnferð* into Ægisfjörðr by Bjarkarey-native Viðkunn Erlingsson, on orders from Sverrir's opponent Magnús Erlingsson:

> Þá sat Víðkunnr fyrir honum inn í Ægisfjörðr ok drap þar Þorgils ok tólf men með honum, tók allt féit ok hafði með sér til Bjarkeyjar.[48]
>
> Víðkunn waited for him in Ægisfjörðr and murdered Þorgils and the twelve men with him, took all the goods [from the trade] and brought it to Bjarkey.

Hákonar saga Hákonarsonar, presumed to have been written in the 1260s,[49] relates how King Hákon Hákonarson's brother-in-law Végarðr ór Veradal is murdered whilst checking the collection of the *finnskatt* in a house south on Hinnøya, in an episode claimed to have taken place in 1221:

> Vegarðr kom einn dag til Hafnar ok bauð Andrési til borðs, en Andrés játtaði. Þá sendi Végarðr heim suma sína menn at setja borðit. Andrés báð Végarð at [finnskatt] eigi spilltisk. Végarðr gekk at húsinu. Þar var fjöl ein sigan ofan. Hann tok af sér stálhúfhuna ok sá inn. Þá hljópu fram tveir sveinar Andréss [...] ok særðu hann banasárum.[50]
>
> Végarð arrived in Hafnar and invited Andrés to his house, and Andrés accepted. Végarð sent some of his men home to set the table. Andrés then told Végarð to find the house where the *finnskatt* was kept and make sure it was not stolen. Végarðr went to the house. A log was latched over the door, he took it off and looked inside. Two of Andrés' men [...] leapt forward and killed him.

Another event in *Hákonar saga*, claimed to have taken place two years earlier (1219), may help contextualise the murder of Végarðr. The text states that King Hákon awarded the stewardship of the northernmost district (Hálogaland, with

---

47 Store norske leksikon, "Sverres saga," snl.no, 04.03.21 https://snl.no/Sverres_saga.
48 *Sv*, 114–15.
49 Ólafía Einarsdóttir, "Om samtidssagaens kildeværdi belyst ved Hákonar saga Hákonarsonar," *Alvíssmál* 5 (1995): 29–80 (33).
50 *Hák 1*, 242.

Finnmǫrk), and thereby also the privilege to pursue *finnkaup*, to both Andrés and Végarðr.[51] While the text does not state how the two *sýslumenn* shared the responsibilities prior to the murder of Végarðr, the murder was undoubtedly motivated by a disagreement in the sharing of the obligations connected to the appropriation of the *finnkaup*. Perhaps the shareholders argued about its collection or distribution, or maybe Andrés simply wished to assert political dominance over his shareholder, and effectively, the kin group he was forced to share the valuable privilege of *finnkaup* with. A similar conflict develops in *Ólafs saga helga* in Heimskringla, when Hárekr ór Þjótta is made to share half the stewardship in Hálogaland and the right to pursue *finnkaup*, with Ásmundr Grankelsson. Hárekr is not happy with the arrangement, but does not refuse it and mentions that:

> En þó gerðu ekki svá inir fyrri hǫfðingjar, at minnka várn rétt, er ættborinn erum til ríkis at hafa af konungum, en fá þá í hendr bóandasonum þeim, er slíkt hafa fyrr ekki með hǫndum haft.[52]

> And yet previous rulers have not acted thus, diminishing our rights, who have a hereditary claim on power, to receive it from kings, but handing it over to sons of farmers who have not previously had control of it.[53]

Hárekr refers to the previous system of maintaining the privilege to trade with the Saami as primarily reserved for kin, obviously disagreeing with the new system of royally appointed *sýslumenn*. Following this, Hárekr and Ásmundr repeatedly fall out, leading to the king having to arbitrate between them.[54] The duo refuse to settle, and Ásmundr ends up killing Hárekr as revenge following the death of Ásmundr's father at the hands of Hárekr.[55] The instance demonstrates the sociocultural changes following the shift from *finnkaup* as mainly kin-based to a royal privilege, as well as the reluctance associated with many high standing Hálogalanders towards royal expansion in the northern territories. These Hálogalanders are portrayed as aligning themselves with the early eleventh-century Danish King Knútr inn ríki, which proves profitable in the texts. When King Knútr reportedly allied himself with the Earls of Hlaðir, powerful earls of Þrǿndalǫg and Hálogaland in the ninth to eleventh centuries opposed to the kings of Norway, promising them authority over the northern territories in exchange for their support, the majority of the Hálogaland chieftains followed suit. By allying themselves with King Knútr,

---

51 *Hák 1*, 228.
52 *Hkr 2*, 211.
53 "Hkr 2," 140.
54 *Hkr 2*, 255.
55 *Hkr 2*, 443.

the chieftains had powerful support against the Norwegian king and could maintain their kin-privileges to the *finnkaup:*

> Þórir hundr hafði farit ór Danmǫrku með Knúti konungi, ok var hann þar. Hárekr ór Þjóttu var ok þá þar kominn. Gerðusk þeir Þórir lendir menn Knúts konungs þá ok bundu þar svardǫgum. Knútr konungr gaf þeim veizlur stórar ok fekk þeim Finnferð.[56]
>
> Þórir hundr had left Denmark with King Knútr, and he was present. Hárekr from Þjótta was also come there then. Then he and Þórir were made King Knútr's landed men and confirmed it with oaths. King Knútr gave them great revenues and granted them the trade with [the Saami].[57]

Sometimes, these conflicts occurred at the highest levels of society. In the aforementioned *Þinga saga*, related in Morkinskinna, an argument between the brothers and reported early twelfth-century co-rulers King Sigurðr Jórsalafari and King Eysteinn Magnússon is rooted in their different views on the appropriation of Saami taxation.[58] Sigurðr Hranason, a farmer granted the right to *finnferð* by King Eysteinn in the text, is accused by King Sigurðr of being dishonest in the royal distribution of *finnkaup*. Sigurðr Hranason, married to the brothers' paternal aunt, is protected by King Eysteinn who quashes the evolving legal case. This only magnifies the conflict between the brothers, which concludes with Sigurðr Hranason offering to settle in order to reconcile the co-rulers.[59] The royal involvement, I would argue, clearly demonstrates the national significance of *finnkaup*. Indeed, according to Hansen and Olsen, *finnkaup* and *finnskatt* became one of the main sources of income for the Norwegian kingdom from the twelfth century onwards.[60] The royal motivation behind appropriating *finnkaup* and the valuable goods it procured is also evident in the accounts relating Icelandic involvement in the trade, discussed below, and the abovementioned instance from *Hákonar saga*, including Novgorod.[61]

As previously noted in section 4.3.1, the growth of the expanding city state of Novgorod, particularly from the late twelfth century onwards, led to several changes in the Saami market trade. By securing and appropriating relationships with other Finno-Ugric groups in the White Sea region, groups previously involved in the large-scale Saami exchange network, the city state changed the economics

---

56 *Hkr 2*, 306.
57 "Hkr 2," 206.
58 *Mork 2*, 117–30.
59 *Mork 2*, 130.
60 Hansen and Olsen, *Hunters*, 144.
61 See sections 5.3.2 and 4.3.1.

and politics of the northern hemisphere as the Saami trade monopoly swapped hands.[62] In an attempt to quell the cross-cultural argument and hinder the growth of an international conflict, King Hákon reportedly sends his own messenger eastwards to Novgorod.[63] *Hákonar saga* then informs us that the kings made peace between their tributary lands, but the peace was not kept for long.[64]

A thought provoking exception to the conflicts above is related in Morkinskinna's *Gull-Ásu-Þórðar þáttur*, which relates an early twelfth-century conflict between the Bjarkarey-elite and an Icelander.[65] The chieftain Viðkunnr Jónsson tells his men to:

> Farið nú ok hittið Sigurð Hranason ok biðið hann hér koma, ok ef hann hefir nǫkkura undanfœrsla þá minnið hann á þat hverr honum dugði bezt þá er Finnar tóku bú hans.[66]
>
> Go now and find Sigurð Hranason, and tell him to come here. If he makes any pretext, remind him who helped him when the [Saami] seized his farm.[67]

The instance precedes the aforementioned conflict related in *Þinga saga*, where the same Sigurðr Hranason is accused of abusing his privileges to *finnkaup* and claiming a higher share of it than he should.[68] *Gull-Ásu-Þórðar þáttur* and the statement "minnið hann á þat hverr honum dugði bezt þá er Finnar tóku bú hans" [remind him who helped him when the Saami seized his farm],[69] theoretically reveals that the Saami wronged by Sigurðr's abuse of his privileges took revenge and seized his farm. As I see it, the Saami appropriation of Sigurðr's farm is one of the most significant moments across the saga material in relation to Norse-Saami dealings, since it so clearly asserts Saami active agency and involvement. Although it is short and does not specifically mention *finnkaup*, *Gull-Ásu-Þórðar þáttur* appears in a contextual framework discussing the Saami trade (and Sigurðr's appropriation of it), and I would therefore argue that the motivation behind the Saami squatters could be directly connected to Sigurðr's inability to follow protocol regarding *finnkaup*. Regardless of the motivation of the Saami, and whether or not their occupancy is a literary tool to shame Sigurðr and amuse the audience, the fact that they are portrayed as capable of seizing his farm and that Si-

---

62 See section 5.3.2. Hansen and Olsen, *Hunters*, 155–58.
63 *Hák 2*, 155.
64 *Hák 2*, 155.
65 *Mork 2*, 108–13.
66 *Mork 2*, 111.
67 Theodore M. Andersson and Kari Ellen Gade, eds., *Morkinskinna: The Earliest Icelandic Chronicle of the Norwegian Kings (1030–1157)* (London: Cornell University Press, 2000), 332.
68 *Mork 2*, 117–30.
69 *Mork 2*, 111.

gurðr needs help from higher places to reclaim it, should in my opinion be read as indicative of the Saami here being viewed as active agents in their own right.

In sum, the conflicts accompanying the Saami fur trade in the texts above displays the significance of *finnkaup*. The politically charged murders of royal *sýslumenn* in Hálogaland who had been awarded with the right to collect the goods from the Saami, demonstrates the economic benefits for the Norse participants in the trade. Furthermore, these murders express the reaction of the high standing Hálogaland elite following the change from *finnkaup* mainly being reserved for the kin of this elite, to becoming a royally appointed privilege. The legal case related in *Þinga saga* shows how important the collection of the valuable Saami products acquired in the *finnkaup* was for the Norwegian kingdom, since it was a significant part of the realm's income. Consequently, the conflict between King Hákon and the prince of Novgorod in *Hákonar saga* again points to the national significance of maintaining geopolitical dominance in Saami settlement areas in the far north, since this procured the rights to appropriate the Saami fur monopoly in these areas. All the conflicts related in this section demonstrate changes affecting Saami societies and economies in the north. However, as the remark from *Gull-Ásu-Þórðar þáttur* asserts, the Saami were not necessarily the "helpless victims" of these changes and sometimes took advantage of the changing circumstances, negotiating the terms of *finnkaup* themselves.

5.2.3 Taxation of the Saami

Scholars disagree on matters relating the taxation of the Saami. From my perspective, certain discussions concerning Norse taxation of the Saami sometimes reinforce the dualism mentioned in sections 1.2 and 5.1, particularly concerning notions of superiority as Saami hunting societies were predominantly viewed as subjects of exploitation by Scandinavian chieftains.[70] In the following subsection I problematise the term *finnskatt* and the debates about it and discuss the nature of Norse taxation of the Saami.

Despite the increasing focus on the mutually beneficial interaction between the Norse and the Saami in the medieval period, several medieval sources refer to uneven power relations between the Norse and the Saami. Ohthere's reported account to King Alfred in 890 is the primary source describing the Norse taxation of the Saami:

---

70 Olsen, "Oppressed Hunters?," 28.

> Ac hyra ar is mæst on þæm gafole þe ða Finnas him gyldað. Þæt gafol bið on deora fellum and on fugela feðerum and hwæles bane and on þæm sciprapum þe beoð of hwæles hyde geworht and of seoles. Æghwilc gylt be hys gebyrdum. Se byrdesta sceall gyldan fiftyne mearðes fell and fif hranes and an beran fel and tyn ambra feðra and berenne kyrtel oððe yterenne and twegen sciprapas, ægþer sy syxtig elna long, oþer sy of hwæles hyde geworht, oþer of sioles.[71]

> Their wealth is mainly in the tax that the Sami pay them. The tax takes the form of animal skins, bird feathers, whalebone, and the ships' ropes which are made from the skin of the whale and the seal. Everyone pays according to his rank. The highest born has to give the skin of fifteen martens, five reindeer and one bear, ten measures of feathers, a coat made of bearskin or otterskin, and two ships' ropes, both sixty ells in length, one of whaleskin and the other of sealskin.[72]

Lars Ivar Hansen and Bjørnar Olsen argue that since the taxation mentioned in the account is generally very extensive and differentiated according to rank, it could possibly have been levied on a collective Saami community.[73] The text obliquely mentions other chieftains ("their wealth"), and this might indicate that the Hálogaland elite had arrived at an agreement concerning the distribution of the exchange received from the Saami. This exchange paid by the Saami to the Hálogaland elite, should be understood as tribute according to the majority of scholars.[74] Tribute is the payment made by one group or its ruler to another in acknowledgement of submission or as "taxation" levied as the price of protection. Other medieval sources also claim that the Saami paid tribute to the Norse, with *Historia Norwegie* stating that:

> Ibi infinita numerositas bestiarum, scilicet ursorum, luporum, lyncorum, uulpium, sabelorum, luctrearum, taxonorum, castorum [...] Sunt eciam apud Finnos scuriones quam plures ac mustele. De quarum omnium bestiarum pellibus regibus Norwegie, quibus et subiecti sunt, maxima tribute omni anno persoluunt.

> In that region there live vast numbers of animals, including bears, wolves, lynxes, foxes, sables, otters, badgers and beavers [...]. In Finnmarken there are also very large numbers of squirrels and ermines. From all these animals' pelts, the people pay a large tribute every year to the Norwegian king, who are their overlords.[75]

Both Ohthere and *Historia Norwegie* then, discuss tribute paid by certain Saami groups to Norse chieftains or the Norwegian king. Inger Storli criticises the idea

---

71 *OEH*, 40.
72 *OEH*, 41.
73 Hansen and Olsen, *Hunters*, 62.
74 Hansen and Olsen, *Hunters*, 55.
75 *HN*, 58–61. See also Saxo, 343.

that the early medieval Saami were a population of migrating hunters and fishers who paid tribute to the Hálogaland chieftains, claiming that this view has been "axiomatic to archaeological as well as historical research."[76] Storli posits that the changes to medieval Saami societies as witnessed by archaeological material was not a result of external factors such as the Norse trade, but rather, of internal factors revolving around the adaption to reindeer pastoralism.[77] While I completely agree with Storli's claim that we as scholars need to problematise established dichotomies and I do not reject the reindeer theory, I disagree with the interpretation of the Norse trade as being an external factor to Saami societies. As discussed above and throughout, *finnkaup* and *finnskatt* was based on Saami specialisation in hunting and fur preparation, and the Saami actively participate as independent agents in this trade.

In my opinion, the last part of the *Historia Norwegie*-extract claiming Norwegian lordship over the Saami helps clarify the question of tribute and the nature of the *finnskatt* as described in the saga material. As with the majority of the instances involving the term *finnskatt*, contrasting *finnkaup* and often in relation to the *finnferð*, *Historia Norwegie* depicts the royal ambitions to be increasingly involved in the trading with the Saami. The term *finnskatt*, interpreted by most scholars as meaning the taxation of or the tribute paid by the Saami, predominantly appears in contexts when royal *sýslumenn* are involved.[78] I do not disregard Ohthere's mention of the tribute paid by certain Saami communities and the possible archaic roots of *finnskatt* (if the tribute later developed to organised taxation). Nevertheless, I suggest that the term *finnskatt* and direct taxation of the Saami are later medieval developments associated with the introduction of stately appointed *sýslumenn* from the late twelfth century onwards. Various sources mention tax levied on the Saami by the Norse, and so it is likely that different Saami groups were taxed by different Norse groups/chiefdoms or the growing Norwegian state.

Automatically assuming that the Saami were oppressed by Norse chieftains or the Norwegian state in the medieval period reinforces a colonial viewpoint and the dualism associated with it. In my opinion, taxation could just as likely be interpreted as the attempted consolidation of the early "nation" formed by several sociocultural groups, including the Saami. This consolidation of the Norwegian nation state needs to be interpreted in light of the increasing pressures from the other growing

---

76 Storli, "Paradigm," 1.
77 Storli, "Paradigm," 20.
78 *Hák 1*, 242; *Mork 2*, 117–30. See Dictionary of Old Norse Prose, "Finnskattr," ONP, https://onp.ku.dk/onp/onp.php?o20687. An exception is *Egils saga*, which states (prior to the events leading to *finnkaup* becoming a royal privilege) that Bjǫrgólfr hálfbergrisi "hǫfðu lengi haft finnferð ok finnskatt" [long had *finnferð* and *finnskatt*], 18.

states like Sweden and Novgorod, all seeking to appropriate traditional Saami settlement areas, as previously discussed.[79] The fact that the tax is levied on the Saami, just as on the Norse population under the Norwegian king, could demonstrate a view of the Saami as part of Norse/Norwegian culture and self-expression.

In the *Hákonar saga*-incident mentioned in section 5.2.2, Finnmǫrk is notably referred to as "skattland" [taxland] when the peace agreement between Norway and Novgorod is related: "settu þeir þá frið at sinni milli skattlanda sinna" [they made peace at once between their [taxlands]].[80] The term *skattlǫnd* denotes (overseas) territories of the Norwegian realm that paid "skatt" or tribute to the king of Norway, with the term first appearing in *Hákonar saga* from the 1260s but increasingly appearing in legal texts following this.[81] These territories were incorporated from the early thirteenth century onwards and included Orkney, Shetland, the Faroes, Iceland, and Greenland, and were "linked by their linguistic, cultural and socio-legal similarities [...] and linked to the centre (Norway) through their relationship to the king and [...] shipping routes."[82] The reference to Finnmǫrk as *skattland* is therefore curious, since while tax was imposed on the Saami in this area, we can question the extent to which we can assume "linguistic, cultural and socio-legal similarities" between Saami people in Finnmǫrk and the Norwegian state, at least compared to that of Iceland and Orkney. It has been argued that because the tax imposed on Finnmǫrk predominantly rested on individuals and not a defined territorial area like the other *skattlǫnd* with more fixed borders, Finnmǫrk should not be included in our treatment of this concept.[83] On the other hand, the term does demonstrate the possibilities of the Saami (at least in Finnmǫrk) being perceived (or presented) as part of Norwegian self-expression. Finally, Norse or Norwegian (or other governmental) taxation of the Saami does not equal taxation of all Saami people, and again we should remind ourselves of the heterogeneity and regional variation of medieval Saami peoples.

Hansen and Olsen propose that the earliest taxation of the Saami potentially functioned as return payment for political protection against hostile groups.[84] Different Saami groups might have benefitted from taxation in the form of the main-

---

[79] Hansen and Olsen, *Hunters*, 157.
[80] *Hák 2*, 155.
[81] Ann-Marie Long, *Iceland's Relationship with Norway c.870 – c. 1100: Memory, History and Identity*, The Northern World 81 (Leiden: Brill, 2017), 155.
[82] Long, *Memory, History*, 155.
[83] Randi B. Wærdahl, *Norges konges rike og hans skattland: Kongemakt og statsutvikling i den norrøne verden i middelalderen* (PhD thesis, Norwegian University of Science and Technology, 2006), 31.
[84] Hansen and Olsen, *Hunters*, 54.

tenance of fur trails, which would allow the continuation of the large-scale trade and its extension abroad, political protection from other actors, and the preservation of the existing sociocultural dynamic that allowed for cultural variation "protecting" Saami culture(s). This does not necessarily mean that the different Saami groups wanted to be included. While no (known) medieval source examines the Saami response to taxation, several incidents in the saga material concern the response of Norwegian and Swedish regional groups when faced with the imposition of tax. In particular, the inhabitants of Jamtaland (repeatedly swapping hands between Norwegian and Swedish kings), the Þrœndir, Icelanders, and Faroese people reject the imposition of tax on several occasions.[85] Despite the lack of sources, we can expect a similar varied response from different Saami groups to the imposition of tax, where some responses may have been positive. Nevertheless, the collective appropriation of Saami settlement areas, particularly in the northeast, resulted in the double- and triple-taxing of several Saami communities, since certain areas in northernmost Fennoscandia were treated as collective tax land.[86] Taxation of the Saami by the nation states became more systematic later in the medieval period and although it meant being included in the nation state's mentality or as part of its self-expression, taxation was grounded in the promotion of the nation state's interests.

In sum, I argue that organised taxation of the Saami appears to be a later medieval development associated with the growth of the nation state and the appropriation of traditional Saami settlement areas. This interpretation aligns with the understanding that medieval Saami societies were dynamic and regionally varied. As stated in section 5.2.1, it is important to keep in mind that the Norse-Saami exchange network was founded on Norse market demand for Saami products, not vice versa. By treating all of the goods traded between the Norse and the Saami as tax paid or tribute offered by the Saami in acknowledgement of Norse dominance over the Saami, we disempower the Saami groups involved in the Norse-Saami trade.

5.3 Western Trading Networks and Saami Perspectives

The Saami trade is not exclusive to Hálogaland, with several pseudohistorical references to Dofri, and harrying expeditions to both Bjarmaland and Finnland.[87] Dif-

---

85 *Hkr 1*, 220–21. *Hkr 2*, 214–19, 241–42. *Hkr 3*, 158.
86 Hansen and Olsen, *Hunters*, 147, 161.
87 *Ágr*, 5–6; *Hkr 1*, 125; *Hkr 2*, 227–34; *Hkr 2*, 10, 115.

ferent Saami groups participated in this exchange network, and traded with several different peoples including the Norse, the Bjarmar, the Kirjálar, the Kvenir, Finnish peoples, Novgorodian/Russians, and other peoples. In other words, different Saami groups were active participants in a large-scale trading network that connected several other peoples, particularly in the east. In this section I analyse the Western trading networks and possible Saami perspectives illuminated by the source material. As discussed throughout chapter 4, participation in and control of the Saami fur trade was crucial for the growing nation states aiming to monopolise the wealth associated with the trade and the geopolitical areas associated with it. Later in the medieval period, northern Norwegian coastal Saami groups became intimately involved in the Bergen and Hanseatic League trade and participated in the growing dried fish industry.[88] In addition to the eastern ties to Bjarmaland and beyond, internally in Norway and Sweden, the Saami are also portrayed as participating in trade with other less-discussed participants. A handful of sources discuss Icelanders participating in trading activity with the Saami north in Finnmǫrk, and there are also indications that the Saami were directly involved with English trading networks. In the following, I discuss the possible Saami exports to England and the direct involvement of the Saami in this exchange, as well as the Icelandic *finnkaup* and its portrayal in the textual material.

5.3.1 *Englandsfar:* Saami Exchange in England

The Saami trading tradition in England can be traced back to Ohthere, who reportedly brings walrus ivory from Saami and Bjarmian settlements to King Alfred's court in 890.[89] The journey taken by Ohthere from Hálogaland to England must have proved successful, since the later saga material stresses similar trading ventures with Saami exports to England.

In Heimskringla's *Ólafs saga helga*, Þórir hundr is depicted as tricking King Óláfr, and his men leave for England with great riches acquired during *finnkaup*, including money, grey furs, beaver, and sable.[90] Þórir hundr's journey is related to his reported loyalties to the Danish King Knútr, who also ruled England at the time. Although the journey is multifactorial, Þórir's loyalties are connected to the Hálogaland elite and the affiliations of the Earls of Hlaðir with the Danish kings. These affiliations were maintained by the mutual wish for power over Norwegian geo-

---

88 Hansen and Olsen, *Hunters*, 174.
89 Hansen and Olsen, *Hunters*, 56.
90 *Hkr 2*, 252–53.

political and sociocultural landscapes and offered ways for the Hálogaland elite to maintain autonomy over the northern Norwegian areas and the Saami fur trade.⁹¹ In *Egils saga*, Þórólfr readies a ship for England and stocks it with dried fish and goods from his trade with the Saami, such as "húðir ok vǫru ljósa; þar lét hann ok fylgja grávǫru mikla ok aðra skinnavǫru, þá er hann hafði haft af fjalli, ok var þat fé stórmikit" [hides and ermine, and a great quantity of squirrel skins and other furs from his expedition to the mountains, a very valuable cargo].⁹² Similarly, when the Hálogalanders Sigurðr and Haukr sail to England as is described in *Óláfs saga Tryggvasonar en mesta*, it is not unlikely that their cargo also consisted of exports from the Saami.⁹³ That these texts narrate similar journeys to England, with exports from the Saami fur trade, suggests that the purpose of trade and exchange with the Saami formed part of a tradition encompassing an extensive trading complex. *Sverris saga* addresses this trade, claiming that the English goods exchanged for the Saami commodities included fish like halibut, linen, and clothing, canvas, flour, wax, and honey.⁹⁴ In *Egils saga*, the Saami goods are exchanged for English wheat, honey, wine, and clothing.⁹⁵

Grettis saga Ásmundarsonar and *Finnboga saga*, both believed to have been first written in the fourteenth century, mention the presence of English ships harbouring in Vágar to participate in the northern Norwegian trade markets.⁹⁶ In the later medieval period, stockfish became increasingly important in the English trade and the Hanseatic League became increasingly involved in the northern Norwegian markets from the late thirteenth century onwards.⁹⁷ However, Saami fur traders and sellers could still participate in the northern Norwegian trading markets, such as the one on Vágar. In this way, the Saami traders would have the chance to involve themselves directly in the trade with foreign and particularly English partakers. I would also like to stress the opportunities for and possibilities of direct Saami involvement in the English exchange from the introduction of this trading network. As will be discussed in chapter 6, Norse-Saami co-operation in the fur trade, in addition to other factors, facilitated personal relations including trad-

---

91 Hansen and Olsen, *Hunters*, 143.
92 *Eg*, 42. "Eg," 50.
93 *Mesta 2*, 143–44.
94 *Sv*, 159–60.
95 *Eg*, 42.
96 *Gr*, 73–78. *Finnb*, 275–76.
97 Hansen and Olsen, *Hunters*, 166–67. Christian Keller, "Furs, Fish and Ivory: Medieval Norsemen at the Arctic Fringe," *Journal of the North Atlantic* 3 (2010): 1–23 (7). This affected the Saami fur trade and followed a trend eventually seeing the re-distribution of the luxury furs from being monopolised in predominantly Saami areas to a centre in Novgorod.

ing alliances and economic loyalties, and more intimate arrangements such as fostering and marriage. Saami people were frequently associated with and attached to the Hálogaland elite. As allies, kin, passengers, or traders in their own right, Saami people travelled to England for trading purposes.[98] These possibilities help contextualise the *Diplomatarium Norvegicum* letter dated to the early thirteenth century discussed in section 2.7.3, relating the rights of several Nordic peoples' rights in London, including the *Lappa*.[99] The letter indicates that Saami people travelled to London, potentially as part of the large-scale (Saami) fur trade to England.

The fact that sailing to England with Saami goods is kept up, at least according to the textual material, from the ninth to the thirteenth century and probably longer, demonstrates the long-standing and far-reaching importance of trade with the Saami in the medieval period. Interpreting the sources with the Saami as active trading agents in mind creates room for the Saami on the ships travelling to England with export from the fur trade.

5.3.2 Icelandic *finnkaup*

In the short stories *Sneglu-Halla þáttr* and *Odds þáttr Ófeigssonar*, both found in Morkinskinna and supposedly portraying events from the eleventh century but presumed to have been compiled in the 1220s, a new conflict related to *finnkaup* occurs. Here, Icelanders attempting to partake in trade with the Saami in Finnmǫrk are met with resistance from the Norwegian *sýslumenn* appointed with *finnkaup*. In *Sneglu-Halla þáttr*, Einarr flúga, son of the infamous Hárekr ór Þjótta, and King Haraldr harðráði's *sysselmaðr* in charge of the *finnkaup*, explains to the king:

> Næstum, herra, er vér várum norðr þá hittum vér Íslandsfar eitt, ok bárum vér á hendr þeim at þeir myndu kaup hafa átt við Finna fyrir várt leyfi fram. Ok er þeir vildu verja málit fannsk á orðum þeira at þeir myndu eigi skírir til lykða ok lǫgðum at þeim síðan.[100]

---

[98] Viking-Age combs made from reindeer antler found in England may offer an interesting insight into the possible Saami trading presence, or the possible trading of Saami products, in England: Steven Ashby, Ashley N. Coutou, and Søren Michael Sindbæk, "Urban Networks and Arctic Outlands: Craft Specialists and Reindeer Antler in Viking Towns," *European Journal of Archaeology* 18, no. 4 (2015): 679–704. See also Jørgen Rosvold, Gitte Hansen, and Knut H. Røed, "From Mountains to Towns: DNA from Ancient Reindeer Antlers as Proxy for Domestic Procurement Networks in Medieval Norway," *Journal of Archaeological Science* 26 (2019): 1–9.

[99] *Diplomatarium Norvegicum*, vol. 19, no. 112," https://www.dokpro.uio.no/cgi-bin/middelalder/diplom_vise_tekst.cgi?b=16086&s=n&str=.

[100] *Mork 1*, 279.

The last time we were in the north, sire, we encountered a vessel from Iceland, and we charged them with engaging in the Saami trade without our permission. When they denied it, their words made it clear that they were in fact guilty, and we attacked.[101]

In *Odds þáttr Ófeigssonar*, we follow the story of the Icelander Oddr Ófeigsson who risks the consequences of sailing to Finnmǫrk in order to trade with the Saami. Despite explicitly stating the possible consequences to his crew, they agree to the journey and return with Saami goods.[102] However, upon arriving in Mjǫla (Meløy), potentially a landing stage from Hálogaland to Iceland, Oddr and his crew are confronted by King Haraldr harðráði and Einarr flúga. With the help of a kinsman of Þórir hundr, Oddr manages to hide the *finnskatt* and returns to Iceland with the goods.[103] Although both instances are meant to have taken place in the eleventh century, the appointment of royal *sýslumenn* was not officially introduced in Norway until the end of the twelfth century, as discussed previously.[104] I therefore suggest that the stories portraying Icelandic active and organised involvement in the Saami trade function as representations of Icelandic perceptions of Norwegian fears about Icelanders and their appropriation of perceived Norwegian resources and privileges at the time of assumed composition in the 1220s or as remnants of recent anxieties experienced in the late twelfth century. Such an appropriation risked obstructing the power balance in the northern territories and added to the stresses connected to the Norwegian and Novgorod geopolitical expansion into Saami settlement areas. More importantly, however, the *þættir* demonstrate that Icelanders could and wanted to be directly involved with the Saami, minimally as trading partners. Despite the apparent legal restrictions against Icelandic participation in *finnkaup*, *Odds þáttr* and *Sneglu-Halla þáttr* indicate that the revenues outweighed potential negative consequences. The *þættir* also point to Saami agency independent of Norwegian "governance" and illustrate that Saami groups most likely had the power to control parts of the trade themselves, regardless of the increasing pressure from the nation states through geopolitical expansion.

With the textual evidence for illegal Icelandic trade with the Saami on the northern coast of Finnmǫrk in the medieval period in mind, Hansen and Olsen offer a fascinating interpretation of the so-called multi-room houses. Predominantly appearing along the northernmost coast of the present-day Norwegian county Finnmark (but stretching from Laukøy in Troms to Soim in Murmansk Oblast)

---

101 "Mork," 243.
102 *Mork 1*, 293.
103 *Mork 1*, 296.
104 Hansen and Olsen, *Hunters*, 49.

from c. 1200 to the mid-fifteenth century, these turf houses consist of a cluster of connected rooms surrounded by a common or continuous outer wall.[105] The houses seem to have fulfilled several tasks throughout their period of usage and archaeological material from excavations show no clear-cut cultural or ethnic framework.[106] However, similar building traditions are found in the medieval Icelandic (and Norse Greenland) passageway farm house.[107] It is therefore possible that these remains, with no predecessors in either Norwegian, Karelian, Russian, or Saami domestic architecture, are the archaeological remnants of Icelanders involved in trading with the Saami in the medieval period. The chronology of the multi-room houses, appearing from the early 1200s to the mid-fifteenth century, generally falls within the time of the recording of *Odds þáttr Ófeigssonar* and *Sneglu-Halla þáttr* in Morkinskinna around 1220 and the increased geopolitical stress in Finnmǫrk in the same period. This overlap strengthens the suggestion that the *þættir*, depicting events during King Haraldr harðráði's reign in the eleventh century, actually mirror real life Norwegian anxieties revolving around the Icelandic appropriation of perceived Norwegian rights to the Saami fur trade. Another, less political interpretation of these multi-room houses is that they were built by Icelanders with kin ties to the Saami living along the northern coast of Finnmǫrk.[108] Given the close personal ties between the Saami and the Hálogalanders, sometimes also creating room for culturally fluid groups based on amalgamations of Norse and Saami (and other) identities, it is not entirely unlikely that the Icelandic-styled houses were built by Icelanders with Saami ties.[109]

---

105 Hansen and Olsen, *Hunters*, 206–7.
106 Hansen and Olsen, *Hunters*, 210.
107 Hansen and Olsen, *Hunters*, 212–13.
108 See section 2.5.
109 See Kendra Willson, "A Putative Sámi Charm on a 12th c. Icelandic Spade: Runic Reception, Magic and Contact," in *Finno-Ugric Folklore, Myth and Cultural identity*, ed. Cornelius Hasselblatt and Adriaan Van der Hoeven (Groeningen: University of Groeningen, 2011), 267–81, for an analysis of a twelfth century spade found in West Central Iceland, with a runic inscription possibly including a Saami word, see discussion in section 6.3.2. For a discussion of the multi-room houses as part of a multicultural landscape on the coast of Finnmark, see Jørn Erik Henriksen, *Kulturmøte og identitet på Finnmarkskysten i tidlig historisk tid: Tolkninger basert på arkeologiske analyser av mangeromstufter* (PhD thesis, University of Tromsø, 2016).

5.3.3 Saami Perspectives?

The sources naturally present *finnkaup* from a Norse point of view. Nevertheless, there are some pointers in the saga material that can help shed light on Saami perspectives.

In Heimskringla's *Óláfs saga helga*, it is explained that the Norse traders brought many goods with them, but does not specify what type.[110] According to *Vatnsdœla saga*, the *semsveinar* agree to help Ingimundr in exchange for butter and tin.[111] In *Helga þáttr Þórissonar* the protagonist brings pork and butter to trade with the Saami,[112] and similarly, in *Ketils saga hœngs*, Ketill brings a barrel of butter to Finnmǫrk, sharing it with his Saami kin who state that "mannfögnuðr er oss at smjöri þessu" [this butter is a great banquet for us].[113] Phil Cardew recognises the textual motif associated with the Saami and butter in the texts and interprets it as a way of portraying the Saami as less sophisticated since they lack "human skills – like butter-making."[114] Although Cardew acknowledges that butter may have been a luxury for some Saami communities as the milk produced from cattle is more substantial compared to that from the reindeer, his theory of the Norse portrayal of the Saami as less sophisticated because of the recurring butter motif in these texts is problematic. Primarily, dehumanising Saami characters on the grounds that they are portrayed as unable to make butter is ill-advised, but it should also be noted that the Saami are not portrayed as unable to make butter, but that butter is portrayed as desirable for some Saami characters. Lastly, it should also be mentioned that butter-making skills is not a prerequisite for being human, neither in medieval texts nor today. We need to be wary of not creating dichotomies supporting a structuralist approach where the Saami fall outside of the Norse, and effectively our current, idea of "development" and sophistication.

Butter (and bacon) appears to be a stereotypical desirable good associated with Saami people in the saga material. This could be a reflection of actual medieval exchanges, as butter might well enough have been a valuable swap for fur products and other Saami goods, but it should be noted that the texts above are

---

110 *Hkr 2*, 229.
111 *Vatn*, 34–35.
112 Guðbrandur Vigfússon and Carl Richard Unger, eds., *Flateyjarbok: En Samling af norske Konge-Sagaer med indskudte mindre Fortællinger om Begivenheder i og udenfor Norge samt Annaler*, vol. 1 (Christiania: P.T. Mallings Forlagsboghandel, 1860), 359.
113 *Ket*, 118.
114 Phil Cardew, "'Mannfögnuður er oss at smjöri þessu': Representations of the Finns within the Icelandic Sagas," in *Text and Nation: Essays on Post-Colonial Cultural Politics*, eds., Andrew Blake and Jopi Nyman (Joensuu: Joensuun Yliopisto, 2001), 146–58.

all believed to date to the fourteenth century (*Vatn:* early; others: late) and that *Helga þáttr* and *Ketils saga* are *fornaldarsögur* and therefore prone to more fantastical narration of Saami characters. We should also be wary of painting a picture where the Saami are only associated with reindeer and the Norse with cattle or other livestock. Ohthere's account relates that the Norse chieftain had few livestock (cattle, pig, sheep, horses), but around six hundred domesticated reindeer.[115] As mentioned in section 2.7.2, there are some indications that the Saami kept sheep (or goats), so we cannot completely endorse the theory that the Saami had no independent access to more fatty butter from livestock. It is nevertheless not unlikely that the textual tradition of associating Saami demands for butter was rooted in actual meetings where butter had been desirable. In addition to pork and butter, tin and other metals appear to be valuable commodities for the Saami in *Vatnsdœla saga*.[116] This could be a reflection of the suggested principal role held by metal in early Saami belief systems, with silver being especially prominent.[117]

Although the textual sources sometimes portray a unified image of the Saami as a fixed and unchanging group, the medieval Saami settlement area did not comprise an overall static population. Different Saami groups had loyalties to different societies, based on geographical location, kin relations, and language. Although related, Saami languages diverge from one another, which is not surprising given the vast geographical distribution of the Saami in the medieval period:

> In the Iron Age and the Middle Ages, the "Saami," as a linguistic group, have formed a heterogenous network of communities that greatly differed from each other in terms of subsistence strategy, culture [...].[118]

When we acknowledge the great diversity found in medieval Saami societies, Norse-Saami relations are established as more multifaceted than what the saga literature sometimes seems to portray on the surface. Different Norse groups met, traded, and fostered personal relations with different Saami groups, and vice versa. This diversity will become particularly clear in the following chapters, discussing personal relations, sociocultural fluidity, and Saami presence in the south. In addition, while this chapter is mainly based on the Norse/Western

---

115 Hansen and Olsen, *Hunters*, 56.
116 *Vatn*, 34–35.
117 Marte Spangen, "Coast as Meeting Place for Believes [sic] and Traditions: Silver Hoards in North Norway," in *Kystkultur: Aktuel arkæologi i Norden*, ed. Anna Beck et al., Kontaktstencil, vol. 44 (Copenhagen, 2004), 85–93 (88–93).
118 Ante Aikio, "An Essay on Ethnolinguistic Prehistory," in *A Linguistic Map of Northern Europe*, ed. Riho Grünthal and Petri Kallio, vol. 266, *Mémoires de la Société Finno-Ougrienne* (Helsinki: Suomalais-Ugrilainen Seura, 2012), 63–117 (93–95).

trade with the Saami, the eastern trading routes were crucial to the Saami fur industry and archaeological evidence shows clear Saami affinities to eastern societies.[119]

In the later medieval period, from the thirteenth and fourteenth century onwards, northern Scandinavian societies were restructured as a result of increasing religious and governmental activities in northern Fennoscandia. In northern Sweden, the number of Saami sacrificial sites containing offerings of coins, jewellery, and ornaments with an eastern origin decreases after 1350, a consequence of the restructuring of trade and the decline of Novgorod as a trading centre.[120] The restructuring of trade and the increasing Norwegian, Swedish, and Novgorodian settlement of northern Fennoscandia led to significant changes for Saami communities, particularly in the interior. New groups of traders and tax collectors become visible, with the aforementioned *birkarlar* on the northern coast of the Gulf of Bothnia representing the "beginnings of an integration of Lapland [Sweden] into the Medieval feudal society."[121] Following the large-scale changes to northern Fennoscandian societies, the Saami lose monopoly of the trade in the northern areas and the growing nation states quickly appropriate Saami land and focus on taxation of the Saami. Inga-Marie Mulk notices the decrease of metallic gifts such as jewellery and coins in northern Swedish Saami sacrificial sites and connects it to the economic monopolisation of trade by the Swedish state in the later medieval period.[122] This decrease of metal gifts, Mulk claims, is a direct reflection of a more authoritarian system and increased tax burden, where the goods received by the Saami cease to correspond to the goods they produced.[123] These developments effectively saw the Saami loss of monopoly over the fur trade and its surplus value changing hands to agents of the state.

Stereotypically, the Saami are portrayed as receiving butter, meat from cattle or other livestock, and metals, in exchange for their fur products.[124] Although these "luxury goods" seem somewhat clichéd, they might have some roots in reality and may have been seen as desirable goods in exchange for the fur products hunted for the trade. In the later medieval period, the restructuring of northern Fen-

---

[119] Inga-Marie Mulk, "The Role of the Sámi in Fur-Trading During the Late Iron Age and Nordic Medieval Period in the Light of the Sámi Sacrificial Sites in Lapland," *Acta Borealia* 13, no. 1 (1996): 47–80 (50, 75).
[120] Mulk, "Fur-Trading," 75. See section 6.2.1 for typical Saami identity markers in the archaeological material (like objects with eastern origin).
[121] Mulk, "Fur-Trading," 75.
[122] Mulk, "Fur-Trading," 75.
[123] Mulk, "Fur-Trading," 76.
[124] Stereotypically, the Norse are portrayed as receiving fur products from the Saami.

noscandia and increasing colonisation of northern Saami settlement areas removed the majority of Saami independent agency in the fur trade.

5.4 Conclusion

Finnkaup, the Norse conceptualisation of the Saami fur trade, should in my opinion be understood as a reciprocal exchange system based on mutual benefits and revenue for both groups. The sources repeatedly emphasise the mutual obligations for both groups involved, and in exchange for high standard Saami fur products, Norse traders reciprocated with butter, metal, and other goods that were in demand in Saami communities.[125]

Before becoming a royal and increasingly governmentally organised privilege in the late twelfth century, the rights to pursue large-scale trade with the Saami was a kin-based prerogative for different families of the Hálogaland elite. This elite had close ties to the Saami communities and trade was not the only aspect of their relationships.[126] The Saami exchange network was not isolated to Hálogaland, however, and the sources emphasise trading links westward to both Iceland and England, as well as elsewhere. That the bestowment of the trading privilege and the conflicts associated with *finnkaup* are the most prominent themes in the texts relating to the Norse-Saami trade, is not surprising. The bestowment of *finnkaup* to people affiliated with the state and its institutions became a tangible strategy for those institutions to establish dominance later in the medieval period onwards. I therefore argue that the many *finnkaup*-related conflicts accompanying unruly Hálogalanders, and sometimes Icelanders, across the texts should be understood as reflecting current anxieties at the time of composition, primarily in the thirteenth century, connected to the appropriation of perceived governmental "rights" to Saami areas. I suggest that since direct descriptions of Norse taxation of the Saami, with the exception of Ohthere's account, primarily appear in contexts relating to the *sýslumenn*, indicates that the implementation of systematic taxation was a later development associated with the emergence of governmental and religious institutions in the far northern areas from the mid-twelfth century onwards. I have also proposed the possibility that tax reportedly levied on the Saami should not necessarily always be read as a negative force or as equal to subjugation but rather, could be interpreted as a consolidating factor. It goes without saying though, that the large-scale systematic taxation of Saami communities from the later me-

---

125 See section 5.3.3.
126 See section 6.2.

dieval period and onwards was rooted in structures that ultimately served the interests of the nation states.

While relations between the Norse and the Saami were not isolated to trading alone, *finnkaup* was, however, very significant for the relations and interactions between different Norse and Saami groups. Different Saami groups with different loyalties, ambitions, and agendas traded with different Norse groups, also with various ambitions and ties. Because of this, trading relations will have depended on regional variations and although trade with the Saami is treated as systematic in the textual material, different experiences, meetings and relations between the trading partners will have taken place.

Chapter 6: Liminal Identities and Fluid Spaces? Norse-Saami Personal Relationships

6.1 Introduction

As the previous chapters have demonstrated, Norse and Saami people lived in close proximity to each other and frequently sought one another out for social, economic, political, and ritual purposes. Humans are social beings and unsurprisingly, Norse-Saami interactions sometimes developed into personal relationships. By personal relationship, I refer to close emotional connections between people maintained by feelings and expectations of mutual social obligations, such as marriage and friendship, but also through the creation of alliances that fostered feelings of loyalty, that might have initially been founded on economic or political grounds.

Personal relationships between the Norse and the Saami appear frequently across the texts and are especially visible in the sagas. Here, relationships between Norse and Saami people are initiated on various grounds, in different contexts, are maintained in different ways and have different results. Contrary to some of the modern day portrayals of Norse-Saami interactions,[1] these relationships appear multifaceted in medieval texts and cultural and ethnic lines are often blurred in the portrayal of people from blended families. In my opinion, this multifaceted portrayal is striking and can demonstrate the many opportunities for identity negotiation in the overlap between cultures that has increasingly been emphasised in archaeological research.[2] This emphasis is rooted in postcolonial theory and has highlighted the diversity of some of the archaeological material and helped break up the Norse-Saami dichotomy in research. Highlighting this diversity is crucial in the opposition of the white supremacy pervading the perception of the Viking Age, and the Nordic medieval period in general, in popular culture, and particularly the imagined notion of a "pure Nordic bloodline." This chapter challenges this notion by presenting the possible textual and archaeological evidence for Norse-Saami personal relationships in order to demonstrate the many opportunities for identity negotiation in medieval Fennoscandian societies. To achieve this, I utilise existing interpretations of certain archaeological finds as identity expressions of Norse-Saami cultural fluidity and blended social milieux and develop a similar framework appropriate for the textual source material.

---

[1] Jeremy DeAngelo, "The North and the Depiction of the 'Finnar' in the Icelandic Sagas," *Scandinavian Studies* 83, no. 3 (2010): 257–86 (269, 279–80).
[2] See section 6.3.

6.2 Norse-Saami Personal Relationships in Literature

6.2.1 Kinship and Intimate Family Relationships

Regardless of the purposes and the background of such relations, medieval texts repeatedly refer to the creation and maintenance of deeply personal relationships between Saami and Norse people. The establishment of kin relations such as marriage, childrearing, and fostering occur "effortlessly"[3] across the sources and portray close connections between the Saami and the Norse. In this section I present an overview of how these relations appear in the source material.

The most famous example of such an "intimate relation" is undoubtedly the account of the marriage between King Haraldr hárfagri and the Saami "princess" Snæfríðr, discussed in sections 2.6.2 and 3.2.1. The relationship is portrayed in *Ágrip* and in *Haralds saga hárfagra* in Heimskringla and is initiated by Snæfríðr's father, the *Finnakonungr* Svási, who insists on the king marrying his daughter.[4] Else Mundal interprets Svási's demand as that of a chieftain solidifying his power by forming an alliance with the king of Norway.[5] Furthermore, the marriage is often assumed to be a later mythical construction supposed to assert Saami obligations to the king of Norway through bonds of kinship and thereby proclaiming Norwegian rights to Saami land.[6] As already discussed in chapter 3.2.1, the account appears in a context relating King Haraldr's growing control over vast areas of land through the establishment of kinship relations with powerful families allowing for the expansion of his kingdom. In this sense, the account has been interpreted as an illustration of the attempt to unify Norse and Saami people in what would become Norway through the creation of kinship between the high standing members of Norse and Saami societies.[7] While I agree with this interpretation, I also think it is important to emphasise the other, simpler "meaning" of the marriage, which in itself demonstrates the possibility and normality of a Norwegian high standing man marrying a high standing Saami woman.

---

3 Asgeir Svestad, "Svøpt i myra: Synspunkter på Skjoldehamnfunnets etniske og kulturelle tilknytning," in *Viking*, ed. Herdis Hølleland et al., Norsk arkeologisk årbok, vol. 80 (Oslo: Norsk Arkeologisk Selskap, 2017), 129–56 (150).
4 See section 3.2.1. *Ágr*, 6. *Hkr 1*, 126.
5 Else Mundal, "The Relationship Between Sami and Nordic Peoples Expressed in Terms of Family Associations," *Journal of Northern Studies* 2 (2009): 25–37 (31).
6 Gro Steinsland, *Det hellige bryllup: En analyse av Hierogami-myten i Skírnismál, Ynglingatál, Háleygjatál og Hyndluljóð* (Larvik: Solum Forlag, 1991). Mundal, "Family," 31. Lars Ivar Hansen and Bjørnar Olsen, *Hunters in Transition: An Outline of Early Sámi History*, The Northern World 63 (Leiden: Brill, 2014), 52.
7 See Saxo, 39.

Eleanor Rosamund Barraclough, however, reads the story of King Haraldr and Snæfríðr as a textual representation of the "quintessential horror of the magical outsider allowed into the intimate domestic sphere."[8] Similarly, Jeremy DeAngelo states that examples like this, alongside other cases of Norse-Saami marriages, "serve as cautionary tales of the suffering that results from such unions for both the Norse partner and the Norse people as a whole."[9] Hermann Pálsson describes Snæfríðr as "seductive, deceitful," as a "wicked bride," and as not "the only lady of the kind."[10] I disagree with these statements since they, consciously or subconsciously, emphasise Snæfríðr's Saami affiliation as the root of her negative portrayal in the narrative. In doing so, the distance between the Saami and the Norse is broadened, with DeAngelo's statement reinforcing colonial notions of Indigenous strain on the majority population. I would argue that, as emphasised in section 3.2.1, while Snæfríðr's magical abilities were most likely perceived as more powerful by a medieval audience because of her Saami identity, it is her paganism, through the implied practise of magic, that poses a problem in the text, rather than her cultural affiliation.[11] This interpretation is strengthened by the aforementioned Biblical account (2 Maccabees 9.8–9) describing Antiochus IV Epiphanes's death. Furthermore, the fact that Snæfríðr and Haraldr's sons are included in King Harald's partition of the realm (see chapter 7), related in *Haralds saga hárfagra* in Heimskringla, speaks in my opinion against the interpretation of the presence of the Saami in the Norse domestic sphere as something inherently unacceptable.[12] Once again, I would emphasise the possibility of a less polarised implication of the marriage, and propose that the story reflects the normality of Norse-Saami marriages, even in a southern context.

This normality becomes clear across the textual sources, where arrangements of marriage between Norse and Saami people occur in both mythical and "historical" contexts, across the different genres. Saxo relates the marriage of the mythical founder of Hálogaland to the daughter of the "Finnorum Byarmorumque principis" [prince of the Saami and the Bjarmar],[13] and *Ynglinga saga* (Heimskringla) relates the marriage between the possible Saami goddess Skaði and Óðinn, in addition to the short-lived marriage between the mythological Swedish king Vanlandi to the Saami woman Drífa, and the marriage of another mythological king of Swe-

---

8 Eleanor Rosamund Barraclough, "Arctic Frontiers: Rethinking Norse-Sámi Relations in the Old Norse Sagas," *Viator* 48, no. 3 (2017): 27–51 (45).
9 DeAngelo, "North," 264.
10 Hermann Pálsson, "The Sami People in Old Norse Literature," *Nordlit* 5 (1999): 29–53 (38).
11 See section 6.3.2.
12 *Hkr 2*, 137.
13 Saxo, 150–51.

den, Agni, to the Saami woman Skjálfr.[14] *Ketils saga hœngs* portrays the marriage between Ketill and the Saami woman Hrafnhildr.[15] When the powerful Vík-*hersir* Haraldr remarries in *Gríms saga*, the text reports it is to the magically skilled Grímhildr from Finnmǫrk, who can be interpreted as Saami.[16] In *Hrólfs saga kraka*, King Hringr marries the Saami "princess" Hvít from Finnmǫrk, also a practitioner of magic.[17] Interestingly, Hvít is described as the daughter of a *Finnakonungr* and his mistress Ingebjǫrg, the latter of whom could be interpreted as Norse, again pointing to the normality of intercultural relationships in the textual material.[18] These accounts exclusively describe elite relationships between the Norse and Saami, demonstrating both the neglect of people not from this elite (the majority), but also, the significance of status and power in the establishment of these relationships. Inger Zachrisson argues that Saami women marrying into the Norse elite functioned as mediators between Norse and Saami societies and therefore had high status in both societies.[19] Personal relationships between Saami and Norse elites could have functioned as alliances that validated and justified certain privileges, such as access to spatial resources like landscape management/appropriation, and sociopolitical resources like *finnkaup*, in turn consolidating the power of both parties involved. In *Landnámabók*, one of the first inhabitants of Iceland traces their family back to Saami royalty:

> Sonr Þorsteins ok Lopthœna var Hrosskell, er átti Jóreiði Ǫlvisdóttur sonar Mǫttuls Finnakonungs.[20]

> Thorstein and Lopthæna had a son called Hroskell, who married Joreid, daughter of Olvir, son of King Mottul [of the Saami].[21]

I would argue that the sources above are indicative of Saami family ties and status being interwoven and that Saami ties strengthened the power of a given kin group through the gaining of both symbolic and actual power. It is also valuable to emphasise that the initiation of these relationships was not necessarily always

---

14 *Hkr 1*, 28–29, 37–38.
15 *Ket*, 123.
16 *GrL*, 144.
17 *Hrólf*, 48.
18 *Hrólf*, 47–48.
19 Inger Zachrisson, "Samiska och nordiska kvinnor," in *Kvinner i vikingtid*, ed. Nancy Coleman and Nanna Løkka (Oslo: Scandinavian Academic Press, 2014), 243–68.
20 *Ldn*, 82.
21 *Landnáma*, 33. On Saami lineage in medieval Icelandic contexts, see Sirpa Aalto and Veli-Pekka Lehtola, "The Sami Representations Reflecting the Multi-Ethnic North of the Saga Literature," *Journal of Northern Studies* 11, no. 2 (2017): 7–30 (20).

based on a profound political or economic meaning and was not exclusive to high standing members of society alone. In areas comprising shared cultural landscapes and culturally fluid meeting places, people with different backgrounds met and sometimes developed deep intimate relationships without any reasons other than attraction, as people do today. These relationships seem (mostly) uncomplicated in the sources, which rarely offer any remarks other than the spouse being Saami, which in my opinion strengthens the likelihood of the societal normality of these interactions.

It should be mentioned that the texts traditionally portray Norse men marrying Saami women. This is not the case for other intimate relationships such as fostering and childrearing, where both Saami women and Saami men are represented. In addition, I would also like to point out that the Norse man + Saami woman "marriage equation" is not necessarily reflective of actual events. Some scholars have interpreted this "equation" as reflective of mythological patterns related to Old Norse ideas of kingship. Gro Steinsland argues that the literary prototype of the Old Norse king was a descendant of a god and a giantess, with the union of opposite forces creating something innovative and inherently heroic.[22] In addition, Steinsland reasons that female giants were mythological personifications of the earth, allowing for the reading of marriages between gods/kings to giants as representations of the consolidation of land rights.[23] According to Steinsland then, the marriages between Norse kings and Saami women in the textual material should be understood as representations of these patterns. Else Mundal agrees with Steinsland's interpretation and asserts that the marriage between King Haraldr and Snæfríðr "must be read in the light of Old Norse myths" and specifically, the marriages between gods and giantesses.[24] Sirpa Aalto and Veli-Pekka Lehtola pursue this notion and claim that the mythical giants could be replaced by the historical Saami since they both "lived somewhere between the known civilized world and the unknown periphery."[25] I generally find these interpretations problematic, since they, in my opinion, overly emphasise the Saami as "exclusive" Others in Norse society.[26] While I agree with parts of Steinsland's theory, I think it is important that it is contextualised so that subconscious notions of the Saami as uncivilised are avoided. As stated in chapter 3.2.1, I do to some extent agree with the theory that the Saami sometimes replace giants in Norse texts, and so it is important to

---

22 Steinsland, *Hierogami-myten*.
23 Steinsland, *Hierogami-myten*.
24 Mundal, "Family," 31.
25 Aalto and Lehtola, "Representations," 14.
26 See section 3.2.1.

emphasise that giants also represented positive values.[27] These values include attractiveness and fertility, but more importantly the possession of desirable objects and knowledge. Nevertheless, I do strongly argue that the association between the Saami and representations of giants in the texts have been extensively covered in past scholarship, and that it is time to look beyond this accepted idea, question it, and rather, investigate other aspects of the Saami in Norse texts. It should be noted that Steinsland's theory has been criticised for not acknowledging that the texts she bases her analysis on are editorial products and not unbiased accounts of the Fennoscandian past and for disregarding the narrative content of the sources themselves.[28] When it comes to the portrayal of the marriage between Snæfríðr and King Haraldr, Steinsland's theory can be criticised on the grounds that neither of their sons are portrayed as the literary prototype of Old Norse kings (none of them become kings) nor as specifically innovative or heroic. The same could also be argued for the other Norse-Saami marriages discussed previously.

Conflict resolution through the creation of marriage alliances (in non-Saami contexts) is common across the sagas, and it is therefore not unlikely that marriages between Norse and Saami people should also be understood in this way.[29] Conflict solving is the background of the marriage between the skiing deity Skaði and the Norse god Njörðr as related in *Skáldskaparmál*. As discussed in section 2.7.1, Skaði is often assumed to have been perceived as Saami by the audience. In *Skáldskaparmál*, Skaði's father, the giant Þjazi, is killed by the Norse gods following a conflict involving Loki and the abduction of the deity Iðunn.[30] In order to avoid vengeance being taken by Skaði, the gods agree that she could choose a husband from amongst them. Norse-Saami marriage alliances in the textual source material could be read as reflections of real-life practical strategies adopted by people living in close proximity with each other, both in the past the texts portray but also at the time of composition. Through the initiation of personal alliances that fostered feelings of loyalty and mutual belonging, conflicts concerning land rights or spatial resources could be avoided.

Unsurprisingly, intimate relationships between Norse and Saami people in the texts sometimes lead to the birth of children. As I have shown, across the textual source material, Saami descent is alluded to repeatedly, referring to a person's

---

27 Mundal, "Family," 30.
28 Margaret Clunies Ross, "Royal Ideology in Early Scandinavia: A Theory Versus the Texts," *The Journal of English and Germanic Philology* 113, no. 1 (2014): 18–33 (18–19, 32–33).
29 Mundal, "Family," 30.
30 *Skáldskaparmál*, 2.

Saami parentage or heritage.³¹ Previously mentioned characters associated with terms like *hálftrǫll* or *hálfbergrisi* are often assumed to be indicative of Saami descent due to the association between the Saami and the supernatural in certain contexts. As problematised in section 3.2.1, this association is not straightforward and we should therefore be cautious of accepting that these characters are Saami on the basis of supernatural nicknames, especially when these are significantly more Othered than other instances involving the Saami in the same text. If we do nevertheless play with the possibility that these characters were indeed understood as having Saami descent at the time of composition or dissemination, it should be noted that while Bjǫrgólfr hálfbergrisi's parentage is not elaborated, Hallbjǫrn hálftrǫll's father is named and described as a farmer in the text, leading to the possibility that his mother was perceived as Saami.³² Again, it should be accentuated that this is an assumption, and that both of Hallbjǫrn's parents might have had Saami descent, or that his father was the one with the Saami link. Regarding the uncertainty of the descent based only on the occasional association between the Saami and supernatural beings (expressed in the nicknames), the Saami descent should in my opinion not be accepted in these instances. Hallbjǫrn's grandson on the other hand, Grímr lóðinkinna, is explicitly stated as having Saami descent through his Saami mother, Hrafnhildr.³³ The soothsayer Drauma-Finni is reported as being the son of the Saami woman Leikny, with both his name and abilities referring to his Saami descent.³⁴ As stated previously, King Haraldr and Snæfríðr's sons are Othered in the stories about them, but they are nevertheless included in the partition of their father's realm following his death, as related in Heimskringla, indicating that their rights as royal sons were not affected by their Saami parentage.³⁵ King Haraldr reportedly initially neglects his sons with Snæfríðr due to the accusations of spellbinding, but is later advised to include them as rightful sons, which stands out as an interesting example of the active inclusion of high standing Saami or culturally fluid actors into the Norse elite.³⁶

As already established, characters with Saami descent are often ascribed with special abilities associated with such descent, most often the predisposition to perform magic, but also archery skills and other connotations with the Saami Motif-

---

31 See *Gautr*, ch. 7; *Ǫrv*, ch. 1; *Ágr*, ch. 2; *Eb*, ch. 7; *Finnb*, ch. 8; *Kjaln*, ch. 14 and 18; *HN*, ch. 11; *Fsk*, ch. 14, for characters with explicit or implicit Saami descent through associations with the Saami Motif-Cluster and/or Saami parentage.
32 *Eg*, 16. See sections 3.2.1 and 3.2.5.
33 *Ket*, 117.
34 *Finnb*, 268. In *Landnámabók*, Lekný is described as "útlend" [foreigner], 275.
35 *Hkr 1*, 137. See section 7.4.2.
36 *Hkr 1*, 127–28.

Cluster. Intimate relationships between two people coming from different cultural backgrounds can result in a blended culture through their children, with Barraclough noting that "it is in hybrid characters and cross-cultural love affairs that imaginary lines drawn between cultures fade away, and the middle ground is most fully realised."[37] Perhaps then, the tendency to Other characters with Saami descent is a literary tool to emphasise this "middle ground" and the fluid cultural expressions of blended families. Depending on the context, the suggested emphasis on this "middle ground" can be positive, negative (characters that do not conform to Christian standards), or even neutral. I therefore suggest that characters who are not explicitly stated as Saami in the texts but are described in ways following the Saami Motif-Cluster can be interpreted as textual expressions of people coming from blended social milieux. This Othering is particularly clear in the list of King Haraldr hárfagri's male heirs as it is presented in *Ágrip*, including his sons by Snæfríðr:

> Sigurðr hrísi, Guðrøðr ljómi, Hálfdan hvítbeinn, er sumir kǫlluðu háfœtu, Rǫgnvaldr reykill, er sumir kalla Ragnar, er var sunr Finnkonu einnar er kǫlluð var Snjófríðr, dóttir Svása Finnkonungs, ok brá honum til moður sinnar. Var hann kallaðr seiðmaðr – þat er spámaðr – ok var staðfastr á Haðalandi ok síddi þar ok var kallaðr skratti.[38]

> Sigurðr hrísi [the giant],[39] Guðrøðr ljómi [the bright], Hálfdan hvítbeinn [the pale-legged], whom some called háfœtu [long-legs], Rǫgnvaldr reykill,[40] whom some call Ragnarr. He was the son of the Saami woman called Snæfríðr, the daughter of Svási [*finnakonungr*], and he took after his mother. He was called a [*seiðmaðr*] – that is to say a soothsayer – and lived in Haðaland where he practised sorcery and was called a warlock.[41]

The Othering of Haraldr and Snæfríð's sons is elaborated in *Haralds saga hárfagra*, which directly depicts their maternal descent in a negative light: "því at fúsir væri þeir at eiga betra móðerni, ef þú hefðir þeim þat fengit" [for they would have willingly had better maternal descent if you had let them have it].[42] In the slightly ear-

---

37 Barraclough, "Frontiers," 44.
38 *Ágr*, 4. Each heir is listed as one of twenty sons in the text, but I have removed the numbers from the extract to ease reading. Haraldr's male heirs with Snæfríðr are listed from seventeen to twenty and are numbered chronologically as they appear above.
39 See Else Mundal, "Når den 'rette' teksten er rang: Tolkinga av tilnamnet Sigurd Rise," *Scandinavian Philology* 15 (2017): 248–60.
40 "Reykill" seems to be a hapax legomenon and might have something to do with Old Norse "reykr" [smoke], but this is a guess.
41 *Ágr*, 5. I have kept *finnakonungr* and *seiðmaðr* in the original Old Norse since I have done so elsewhere. Soothsayer and warlock are both problematic terms but are based on the cited translation.
42 *Hkr 1*, 128.

lier *Ágrip*, the Othering of Snæfríðr's sons is reflected in nicknames like *hrísi* (giant) and the ability to practise magic, but their descent is never explicitly stated as something negative. In the slightly later *Haralds saga hárfagra* of Heimskringla however, their maternal descent is specifically said to be undesirable. While it has been argued that this "negatively charged" descent alludes to the sons' Saami cultural affiliation through their mother, I would again assert my interpretation that the "inherited" pagan associations function as negative factors in the text rather than their "Saaminess." The only negative associations with Snæfríðr in the stories about her are connected to her reported bewitchment of King Haraldr, *i.e.*, an inherently unchristian practice, and generally, both Snæfríðr and Svási are described in predominantly positive language or language that emphasises their high status. In the following chapter of *Haralds saga*, this "inherited" negative association with paganism is made explicitly clear, when King Haraldr is directly depicted as disproving of *seiðmenn* (practitioners of *seiðr*) and orders Rǫgnvaldr, his son with Snæfríðr, to be killed (by their half-brother) for practising *seiðr:*

> Rǫgnvaldr réttilbeini átti Haðaland. Hann nam fjǫlkynngi ok gerðisk seiðmaðr. Haraldri konungi þótti illir seiðmenn. Á Hǫrðalandi var sá seiðmaðr, er hét Vitgeirr. Konungr sendi honum orð ok bað hann hætta seið. Hann svaraði ok kvað:
>
> Þat sá vǫ lítil,
> at vér síðim,
> karla born
> ok kerlinga,
> es Rǫgnvaldr síðr
> réttilbeini,
> hróðmǫgr Haralds,
> á Haðalandi.
>
> En er Haraldr konungr heyrði þetta sagt, þá með hans ráði fór Eiríkr blóðøx til Upplanda ok kom á Haðaland. Hann brenndi inni Rǫgnvald, bróður sinn, með átta tigu seiðmanna.[43]
>
> Rǫgnvaldr réttilbeini had Haðaland. He learned witchcraft and became a [*seiðmaðr*]. King Haraldr thought [practioners of *seiðr*] were evil. In Hǫrðaland there was a [*seiðmaðr*] who was called Vitgeirr. The king sent him word and commanded him to cease casting spells. He replied and said:
>
> It does little harm
> if we do magic,
> the children
> of churls and crones,
> if so does Rǫgnvaldr
> réttilbeini,

---

43 *Hkr 1*, 138–39.

great son of Haraldr,
in Haðaland.

And when King Haraldr heard this said, on his instruction Eiríkr blóðøx went to Upplǫnd and reached Haðaland. He burned his brother Rǫgnvaldr in his house with eighty [seiðmenn], and this deed was greatly praised.⁴⁴

In my opinion the extract above should be understood as textual representations of the anxieties connected to the pre-Christian religion(s), rather than negative textual depictions of the Saami. While Rǫgnvaldr's Saami descent strengthens his pagan portrayal, it is never at the forefront of his negative portrayal in the text. That the "inherited" pagan associations function as negative factors in the text rather than the "Saaminess," is in my opinion furthered by the aforementioned inclusion of the *Snæfríðarsynir* in the partition of the realm after King Haraldr's death, which I would suggest demonstrates the inclusion of high standing people with Saami or culturally fluid descent into high standing Norse society. Similarly, the fact that Haraldr is reprimanded for his initial exclusion of his sons with Snæfríðr,⁴⁵ also points, I would argue, to the fact that including Saami people or people with Saami ties in the highest strata of Norse society was not frowned upon, at least not textually. In addition, I argue that this inclusion is evident in the abovementioned reported statement by the *seiðmaðr* Vitgeirr. Vitgeirr distances himself from Rǫgnvaldr by emphasising Rǫgnvaldr's royal descent, followed by a comment on his own descent from "karla[r] ok kerlinga[r]" [churls and crones]. If the negative portrayal of Rǫgnvaldr was rooted in his Saami descent through Snæfríðr, I would argue that it would have been natural to include Rǫgnvaldr in the *karla[r] ok kerlinga[r]* category in the text. It should be mentioned that these terms are primarily social markers, and that the text does not dispute Snæfríðr's high status. I nevertheless believe that if the goal was to alienate Snæfríðr because of her Saami descent, it would be natural to include her in the less favourable category. Once again then, it is necessary to emphasise that there are no direct connections between the negative depiction of the sons of Snæfríðr, or even Snæfríðr herself, and their Saami cultural affiliation. To conclude this section, it is also critical to emphasise that Saami descent typically strengthens the status of the characters, through abilities connected to the Saami Motif-Cluster, as examined in chapter 3.

---

44 Snorri Sturluson, *Heimskringla*, trans. Alison Finlay and Anthony Faulkes, 3 vols (London: Viking Society for Northern Research, 2014), "Hkr 1," 80–81.
45 *Hkr 1*, 128.

King Haraldr hárfagri's personal relationship with the Saami is not limited to marriage or childrearing, and Else Mundal has called him the "foster son" of the Saami.[46] Both *Kjalnesinga saga* and *Hálfdánar þáttr svarta*, first written in the early and late fourteenth century respectively, narrate the fostering of Haraldr by the mountain dweller Dófri, whom Else Mundal has described as a Norse "representation" of the Saami.[47] Mundal interprets the fostering of the Norwegian King Haraldr by Dófri as forming parts of the previously mentioned foundation myth of Norway as a result of Norse-Saami fostering arrangements.[48] While foster parents normally had lower social status than the biological family of the foster child, the institution created strong and often lifelong relationships founded on the establishment of symbolic kinship relations that often developed into a sense of loyalty.[49] Regardless of the status of the foster parent, in the stories relating King Haraldr's relations to his foster father, Dófri is always treated as more amicable than Haraldr's biological father.[50] According to Mundal, King Haraldr emerges as a symbolic expression of community as the foster son of the Saami people (Dófri) in these texts,[51] a textual motif that could also be used to strengthen medieval Norwegian governmental claims in more Saami areas. If we accept the idea that Dófri was indeed understood as a Saami character, I would also suggest that the story describes a possible and practical relationship between Norse and Saami people living in close proximity and sharing certain societal features, where kinship with the other group could reinforce status and power. However, as I explore further in section 7.4.2, I am unsure whether Dófri can be said to have been understood as a Saami "representation." Nevertheless, similar Norse-Saami fostering arrangements appear in Fagrskinna, with the fostering of the Hálogalander Gunnhildr in Finnmǫrk by Mǫttul Finnakonungr.[52] The previously mentioned story about Eyvindr kinnrifa could also be interpreted as a Norse-Saami fostering arrangement, where the foster parents are Norse. The fact that the fostering arrangements in these texts again concern characters from the highest social strata, demonstrates cross-cultural recognition of social stratification and that the establishment of these arrangements could be crucial in the maintenance of the connection be-

---

46 Mundal, "Family," 32
47 *Kjaln*, 28. Daniel Sävborg, "Den 'efterklassiska' islänningasagan och dess ålder," *Arkiv för nordisk filologi* 27 (2012): 19–58 (19). *HálfdSv*, 175.
48 Mundal, "Family," 31–32.
49 Lorenzo Lozzi Gallo, "The Giantess as Foster-Mother in Old Norse Literature," *Scandinavian Studies* 78, no. 1 (2016): 1–20 (13).
50 *Kjaln*, 28. *HálfdSv*, 171–75. See section 7.4.2.
51 Mundal, "Family," 32.
52 *Fsk*, 79.

tween the groups. Furthermore, since higher levels of society are narrated as utilising fostering as a means of facilitating personal relationships, the arrangement was normalised and most likely occurred regularly in families of lower social status, especially in areas with shared cultural landscapes appropriating the same resources.

It should also be emphasised that Saami cross-cultural personal relationships were not isolated to the Norse alone. Saami-Bjarmian relations are well represented in the source material, and we should to some degree expect similar types of relationships being facilitated between Saami and Bjarmian peoples, as well as other peoples in close proximity to the Saami, as with the Norse. Marriage is the most common type of intimate relationship between the groups, something that is also reflected in characters having both Saami and Bjarmian descent.[53] The Norse also initiate relationships with the Bjarmar, and in *Hauks þáttr hábrókar*, King Haraldr's foster mother is portrayed as Bjarmian.[54] Through these instances we are once again reminded of the many diverse realities of different Saami characters across the texts and how these characters often and unsurprisingly act independently of the Norse.

The creation and maintenance of deep personal relationships between Norse and Saami people in the literature appear somewhat effortless, facilitated through marriages, childrearing, and fostering arrangements. Scholars sometimes read these relationships, particularly marriages, as reflections of Norse anxieties connected to the Other. I suggest that the Other should primarily be understood as the non-Christian Other rather than the Saami or foreign Other. In emphasising the differences between the Norse and the Saami as inherently based on the distancing of Norse people (or minimally, the writers of the text) from the Saami, I believe that scholars contribute to the polarisation of the Norse and Saami in historical research and unconsciously affirm colonial frameworks. Instead, I have argued that the Othering of characters with Saami descent can also be understood as a literary tool used to portray the culturally fluid identity expressions of people from blended social milieux, rather than as a way of alienating the Saami. In general, I think that the relationships discussed above should be read as demonstrating the normality of Norse-Saami relationships in and to society, as well as being representative of realistic and practical relationships between people living in close proximity with each other. Nevertheless, even if these relationships did not have any basis in actual physical interactions, the expression of the relationship between the Norse and the Saami in terms of married partners, parent/child, or

---

53 Saxo, 67, 151. *Qrv*, 240–41.
54 *HHábr*, 202–3. See also *Ldn*, 150.

foster child/foster parent creates strong textual images whereby the Norse and Saami have bonds of kinship.

6.2.2 Business Partners, Cohabitation, and Saami Soldiers

Personal relationships do not necessarily have to be kinship-related or intimate to facilitate longlasting feelings of loyalty or to be important. Throughout the source material, other types of personal relationships such as friendship, alliances, apprenticeships, and neighbourliness reflect the normalised presence of the Saami in Norse society.

Norse-Saami co-operation in the fur trade facilitated personal relationships such as trading alliances and economic loyalties, in addition to more intimate relationships. In *Egils saga*, the text states that the organised trading between Þórólfr and the Saami occurred under friendly circumstances, partly because of the *hræzlugœði* reportedly experienced by the Saami.[55] The loyalties built between the trading parties may therefore have functioned as another justification behind the reported Saami group's apparent dislike of the *Hildiríðarsynir*.[56] Similarly, the fact that Þórólfr continues to trade with the Saami even after losing the privilege to *finnkaup* should in my opinion be read as indicative of more personal motivations such as feelings of loyalty, possibly connected to trading alliances, between Þórólfr and the Saami groups. As discussed in section 5.2.2, *finnkaup* was mainly a kin-based prerogative prior to becoming a royally appointed privilege. I would argue that the nature of *finnkaup* as a perceived right inherited from generation to generation must have had deep-rooted implications for feelings of trust as well as expectations between Norse and Saami business partners. Even if these were mainly founded on economic grounds, certain personal relationships will have been maintained through annual contact and communication, business agreements, and the like. *Historia Norwegie* reports that Hálogalanders and Saami people cohabited and had frequent transactions between them.[57] Similarly, when Þórir hundr's stays with his Saami partners over two winters it is related that he "átti margs konar kaupa við Finna" [did various kinds of trade with the Saami].[58] Both instances indicate that Norse and Saami people were perceived as spending time together frequently while trading and establish that some type of social interaction (cohabitation) took place in addition to the emphasised economic aspects. As

---

55 *Eg*, 27.
56 See section 5.2.2. *Eg*, 43.
57 *HN*, 56–57.
58 *Hkr 2*, 344–45.

discussed in chapter 3.2.4 and related in Heimskringla's *Haraldssona saga*, Morkinskinna, and Fagrskinna, the alleged son of King Magnús berfœttr, Sigurðr Slembidjákn, is portrayed as living with Saami boatbuilders after fleeing northwards sometime in the early twelfth century:

> Sigurðr var með Finnum, þá er þeir gerðu skúturnar, ok hǫfðu Finnar þar mungát ok gerðu honum þar veizlu.⁵⁹
>
> Sigurðr stayed with the [Saami] while they were building the ships, and the [Saami] had beer there and put on a banquet there for him.⁶⁰

The version above sees Sigurðr staying with his Saami friends in Tjaldasund on Hinnøya and prior to the above paragraph, it is stated that Sigurðr and his entourage were provisioned by what are seemingly Norse actors during the winter.⁶¹ The account also, once again, relates close relationships between Norwegian royalty and Saami groups. According to Heimskringla and *Óláfs saga Tryggvasonar en mesta*, Gunnhildr lived together with the two Saami men she was apprenticing under to learn magic in Finnmǫrk.⁶² Living with someone has implications for your relationship with them and involves matters of communication and traditions. The fact that the texts nonchalantly mention cohabitation indicates, I would argue, some sort of normality or at least, the textual predictability of such arrangements which in itself is important.

As discussed in section 5.2.2, Hansen and Olsen offer the interpretation that parts of *finnskatt* functioned as return payment from Saami groups to Norse chiefdoms for political protection against hostile groups.⁶³ While there are no examples of such an agreement as far as I am aware, there are instances where Saami people partake in seemingly "Norse" military contexts, often as archers and as part of the royal retinue. In Heimskringla's *Óláfs saga Tryggvassonar*, Jarl Eiríkr's Saami bowman becomes the final catalyst for the defeat of King Óláfr at the battle of Svǫlðr.⁶⁴ In *Helgisaga Óláfs konungs Haraldssonar*, "fiðr æinn i liði Ólafs" [a Saami man in Ólaf's army] foretells that the king's opponent would attack and take them all hostage.⁶⁵ Although initially discouraged by the other soldiers, King Óláfr listens to the Saami man, leading to the king's success.⁶⁶ While the

---

59 *Hkr 3*, 311.
60 "Hkr 3," 191.
61 *Hkr 3*, 311.
62 *Hkr 1*, 135–36. *Mesta 1*, 8–10.
63 Hansen and Olsen, *Hunters*, 69.
64 *Hkr 1*, 362–63.
65 *Helgisaga*, 16.
66 *Helgisaga*, 17–18.

Saami man's abilities are remarkable and certainly follow the Saami Motif-Cluster, I find the lack of remarkability associated with his presence as part of the king's army very telling. Alongside the presence of Finnr in Jarl Eirík's army at the battle of Svǫlðr, the unexceptional presence of a Saami man in the royal army can demonstrate the normality of Saami people in Norse military contexts and that regardless of the reasoning behind it, Saami people were included in this context. In *Hákonar saga Hákonarsonar*, this inclusion is reflected in stanza 1 of Sturla Þórðarson's *Hrafnsmál*, relating King Hákon's journey to Scotland to defend his rights to the Scottish isles:

> Sóttu sóknhvattar
> sveitir háleitan
> geira glymstæri
> glyggs ór Finnbygðum.
> Alt brá jarðbeltis
> austan sigrflaustum
> gjálfr af Gautelfi
> gætis hásæta.
>
> Battle-keen companies sought the sublime din-increaser of the storm of spears [BATTLE > WARRIOR] from the settlements of the Saami. The surge of the earth-belt [SEA] drove the victory-vessels of the guardian of rowing-benches [CAPTAIN] all the way west from the Götaälv.[67]

The stanza appears in a context describing the large army of King Hákon, emphasising the presence of Saami soldiers. The presence of the Saami army in King Hákon's forces may have been the result of a sort of national conscription and could reflect the growing Norwegian interest in Saami resources. A story related in Heimskringla's *Óláfs saga helga*, however, demonstrates that individual "career choices" could also be the motivation behind these so-called Saami "soldiers." Here, the "stereotypical" Saami character Finnr litli works as a type of mercenary for the petty king Hrœrekr.[68] Similarly, *Sǫrla saga sterka*, most likely first written in the fifteenth century, relates that both Sörli and his father King Erlingr had Saami men in their armies, called Ívarr and Sverri respectively, from "Finnmörkr austan" [Finnmǫrk in the east].[69] In Heimskringla's *Óláfs saga Tryggvasonar*, potential military alliances founded on sociopolitical loyalties are alluded to in the introduction of the Hálogaland chieftain Rauðr inn rammi: "Hann var ríkr maðr. Fylgði

---

67 Kari Ellen Gade, "Sturla Þórðarson, *Hrafnsmál* 1," in *Poetry from the Kings' Sagas 2: From c. 1035 to c. 1300*, ed. Diana Whaley, Skaldic Poetry of the Scandinavian Middle Ages 2 (Turnhout: Brepols, 2009), 728.
68 *Hkr 2*, 120.
69 *SǫrlaSt*, 436, 440.

honum mikill fjǫlði Finna, þegar er kunnigr. Hann var vinr mikill ok mjǫk fjǫlkunnigr" [He was a rich man. A large number of (Saami people) attended him when he needed them. Rauðr was a great pagan and very skilled in magic].[70]

Whether as a result of more organised processes such as conscription, individual career choices (mercenaries, archers, and the like), or sociopolitical alliances and loyalties, the presence of Saami people in Norse military contexts in the textual source material once again demonstrates the overall normalised presence of the Saami in Norse society. The appearance of so-called Saami "soldiers" emphasises the many possibilities of Saami actors in Norse society, at least in these texts. Furthermore, we should also not be surprised that the Saami are portrayed as initiating military alliances with other actors than the Norse, particularly the Bjarmar.[71] Regardless, the portrayal of the Saami as contributors to and participants in Norse military contexts carries clear meaning whereby the Saami have military loyalties to the Norse. If these portrayals are based on real life observations, feelings of friendship, loyalties, obligations, allegiances, and camaraderie will have shaped the personal experience of the people fighting together, regardless of their cultural or ethnic background.[72] Returning to Hansen and Olsen's interpretation that *finnkaup* may have functioned as return payment from Saami groups for political protection against hostile groups,[73] the exchange of so-called Saami soldiers to Norse armies could even have worked as a similar type of payment in return for political protection or inclusion in sociopolitical affairs. The presence of these Saami soldiers could also be representative of less politically charged relations, such as the social systems of reciprocity relevant in Norse societies that were dependant on mutual obligations and expectations. In areas where the Saami and the Norse were in close contact or had entered alliances together, these aspects of reciprocity may have been expressed in Saami contributions to Norse armies, and vice versa.

Medieval texts portray personal relationships such as business arrangements, friendships, alliances, apprenticeships, amongst others, between Norse and Saami people. While *finnkaup* is often treated as purely economic, the trading alliances and feelings of loyalty evident in *Egils saga* demonstrate the importance of not underestimating the personal bonds facilitated between business partners. Similarly, I would suggest that the textual predictability of Norse-Saami cohabitation in certain areas such as Hinnøya indicates that shared spatial belonging was common, which is not surprising given the archaeological material discussed below. The por-

---

70 *Hkr 1*, 324. "Hkr 1," 202.
71 Saxo, 343, 651.
72 See for example, *Eg*, 35–36.
73 Hansen and Olsen, *Hunters*, 69.

trayals of Saami people participating in Norse military contexts also indicate social awareness of Saami people as direct contributors to Norse society.

6.2.3 "Fiðrenn svarar": Communication, Language Barriers, and Bilingualism

Despite Norse, a Germanic language, and Saami, a group of Uralic languages,[74] being neither related nor mutually intelligible, there are no reported language barriers between the Norse and the Saami in the saga material or similar as far as I am aware.[75] This is strange and raises questions about communication and language understanding, since after all, Norse and Saami characters are depicted partaking in arrangements where communication will have been key to the creation and maintenance of the relationship. In fact, communication between the groups seem to be entirely unproblematic in the textual sources, as demonstrated by Ingimundr's angry response to the Saami seeress's prophecy in *Vatnsdœla saga* mentioned previously.[76]

The unproblematic nature of communication between the Norse and the Saami across the textual material indicates that communication, despite the expected language barrier, was perceived as possible and/or not a hindrance worthy of mentioning by the writers of these texts. Interestingly, this communication is not always possible with the Bjarmians, whose language sounds like "fuglaklið" [birds twittering] to Oddr and Ásmundr in *Qrvar-Odds saga*,[77] whereas their previous communication with the Saami had been uncomplicated and unremarked on in the text.[78] Ohthere, on the other hand, relates the many stories told to him by the Bjarmar, explaining that the Saami and Bjarmar "spoke practically one and the same language."[79] The portrayal of communication with the Saami as unproblematic is significant, since it might reflect actual perceptions of communication at the time of writing, or at least the portrayal of a time when communication was possible. Triin Laidoner argues that the linguistic dissimilarity was bound to com-

---

74 Ante Aikio, "An Essay on Ethnolinguistic Prehistory," in *A Linguistic Map of Northern Europe*, ed. Riho Grünthal and Petri Kallio, vol. 266, *Mémoires de la Société Finno-Ougrienne* (Helsinki: Suomalais-Ugrilainen Seura, 2012), 63–117.
75 *Helgisaga*, 16: "Fiðrenn svarar: 'Ef æigi værðr a þessum degi sem ec sægi, þa lat mik slicum dauða dæyja sem þú villt" [The Saami answers: If today does not transpire as I have foretold, then kill me however you see fit].
76 *Vatn*, 30.
77 *Qrv*, 175.
78 *Qrv*, 174.
79 Hansen and Olsen, *Hunters*, 55.

plicate social intercourse and impact the level of trust among the Norse and the Saami,[80] which may have well been the case, but this is not apparent in the texts. Since the sources indirectly claim that Norse and Saami people communicated regardless of the language differences, this communication must have occurred through bilingualism and/or the use of interpreters. Both ways of communication are probable and well documented in the textual material.

Bilingualism is the phenomenon of speaking and understanding two languages. In shared landscapes and sociocultural spaces where Norse and Saami characters often meet, such as in Hálogaland and Upplǫnd, bilingualism was probably the most efficient tool for communication. Potentially, people might have had the ability and knowledge to speak and understand both Norse and Saami languages, using it in everyday situations and contextually swapping between the two. Since no interpreter is present when Gunnhildr stays with the Saami men to learn magic, the stated communication is implied textually as having occurred directly between the characters themselves.[81] Bilingual knowledge might have been grounded in personal relations, for example if Saami was the mother tongue but Norse the dominant spoken language of the group, like for Grímr lóðinkinna at Hrafnista.[82] A similar case is that of Óláfr pái in *Laxdœla saga*, who is reportedly taught Irish from an early age by his Irish mother, later allowing him to communicate with his Irish kin.[83] Therefore, bilingualism seems to have been perceived as possible and useful by medieval Icelandic writers, and this possibility may be reflected in the lack of commentary on Norse-Saami communication.

The language used by a given family could have been interchangeable or varied depending on the overall context. Language plays a prominent part in identity formation, and for cross-cultural families, the choice of spoken language could have been politically motivated. Given the suggested high number of intermarriages and similar close personal relationships appearing in the textual sources as demonstrated previously, the effect of spoken language and communication on large- and small-scale levels between kin groups will have been significant and shaped the worldviews of the group(s). Language could have been passed on to newer generations or used in certain contexts such as during rituals or in more

---

[80] Triin Laidoner, "The Flying *Noaidi* of the North: Sámi Tradition Reflected in the Figure Loki Laufeyjarson in Old Norse Mythology," *Scripta Islandica* 63 (2012): 59–93 (66).
[81] *Hkr 1*, 135–36. *Mesta 1*, 8–10. *Fsk*, 79. We can assume that Gunnhildr speaks Norse to Eiríkr blóðøx, and it is reasonable to suggest that her character, or the Saami men she stays with, had bilingual skills (Norse and Saami).
[82] *Ket*, 123.
[83] Einar Ól. Sveinsson, ed., *Laxdœla saga*, Íslenzk fornrit 5 (Reykjavík: Hið íslenzka fornritafélag, 1934), 27, 57.

mundane everyday expressions. The (briefly) previously mentioned (footnote 107, chapter 5) twelfth-century Icelandic spade with the inscription "boat tiat," interpreted as the North Saami verb *boahtit* (to come), could potentially be understood in this light, or as an expression of identity or descent.[84] Bilingual knowledge may have also been acquired specifically for professional contexts, enabling the communication reported during the many descriptions of *finnkaup* as well as in contexts where the Saami function as ritual performers. Moreover, receptive bilingualism – when a language is understood but not spoken, might have been a useful and efficient tool for many people, especially in areas of repeated but limited contact. It is not unlikely however, that in the creation of so-called blended social milieux, a sort of mixed language was spoken, with influence from both Norse and Saami.

Another useful language strategy could have been the usage of interpreters, enabling a common understanding of meaning despite initial and distinct differences in language structure. Interpretation is a translational activity, and an interpreter is a person working as an intermediary across language barriers, transferring meaning (orally) and context (subjectively) from one language to another. Interpreters would have been bilingual and were conceivably people from Norse-Saami families, in turn making people from blended families desirable in this context (among others) as linguistic mediators. In the aforementioned episode in *Ǫrvar-Odds saga*, a Bjarmian man functions as an interpreter between the Bjarmians and Oddr's crew, utilising the language confusion of the Norse to his favour in order to trick them.[85] The tenth-century Arab traveller Ahmad ibn Fadlān reportedly used an interpreter whilst visiting the Volga "Vikings," again demonstrating that the people inhabiting Fennoscandia and beyond were familiar with the practice of interpretation.[86] I therefore propose that people from mixed Norse-Saami backgrounds could specialise as interpreters and profit from it. These could be the people that characters like the *Snæfriðarsynir* and Finnr litli were based on.

Although Norse and Saami languages were unrelated, some language loans have occurred and should be expected considering the close proximity of Norse and Saami societies.[87] While the traditional focus of scholarship was on the study of Norse loan words in the Saami languages, recent research creates a

---

84 Kendra Willson, "A Putative Sámi Charm on a 12th c. Icelandic Spade: Runic Reception, Magic and Contact," in *Finno-Ugric Folklore, Myth and Cultural identity*, ed. Cornelius Hasselblatt and Adriaan Van der Hoeven (Groeningen: University of Groeningen, 2011), 267–81 (277–78).
85 *Ǫrv*, 176.
86 Paul Lunde and Caroline Stone, eds., *The Land of Darkness: Arab Travellers in the Far North* (London: Penguin Group, 2012), 54.
87 See Hansen and Olsen, *Hunters*, 79–81.

more balanced picture whereby loans have occurred in both directions.[88] Nevertheless, the fact that the Scandinavian languages might have been affected by the Saami languages is still a sensitive topic for many.[89]

While earlier sources portray uncomplicated communication between the Norse and the Saami, an extract from an Icelandic encyclopaedic manuscript from 1387 relates a marked change in the representation of language comprehension.[90] Here, a priest from Hálogaland sailing with tradesmen to "Finnmarkar" communicates with the Saami through interpreters:

> i hverium stad margir Finnar komu til þeira til kaupstefnu, svo sem sidur ær til, ok haufdu hvorertveggiu ser tulka, þviath Finnar þeir, á enda Finnmarkar allt nordur vidr Gandvik, æru allir allheidnir ok hafva adra tungu en ver Nordmenn.[91]
>
> in each place many Saami people came to their markets, as is the custom, and they each had their own interpreters, since the Saami that live in [Finnmarkar] all the way north to Gandvik, are all heathen and speak a different language than Norwegians.

Although interpretation was a probable communication tool used in contexts between the Norse and the Saami prior to this, the extract is the first direct mention of the need for such tools. In my opinion, this marked need for an interpreter could stem from the sociopolitical changes involved in the governance of the Norwegian kingdom. These changes increasingly moved the context in which Norse-Saami relations occurred from mainly based on similarities and common understanding into more isolated groups as a result of the growth of the Norwegian state and the colonisation of Saami areas. While it is not clear whether the statement "haufdu hvorertveggiu ser tulka" [they each had their own interpreters] refers to the priest and the tradesmen each bringing interpreters, or the priest and the Saami each bringing interpreters, the latter interpretation would be indicative of high levels of distrust between the Saami groups and the priest. Archaeologically, the later medieval period is marked by a decrease and then disappearance of culturally fluid material and more striking Saami identification markers, possibly referring to the marked differences between Norwegian and Saami people follow-

---

88 Tove Bull, "Samisk påverknad på norsk språk," *NOA* 27, no. 1 (2011): 5–32 (6–9). Jurij Kusmenko, "Sámi and Scandinavians in the Viking Age," *Scandinavistica Vilnensis* 2 (2009): 65–94 (89).
89 Bull, "påverknad," 8.
90 Arnamagnæanske samling, "AM 194 8vo, f.34r-f.35r," handrit.is, https://handrit.is/en/manuscript/imaging/da/AM08-0194#page/34v++(87+of+124)/mode/2up.
91 Ian McDougall, "Foreigners and Foreign Languages in Iceland," *Saga-Book* 22 (1986–89): 180–234 (217).

ing the societal changes imposed by Norse and Novgorod-driven geopolitical forces.[92]

Although language is rarely uncomplicated, the textual material portrays Norse-Saami communication as straightforward. In my view, the unproblematic nature of Norse-Saami communication in the source material, despite the distinct differences between the languages, is significant and should be read as indicating the normalised presence of Saami people in Norse society. Minimally, the textual representations of Norse-Saami communication as hassle-free suggests that communication was perceived as possible by writers and their audience. I would argue that if the goal of the writers was to alienate the Saami from the Norse or if this was the social reality at the time of composition, more focus would be laid on the reported language differences.

6.3 Both, and: Liminal Identities and the Archaeological "Inbetweeners"

In my opinion, the portrayal of normalised Norse-Saami relationships in the sources contextualises culturally fluid characters and demonstrates that expressions of identity and sense of belonging were negotiable factors, at least textually. Characters with both Norse and Saami connections materialise as mediators between worlds, emphasising a sort of cultural "middle ground" and the many cultural expressions of blended families and/or spatial groups. The emphasis of this "cultural middle ground" or so-called "inbetweeners" has already been established by archaeological scholars adopting postcolonial methods and anthropological theories of cultural belonging and identity formation.[93] Through these interpretations, alternative identities have emerged in the archaeological record. It is nevertheless important to acknowledge that the established dualism between two large Fennoscandian cultural groups is not a random construction, and that archaeological, textual, and linguistic sources demonstrate certain defined distinctions between the Norse and the Saami.[94] To some extent, these distinctions allow archaeologists to sometimes use expansion of Norse settlement as a counterfactor to Saami settlement, although this approach is criticised for skewing the archaeological past in

---

92 Hansen and Olsen, *Hunters*, 65.
93 See section 1.3.
94 Marte Spangen, "Coast as Meeting Place for Believes [sic] and Traditions: Silver Hoards in North Norway," in *Kystkultur: Aktuel arkæologi i Norden*, ed. Anna Beck et al., Kontaktstencil, vol. 44 (Copenhagen, 2004), 88–93 (86–87, 89, 92).

favour of Norse settlement.[95] In my opinion, this dualism is already well represented across the scholarly fields, both previously and at present. Nevertheless, I think Norse and Saami cultures should be read as a spectrum, both in the textual and archaeological material, with room for both distinctly different cultures, as well as cultural overlap, depending on context, degree of contact, and levels and nature of interactions. Inga Malene Bruun shares this notion, stating that:

> Iron Age and early medieval northern Norway can only roughly be understood as consisting of two ethnic groups with different practices, ways of life and resource exploitation. Within these groups there existed different subgroups and there were interactions across these cultures.[96]

As becomes clear in chapter 7, I argue that the different subgroups and cultural interactions observed by Bruun in the Northern Norwegian archaeological material were also present elsewhere in Fennoscandia. In treating Norse and Saami cultures as forming parts of a spectrum, we allow for the acknowledgement of Norse and Saami cultures as different cultural entities whilst simultaneously also allowing for regional variation, degrees of cultural blending, and less easily categorised groups between this polarity. Instead of debating whether the recorded material, be it textual or archaeological, is either Norse or Saami and thereby obscuring signs of groups with alternative identities, it can be more productive to interpret some of the material as "both, and."[97] Such an interpretation also allows for the concept of fluid spatial awareness suggested in section 4.2.1. The following sections contextualise the personal relationships discussed in section 6.2 through an investigation of the evidence for Norse-Saami cultural blending in the archaeological material and some possible strategies adopted by these "unsolidified" cultural groups.

6.3.1 Blended Archaeology and Blended Social Milieux?

Inger Zachrisson's schematic map of Nordic (horizontal) and Saami (vertical) culture in the eleventh century (figure 5), based on archaeological material, demonstrates that a large geographical area of Fennoscandia can be interpreted as an in-

---

95 See Spangen, "Coast," 87.
96 Inga Malene Bruun, *Blandede graver: blandede kulturer? En tolkning av gravskikk og etniske forhold i Nord-Norge gjennom jernalder og tidlig middelalder* (MA diss., University of Tromsø, 2007), 84. My translation.
97 Bruun, *Gravskikk*, 84.

terface between Norse and Saami people early in the medieval period. Tying these maps to my own map based on the textual representation of toponymy (figure 3), it becomes quite evident that the presence of blended cultural groups in medieval Fennoscandia should be expected. According to Marte Spangen, it is in these interface zones that we should be particularly conscious about looking for signs of Norse-Saami fluidity in the early medieval period.[98] The maps compare quite well to the personal relationships portrayed across the textual source material, which highlights northern Norway, the Dovre-mountain range, Østerdalen, and Hadeland in Norway, and Jämtland in Sweden. The occurrence of fluid cultural expressions in more southern localities is discussed in chapter 7, and the following section mainly focuses on northern Norwegian conditions.

The map above reflects the archaeological record and is therefore based on archaeological finds that display more or less typical Norse and Saami features, or a mix of both. Norse features are characteristically associated with farmsteads, longhouses,[99] boathouses, burial mounds/cairns, objects with southern and western continental influences or origin, and are typically located by the outer coast and on the islands.[100] Saami features are characteristically associated with the scree burial and birchbark swaddles, round houses, hunting facilities like reindeer fences and pitfall systems, bear graves, sacrificial sites at "unique" places in nature, and objects with eastern influences or origin.[101] Numerically, the Saami grave material generally displays an even distribution of men and women, with children receiving the same treatment as adults.[102] The apparent equal early medieval Saami burial traditions contrasts typical Norse burials, where men form the majority and women and especially children are underrepresented in the archaeological material.[103] Another typical feature of the Saami archaeological record is that it is most often found in inland areas and the inner fjord, appearing increasingly towards the outer coasts (on the Norwegian and Swedish sides) further north. However, the Saami archaeological record is less visible in the landscape than the Norse record, in addition to being overlooked both previously and pres-

---

98 Spangen, "Coast," 86. Other identities may have also formed, especially at cultural interfaces with other peoples (Bjarmar, Finnish and Russian peoples, etc.).
99 Marte Spangen and Johan Eilertsen Arntzen, "Sticky Structures and Opportunistic Builders: The Construction and Social Role of Longhouses in Northern Norway," in *Re-Imagining Periphery: Archaeology and Text in Northern Europe from Iron Age to Viking and Early Medieval Periods*, ed. Charlotta Hillerdal and Kristin Ilves (Oxford: Oxbow Books, 2020), 11–32 (14–24).
100 Spangen, "Coast," 86–87. Bruun, *Gravskikk*, 30–33.
101 Spangen, "Coast," 87. Bruun, *Gravskikk*, 27–30.
102 Bruun, *Gravskikk*, 30, 49.
103 Bruun, *Gravskikk*, 32.

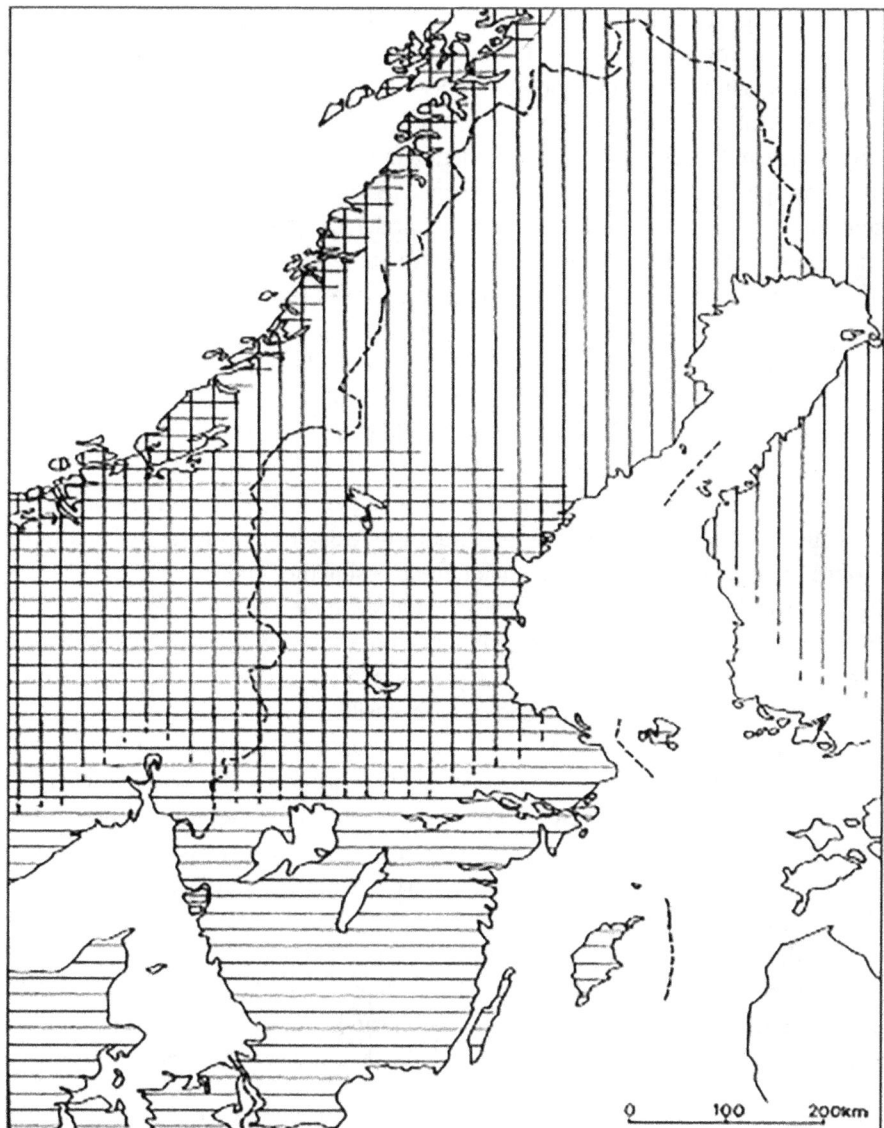

Figure 5: *Schematic picture of the distribution of Saami (vertical) and Norse (horizontal) archaeological culture, c. 1000 by Inger Zachrisson, from* Möten i gränsland: Samer och germaner i Mellanskandinavien, Monographs 4 *(Stockholm: Statens Historiska Museum, 1997), 219.*

ently in the national historical and archaeological narrative (at least in areas south of modern day Finnmark), and the Saami record is therefore underrepresented in archaeological studies. In addition, while these features are stereotypically associated with the traditional Norse or Saami archaeological identity markers, they are not always decisive or rigid and can appear as mixed. Marte Spangen and Johan Eilertsen Arntzen note that both Norse and Saami house structures vary considerably in size and form, depending on function and location, and that it is "not viable to define specific house shapes as unanimously representative of one cultural [...] context."[104] Similarly, Bruun claims that the archaeological record in northern Norway appears so mixed that it is almost entirely unhelpful to use the typical features mentioned previously to "separate" Norse and Saami culture.[105] Nevertheless, it is through the appearance, incorporation, and overlap of features with both Norse and Saami stereotypical identity markers that more alternative identities and fluid cultures emerge.[106] While the categorical features should be treated with caution, they are very helpful for the identification, or even validation, of alternative and culturally fluid identities.

Marte Spangen's previously mentioned interpretation of the northern Norwegian silver hoards as expressions of a dual Norse-Saami identity actualised in interface areas demonstrates the value of emphasising the fluidity of the archaeological record.[107] Silver hoards are interpreted as a Norse tradition and are common in the archaeological record throughout Scandinavia, the Baltic Sea, and the British Isles, and seem to have been particular common between the tenth and twelfth centuries.[108] The hoards usually consist of hacksilver, coins, and ornaments, intentionally deposited with no apparent connection to graves or similar. Spangen notes that the northern Norwegian silver hoards differ from the stereotypical hoard in that they mix both western and eastern ornaments, with the eastern ornaments displaying clear Saami associations, as well as being found outside of core Norse and Saami areas. She accentuates five early medieval hoards found in Troms that are particularly interesting, where four are found in scree contexts, emphasising the dual cultural expression through the combination of the Norse tradition of hoarding with Saami elements like the scree deposition and eastern ornaments.[109] The possible background for this combination can be interpreted as based on identity negotiation in a time of change and is further discussed in section 6.3.2.

---

104 Spangen and Arntzen, "Longhouses," 14–15.
105 Bruun, *Gravskikk*, 39.
106 See for example Spangen and Arntzen's discussion, "Longhouses," 27–29.
107 Marte Spangen, "Silver Hoards in Sámi Areas," in *Recent Perspectives on Sámi Archaeology in Fennoscandia and North-West Russia*, ed. Petri Halinen et al. (Helsinki: Finnish Antiquarian Society, 2009), 94–106 (103).
108 Spangen, "Coast," 88.
109 Spangen, "Coast," 91.

A parallel to the mixed composition of the silver hoards is Gerd Stamsø Munch's interpretation of the archaeological finds from two localities just south of Bodø, dated to the eleventh and twelfth centuries. Archaeological excavations at Vestvatn (Misvær) and Eiterjord (Beiarn) in the early 1960s revealed remains of houses and signs of farming, interpreted as typical features of Norse presence, in addition to eastern artefacts carrying strong Saami associations such as bronze objects and bone tools, and the sighting (but not excavation) of possible round turf-houses.[110] Stamsø Munch therefore concludes that the finds indicate Norse "habitations with a marked [Saami] influence [...] as the [Saami] certainly have travelled wide in these tracts and thus easily may have acted as intermediaries."[111] In my opinion, there is also a strong possibility that the finds from Vestvatn and Eiterjord can be read as expressions of mixed Norse-Saami identity and the traces of the living spaces of blended families.

Grave material has proved to be useful in the search for culturally fluid identities in the archaeological record.[112] In her Master's dissertation, Inga Malene Bruun presents a schematic analysis of thirteen selected northern Norwegian graves with mixed grave material, dated from around the year 0 to approximately 1250. Through her analysis of these graves, with locations in Nordland (five), Troms (six), and Finnmark (two), she highlights the fact that "cultural blending," *i.e.*, the mixing of Norse and Saami archaeological identity markers, is traceable on an individual level in female, male, and children's graves.[113] Furthermore, she claims that the burials with blended features might have been reserved for specific individuals within society, but that these belonged to a group of people from within the same social milieu.[114] This social milieu might have been formed by people with both Norse and Saami affiliations, such as the characters discussed in chapter 6.2 and the people living at Vestvatn and Eiterjord.

Fluid archaeological expressions are particularly visible in and around the Tromsø area, and several scholars argue that the area seems to have been a hub for cross-culturalism early in the medieval period.[115] As previously mentioned,

---

110 Gerd Stamsø Munch, "Funnene fra Eiterjord i Beiarn og Vestvatn i Misvær," in *Viking*, ed. Bjørn Hougen and Arne Skjølsvold, Norsk arkeologisk årbok, vol. 31 (Oslo: Norsk Arkeologisk Selskap, 1967), 99–122 (117).
111 Stamsø Munch, "Beiarn og Vestvatn," 119.
112 See Johan Eilertsen Arntzen, "En sen vikingtids våpengrav med østlige trekk fra Løding, Bodø k," *Arkeologiske Undersøkelser Tromsø Museum: Universitetsmuseet* (2015).
113 Bruun, *Gravskikk*, 49, 84.
114 Bruun, *Gravskikk*, 84.
115 Bruun, *Gravskikk*, 51–53. Astrid Mellem Johnsen, *Troms som etnisk sammensatt grenseområde ca 600–1600* (forthcoming PhD thesis, University of Tromsø).

the area around Tromsø emerges as something of a liminal stage or border between Norse and Saami cultural groups. The abundance of a fluid archaeological record in the area is therefore not surprising, since it is precisely in interface areas that fluid cultural expressions are most common. Nevertheless, this "social milieu" was probably quite widespread, especially in Hálogaland and in the southern areas discussed in chapter 7. The culturally fluid two-person grave found on Helløya just north of Bjarkøy and dated to 700 intimately combines Norse and Saami elements through the ornament styles in what is presumably a female burial: the deceased was found with fragments of two oval brooches, probably the most familiar component of Norse female fashion, as well as a bronze pendant shaped like a bird's foot, of Finno-Ugric import, probably the most familiar component of Saami female fashion.[116] Inger Storli reads the grave in relation to Norse and Saami marriage alliances, but does not account for the other remains in the grave.[117] The other remains were found together with a spinning whorl of soapstone and some iron fragments.[118] The close proximity to Bjarkøy is interesting in relation to the Hálogaland power centre on Bjarkøy, and helps contextualise Þórir hundr's different types of interactions with Saami people, although there is admittedly substantial chronological distance from the grave to the stories about Þórir.[119] Nevertheless, perhaps Þórir's winters spent with the Saami did not occur too far from home after all.

Another example of such a blended social milieu is the well-known and often-discussed Skjoldehamn-grave, found on Andøy. The grave itself is dated to the latter half of the eleventh century and points to the culturally fluid burial of a high standing person with ties to both Norse and Saami society.[120] The grave is, in my opinion, one of the most telling examples of the intimate relationships between Norse and Saami people in the early medieval period. The burial revealed the remains of a short 40–50-year-old person with a coastal diet, swaddled in birchbark, and wearing an outstandingly well-conserved tunic with a metal belt with hanging tin beads and pearls, a hood, and shoes made from skin with colourful woven ribbons, laid on a reindeer skin. Six surrounding burial mounds, from approximately the same time, conform to a Norse context, but the costume found in the burial indicates a strong Saami connection:

---

116 Bruun, *Gravskikk*, 51.
117 Inger Storli, *"Stallo"-boplassene: Spor etter de første fjellsamer?* (Oslo: Novus, 1994), 113.
118 Bruun, *Gravskikk*, 51.
119 *Hkr* 2, 344–45.
120 Svestad, "Skjoldehamnfunnet," 133, 146–47. The dating is based on radiocarbon dating of the costume.

judging from the characteristic features of the outfit, being the shoes, anklets, and the tin-buttons, -pearls, and -rings, the find points to Saami affiliation.[121]

The Saami affiliation is also strengthened by the birchbark swaddling, the usage of sinew-thread, and the reindeer skin. Svestad hypothesises that because of the strong Saami identity markers in the burial and the surrounding Norse context, the burial might have belonged to a Saami person buried by Norse people.[122] The thoughtfulness and care awarded the burial indicates that the person buried was important to the people left behind. Svestad argues that this importance is reflected in the hanging metal belt that potentially indicates a person with magical expertise. However, the remains could also have belonged to a person with deep ties to the inhabitants of the area, if they were not an inhabitant themselves – which I think is just as likely – potentially a spouse, a parent, a friend, an ally, or a partner.

The culturally fluid material discussed here reflects a diverse and versatile Fennoscandian society early in the medieval period. The material is significant since it demonstrates that the cultural borders between Norse and Saami people, at least in certain areas, were less rigid than often assumed. In my opinion, the archaeological material supporting the notions of so-called blended social milieux can function as reflections of the liminal identities portrayed in the textual material. However, these milieux were not isolated to northern Norwegian conditions, which I emphasise in chapter 7.

6.3.2 Common Ground: Religion, Ritual, and Reorganisation of Identities

Since Saami and Norse people were closely connected through different levels of interactions, they must have had knowledge and perceptions of each other's particular lifestyles and belief systems. Several scholars have pointed out that a significant basis for these close connections was that Norse and Saami peoples shared central religious features allowing for common understanding and mutual respect.[123] Features such as spirit journeys, shapeshifting, weather magic, animal spirits, and personifications of nature, magical clothing, and weapons, in addition to aspects connected to ecstatic ritual performance, are connected to both Norse and Saami belief systems in the textual and archaeological material and, if reflections

---

121 Svestad, "Skjoldehamnfunnet," 146–47. My translation.
122 Svestad, "Skjoldehamnfunnet," 148.
123 Svestad, "Skjoldehamnfunnet," 194. Hansen and Olsen, *Hunters*, 50–51. Else Mundal, "Sami Sieidis in a Nordic Context?," *Journal of Northern Studies* 12, no. 1 (2018): 11–20 (11–13).

of actual ritual performances, will have provided some common ground during different types of interactions.[124] These shared features can, according to my understanding, contextualise the trips made by (seemingly) Norse characters to Saami groups when learning magic and the invitation of Saami characters to perform magic rituals during (seemingly) Norse ceremonies across the textual material.[125] However, following the large-scale conversion to Christianity, the common ground between Norse and Saami people through these shared features was removed.[126] In light of this, archaeologists have proposed that parts of the blended Norse-Saami archaeological material discussed here might actually reflect strategies of cross-cultural societies and/or blended families, who rather than converting to Christianity chose to reclaim their pre-Christian identities and associate themselves more closely with Saami culture.[127] This section will examine this strategy, and whether it appears in the textual material.

In the aforementioned *Eiðsivaþingslǫg* and *Borgarþingslǫg*, the law codes covering the eastern Norwegian inland and the area around the Oslo fjord, there are prohibitions on believing in the magical powers of the Saami and on seeking the Saami out specifically for acting on these beliefs.[128] Both law codes were written in a Christian context for Christian people, indicating that following the conversion, Christian people (Norwegians, Saami, and people from blended families) still sought out the Saami for magical help and participated in Saami ritual ceremonies.[129] The conversion to Christianity was closely connected to the employment of new social structures of centralisation and the growth of the nation state under the rule of a single (royal) person. Spangen notes that the harsh measures to obtain these large-scale sociopolitical changes was mainly directed at the Norse population, whereas the missionary activity among the Saami was not intensified until after the Reformation.[130] In areas of shared landscapes and of frequent cultural overlap, converted Norwegians or people reluctant to convert might therefore have chosen to associate themselves with the Saami to reclaim parts of their pre-

---

[124] See section 3.2.1. For the archaeology of some of these features, see Neil Price, *The Viking Way: Magic and Mind in Late Iron Age Scandinavia*, 2nd edition (Oxford: Oxbow Books, 2019), 217–71.
[125] Like during the previously mentioned stay of Gunnhildr with Mǫttul and during the ceremony with the Saami seeress at Ingimundr's farm, *Fsk*, 79. *Vatn*, 30.
[126] Traditionally, the Saami were not subjected to large-scale conversion until after the Reformation. However, this will have been subject to regional variation; Mundal, "Sieidis," 18.
[127] Spangen, "Hoards," 103. Svestad, "Skjoldehamnfunnet," 134.
[128] *NGL 1*, 371, 389–90. See section 2.4.1.
[129] *HN*, 62–63. See also section 3.2.1.
[130] Spangen, "Hoards," 103. There is evidence that Saami people across Norway converted, either voluntarily or by force, to Christianity in the medieval period, as discussed in section 3.2.

Christian identities.¹³¹ In doing so, they may not have been identified as Saami by more uniform Saami communities, but it would be adequate to be identified as Saami by agents of the nation state or the church.¹³²

This reclaiming of a pre-Christian identity may also be visible in the saga material, which principally focuses on the difficulties connected to the conversion of the Hálogaland elite, whose relationship with different Saami groups is emphasised. However, as already stressed, it is important to note that the negative portrayals of Hálogalanders is never directly connected to their relationships with the Saami, but inherently because of their refusal to convert to Christianity.¹³³ The texts do stress that Hálogaland chieftains such as Hárekr ór Þjótta, Rauðr inn rammi, Þórir hjǫrt, and Þorir hundr co-operated with and fought alongside their Saami associates against the Christian kings and in opposition to the conversion to Christianity.¹³⁴ These portrayals of (presumed) chieftains of the past could have been strengthened by observations or current anxieties about people not conforming to Christianity in Hálogaland at the time these texts were compiled. I would argue that it is in precisely this co-operation against conversion and in the wish to maintain the pre-conversion ways of life, that the numerous opportunities for negotiation of identity and cultural belonging in Norse, Saami, and culturally fluid societies becomes clear. In the context of Hálogaland, the wish to maintain a pre-Christian identity was most likely also connected to the rejection of state power and royal authority which affected the previously Hálogaland privilege to *finnkaup*, as discussed in sections 4.2 and 5.2. With this opposition of state power in mind, Marte Spangen and Johan Eilertsen Arntzen notes that in northern Norway, the tradition of building longhouses continued well into the Middle Ages. They see this continuation of the common building tradition in the far north as associated with previous power systems and social organisation like chieftaincies and argue that this continuation was an active rejection of state power and royal authority.¹³⁵

Returning to the re-actualisation of pre-Christian identities, I would suggest that the negotiation of identity and cultural belonging is particularly visible in the previously mentioned elaboration of Eyvindr kinnrifa's story in *Óláfs saga Tryggvasonar en mesta*. The Saami characters only agree to help the childless couple with childbearing after the couple promise with an oath that the child "skal alt til dauðadags þjóna Þór ok Óðni, ef vér megum öðlast þat barn er líf ok aldr hafi

---

131 Spangen, "Hoards," 103.
132 Spangen, "Hoards," 103.
133 See sections 3.2.1 and 4.2.1.
134 *Hkr 2*, 344–45. *Hkr 1*, 326.
135 Spangen and Arntzen, "Longhouses," 29.

til" [shall serve Thor and Odin till the day of its death, and that we may have him when he is old enough].[136] It is interesting that the text explicitly states the Norse pre-Christian gods rather than Saami deities or simply "heathen" gods, something which may have been the limitations of knowledge of the writer[137] and fits in with the overall conversion narrative in chapter 3.2.1. As I see it, however, it is not necessarily the requirement that Eyvindr should devote himself to the Norse gods that stands out in this context, but rather, the demand that he should return to Saami society in adulthood. This fairy tale – like motif may be just that (a fairy tale motif), but it might also be a textual reflection of the archaeological interpretation of fluid grave material such as the Skjoldehamn-burial as representing the choices given to bicultural people to emphasise their Saami identities over their Norse in order to maintain their pre-Christian beliefs. The northern Norwegian silver hoards, as discussed in sections 6.3.1 and 4.2.1, are also interpreted in this light, since they seem to be found in cultural interfaces between areas inhabited by Norse and Saami people and mix material typical of both cultures, and could therefore be expressions of a dual Norse-Saami identity, as Spangen puts it:

> This dual connection may have been a part of the identity of these border groups that had been previously taken for granted, but that was actualized during the process of Christianization in northern Norway.[138]

Within this dual connection offered by blended families and border groups, it is likely that a type of fluid belief system developed that allowed for new ways of thinking and the mixing of both Norse and Saami elements. As stated in section 3.2.1, sociologists claim that people come to think alike when they find themselves in comparable situations, which allows for the blending of "religious" or ritual fields following meetings of cultures. Mundal claims that *Landnámabók* portrays possible evidence for the borrowing of the Saami *sieidi* tradition into Norse culture in Iceland.[139] Here, the Hálogaland-born Eyvindr Loðinnsonr is portrayed as taking land in "Flateyjardal upp til Gunnsteina ok blótaði þá" [Flateyjardal up to Gunnsteinar, and held the boulders there sacred].[140] While I think Mundal's theory of the Gunnsteinar being borrowed from Saami tradition is slightly farfetched since

---

136 *Mesta 2*, 168.
137 The text's emphasis on the pre-Christian Norse rather than Saami deities might have been completely made up, or an outsider's interpretation.
138 Spangen, "Hoards," 103.
139 Mundal, "Sieidis," 15.
140 *Ldn*, 273. *Landnáma*, 104.

the ritual veneration of stones can also be traced in pre-Christian Norse cults,[141] the instance is also included in Hermann Pálsson's list of notices with possible Saami influence. However, Hermann Pálsson does not see the instance as reflecting the borrowing of Saami *sieidi* tradition, but rather in connection with a cult of stone-living spirits also found in other Old Norse texts.[142] Either way, the connection is plausible since it is expected that Norse and Saami people, particularly in areas of cultural interfaces, participated in each other's ritual ceremonies. The connection also highlights the similarities between the belief systems. The *sieidi* interpretation is therefore not entirely unlikely, as discussed in the subsection on Saami ritual performance in 3.2.1, and the *Eiðsivaþingslǫg* does prohibit the belief in "blót" [sacrifice] and "rót" [root of a tree] in a Saami context.[143] I suggest that another potential link to the veneration of a *sieidi*-like figure can be found in the previously mentioned conversion narrative of the Guðbrandsdalr farmers in *Ólafs saga helga*.[144] Here, the destruction of a wooden effigy idolised by the farmers leads to the outpouring of different unwanted animals, directly mirroring the quick decomposition of Snæfríðr's corpse following its removal.[145] The Guðbrandsdalr area falls under the southern region associated with the Saami in Norse sources. It is therefore possible that the farmers had either adapted a form of the Saami *siedi* ritual or that the farmers themselves formed part of a blended social milieu, and as Mundal writes, it is not surprising "that in areas where Norwegians and Sami lived in close contact, Sami cult had spread among their Norwegian neighbours" and vice-versa.[146] Rituals such as the deposition of silver or connected to the veneration of shared idols or deities may have functioned as important symbolic connectors between Norse and Saami people and/or blended families and groups on the borders between norse and Saami cultures.

Considering shared ritual aspects there is a fascinating Norse loan word in the Saami languages. The North Saami word "skeaŋka" means "gift," whereas in Norse, the word "skenkja" means to "serve" (a drink) or to "pour."[147] Ceremonial drinking played a significant role in Norse rituals as well as in the creation and mainte-

---

141 The cultic place name "hǫrgr" is a good example of pre-Christian Norse cults connected to stones, since it translates as stone-circle, scree or cairn.
142 Hermann Pálsson, *Úr landnorðri: Samar og ystu rætur íslenskrar menningar* (Reykjavík: Bókmenntafræðistofnun Háskóla Íslands, 1997), 81.
143 Marte Spangen, *Circling Concepts: A Critical Archaeological Analysis of the Notion of Stone Circles as Sami Offering Sites*, Stockholm Studies in Archaeology 70 (Malmø: Holmbergs, 2016), 40–42. See section 3.2.1.
144 See section 3.2.1.
145 *Hkr 2*, 189. *Ágr*, 5–6.
146 Mundal, "Sieidis," 18.
147 Hansen and Olsen, "Hunters," 76.

nance of political alliances and friendships, social phenomena upheld by the pouring and sharing of drinks and symbolic gift exchange.[148] Audhild Schanche therefore proposes that a language loan from the Norse "pouring a drink" to the Saami meaning "gift" suggests that ceremonial drinking and subsequent gift exchange played an important role in the formal exchanges between Norse and Saami people.[149] In my opinion, Schanche's interpretation is very convincing, and several meetings between Norse and Saami people in the saga material revolves around the sharing of drink. When King Haraldr is first introduced to Snæfríðr, she reportedly offers him a cup of mead (following the Norse protocol of greeting a guest), and in the stories relating Sigurðr Slembidjákn's stay with the Saami boatbuilders, their sharing of drink is emphasised.[150] Although these are textual instances, ceremonial drinking may have contributed to the solidification of personal relationships such as romantic interactions, friendships, and alliances between the groups in real life, as it also did in Norse contexts.[151]

The Norse and the Saami shared central religious features that allowed for a common understanding, in turn enabling the participation in and contribution to each other's respective ritual ceremonies. Following the conversion to Christianity, this common ground was gradually lost and archaeologists have interpreted some of the mixed Norse-Saami archaeological material as reflections of strategies of Norse or bicultural people to increasingly associate themselves with Saami identities in order to maintain a pre-Christian identity.[152] I suggest that these strategies are also visible in the textual material, particularly in the eastern law codes prohibiting Norwegians from seeking out and believing in Saami magic. Furthermore, I would argue that the portrayal of Hálogalanders relying on their Saami associates in the "fight" against Christianity should be read as knowledge of similar strategies of leaning on Saami affiliates in the reclaiming of their pre-Christian identity.

---

148 Lisa Turberfield, *Intoxicating Women: Old Norse Drinking Culture and the Role of Women* (PhD thesis, University of Aberdeen, 2016), 31, 99–100. See also Spangen and Arntzen, "Longhouses," 28–29.
149 Audhild Schanche, *Graver i ur og berg: Samisk gravskikk og religion fra forhistorisk til nyere tid* (Karasjok: Davvi Girji, 2000), 305.
150 *Ágr*, 5. *Hkr 3*, 311.
151 Turberfield, *Intoxicating Women*, 31.
152 Spangen, "Hoards," 103. Svestad, "Skjoldehamnfunnet," 134.

6.4 Conclusion

This chapter argues that Norse-Saami personal relationships are visible in both the textual sources and in the archaeological material. To allow for the acknowledgement of Norse and Saami as being two distinct entities as well as allowing for regional variation and cultural blending, I have chosen to interpret Norse and Saami cultures as forming parts of a spectrum. In addition, I chose to develop the archaeological interpretation of blended Norse-Saami material as expressions of culturally fluid identities or identity strategies into a framework suitable to interpret the texts. Through this framework, I understand expressions of identity, sense of belonging, power structures, and communication as negotiable factors in the creation and maintenance of Norse-Saami personal relationships. I would argue that these negotiations are visible in the textual material through the portrayal of characters associated with both Norse and Saami descent or connections, like the Saami "princess" Hvít, but also seemingly Norse characters like Gunnhildr, and characters conveying an expressed dual identity like Eyvindr kinnrifa. These characters and their possible archaeological counterparts (for example individuals buried with culturally fluid grave goods) may have functioned as mediators between worlds, conformed to different contexts, and purveyed liminal identities that had consequences both on individual and group levels, related to social network, lifestyle, language, ritual, customs, and traditions. I therefore propose that the Othering of such characters can be understood as a literary tool used to portray liminal identities and the different identity strategies of blended Norse-Saami social milieux. Returning to the Othering-discussion of Saami characters that I predominantly connect to the anxieties associated with non-Christians, an interesting link could be drawn to the interpretation of fluid archaeological material as reflections of strategies adopted by people in interface areas to associate themselves with Saami culture in order to re-actualise their pre-Christian identities. To conclude, I suggest that both the textual and archaeological material should be read as representations of practical relationships between people living in close proximity to each other, including conflict-solving measures, which are indications of the normalised presence and social and spatial belonging of the Saami in and to societies we would consider "Norse."

Chapter 7: Saami in the South: Sources and Societies

7.1 Introduction

Saami presence further south than the traditional northern Fennoscandian landscapes discussed in sections 4.2 and 4.3 is portrayed surprisingly often across medieval texts. While Saami presence in more southern landscapes should not be surprising,[1] the failure to mention this prevalence in the secondary literature is. Despite the prevalence of Saami actors in southern contexts, the exclusive association between the Saami and the far north has often been adopted by scholars focusing on the Saami in Norse society, leading to the overall assumption that Saami people of the medieval period were foreigners confined to "exotic arctic snowscapes" who did not contribute to Norse society.[2] This assumption leads to a lack of attention to the sources mentioning Saami people in the south, in addition to a scholarly inability to challenge the colonial claim that the Saami were not present in southern Scandinavia until later in the early modern period.[3] Through this interpretation, the dichotomy between the Norse and the Saami is fully realised, visible in the tendency to neglect the Saami in historical research as well as in more direct statements like Jeremy DeAngelo's interpretation:

> The *Finnar* [Saami], for their part, appear to be especially allergic to the areas in which the Norse subsist [...] they are never associated with towns or southern locales in the sagas, but rather remain in the dark forests of the north and east.[4]

Following the initiation of the *Sörsamiska projektet* led by Inger Zachrisson in 1984, archaeological research has increasingly pointed to the continuous presence of Saami people or people with Saami ties in what today forms the traditional

---

[1] Minerva Piha, *Eteläsaamelaiset rautakautisessa Pohjolassa: Kielitieteellis-arkeologinen näkökulma*, Scripta Lingua Fennica Edita 498 (Turku: Painosalama, 2020), 7.
[2] Neil Price, *The Viking Way: Magic and Mind in Late Iron Age Scandinavia*, 2nd edition (Oxford: Oxbow Books, 2019), 193.
[3] Håkon Hermanstrand et al., eds., *The Indigenous Identity of the South Saami: Historical and Political Perspectives on a Minority within a Minority* (New York: Springer, 2019), 50–51.
[4] Jeremy DeAngelo, "The North and the Depiction of the 'Finnar' in the Icelandic Sagas," *Scandinavian Studies* 83, no. 3 (2010): 257–86 (272).

South Saami area, as well as south of this, from before the Viking Age.[5] Regardless of the archaeological and historical material pointing towards a culturally diverse southern Fennoscandia, the overall academic community[6] and the general public still tend to uphold the association between Saami people and the far north, sometimes directly disregarding the evidence that point to Saami presence in the south prior to the early modern period. In this chapter, I challenge this commonly perceived "exclusive" historical association by focusing on the archaeological and textual material that indicate Saami presence in the south in the medieval period. Before going into this material, however, the intricacies of the politics concerning Saami presence in southern contexts will be problematised.

7.2 Politics, Pre-History, and the South Saami

The common perception of the South Saami (Indigenous) area today stretches from Saltfjellet in Nordland county to northern Hedmark on the Norwegian side, and in Sweden, most South Saami people live in Västerbotten, Jämtland, Härjedalen and Dalarna (figure 6).[7] The South Saami group differs from other Saami groups on linguistic grounds, in ornamentation and traditional clothing, building customs and other cultural expressions, as well as in subsistence strategies.[8] From a state point of view, the South Saami geographical area is defined by people speaking South Saami (Åarjelsaemien). Language is not the most considerate identity marker, since only a fraction of South Saami people today master the language and Åarjelsaemien is listed as "severely endangered" on UNESCO's list of languages in danger.[9] Recent political and cultural campaigns focused on the preservation and continuation of the Saami languages, particularly South Saami, have, nevertheless, fostered some increase in the amount of South Saami speakers.[10] Because South Saami peoples have lived and continue to live in a wide area, South Saami peoples have been seriously subjected to colonising strategies like forced assimilation into Norwegian or Swedish majority society and to external stress factors like the *fram-*

---

5 Hege Skalleberg Gjerde, *Sørsamisk eller førsamisk? Arkeologi og sørsamisk forhistorie i Sør-Norge: en kildekritisk analyse* (PhD thesis, University of Oslo, 2015), 14.
6 *I.e.*, historians or archaeologists not preoccupied with matters relating to the Saami.
7 Hermanstrand et al., *South Saami*, 6–7.
8 Hermanstrand et al., *South Saami*, 23–24.
9 UNESCO, "UNESCO Atlas of the World's Languages in Danger," Unesco.org, http://www.unesco.org/languages-atlas/index.php.
10 Sámediggi, "Hjertespråket," https://sametinget.no/sprak/hjertespraket-vaajmoegiele-vajmo-giella-vaibmogiella-utredningen/.

rykningsteori discussed in section 1.2, which rejected South Saami presence and historicity prior to the 1500s. This subsection will quickly summarise the politics of South Saami pre-history, since it is crucial to be conscious of colonial remnants still lingering in the narration of Saami history in southern contexts today.

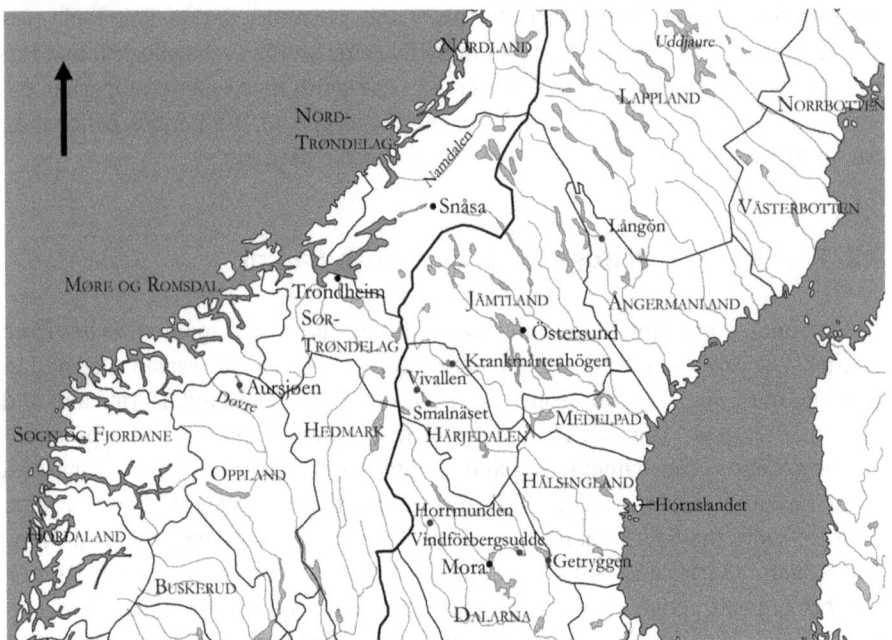

Figure 6: *Map of the South Saami area by Carl-Gösta Ojala and Karin Bengtsson, in Carl-Gösta Ojala,* Sámi Prehistories: The Politics of Archaeology and Identity in Northernmost Europe, *Occasional Papers in Archaeology 47 (Västerås: Edita Västra Aros, 2009), 142.*

Being a minority within the minority, the telling of South Saami history is inherently political and claims to historicity are intertwined with legal and cultural protection within a given area. From the end of the nineteenth century to the end of the twentieth century (1980s), aforementioned factors like Social Darwinism and Yngvar Nielssen's accepted *framrykningsteori* presupposed that the Saami were a static people and that the South Saami population had been early modern settlers in the regions south of northern Trøndelag in Norway and adjacent areas in Sweden.[11] As Hege Skalleberg Gjerde poses, South Saami pre-history was therefore for

---

11 Yngvar Nielsen, "Lappernes fremrykning mot syd i Trondhjems stift och Hedmarkens amt," in *Det norske geografiske selskaps årbog*, vol. 1 (1889–90).

a long time seen as contradictory within both historical and archaeological research.[12] As mentioned in the introduction, a significant factor behind the marked change in interpreting and narrating the medieval history of Saami peoples, especially in southern contexts, was a result of the debate between Knut Bergsland and Jørn Sandnes in Historisk Tidsskrift throughout the 1970s.[13] The most significant factors in this discourse were Bergsland's argument that both Norwegian and Swedish medieval documents referred to the presence of Saami peoples in southern contexts, and Sandnes' support of the *framrykningsteori* and his understanding that there was no proof of any "Finnmǫrk" south of Hálogaland.[14] While their discussions were significant and led to the development of historiography, it in no way settled the debate on Saami historicity in the south.

The idea that the South Saami people were early modern or modern settlers in regions south of Trøndelag is unfortunately still a prevailing cultural notion, also within historiography. This prevalence contributes to the exclusion of Saami history in large regions, since Saami history prior to the sixteenth and seventeenth centuries is not viewed as relevant for these areas. The reluctance felt by both researchers and others to acknowledge Saami historical presence south of northern areas have "served as support for colonialism,"[15] and has also been used in court decisions regarding Saami rights to land such as the Norwegian Trollheimsak in 1981 and the Swedish Härjedalsdomen in 2002. In 2007, the Norwegian Official Report put forward by Samerettsutvalget II (Saami Law Committee)[16] used historical and archaeological research to clarify Saami nature use and judicial situation from Hedmark to Troms.[17] The committee found that the *framrykningsteori* was "very hard to support based on the [historical and archaeological] evidence."[18] The theory is, nevertheless, still weighted heavily in the cultural debate, particular-

---

12 Gjerde, *Sørsamisk eller førsamisk*, 15.
13 Knut Bergsland, "Om middelalderens Finnmarker," *Historisk tidsskrift* 49, no. 4 (1970): 365–409; "Synsvinkler i samisk historie," *Historisk tidsskrift* 53 (1974): 1–36. Jørn Sandnes, "Om samenes utbredelse mot sør i eldre tid," *Historisk tidsskrift* 52, no. 3 (1972): 113–37; "Sørsamenes eldre historie igjen," *Historisk tidsskrift* 53 (1974): 415–21.
14 See Bergsland, "Synsvinkler," 12–13. Sandnes, "Om samenes utbredelse," 121, 133.
15 Hermanstrand et al., *South Saami*, 50.
16 The Saami Law committee is a state-appointed committee tasked with clarifying the relationship of the Norwegian state to Saami culture and legal status. The committee was first appointed in 1980 as a response to the Alta controversy in the late 1970s, and secondly in 2001 to clarify Saami rights to land and water south of the county Finnmark.
17 Jon Gauslaa and Bjørn Bjerkli, "Samisk naturbruk og rettssituasjon fra Hedmark til Troms," Norges Offentlige Utredninger 14, 03.12.2007 https://www.regjeringen.no/no/dokumenter/nou-2007-14/id584312/.
18 NOU 14, 42.

ly in areas where rights to land and water are contested.[19] The inclusion, or lack thereof, of Saami people in the three-volume history of the Trøndelag region published in 2005,[20] is also worth mentioning since the controversy around the compilation illuminates the problems surrounding nation state historiography that unconsciously or consciously neglects the Indigenous population. The compilation received criticism from academics and Indigenous communities, both prior to publication and after, based on the neglect to include the South Saami in the *longue durée* history of Trøndelag and the resistance to include alternative Saami histories.[21] Leiv Sem emphasised the ideologies behind the decisions to disregard the South Saami in the history-telling of the region:

> The fundamental limitation of the depiction of the Saamis in the text as a whole is not a question of sources. Rather it is a question of the narrative and rhetorical structure of the text, and by extension: of the ideologies of the discourse of the historical community.[22]

Sem emphasises the power within considering the presence of a marginalised group and then choosing to ignore or neglect it, rather than finding alternative ways of narrating this group's history.[23] Jostein Bergstøl and Gaute Reitan made a similar remark in 2006, when they requested more focus on South Saami history as a wholesome and fully valuable entity in itself, so that not every piece of work on the topic has to use up big parts of the content "just" to argue for Indigenous presence.[24]

It is worth discussing the aforementioned view that treats the appearance of Saami people in southern contexts in texts from the 1500/1600s as indicative of a sudden shift in Saami population patterns (the *framrykning*). Rather than questioning this "sudden" emergence of Saami people in the south, we should question why there was a sudden need to write about Saami peoples in these areas. As Bergsland has noted, the early modern texts often treated as proof of the *framrykning* of the South Saami people are predominantly legal in nature and related to complaints regarding land conflicts and hunting rights.[25] These complaints, Bergs-

---

19 Tore Østby, Hanne Magga and Sara Kristine Bransfjell, "Hva var rasistisk ved Selbu Utmarksråd sitt møte?" Rørosnytt, 09.06.2019 https://rorosnytt.no/hva-var-rasistisk-ved-selbu-utmarksrad-sitt-mote/?fbclid=IwAR2h7DZVLzqmS6pFsvGkAwlm32TG50UZ67sx96haYC7R2mMLSlZdiabmdqI.
20 Ida Bull, ed., *Trøndelags historie*, 3 vols (Trondheim: Tapir akademiske forlag, 2005).
21 Leiv Sem, "Om framstillinga av sørsamar i *Trøndelags historie*," *Heimen* 54, no. 2 (2017): 130–44.
22 Sem, "Om framstillinga," 130. My translation.
23 Sem, "Om framstillinga," 143.
24 Jostein Bergstøl and Gaute Reitan, "Samer på Dovrefjell i vikingtiden: et bidrag til debatten omkring samenes sørgrense i forhistorisk tid," *Historisk tidsskrift* 87 (2008): 9–27.
25 Bergsland, "Synsvinkler," 28.

land argues, should be seen as reflections of the popularisation of firearms among Norwegian farmers in the early modern period which led to an increased usage of mountainous resources. In turn, the use of firearms led to a conflict with the Saami people who were already present in the region, who had previously been the primary appropriators of the mountainous resources.[26] This clash was then reflected in legal texts relating the complaints of farmers wishing to appropriate resources previously dominated by the Saami. I find this theory persuasive, especially since the medieval texts discussed in section 7.4 indeed indicates the presence of Saami peoples in southern regions prior to the early modern period.

Increasing interest directed towards the South Saami people in public history narratives like Leif Braseth's *Samer sør for midnattsola* (2014), the multi-authored *The Indigenous Identity of the South Saami: Historical and Political Perspectives on a Minority Within a Minority* (2019), and the funding for a new and modern building for the South Saami museum and cultural centre *Saemien Sijte* in Snåsa (commenced in 2020) contributes to the strengthening of South Saami historicity.[27] Similarly, the launch of the website *Gaavnoes.no* ("that which exists") in 2018 forms part of the attempt to digitise South Saami history and make it more accessible to both Indigenous communities and others.[28]

As will be elaborated below, archaeological excavations of possible Saami material cultures in southern Fennoscandia have been paramount in the strengthening of South Saami historicity, since it has helped illuminate the likelihood of pre-early modern presence of Saami people in the south, especially in areas where a (perceived) lack of historical sources has been used to reject Saami presence. Section 7.4 challenges this perception by emphasising the source material listed in chapter 2 that alludes to Saami presence in the south. It is, however, important to accentuate that while the archaeological material record and the textual material may not be based on direct historical portrayals of the people known today as South Saami, these portrayals could form the early roots of what later developed into the South Saami identity. Whether or not the material can be successfully "categorised" as pre-Saami, South Saami, Saami, culturally fluid or Norse, it is nevertheless important that as academics, we are conscious of the inclusion of Saami people in southern contexts in our narration of history today, since it directly impacts current political debates and notions of Indigeneity.

---

26 Bergsland, "Synsvinkler," 26–28.
27 Leif Braseth, *Samer sør for midnattsola: Sørsamenes forhistorie, kultur og levemåte* (Bergen: Fagbokforlaget, 2015). Hermanstrand et al., *South Saami*. Saemien Sijte (website), https://saemiensijte.no/.
28 Sørsamisk Digitalt, "Gaavnoes" (website), https://gaavnoes.no/.

7.3 A South Saami Archaeology?

The archaeological bias, whereby there has been a tendency to overlook the Saami archaeological record on the grounds of lingering colonial structures, has been particularly relevant in southern contexts. However, archaeological source material became an increasingly important tool in the telling of a South Saami pre-history from the 1980s with Inger Zachrisson's excavations at Vivallen in Härjedalen (Sweden).[29] The interdisciplinary Norwegian-Swedish project *Sörsamiska projektet* initiated in 1984 sought to answer whether there were Saami people in Jämtland, Härjedalen, and Hedmark early in the medieval period, with the excavation of Vivallen and Zachrisson's interpretation of it as part of a South Saami settlement between 800–1200 being particularly important.[30] Zachrisson noted similarities between the burials at Vivallen with early medieval Saami burial traditions in northern Sweden (particularly stone settings, inhumation graves, and birchbark swaddles), and declared the paradox that had the graves at Vivallen been found in the north, they would have undoubtedly have been categorised as "Saami."[31] The project culminated in the co-authored 1997 publication *Möten i gränsland: Samer och germaner i mellanskandinavien*. Since Zachrisson's excavations of Vivallen, several archaeologists have started focusing on premodern Saami presence in southern regions, through new excavations and finds as well as reinterpretations of older finds as Saami.[32] This material and its research tradition has been summarised and discussed elsewhere, notably in Hege Skalleberg Gjerde's 2015 doctoral thesis. In this section, I will review some of the archaeological material in light of my own analysis.

As mentioned in section 6.3.1, Norse and Saami archaeological categories can be helpful for "identifying" cultural affiliations in the archaeological material. With increasing acknowledgement of medieval Saami presence in southern contexts and a growing distancing from colonial strategies, archaeological finds falling within the Saami archaeological category in the south have been increasingly identified or reinterpreted as representing medieval Saami presence.[33] Archaeologists excavating possible early Saami material in southern contexts have primarily em-

---

[29] Gjerde, *Sørsamisk eller førsamisk*, 14.
[30] NOU 14, 39.
[31] Inger Zachrisson et al., eds., *Möten i gränsland: Samer och germaner i Mellanskandinavien*, Monographs 4 (Stockholm: Statens Historiska Museum, 1997), 117.
[32] Gjerde, *Sørsamisk eller førsamisk*, 14.
[33] Gjerde, *Sørsamisk eller førsamisk*, 15. One previous interpretation was that rather than representing Saami historical presence, the material with similarities to Saami archaeological categories represented an otherwise unknown Germanic/Norse hunting society.

phasised birchbark swaddles, eastern ornaments (especially pendants) or decoration, the so-called (and much debated) hunting-ground graves, trapping systems for hunting,[34] hearth row sites, and sacrificial sites, amongst other archaeological interpretations of recognisable Saami "elements." The "sensational" discovery of several hearth rows dated between years 700–900 at Aursjøen in Lesja (Norway) in 2006 was interpreted by Jostein Bergstøl as a Saami settlement site.[35] Similarly, Hege Skalleberg Gjerde interprets some twenty circular foundations found in Hallingdal (Buskerud, Norway) as traces of possible Saami settlement sites, eleven of which have been dated and span from the year 600 to 1450.[36] Gjerde bases her interpretation on the circular foundations' floor systems, and links them to the traditional Saami organisation of floor space that can be traced to historical Saami settlements.[37] She also emphasises that the organisation and structure of the circular foundation sites differ from typically Norse buildings, and emphasises the clear cross-cultural situation evident in southern Norway.[38] Inger Zachrisson and Elisabeth Iregren also read the traces of settlements surrounding the graves at Vivallen as Saami hearth row sites due to the similar floor organisation to older Saami settlement sites found in northern Sweden.[39] One of the most significant Saami elements for Inger Zachrisson was that some of the buried individuals at Vivallen had been swaddled in birchbark.[40] Another fascinating pointer to Saami affiliation at Vivallen could also, in my opinion, be reflected in the seemingly equal distribution of men, women, and children in the graves, a common feature of medieval Saami burials, as noted in section 6.3.1. Asgeir Svestad notes that some of the pre-medieval (Vendel period) and early medieval burials at Vendel and Valsgärde also contain birchbark, with one grave (Vendel 7) containing a birchbark mat showing significant decorative similarities to a birchbark swaddle found in a Saami grave from

---

34 Hilde Rigmor Amundsen and Kristin Os, "Funnel-Shaped Reindeer Trapping Systems in Hedmark: Saami or Norse?," in *Currents of Saami Pasts: Recent Advances in Saami Archaeology*, ed. Marte Spangen et al., Monographs of the Archaeological Society of Finland 9 (Helsinki: Archaeological Society of Finland, 2020), 16–34 (17).
35 Bergstøl and Reitan, "Dovrefjell," 9. See section 3.5.
36 Hege Skalleberg Gjerde, "Samiske tufter i Hallingdal?," in *Viking*, ed. Ellen Høigård Hofseth and Egil Mikkelsen, Norsk arkeologisk årbok, vol. 72 (Oslo: Norsk Arkeologisk Selskap, 2009), 197–210 (202).
37 Gjerde, "Samiske tufter?," 208.
38 Gjerde, "Samiske tufter?," 208.
39 Zachrisson et al., *Möten i gränsland*, 117–24.
40 Zachrisson, *Möten i gränsland*, 54–60.

Varanger in Finnmark.⁴¹ More curiously, Svestad mentions three burials at St. Clemens cemetery in Oslo, dating from the late 900s to early 1100s, that contained individuals swaddled in birchbark.⁴² These graves, according to Svestad, are seemingly demarcated in the cemetery, and he therefore interprets them as representing a specific type of people, either Saami people or people from a fluid Norse-Saami milieu.⁴³ Single loose finds found in southern contexts like z-shaped leather scrapers, a specific ski-type (Bothnian skis), arrowheads, and jewellery or ornaments with eastern origin, are also often assigned Saami affiliation due to their prevalence in Saami graves in the north.⁴⁴ These loose finds are not unproblematic, and while they certainly demonstrate Saami affiliation, they should not always or unquestionably be read as indicating Saami identity.⁴⁵ They do, however, indicate clear social meaning as associated with the Saami, and the usage of what must have been perceived as "Saami jewellery," for example, either by people identifying as Saami, culturally fluid, or Norse, indicates some Saami influence in these southern areas. As Gjerde writes, the presence of these Saami elements is hardly random.⁴⁶

While Zachrisson repeatedly stresses the South Saami affiliation of the aforementioned material, other archaeologists have demonstrated more scepticism in categorising the material as "only" Saami, and instead focus on the fluidity expressed by the southern material. Camilla Olofsson, for example, claims that the antler deposits of elk and reindeer found at two pre-medieval gravefields in Härjedalen (Krankmårtenhögen and Smalnäset), which Inger Zachrisson has interpreted as representing South Saami burial tradition, are illustrative of:

> the strategies of people who identified themselves just as living on the intersection point between, and interacting with, more distinctively defined Saami and Germanic ethnicities.⁴⁷

---

41 Asgeir Svestad, "Svøpt i myra: Synspunkter på Skjoldehamnfunnets etniske og kulturelle tilknytning," in *Viking*, ed. Herdis Hølleland et al., Norsk arkeologisk årbok, vol. 80 (Oslo: Norsk Arkeologisk Selskap, 2017), 129–56 (142).
42 Svestad, "Skjoldehamnfunnet," 142.
43 Svestad, "Skjoldehamnfunnet," 142–43.
44 Gjerde, *Sørsamisk eller førsamisk*, 167–83.
45 Gjerde, *Sørsamisk eller førsamisk*, 183.
46 Hege Skalleberg Gjerde, "Tilfeldig? Neppe: Finsk-Ugriske smykker i Sør-Norge," in *Viking*, ed. Britt Solli, Zanette Tsigaridas Gjørstad, and Egil Mikkelsen, Norsk arkeologisk årbok, vol. 73 (Oslo: Norsk Arkeologisk Selskap, 2010), 49–60: 58–59.
47 Camilla Olofsson, "Making New Antlers: Depositions of Animal Skulls and Antlers as a Message of Regeneration in South Saami Grave Contexts," *Norwegian Archaeological Review* 43, no. 2 (2010): 97–114 (111).

Within this intersection, Olofsson sees the first signs for a dawning South Saami identity.⁴⁸ Personally, I find Olofsson's interpretation of the later development of South Saami identity within this intersection of more pronounced Norse and Saami cultures particularly useful, especially given the prevalence of culturally fluid characters in and around the same landscapes as expressed in the textual material discussed below. I therefore agree with Hege Skalleberg Gjerde, who emphasises that:

> The [fluid] archaeological material can in fact also contribute to the telling of a South Saami pre-history by multiplying it, for example by demonstrating the variations of "Saaminess" in time and space.⁴⁹

Jostein Bergstøl writes that the attempts to "reduce the material so that it can be assigned to one or two known ethnic groups can contribute to the simplification of the complexity and dynamic present in ethnic processes."⁵⁰

A good example of the benefits of reading items categorised as either Norse or Saami in light of more dynamic cultural relations, is the famous *vietjere* found in Rendalen in Hedmark (figure 7). A *viejtere* is a typical Saami object similar to a hammer used for beating on the *gievrie* (South Saami for ritual drum) by a ritual performer during ceremonies, as mentioned in section 3.2.1. The traces of iron on the Rendalen-*vietjere* have been dated to the 1400s, but the hammer itself is assumed to have been made between 1160–1260. The object is often used as the archaeological epitome of Saami presence in Østerdalen in the medieval period.⁵¹ Gjerde has emphasised the uncertainty of the find context and the ambivalence of the object itself, but she does highlight the significance of the clear Saami ritual usage of the object, in addition to the mixed decoration of the hammer.⁵² The mixed decoration is thought provoking since it illustrates a sort-of Norse-Saami "cultural dialogue" as the hammer is decorated with geometric ribbon ornament that is common in Saami ornamentation from the 1050s onwards,⁵³ and the typically "Norse" Ringerike-style on the other, common in Norse contexts like early

---

48 Olofsson, "Regeneration," 111.
49 Gjerde, *Sørsamisk eller førsamisk*, 229. My own translation.
50 Jostein Bergstøl, *Samer i Østerdalen? En studie av etnisitet i jernalderen og middelalderen i det nordøstre Hedmark*, Acta Humaniora 325 (Oslo: Unipub, 2008), 211.
51 Gjerde, *Sørsamisk eller førsamisk*, 167. It even features on the cover of *Möten i gränsland*.
52 Gjerde, *Sørsamisk eller førsamisk*, 168–70.
53 The ribbon ornament was typical on many Norse objects (pre 1050s), but became a Saami style later. See Gjerde, *Sørsamisk eller førsamisk*, 172–73.

churches and on runestones in the tenth and eleventh centuries.⁵⁴ The third side has an otherwise unknown geometric pattern, and the fourth side has not been carved, suggested as representing a space left for future generations to carve with symbols relevant to them.⁵⁵

Figure 7: Vietjere from Rendalen, by Erik Iregren, "C26831: runebommehammer," KHM (CC BY-SA 4.02).

In my opinion, it is unquestionable that the main function of the hammer belonged within the field of Saami ritual performance. The mixing of otherwise "separate" cultural categories is nevertheless significant, and I would propose that the object should be read as representative of being a connector between Norse and Saami cultures, or created for the people on the intersection of these. Either way, the object shows a kind of intimacy in the integration of the Norse and Saami. With that in mind, it is also possible that the adoption of Norse ornamentation on the otherwise Saami object symbolises a welcoming gesture to Norse neighbours or family members to participate in Saami rituals. I would argue that this strategy should be understood as parallel to the identity strategies reviewed in section 6.3.2, whereby

---

54 Hege Skalleberg Gjerde and Jostein Bergstøl, "Sámi Vikings?," in *Vikings Across Boundaries*, ed. Hanne Lovise Aannestad et al., Viking-Age Transformations 2 (London: Routledge, 2020), 166–78 (172–73).
55 Gjerde, *Sørsamisk eller førsamisk*, 174.

Norse or Norse-Saami peoples could more increasingly associate themselves with Saami traditions in order to maintain their pre-Christian identity and thereby avoid the stress of conversion. The Christianisation of the inner forested parts of eastern Norway is comparable to that of Hálogaland and Finnmǫrk, and took longer than in more central parts of Norway.⁵⁶ Either way, the *vietjere* could signify several different things, but the overall fluidity clearly demonstrates that Norse and Saami people living in Hedmark in the medieval period were in close contact. It should also be noted that the *vietjere's* assumed dating is consistent with that of the composition of the *Eiðsivaþingslǫg*, which would have incorporated the find context and forbids participation in Saami ritual performance.

As discussed by both Hilde Rigmor Amundsen and Jostein Bergstøl, the main archaeological patterns and inherent processes of change suggest that the inland area of southeast Norway was one of several regions constituting both borders and contacts between early Saami and Norse groups.⁵⁷ Despite the conspicuous increased Norse influence on the region of Hedmark in the period before the Viking Age according to the archaeological material, finds that are typically ascribed to either Saami or Norse-Saami traditions like hunting-ground graves indicate that contact with Saami-affiliated groups continued.⁵⁸ Jostein Bergstøl interprets the hunting-ground graves as a product of an independent fluid complex, precisely because they often include a mix of both Norse and Saami cultural identity markers. This is reinforced by the interpretations of Hilde Rigmor Amundsen, who states that in the meeting of Norse and Saami culture in early medieval shared cultural landscapes, "some people could choose to hold a mix of Saami and Norse identities and worldviews."⁵⁹

Joint Norse-Saami ritual performance may also be visible in the remains of what has been interpreted as a sacrificial tree found under the church at Frösön in Jämtland.⁶⁰ The birch tree had received regular animal sacrifices until it was cut down and a church building was constructed on top of it, and the

---

56 See section 6.3.2.
57 Hilde Rigmor Amundsen, "Changing Histories and Ethnicities in a Sámi and Norse Borderland," *Acta Borealia* 34, no. 2 (2017): 178–97 (192). Bergstøl, *Østerdalen*. See also Hege Skalleberg Gjerde, "Common Ground: Saami-Norse Interactions in South Norway During the Late Iron Age and Early Medieval Period," in *Currents of Saami Pasts: Recent advances in Saami archaeology*, ed. Marte Spangen et al., Monographs of the Archaeological Society of Finland 9 (Helsinki: Archaeological Society of Finland, 2020), 149–59.
58 Bergstøl, *Østerdalen*, 188–89.
59 Amundsen, "Borderland," 190.
60 Eva Ryynänen, "*Karjalen Kukkiva Puu (The Flowering Tree of Karelia)* and Continuity Uncovered," in *Sacred to the Touch: Nordic and Baltic Religious Wood Carving*, ed. Thomas DuBois (Seattle: University of Washington Press, 2018), 38.

tree is interpreted in light of the Norse "blót" [sacrifice] tradition.[61] The island of Frösön represents the northernmost inland extension of agrarian society in Sweden in the early medieval period, and the end of the sacrifices by the tree correspond with the erection of a runestone claiming the Christianisation of Jämtland by a so-called Austmaðr, dated between 1060 and 1090.[62] Surrounding the island is a mountainous area inhabited by Saami people today. The animals sacrificed and buried surrounding the tree stump consists of both domesticated animals as well as wild game like elk, squirrel, and bear. This mixing of both wild and domesticated animals in the sacrificial tradition has been interpreted as a reflection of the area's cultural fluidity, where "Norse agrarian religion mixed syncretically with Saami hunter-gatherer livelihoods and religious traditions."[63] Particularly important for this reading of the sacrificial site is the large prevalence of bear among the wild game deposits, and the fact that the bear was buried anatomically correctly in ways reminiscent of the Saami bear burials discussed in section 3.2.3.[64]

While we should be careful of drawing conclusions based on the dichotomy between hunting and agriculture, I would argue that the fluid symbolism evident in the sacrificial deposits should be read as a reflection of a joint ritual space shared by Norse and Saami peoples. In my opinion, this shared ritual is comparable to the silver hoards discussed in section 6.3.1 and 4.2.1 as expressions of a dual Norse-Saami identity actualised in interface areas. However, the erection of the runestone declaring the Christianisation of the area coinciding with the concluded use of the sacrificial tree indicates that the possible Norse-Saami ritual ceased in this specific locality, as opposed to the silver hoards that are interpreted as a response to conversion. Regional variation is not surprising and shared rituals probably continued after the conversion but was expressed differently. Regardless of whether scholars agree that the sacrifices were deposited in a context involving Saami, culturally fluid, or only Norse actors, it is refreshing to see, as well as significant, that possible Saami influence is discussed. Again, these inclusive interpre-

---

61 Ola Magnell and Elisabeth Iregren, "Veitstu hvé blóta skal? The Old Norse *blót* in the Light of Osteological Remains from Frösö Church, Jämtland, Sweden," *Current Swedish Archaeology* 18 (2010): 223–50 (244–45).
62 Magnell and Iregren, "The Old Norse *blót*," 241. Notably, Adam of Bremen writes about a people possibly identifiable with the Saami in the same region in the same period (mid-to-late eleventh century), see section 2.3.2.
63 Ryynänen, "*Karjalen*," 38.
64 Nina Sandberg, *Offerträdet: Spår av offer, blot och kult under vikingatiden på Frösön, Jämtland* (PhD thesis, University of Stockholm, 2016), 15–16. For differences between the tree deposits and Saami bear burials, see Magnell and Iregren, "The Old Norse *blót*," 243.

tations are significant since they emphasise the long historical Saami ties in areas where Saami presence is contested on the basis of *e silentio* conclusions.

The archaeological material discussed previously indicates that people belonging to two cultural affiliations, Saami and Norse, used the same areas and shared landscapes in southern Norway and mid-Sweden in the medieval period. Due to the current political and cultural debates regarding Saami historical claims and thereby rights in southern areas, discussing Saami presence in the south is not unproblematic. In addition, the mixed cultural expressions of the archaeological material often make it problematic to assign certain finds as either Norse or Saami, and there has been an increasing effort from archaeologists working in southern contexts to emphasise the culturally fluid expressions of the material.[65] Narrating Saami history in southern contexts through interpretations of the archaeological material is therefore complicated, and it is precisely in this complication that I believe the value in continuing to emphasise the evidence supporting medieval Saami presence in these areas lie. Having moved away, at least in most academic environments, from having to solely justify Saami presence and oppose Nielsen's theory, it is now the ways in which the Saami identity in these areas have formed through historical processes that lie at the heart of the debate. I would argue that the archaeological material clearly demonstrates a society where both Norse and Saami actors contributed, and that these actors had varying degrees of contact or distance to and from each other. Within this situation, there was room for identity negotiation that enabled so-called "both and"-peoples and culturally fluid societies. An emphasis on fluidity does not take away from either Norse or Saami cultural expressions, but rather, adds to it.

7.4 Saami Characters in Southern Contexts

While the sources associating the Saami with the north are in the majority, they certainly do not stand alone, and several texts mention Saami people in connection with more southern regions. Despite this, when the southern presence of the Saami in medieval texts actually is discussed, the discussion is more often than not based on the premise that the Saami are literary tools of monstrosity or Otherness or that the depictions represent Norse claims to Saami land (which in itself, presupposes Saami presence).[66] In an already small field of studies concerning the Saami in Norse society, the discussion of Saami characters in southern contexts is still a

---

[65] Gjerde, "Interactions," 156–57.
[66] See section 6.2.1.

topic rarely examined. Nevertheless, Else Mundal asserts that the Saami may have been in the majority in some regions and that "even in Southern Norway, in the mountainous districts and in the inland areas less densely populated by Norwegians, the two peoples may have been more equal in number than we usually think."[67] I agree with Mundal's sentiment, but I do not necessarily think that the geographical prevalence of Saami people always have to be founded on a "lack of Norwegians" (or Norse people). Rather, I support the approach taken by some of the archaeologists referred to previously in which material with Saami identity markers in otherwise Norse contexts can be interpreted as signifying Saami or fluid identity affiliation within these contexts. Moreover, the interpretations of some of the archaeological material as culturally fluid can, I would argue, also be transferred to some of textual portrayals of people with Saami ties in southern contexts. In the following section I provide a systematic overview of the medieval textual portrayal of Saami people in southern contexts, followed by a reading of certain portrayals of characters with associations with the Saami Motif-Cluster as possible representations of fluid Norse-Saami societies. I have adapted Hege Skalleberg Gjerde's method of exposing the fragmentation and inconsistency of the archaeological material that makes supporting a uniform and common interpretation of it difficult, in my reading of the textual source material.[68]

7.4.1 Fínmarkr and Saami Dwelling Spaces in the South

While Finnmǫrk is traditionally associated with the north and northeast of Fennoscandia, it is important to emphasise the points stressed in sections 4.2.1 and 4.4. Here, I argue that the sources indicate that the landscape stretched further south than the traditional northern landscape, and that socioculturally, the concept stretched down the Scandes mountain range all the way south to Eiðskogr and the adjacent areas of Vermaland in Sweden.[69] The spatial concept Finnmǫrk (fínmarkr) should then, in my view, be understood as referring to any areas where the Saami lived, rather than as an isolated northern landscape. As will be elaborated here and in section 7.4.2, I therefore assert that certain incidents involving Saami characters located in Finnmǫrk but otherwise conforming to southern contexts should be understood as occurring south of the traditional northern geo-

---

67 Else Mundal, "Sami Sieidis in a Nordic Context?," *Journal of Northern Studies* 12, no. 1 (2018): 11–20 (12).
68 Gjerde, *Sørsamisk eller førsamisk*, 229.
69 See sections 4.2.1 and 4.4.

graphical landscape. Þrǫndalǫg, the Upplǫnd region (Valdres, Þótn, Haðaland, Hringaríki, Dofri, Guðbrandsdalr, Eystridalr, and sometimes Heiðmǫrk and Raumaríki) in present day Norway, and Helsingjaland, Härjedalen, Jamtaland, Járnberaland, and Vermaland in present day Sweden, are landscapes either connected to Finnmǫrk or to Saami characters. These areas coincide with both present day South Saami cultural and political landscapes as well as areas interpreted by certain archaeologists as including culturally fluid and/or Saami material cultures in the medieval period.

It is particularly the central Norwegian-Swedish border forests between the landscapes above that stand out in the textual material, with the previously mentioned description of Norway in *Historia Norwegie* being a good example of this: "tertia siluestris, que Finnis inhabitur, sed non aratur" [the third is wooded and populated by the [Saami], but there is no agriculture there].[70] The text does not comment on latitude and we should therefore not assume a northern connection on the basis of this description. Instead, the lack of agriculture and the population of Saami people in what is referred to as the wooded habitable zone is emphasised. The previously mentioned landscape description in *Egils saga* also alludes to the presence of Saami people in southern borderscapes with a description of Finnmǫrk as stretching from the north down the Scandinavian mountain range.[71] Similarly, the two eastern Norwegian law codes discussed in section 2.4.1, the *Eiðsivaþingslǫg* and *Borgarþingslǫg*, both suggest that Saami people lived in the areas the legal texts covered and the landscapes mentioned above. The laws were most likely employed prior to their composition, with initial composition for the *Eiðsivaþingslǫg* suggested as taking place in the mid–1100s, and the same for *Borgarþingslǫg*, but can only be securely found as remnants in King Magnús lagabœti's reworked *landslov* from 1274.[72] Covering the Oppland and Viken regions respectively, the law codes prohibit travelling to the Saami to ask for divination or participate in Saami rituals.[73] As Hege Skalleberg Gjerde notes, the prohibitions against believing in and seeking out Saami people in these areas are therefore clear testimonies that there was a Saami population that it was or had been very common to receive "magical" help from.[74] The usage of the term *finnmarkr* in the *Borgarþingslǫg* supports this. Indeed, as Mundal writes, the legal codes are thus the hardest sources to discount when the medieval Saami presence

---

70 *HN*, 51–52. The literal translation from the original Latin is that the area in which the Saami live is "not ploughed."
71 *Eg*, 36.
72 *NGL 1*, IX.
73 *NGL 1*, 372, 389–90.
74 Gjerde, *Sørsamisk eller førsamisk*, 48–49.

in southern Fennoscandia is debated.[75] In addition, it should be emphasised that while the legal texts prohibit Christians from seeking out Saami people in these regions for non-Christian purposes like participating in Saami rituals or for divination, neither legal text prohibits seeking out the Saami for other purposes. In my view, this is a strong indication that other more normalised activities such as trade, participation in cultural affairs, communication, and the initiation of personal relationships between Norse and Saami people were common in these areas, at the time of first recorded composition and earlier. It should also be noted that in a significant part of inland eastern Norway (and parts of the same landscape on the Swedish side) the Christianisation process was slow.[76] This slow conversion of the region opens up possibilities for frequent cultural overlap due to shared sociocultural features and identity negotiation between Saami, Norse, and culturally fluid people, as argued in section 6.3.2. The prevalence of Saami characters or allusions to the Saami in this region may therefore be a result of this cultural overlap.

On the Swedish side, a border agreement between Norway and Sweden from between 1268–73 relate the "landamœre [...] mellim Jœmtalandz ok Finmarkar ok Hœlsingalandz" [border between Jämtland, [Finnmarkar] and Hälsingland] and states that Finnmǫrk was between Jamtaland and Helsingjaland, and that some people from Jamtaland had rights to hunt in certain areas of Finnmǫrk.[77] The concept of Finnmǫrk should therefore be understood as adjacent to both Jämtland and Hälsingland, which would also suggest the normalised presence of Saami peoples in these regions since borders rarely function as absolute delineations in the landscapes. Knut Bergsland analysed an early fourteenth-century Swedish border agreement, repeated in the Swedish law of Hälsingland in the 1320s, that points to the northern part of Jämtland still being regarded as Saami territory at this time.[78] Having also investigated placenames with Saami roots in Swedish legal documents from the same period, Bergsland asserts that on these grounds, Saami people must have been present in Jämtland also prior to the fourteenth century. The previously mentioned Tälje-stadgan decree ordered by the Swedish-Norwegian King Magnus Eriksson in 1328 demonstrates that hunting rights in Saami areas had become a conflict in Helsingjaland, stating that neither *Birkarlar* nor Hälsingar should obstruct the Saami in their hunting.[79] As discussed in section

---

75 Else Mundal, "The Perception of the Saamis and their Religion in Old Norse Sources," in *Shamanism and Northern Ecology*, ed. Juha Pentikäinen (Berlin: De Gruyter, 1996), 97–116 (102).
76 As far as I am aware, the first church to be sanctified in Østerdalen was Tynset (1211).
77 *NGL 2*, 490.
78 Bergsland, "Finnmarker," 378–79.
79 Riksarkivet, "SDHK-nr 3558," https://sok.riksarkivet.se/dokument/sdhk/3558.pdf.

2.3.2, Adam of Bremen also attests the presence of a people commonly interpreted as the Saami (Skritefengi) in Hälsingland and also possibly further south in Värmland (the Fenni).⁸⁰ Adam's statement is significant, since it ties Saami presence in these regions back to the 1060s.

Finally, the Härjedalen/Herdalar debate mentioned in section 4.3.2 should be repeated. An instance related in Heimskringla's *Óláfs saga helga* describes King Óláfr Haraldsson's harrying expedition in the Baltic and states that on his return, he harried in Finnland.⁸¹ However, King Óláfr's court poet, Sigvatr Þórðarson, confuses the narrative by mentioning "Herdala," alongside direct references to the Baltic Sea (Eysýsla and Bálagarðssíða) and the placename Finnland. Since "Herdala" is a toponym predominantly associated with the mid-Swedish landscape Härjedalen, Inger Zachrisson has consequently suggested that the instance must have taken place in Härjedalen and not Finland. Erik Norberg builds on Zachrisson's suggestion and claims that "Saint Olav's third battle was an attack against the Saami living in Herdalir – Härjedalen."⁸² As stated in section 4.3.2, I disagree with Zachrisson's interpretation because the description emphasising a starting point sailing in the Baltic Sea, alongside the toponyms, makes it more feasible that the meeting occurred on the coast of Finland rather than in western Central Sweden. However, the term Herdalir is associated with Härjedalen in other sources, where Saami presence in the area is alluded to. *Sverris saga* relates how King Sverrir Sigurðarson travelled with the *birkibeinar* through Vermaland, Järnberaland, Herdalr (sic), and Jamtaland before reaching Þrǫndalǫg in 1177, with the text calling the area now known as Härjeland for Herdalr.⁸³ The text emphasises that the area belonged to the Swedish king, was filled with great forests, and that the people there were not Christians. These non-Christians could have consisted of people conforming to either or both Norse and Saami cultures.

In the early fourteenth-century *Óláfs saga Tryggvasonar en mesta*, Eiríkr hlaðajarl Hákonarson's retinue during the battle of Svǫlðr is related:

> Þar var þá ok með jarli norrænn maðr, sá er nefndr er Finnr Eyvindarson af Herlǫndum; sumir men segja, at hann væri finzkr; svá er sagt, at hann væri fimaztr við boga ok beinskeyttaztr allra manna í Noregi.⁸⁴

---

80 *Hammaburgensis*, 172–73.
81 *Hkr 2*, 11–12.
82 Zachrisson, *Möten i gränsland*, 169. Erik Norberg, "The Meaning of Words and the Power of Silence," in *The Indigenous Identity of the South Saami: Historical and Political Perspectives on a Minority Within a Minority*, ed. Håkon Hermanstrand et al. (New York: Springer, 2019), 65–89 (83).
83 *Sv*, 21.
84 *Mesta 2*, 320.

> With the Earl there was also a northman, Finnr Eyvindsonr from Härjedalen [Herlöndum], who, some say, was of Saami descent. He was reckoned the most skilful archer and the best marksman in Norway.

Herlǫnd is commonly understood as Härjedalen,[85] and the instance therefore associates the Saami with the area of Härjedalen. At the time of conscription then, Saami presence in the area was expected. Consequently, while I do not agree with Zachrisson and Norberg that the harrying undertaken by King Óláfr Haraldsson on his return from the Baltic was interpreted by a medieval audience as taking place in Härjedalen, I agree that Härjedalen is associated with the Saami in other sources, suggesting Saami medieval presence in the area. Considering the archaeological material presented above, this textual association between the Saami and Härjedalen can contribute to present-day political debates concerning land-rights and heritage in the area.[86] It should also be mentioned that other archaic toponyms consisting of the compound *finn* could also in some instances reveal Saami presence in southern contexts in the medieval period. These toponyms have been thoroughly analysed by historian Leiv Olsen in his book *Sørsamisk historie i nytt lys* and will not be repeated here. However, Olsen's final conclusion should be stressed, claiming that the occurrence of these toponyms should be read as indicative of large-scale Saami presence in southern Scandinavia in the time leading up to the early medieval period.[87]

Medieval landscape descriptions suggest Saami presence further south than often assumed in historical research. The emphasis on regions like Upplǫnd and the adjacent Swedish areas correspond to present-day South Saami cultural and political landscapes, as well as areas interpreted by archaeologists as consisting of Saami and Norse-Saami fluid material cultures in the early medieval period. I would therefore argue that it is not surprising that Saami characters often appear in scenes occurring in southern locations, despite other scholars claiming the opposite.[88] The spatial concept of Finnmǫrk does not stand out as the epitome of the far north but rather, and in line with the toponym, as areas where Saami people lived. The usage of the toponym in southern contexts is therefore significant since

---

[85] Leiv Heggestad, Finn Hødnebø, and Erik Simensen, eds., *Norrøn Ordbok*, 5th edition (Oslo: Samlaget, 2012), 264.

[86] Malin Brännström, "The Enhanced Role of Archaeological and Historical Research in Court Proceedings About Saami Land Rights," in *Currents of Saami Pasts: Recent Advances in Saami Archaeology*, ed. Marte Spangen et al., Monographs of the Archaeological Society of Finland 9 (Helsinki: Archaeological Society of Finland, 2020), 177–88 (180–81).

[87] Leiv Olsen, *Sørsamisk historie i nytt lys*, Senter for samiske studier, skriftserie 17 (Tromsø: Senter for samiske studier, 2010), 23–49 (192).

[88] DeAngelo, "North," 272.

it has implications for the reading of these instances, and I would argue that the evidence should be read as representative of actual Saami dwelling spaces in southern contexts.

7.4.2 Saami Characters in the South

The appearance of Saami characters in southern contexts across the texts is occasionally discussed by historians, who predominantly relate the stories concerning King Hálfdan svarti in Haðaland and the meeting between King Haraldr and Snæfríðr in Dovre.[89] Lars Ivar Hansen and Bjørnar Olsen, for example, in addition to emphasising the eastern Norwegian law codes, state that:

> the extent to which the sagas mention (or state the presence of) "Finns" in areas far outside what is traditionally assumed to have been the Sámi settlement area is remarkable. In the *Saga of Harald Fairhair*, we meet Svåse, King of the Finns [Saami], who has a turf hut not far from the king's estate at Dovre. In the *Saga of Halvdan Black*, the Sámi are referred to in the form of a [Saami man] skilled in sorcery in connection with a Christmas feast at Hadeland.[90]

Hansen and Olsen, alongside Else Mundal, are among the scholars who contextualise the southern location in the saga material and assert that the presence of the Saami in southeastern medieval Norway was common.[91] Despite their assertions, however, Hansen and Olsen do not present additional saga material to the stories involving Haraldr hárfagri to strengthen their claim. Similarly, Mundal has on several occasions emphasised the prevalence of Old Norse sources confirming Saami presence south of Trøndelag but neglects to specifically refer to these texts.[92] This is unfortunate since citing these other and apparently numerous mentions of Saami people in southern contexts in Old Norse texts could have significantly strengthened Saami historicity in the south. As argued throughout, the incidents

---

[89] *Ágr*, 4. *Hkr 1*, 91–92.
[90] Lars Ivar Hansen and Bjørnar Olsen, *Hunters in Transition: An Outline of Early Sámi History*, The Northern World 63 (Leiden: Brill, 2014), 98.
[91] Hansen and Olsen, *Hunters*, 99.
[92] Else Mundal, "Coexistence of Saami and Norse Culture: Reflected in and Interpreted by Old Norse Myths," in *Old Norse Myths, Literature and Society: The Proceedings of the 11th International Saga Conference, 2–7 July 2000, University of Sydney*, ed. Geraldine Barnes and Margaret Clunies Ross (Sydney: University of Sydney, 2000), 346–55: "Quite a lot of Old Norse texts [...] place Saamis in this area [south of Trøndelag]," 347; "Sieidis": "we know from Old Norse sources that Sami people lived [...] in this district," 12.

involving Saami people in Heimskringla's *Hálfdans saga svarta* and *Haralds saga hárfagra* are, the way I see it, frequently interpreted by other scholars as literary tools of Othering or as symbolic of the ideologies of the nation state rather than as historical sources for Saami presence in the south. So, while these instances are often discussed within other theoretical frameworks, I would argue that it is also important to emphasise the spatial context offered by the texts. Establishing a foundation for Saami characters in the south, the discussion of the spatial contexts offered by *Hálfdans saga* and *Haraldr saga hárfagra* will be succeeded by an overview of cases in which Saami characters appear in southern contexts across the source material. As far as I know, the following overview will be the first revised list of Saami characters in southern contexts, as represented by medieval texts.

King Hálfdan is described as receiving a Yule banquet in Haðaland in Heimskringla's *Hálfdanar saga svarta*.[93] Today, Hadeland is a district south of the Randsfjord and is located some 50 km north of Oslo, and during the medieval period it was included in the jurisdiction of the *Eiðsivaþingslǫg*. During the banquet, the food mysteriously disappears, and a Saami man is brought to help:

> En til þess at konungr mætti viss verða, hvat þessum atburð olli, þá lét hann taka Finn einn, er margfróðr var, ok vildi neyða hann til saðrar sǫgu ok þíndi hann ok fekk þó eigi af honum. Finnrinn hét þannug mjǫk til hjálpar, er Haraldr var, sonr hans, ok Haraldr bað honum eirðar ok fekk eigi, ok hleypði Haraldr honum þó í brot at óvilja konungs ok fylði honum sjálfr. Þeir kómu þar farandi, er hǫfðingi einn helt veizlu mikla, ok var þeim at sýn þar vel fagnat.[94]

> But in order that the king might ascertain what was behind this event, he had a [Saami man] brought who had knowledge of many kinds, and tried to compel him to tell the truth and tortured him and yet got nothing out of him. The [Saami man] turned insistently to Hálfdan's son Haraldr for help, and Haraldr begged for mercy for him and it was not granted, and yet Haraldr got him away in spite of the king's opposition and himself went with him. They came on their travels to where a nobleman was holding a great banquet and they were apparently given a good welcome there.[95]

There are several important points to take from this incident. I would argue that the most significant point is undoubtedly the outward normality associated with the presence of a Saami man in Haðaland, at least textually, here in Heimskringla dating to the early thirteenth century. The presence of Saami people in Haðaland is also evident in the previously mentioned *Eiðsivaþingslǫg*, which elaborately de-

---

93 *Hkr 1*, 92.
94 *Hkr 1*, 92.
95 Snorri Sturluson, *Heimskringla*, trans. Alison Finlay and Anthony Faulkes, 3 vols (London: Viking Society for Northern Research, 2014), "Hkr 1," 52.

scribes Saami ritual performance and prohibits Christians participating in these rituals.[96] Interestingly then, King Hálfdan inviting the Saami man to the court under the presumption that the Saami man will conjure back the stolen food using magic, is prohibited in the Christian law code of the region, potentially in use early in the twelfth century (and earlier) but at least in writing from the late thirteenth century. In my opinion, both texts should be read as indicative of the normalised and stated presence of Saami people in the area, with Hálfdan's invitation of the Saami man potentially showcasing the motivation behind criminalising such behaviour in the legal text. With this in mind, it could be argued that Hálfdan seeking out the Saami man specifically for help connected to pre-Christian beliefs was used as a literary tool to reflect the dangers of such behaviour. However, this argument does not hold ground, since Hálfdan's son Haraldr is portrayed as helping the Saami man. In fact, the text implies that Hálfdan's treatment of the Saami man is wrong. Indeed, Mundal directly associates the king's death with his poor treatment of the Saami and states that "in all the literary texts in which the Saami are badly treated, those guilty of such bad treatment are the villains in the story or are being punished for their crimes against the Saami."[97] Hálfdan is unquestionably portrayed in a negative light following his poor treatment of the Saami man, represented in the welcoming nobleman visited by Haraldr and the Saami man's revelation that:

> Furðu mikit torrek lætr faðir þinn sér at, er ek tók visst nǫkkura frá honum í vetr, en ek mun þér þat launa með feginsǫgu. Faðir þinn er nú dauðr, ok skaltu heim fara. Muntu þá fá ríki þat allt, er hann hefir átt, ok þar með skaltu eignask allan Nóreg.[98]
>
> An amazingly damaging loss for himself your father made out of it when I took some food away from him last winter, but I will compensate you for it with joyful news. Your father is now dead, and you must go home. You will then get all the realm that he has ruled, and in addition you will gain all Norway.[99]

Here, the nobleman reveals that it was in fact himself that had taken the banquet food, and that the king had been wrong to punish the Saami man for a crime he had not committed. Haraldr is never sanctioned for helping the Saami man, with the events directly leading to his succession as king. It should be mentioned that Haraldr under no circumstances is depicted as participating in Saami ritual performance but interacts with the Saami man socially. Another point to take from the

---

96 *NGL 1*, 389–90. See section 2.4.1.
97 Mundal, "Perception," 106.
98 *Hkr 1*, 92.
99 "Hkr 1," 53.

extract above is that both Haraldr and the Saami man are "vel fagnat" [given a good welcome] when they appear at the banquet. In my opinion, this should be read as indicative of the Saami man having high social standing similar to Haraldr, and that the Saami's appearance at the nobleman's banquet was not deprecated. Although the cultural affiliation of the nobleman is never mentioned in Heimskringla, some scholars read him as Saami.[100] This is probably due to the elaboration of the story in the late fourteenth-century *Hálfdanar þáttr svarta*, where the nobleman Dófri is released by Haraldr from King Hálfdan's imprisonment in a very similar manner as the Saami man was in *Hálfdans saga*, using a "precious" knife given to him by another unspecified Saami man.[101] Dófri then hosts a banquet for Haraldr, similar to the nobleman in Heimskringla, and fosters him for five years. Dófri is never directly described as Saami, however, but is rather described as a "troll" [troll],[102] and I am therefore wary of identifying him as a Saami "representation."

Haðaland is also later tied to Saami presence, with *Ágrip* and Heimskringla's *Haralds saga hárfagra* relating that Rǫgnvaldr reykill, one of King Haraldr's sons with Snæfríðr, lived in Haðaland where he practised *seiðr*.[103] In addition, Haðaland is, as previously mentioned, also included in the regions inherited by King Haraldr's sons with Snæfríðr as related in the abovementioned *Haralds saga*, which I would suggest strengthens the Saami connection with the area.[104] In light of the above, I would maintain that at the time these sources were written, Saami and fluid Norse-Saami people were associated with and lived in Haðaland and the surrounding vicinities.

The stories relating the marriage between King Haraldr hárfagri and Snæfríðr Svásadóttir, as already extensively discussed, state that the events occur at Þoptar (Dofri). Also happening during a Yule feast, *Haralds saga hárfagra* states that "Haraldr konungr fór einn vetr at veizlum um Upplǫnd ok lét búa sér til jólaveizlu á Þoptum" [King Haraldr went one winter to attend banquets through Upplǫnd and had a Yule banquet prepared for himself in Þoptar].[105] Þoptar was a crown estate during the medieval period and is strategically located just before the Dovre mountain passage on the important trading trail connecting Trøndelag to the southeast and later becoming a common stop as part of the pilgrim route to Niðarós. The Dovre region also materialises as consisting of Saami and fluid

---

100 Bruce Lincoln, *Between History and Myth: Stories of Harald Fairhair and the Founding of the State* (Chicago: The University of Chicago Press, 2014), 69, 61–71. Mundal, "Family," 32.
101 *HalfdSv*, 173. This may be Dófri, but the text is unclear as to who this "finnrinn" is.
102 *HálfdSv*, 173. Mundal, "Family," 32.
103 *Ágr*, 4. *Hkr 1*, 138–39.
104 *Hkr 1*, 137.
105 *Hkr 1*, 124, "Hkr 1," 72.

Norse-Saami material cultures in the archaeological record, and it is therefore not surprising that a Norse-Saami meeting is depicted there. Nevertheless, both *Haralds saga hárfagra* and *Ágrip* emphasise that Svási, Snæfríðr's father, explains that he was "þann Finninn er hann hafði ját at setja gamma sinn annan veg brekkunnar á Þoptyn" [the Saami man whom the king had allowed to set up his hut on the other side of the hill at Þoptyn].[106] The Saami, at least Svási, while close to the crown estate (Haraldr and his men later visits Svási's hut), are described as being on the other side of the hill/mountain slope, which indicates some form of differentiation in spatial belonging. However, the dwelling space of Snæfríðr and her father is in fact described in detail and belongs to the same spatial context as that of the king's farm, making it known, visible, and as such, part of a shared landscape.

This shared landscape may also be referred to in the stories about the journeys of the Faroese cousins Sigmundr Brestisson and Þórir Beinisson across the Dovre mountain passage, as related in *Færeyinga saga*, believed to have first been written in its extant form in the early thirteenth century but only surviving in later fragments.[107] The cousins, twelve and fourteen years old, decide to seek service with Jarl Hákon of Hlaðir, and travel to Norway. Beginning their journey in Vík they travel to Upplǫnd and go east across Heiðmǫrk, before heading north and reaching Dofrafjöll, where they get caught in a snowstorm at the start of winter.[108] After some initial difficulties attempting to cross the mountain passage during the storm, the cousins find an isolated farm located in a depression of the mountain where they are taken in by a farmer's wife and her daughter. The farmer himself is later introduced as "mikill vexti ok í hreinbjálfa ok hafði hreindýri á baki" [large of build and in a reindeer-skin coat and he had a reindeer on his back].[109] In *Óláfs saga Tryggvasonar en mesta*, the farmer explains that the cousins had come off the public road passing through Dofrafjöll, and that dwellings were hard to come by on the mountain side.[110] The cousins are later taken in by the farmer, Úlfr, staying with the family for six years while they are taught archery and other skills, and continuously warned not to enter the forest north of the farm. Naturally, the cousins decide to explore the mysterious forest, where they encounter a bear.[111] In a scene resembling the bear hunt episodes analysed within a Saami ritualistic framework in section 3.2.3,[112] the cousins kill the bear by spearing it.[113] However,

---

106 *Ágr*, 4–5. *Hkr 1*, 126.
107 *Fær*, VIII.
108 *Fær*, 21–23.
109 *Fær*, 23.
110 *Mesta 2*, 99.
111 *Fær*, 27.
112 Clive Tolley, "*Hrólfs saga kraka* and Sámi Bear Rites," *Saga-Book* 31 (2007): 5–21.

fearing their foster father Úlfr's reaction that they had gone against his wish, the boys lift the bear upright, fastening its mouth with a pole so that it looks jerked open and ready to attack, similarly to Oddr's strategy in *Ǫrvar-Odds saga*. The cousins then ask Úlfr for help, pretending the bear is still alive. While Úlfr quickly sees through the cousins' trick and reprimands them for fooling him, he later congratulates them on the slaying of the animal. Following this, Úlfr reveals that he is in fact the hunter and archer Þorkell Þurrafrost (dry frost) from Heiðmǫrk, and that he had been outlawed.[114] Although Þurrafrost is never directly mentioned as being Saami in the text, I would argue that the overall allusions to the Saami Motif-Cluster, including the reindeer, the bear hunt, the allusions to winter weather called forth by his nickname, and the pronounced emphasis on his skills, may be indicative of him being portrayed as Saami or affiliated with the Saami. This Saami affiliation is strengthened by the locations Heiðmǫrk and Dofri, that appear as Norse-Saami meeting places throughout the textual and archaeological material. Again, it could also be argued that Þurrafrost forms part of the portrayals of characters with fluid Norse-Saami affiliations in Norse texts, which is further discussed in section 7.4.3. Regardless of whether he should be understood as one or the other, I would argue that the allusions to the Saami Motif-Cluster in the portrayal of the character in addition to the locations enable the possible reading of the character as being associated with the Saami.

Other texts also point to the normalised presence of Saami people in southern contexts in the medieval period. Before going into more southern localities however, I would like to discuss Saami presence as suggested by the textual material in the area around Þrøndalǫg. Given the overall location of the area as south of Hálogaland (and Naumudalr), bordering Jamtaland on the Swedish side and forming parts of Sápmi today, I find it baffling that there are not more mentions in the texts of Saami characters associated with this area. However, I strongly disagree with the common notion that the first written source mentioning Saami people in and around the area of Trøndelag can only be traced to the 1500s. This notion has unfortunately been used to ensure the continuation of refusing Saami presence and Saami rights in the region today on the grounds that their presence is not historical.[115] As Knut Bergsland notes, the area encompassing the *Frostaþingslǫg* "naturally must have included Saami people."[116] His *rekspegn*-theory mentioned in section 2.4.2 is therefore very interesting, and it should also be noted that the

---

113 *Fær*, 27.
114 *Fær*, 31–32.
115 See section 1.1.2. This notion fails to acknowledge that Indigeneity in Norway is not defined by historical presence, but by ILO 169.
116 Bergsland, "Synsvinkler," 24.

Norwegian-Swedish border agreement cited in section 7.4.1 (Jämtlands landskrå, 1268–73), will have also included significant parts of present day Trøndelag.[117]

In my analysis of the source material, I could only find one instance directly associating and locating Saami characters in Þrøndalǫg. In Oddr munk Snorrason's late twelfth century *Óláfs saga Tryggvasonar*, King Óláfr is depicted as visiting a Saami man living in a dwelling in the mountains of Þjálfahellir, an otherwise unmentioned placename located not far from Agdenes at the entrance of the Trondheimsfjord.[118] While it in some ways stands alone, it is an important observation associating Saami people with the Þrøndalǫg region in a source significantly earlier than the 1500s. Nevertheless, there are other allusions to Saami presence or connections to the region of Þrøndalǫg that contribute to challenging the notion that Saami people were early modern settlers in the region. Primarily, I would argue that the overall location of Þrøndalǫg with Hálogaland to the north, its spatial proximity to the mountainous area on the border to Sweden coinciding with descriptions of Finnmǫrk as well as bordering the Dovre mountain range to the south, is consistent with Saami medieval presence. Bearing the spatial context in mind, incidents involving characters portrayed using references to the Saami Motif-Cluster should in my opinion be read as Saami characters or characters connected to the Saami in one way or another. In Heimskringla's *Magnúss saga Erlingssonar*, the description of the *Birkibeinar*-ally Þorfinnr svarti af Snǫs (Snåsa) may carefully suggest Saami identity or cultural affiliation, which his name (*finnr* here meaning Saami) and the location of Snǫs in northern Þrøndalǫg could imply.[119] The connections between the jarls of Hláðir and Saami descent should in my opinion to some extent be read as consistent with Saami presence in and around Þrøndalǫg in the medieval period. The skaldic poem *Háleygjatál* written by Eyvindr skáldaspillir towards the end of the tenth century to honour his patron Hákon hlaðajarl Sigurðarson, traces the lineage of the jarl back to Óðinn's son with Skaði, called Sæmingr.[120] As discussed in chapters 3 and 6, the skiing deity Skaði is often associated with the Saami. The name of Skaði's son with Óðinn, Sæmingr, is thought provoking on the same grounds as the *semsveinar* dis-

---

117 Bergsland, "Synsvinkler," 21–22.
118 *Odds*, 187–90: "finnr einn á hér byggð í fjálli þessu" [a Saami has his residence here in these mountains].
119 *Hkr 3*, 414–16. These suggestions are not the strongest allusions to the Saami Motif-Cluster, but the significance lies in accepting the possibility that the people that characters like Þorfinnr were based on may have been Saami (or that the characters themselves were understood as Saami).
120 Russell Poole, "(Introduction to) Eyvindr skáldspíllir Finnson, *Háleygjatal*," in *Poetry from Kings' Sagas 1: From Mythical Times to c. 1035*, ed. Diana Whaley, Skaldic Poetry of the Scandinavian Middle Ages 1 (Turnhout: Brepols, 2012), 195–96.

cussed in section 2.6.1. Mundal, amongst others, links the name to the endonym "Saami," and argues that the portrayals of Sæmingr in Old Norse sources should be read with the understanding that he represents Saami people.[121] Albeit quite circumstantial given that the jarls originally hailed from Hálogaland, I would nevertheless argue that the expression of Saami descent in the lineage of the jarls and their connection to the Þrǿndalǫg region minimally suggests some associations between the Saami and the region.

Hálfdanar saga Eysteinssonar, a *fornaldarsaga* dated to the fourteenth or fifteenth century,[122] also traces the lineage of the protagonist Hálfdan to Sæmingr. In addition, the introduction of the saga emphasises northern localities like Hálogaland and Naumudalr, which alongside the connection to Sæmingr strengthens the allusions to the Saami. The main story of the saga takes place in southeastern Norway, with the genealogy of Hálfdan's parents supplementing the evidence for Saami dwelling spaces in southeastern Norway discussed in section 7.4.1. Here, the toponym Finnmǫrk is directly associated with areas in Upplǫnd:

> Eysteinn giftist ok fekk dóttur Sigurðar hjartar, er Ása hét. Hennar móðir var Áslaug, dóttir Sigurðar orms í auga. Eysteinn fekk með henni Finnmörk ok Valdres, Þótn ok Haðaland.[123]

> Eysteinn married Ása, the daughter of Sigurðr hjartar. Her mother was Áslaug, the daughter of Sigurðr "snake in the eye." Eysteinn got from Ása's dowry the provinces of Finnmörk, Valdres, Þótn, and Haðaland.

Since Finnmörk here is coupled with the landscapes of Valdres, Þótn, and Haðaland, I strongly argue that the landscape in this case should be understood as adjacent to the other areas mentioned, rather than being read as located in the more traditional northern landscape of Finnmǫrk. Furthermore, my interpretation is complemented by the *Borgarþingslǫg* mentioned above, which also provides evidence of the term *finmarkr* being used to describe Saami dwelling spaces in southeastern Norway. In addition to this, the aforementioned *Eiðsifaþingslǫg*, which these areas would have fallen under the jurisdiction of, also asserts Saami dwelling spaces in the area, again strengthening the southeastern location of Finnmǫrk given to Hálfdan from his wife's dowry. Another indication that reinforces my

---

121 Else Mundal, "The Relationship Between Sami and Nordic Peoples Expressed in Terms of Family Associations," *Journal of Northern Studies* 2 (2009): 25–37 (28).
122 Dictionary of Old Norse Prose, "HálfdEyst," ONP, https://onp.ku.dk/onp/onp.php?v206. The earliest surviving manuscripts are from the mid-fifteenth century, but the saga itself is assumed to be older.
123 Franz Rolf Schröder, ed., *Hálfdanar saga Eysteinssonar* (Tübingen: Max Niemeyer Verlag, 1917), 91.

reading, is the aforementioned partition of King Haraldr's realm to his many sons, granting his Saami sons precisely these areas in *Haralds saga:*

> Snæfríðarsonum gaf hann Hringaríki, Haðaland, Þótn ok þat, er þar liggr til.[124]
>
> To the sons of Snæfríðr he gave Ringerike, Hadeland, Toten and all that belongs to them.[125]

In my opinion, *Hálfdanar saga Eysteinssonar* and *Haralds saga hárfagra* complement the eastern law codes and should be read as clearly associating these areas with actual historical Saami dwelling spaces, in the thirteenth to fifteenth centuries, and possibly both prior to and after this. This association becomes clear in the descriptions of the "stereotypical Saami" character Finnr or Fiðr litli in *Heimskringla's Ólafs saga helga:*

> Maðr er nefnd Fiðr litli, upplenzkr maðr, en sumir segja, at hann væri finnskr at ætt. Hann var allra manna minnstr ok allra manna fóthvatastr, svá at engi hestr tók hann á rás. Hann kunni mana bezt við skíð ok boga. Hann hafði lengi verit þjónostumaðr Hrœreks konungs ok farit opt ørenda hans, þeira er trúnaðar þurfti við. Hann kunni vega um ǫll Upplǫnd. Hann var ok málkunnigr þar mǫgu stórmenni.[126]
>
> There is a man called Fiðr litli [the small], a man from Upplǫnd, [and] some say that he was [Saami] by descent. He was the smallest of all men and the fastest runner of all men, so that no horse could catch him up when running. He was the most skilled of men with skis and the bow. He had long been a servant of King Hrœrekr and often gone on errands for him that needed to be confidential. He knew the routes over the whole of Upplǫnd. He also knew many important men there to speak to.[127]

Finnr litli is here unmistakably portrayed using images from the Saami Motif-Cluster, with both his name, descent, and abilities associating him with the Saami. Finnr's connection to Upplǫnd is emphasised twice, and I find the claim that "hann kunni vega um ǫll Upplǫnd" [he knew the routes over the whole of Upplǫnd] and that he knew many important people across Upplǫnd particularly interesting. While there is no direct evidence of it, I would suggest the possibility of some of these *stórmenn* being leaders or significant contributors to the Saami dwelling spaces or societies in Upplǫnd, in addition to also consisting of important men from more typical Norse societies. That Finnr is described as knowing the routes across Upplǫnd, in addition to having Saami descent or being Saami himself, would indeed indicate that these routes included the Saami settlements of the area. Fur-

---

124 *Hkr 1*, 137.
125 "Hkr 1," 79.
126 *Hkr 2*, 120.
127 "Hkr 2," 77.

thermore, it should be noted that Finnr was in the service of King Hrœrekr, a petty king of Heiðmǫrk, which once again sees the Saami connected to this landscape, as well as associated with Norse royalty. Similarly, the *fornaldarsaga Sturlaugs saga Starfsama*, most likely first composed in the fourteenth century and with the earliest surviving manuscript from c. 1400,[128] relates the presence of "Finnr ein" [a certain Saami] in jarl Hringr of Heiðmǫrk's retinue.[129] In my opinion, both extracts demonstrate a commonly shared assumptions that there were (or had been) many possibilities and opportunities for Saami people in southeastern landscapes of Norse society. Following Finnr litli's description, *Óláfs saga helga* relates that Hrœrekr had been taken captive by King Óláfr and was kept in Túnsberg (Tønseberg), with Finnr by his side, indicating the normalised presence of Saami people in southern contexts.[130] Túnsberg lies at the south of the Oslo fjord and was included in the jurisdiction of the *Borgarþingslǫg*, again pointing to why Saami presence in this very southern area is not questioned in *Óláfs saga*.

The frequency in which the textual source material portrays Saami characters in southern contexts should, I argue, be read as indicative of widely shared assumptions among the compilers of these texts between the twelfth and fifteenth centuries that there was or had been Saami presence in these areas. Interpretations of archaeological material from the same period in the same area support this interpretation of the saga material and demonstrate the importance of actively searching for Saami characters across saga genres. The apparent normality associated with the majority of these Saami characters is striking and demonstrates an intimate social awareness that is not (necessarily always) grounded in mythical portrayals or economic transactions, but rather based on inhabiting a shared interface area over a longer period of time. The sources mentioned above mainly provide more or less normalised, albeit somewhat mysterious, depictions of Saami characters. Since magic is one of the most common textual tropes associated with the Saami however, the pronounced association between the Saami and abilities associated with pre-Christian beliefs is not surprising, and the eastern law codes and *Hálfdans saga svarta* demonstrate that this association was also a genuine anxiety at the time of writing, at least from more high standing and ecclesiastical perspectives. Nevertheless, on more mundane societal levels as portrayed in the texts, this anxiety was not always pronounced and opportunities for Saami characters in Norse society seem to have been multifaceted. Overall, however, I would argue that the most telling outcome of this section is the highlighting of a

---

[128] Dictionary of Old Norse Prose, "StSt," ONP, https://onp.ku.dk/onp/onp.php?v493.
[129] *StSt*, 613. See section 3.2.1.
[130] "Hkr 2," 77.

direct association between the toponym Finnmǫrk and the areas of Valdres, Þótn, and Haðaland as suggested by *Hálfdanar saga Eysteinssonar*. This association, supported by other, notably earlier, texts associating Saami characters with the Upplǫnd region in particular and specifically Haðaland, stands out to me as the most significant indication that the Saami were perceived as dwelling across these southern landscapes in the medieval period. I would therefore argue that the Upplǫnd region should be understood within the same framework of the fluid spatial awareness appropriate for Hálogaland (and to some extent Finnmǫrk) suggested in chapter 4.2.1. Adopting this framework would allow for an interpretation of the Upplǫnd region as consisting of both Norse and Saami societies in the medieval period, minimally in its earlier stages, with varying degrees of contact and separation. I would suggest that to some extent, within the Upplǫnd region, a variety of societies may have existed, such as

– societies that were geopolitically and socioculturally "Norse," but with ties and connections to the Saami people living close by
– societies that were socioculturally Saami but still geopolitically connected to the Norse, or potentially based on an amalgamation of Norse-Saami societies (i.e., more culturally fluid societies)
– societies that were both geopolitically and socioculturally "Saami," but with ties to Norse people living nearby (on both the "Norwegian" and "Swedish" sides)

This interpretation should also be read in conjunction with my proposal in section 6.3 that Norse and Saami cultures can be understood as a spectrum, with room for both distinctly different cultures as well as cultural overlap, depending on context, degree of contact, and levels and nature of interactions. Overall and in conclusion, Saami people appear in southern contexts stretching from Þróndalǫg and the Dofrifjöll in "the north," through the Upplǫnd region including landscapes such as Hríngaríki, Haðaland, and Þótn, all the way south to Túnsberg. These portrayals demonstrate a culturally diverse southern Fennoscandia.

7.4.3 Fluidity and Saaminess

Returning to the framework suggested and adopted in section 6.3, the following section will analyse the possible portrayals of fluid Norse-Saami characters in southern contexts. This framework sees the Othering of certain characters as a literary tool to portray fluid identity expressions, rather than as a way of alienating the Saami in the texts. As demonstrated in the sections above, Saami presence in the south is not at all surprising and it is therefore also not surprising that textual portrayals of blended social milieux may be traceable in southern landscapes associated with both Norse and Saami peoples. Characters portrayed with allusions to the Saami Motif-Cluster may therefore be textual representations of individuals from societies founded on the intersection of Norse and Saami traditions.

I would argue that the stories concerning the mysterious Arnljótr gellini, who offers aid to abducted agents of King Óláfr helgi in Jamtaland, should be read with such an intersection in mind. When escaping their Swedish captors, Heimskringla's *Óláfs saga helga* relates that the agents cut off the foot pieces of some reindeer skins they found hanging in a storehouse and tied them backwards around their feet and fled.[131] After travelling all night through uninhabited areas, they arrive at the small farmstead of the fashionably cloaked Arnljótr, who helps them flee back to Norway:

> Steig hann [Arnljótr] á skíð. Þau váru bæði breið ok lǫng. En þegar er Arnljótr laust við geislinum, þá var hann hvar fjarri þeim. Þá beið hann ok mælti, at þeir myndi hvergi komask at svá búnu, bað þa stíga á skíðin með sér. Þeir gerðu svá [...]. Skreið Arnljótr þá svá hart sem hann fœri lauss.[132]

> Arnljótr fastened his skis. They were both broad and long. When Arnljótr pushed away with the ski-poles, he was far ahead of them. So he waited for them and said they would get nowhere like that, telling them to step onto his skis with him. They did so [...]. Arnljótr slid along [on his skis] as if he was alone.[133]

Seeking shelter for the night in a hut somewhere in Jamtaland, the men encounter a vicious troll woman whom Arnljótr kills. While Arnljótr is never directly stated as Saami, his portrayal as being an exceptional skier ties into the Saami Motif-Cluster. Supported by the anecdotes about the reindeer skins and the troll woman, and the overall Othering of the landscape introduced in the text, the usage of features recognisable as belonging to the Saami Motif-Cluster should, in my opinion, be read as portraying a landscape inhabited by people with connections to Saami societies. These connections may have been based on the mixing of Norse and Saami cultures, and I think it likely that the distinct portrayal of Arnljótr and the landscape of Jamtaland should be interpreted as reflections of fluid societies, rooted in knowledge, reports or even rumours, made by the compilers to emphasise the blurring of cultural lines in this area. Similarly, the descriptions of the hunter Átti inn dœlski, related by two Gautar at the court of the Swedish king, in the

---

131 *Hkr 2*, 259.
132 *Hkr 2*, 259.
133 "Hkr 2," 173–74.

same text as above, should in my opinion also be read as representative of fluid Norse-Saami societies in the Swedish-Norwegian border forests:

> Átti inn dœlski á Vermalandi fór í vetr upp á markir með skíð sín ok boga. Hann kǫllum vér mestan veiðimann. Hann hafði fengit á fjalli svámikla grávǫro, at hann hafði fyllt skíðsleða sinn, svá sem mest gat hann flutt eptir sér.[134]

> Atti inn dœlski of Värmland went during the winter up into the forest with his skis and bow. We declare him the greatest huntsman. On the mountain, he had taken so many skins that he had filled his sledge to the maximum he could haul with it. Then he turned home from the forest.[135]

Here, there are clear allusions to the Saami Motif-Cluster, notably the hunting, archery, and skiing skills, in addition to the notion that he went "upp á markir" [up into the forest] to hunt. The notion is reminiscent of the trading descriptions of *finnkaup* as discussed in chapter 5.2.1, where Norse traders travel, during winter, *á fjáll upp* to Saami settlement areas or marketplaces. As with Arnljótr, Átti is never explicitly identified as being Saami, however, I think the overall description of him fitting into the Saami Motif-Cluster, the location of Vermaland as well as the aforementioned notion of travelling *upp á markir*, are indicative of him being portrayed as connected to the Saami in the text. Comparably to Arnljótr, I would suggest that the portrayal of Átti in this "Saami way" is a reflection made by the compiler(s) to emphasise the blurring of cultural and ethnic lines in the forests between Norway and Sweden. The upper part of Vermaland coincides with some of the southern Saami settlement areas (*finnmarkr*) discussed in sections 7.4.1 and 7.4.2, and it is therefore not unexpected that Átti may have been from a Saami or fluid Norse-Saami society in this area. My reading of both Arnljótr and Átti as members of fluid Norse-Saami societies is strengthened by interpretations of the archaeological material mentioned in section 7.3, suggesting a possible intersection of Norse and Saami material records and thereby fluid cultural traditions in these landscapes. This is, to me, indicative of the fact that there must have been a conscious understanding of these landscapes as what we would now describe as culturally fluid at the time the texts were written, or an understanding that these landscapes had been fluid in the past, reflected in these characters' portrayals and the emphasis on their spatial belonging.

By extending the argument above, it is possible to read other less "pronounced" Saami episodes occurring in southern landscapes associated with both

---

134 *Hkr 2*, 149.
135 "Hkr 2," 96. The story of Átti is used later in the text as a way of explaining the dangers of bravado. This function does not affect my analysis and is not included here.

Norse and Saami people, as representative of fluid Norse-Saami societies. This representation may be carefully alluded to in Heimskringla's *Ólafs saga helga*, when the scattered inhabitants of the large valley Eystri-Dalr in the Heiðmǫrk district are accused of theft by the unpopular district-overseer at a legal assembly:

> Hann kallaði þá men líkligsta til slíkra hlúta ok illbregða, er sátu í markbyggðum fjarri ǫðrum mǫnnum. Veik hann því máli til þeira, er byggðu Eystri-Dali. Sú byggds var mjǫk sundrlaus, byggt við vǫtn eða rjóðr í skógum, en fastaðr stórbyggðir saman.[136]

> He declared the men most likely for this and [other] bad deeds were those who lived in the forest-areas far from other people. He blamed the inhabitants of Eystri-Dalr. This settlement was very scattered, with settlements by lakes or in clearings in the forest, and only in a few places were there larger settlements.[137]

Following the assembly, the *Rauðssynir* Dagr and Sigurðr are accused of the theft but are acquitted by King Óláfr, in turn leading to the deportation of the actual culprit, the district-overseer himself.[138] The abilities of the *Rauðssynir* include dream interpretation, time telling, and character reading, abilities occasionally connected to the Saami Motif-Cluster. Although a short paragraph, the instance is interesting since it juxtaposes the Christian centralised regions with the scattered habitation of the inland regions, with the latter narrated as Othered in the text. Since Saami people are connected to the Heiðmǫrk district elsewhere, and since Saami people often form a major part of the textual juxtaposition between the Christian and the non-Christian, I would argue that the extract can illuminate possible Saami influences on the inland regions of southeastern Norway. As previously argued in sections 3.2.1 and 6.3.2, I would also suggest that the destruction of the wooden effigy venerated by Guðbrandsdalr farmers also related in the same *Ólafs saga helga*, may be interpreted in a similar light where the farmers form part of a blended social milieu. Previously mentioned characters like Þorfinnr svarti af Snǫs and Úlfr (Þurrafrost) may also be textual representations of individuals from a blended social milieu in southern contexts. I would argue, however, that the best representations of so-called culturally fluid individuals in the textual material are the *Snæfríðarsynir*. These are unquestionably linked to both Norse and Saami societies, reflected in their depicted abilities examined in sections 3.2.1 and 6.2.1, and the spatial belonging discussed above. The brothers undoubtedly participate in the Norse "majority" society as it is depicted, but their portrayal certainly suggests that their Saami descent was still relevant or even crucial to their roles within this society.

---

136 *Hkr 2*, 298.
137 "Hkr 2," 200.
138 *Hkr 2*, 299.

This section sees the benefits of using concepts of the Saami Motif-Cluster as a way of identifying characters with Saami ties in southern contexts. The textual material discussed above definitely suggests regional variation in southern landscapes, and demonstrates that at least in certain areas, the differences between Norse and Saami societies were relatively few. I would therefore assert that the texts support the interpretations of the archaeological material discussed above, establishing that some groups or individuals in southern Fennoscandian landscapes found their identity precisely in the intersection between Norse and Saami cultural affiliations. These possibilities for identity negotiation will not have been possible without the presence of both Norse and Saami groups in these landscapes, and the portrayal of culturally fluid characters therefore presupposes and validates the presence of Saami people in these landscapes.

7.5 Conclusion

With the main objective of decolonising the source material, this chapter has demonstrated the many possibilities obtainable in the material for including Saami people in southern contexts in the narration of medieval history. In my opinion, it is clear that regardless of how the source material is read, Saami people or people with Saami ties are visible in southern contexts stretching from Trøndelag, Dovre, Østerdalen, Hedmark, and even Oslo in Norway, and in Hälsingland, Jämtland (particularly Härjedalen), and potentially also Värmland in Sweden. Similar to Saami characters or interpretations of the archaeological traces of Saami people in northern contexts, the source material demonstrates great regional variation, cultural diversity, and few rigid oppositions between the Saami and the Norse.

Most fascinating, I would argue, are the several realities that are visualised across the source material, but especially the outward normality in the textual material of the presence of Saami people in these southern landscapes. I would argue that had Saami presence not assumed to be common in landscapes like the Upplǫnd region, the inclusion of Saami characters and toponyms associated with Saami people as ordinary features of southern landscapes would have stood out to informed audiences as strange. The calling of a Saami man to King Hálfdan's court at Haðaland, the presence of "Finnr ein" [a Saami man] in a Heiðmǫrkjarl's retinue, and Finnr litli's role as loyal to King Hrœrekr and following him from Heiðmǫrk to Túnsberg, is never portrayed as unexpected across the textual material. Their normalised portrayal should therefore, I would strongly assert, be read as indicative of Saami presence in these southern contexts being unquestionable. The increasing focus on interpretations of archaeological material from the medieval period containing Saami identity markers or objects connected to Saami tradition south of Trøndelag determinedly demonstrate that these textual portrayals were not based solely on literary tools relating to the mystification or Othering of a given people of the far north. Rather, I would assert that, strengthened by interpretations of the archaeological material, the texts represent an actual cross-cultural reality where both Norse and Saami people were important players. Displaying the opposite of a rigid society, this chapter has demonstrated that southeastern medieval Norway and the coinciding Swedish areas consisted of both Norse, Saami, and fluid societies with room for identity negotiation and cross-cultural meetings. I would suggest that the textual material reflects this culturally fluid situation, where some characters connected to southern areas associated with the Saami in other contexts, are portrayed using images from the Saami Motif-Cluster. As proposed in chapter 6, it is not beneficial to overly focus on the "either, or" aspects of a character or the archaeological material for that matter, but rather emphasise the prevalence of both Norse and Saami affiliations. When adding the interpretations of the archaeological material mentioned in section 7.3, the sources depict diverse societies with a wide range of different cultural expressions. Lars Ivar Hansen and Bjørnar Olsen write about medieval Saami presence in the south:

> There is reason to remind those who reject and those who defend a Saami presence (here and in other areas) that, just as the Saami economy and social structure changed over time, cultural manifestations and ethnic signals have also varied in time and space. This fact means we need to understand Saami ethnicity [sic] as a dynamic process and not as a readymade category that has either always existed or one which must have arisen as a result of "migrations" [from the north].[139]

It is therefore my opinion that the source material should be read as indicative of the longstanding assumed presence of Saami people in southern Fennoscandian contexts stretching as far south as just north of the Oslo region in Norway and the adjacent Swedish landscapes.

---

139 Hansen and Olsen, *Hunters*, 100.

Reassessing Norse-Saami Relations in the Medieval Period: Conclusion

This book took its starting point in an investigative analysis of Norse-Saami relations. By actively employing decolonising tools to read these relations in medieval sources, the analysis demonstrates how inclusive readings can display the diverse and varied role of Saami people in medieval Fennoscandian society. The study concentrated on an interdisciplinary approach through the comparative analysis of medieval texts, predominantly Norse, and relevant archaeological material from the medieval period. By employing an archaeological framework based on postcolonial methodologies in my reading of the textual presence and appearance of Saami characters in medieval texts, I emphasised the prevalence of Saami presence in the source material and challenged lingering colonial structures or assumptions about the role of the Saami in Norse society. In the spirit of this approach, the book first identified and then actively confronted the academic tendency to exclusively view Saami characters as symbols of the peripheral or magical Other in Norse society and demonstrated the various other possible readings of Saami characters in medieval texts.

Chapter 1 introduced the historiographic background of the research into Norse-Saami relations and how this research developed following the growing recognition of methodologies rooted in postcolonial frameworks and the increased awareness of Indigenous narratives from the 1980s onwards. By investigating the ways in which Nordic colonialism affected Saami peoples from the late medieval period onwards, particularly focusing on the harsh structures of debasement and dehumanisation enforced in the nineteenth century, the chapter demonstrated the deeply rooted colonial constructions still relevant for Saami people, and by extension, research involving Saami people, today. Through a presentation of the research tradition associated with Saami characters in medieval texts, it was argued that the overemphasis, in my opinion, of Saami characters as the exclusive "Other" in medieval texts sometimes hinders an unbiased reading of the material and can contribute to the perpetuation of harmful beliefs associated with Indigenous people. As a result of this, the chapter emphasised the values of employing decolonising tools in research on Saami characters in medieval texts, and how recent interpretations of medieval archaeological material founded in postcolonial frameworks are useful for our readings of medieval Saami characters. It also argued that the active inclusion of Saami characters and Saami presence or influence in our readings of and writing on medieval literature is crucial for the field going forward.

Chapter 2 presented an overview of the pre-modern textual tradition referring to Saami peoples and analysed the various ways Saami people are portrayed in writing from the classical period to the late fifteenth century. The chapter acknowledged the development of textual motifs associated with the Saami in these texts, while simultaneously establishing the diversity and variety inherent in these portrayals. Given this variation, the chapter argued that the emphasis on Saami people or characters throughout the medieval period actively conveys the sociopolitical gravity held by the Saami in both Norse and continental medieval contexts, a view traditionally contradicted in early modern and modern stereotypical views of Saami people.

Chapter 3 explored the textual motifs associated with Saami peoples and characters across medieval texts and contextualised how these textual images, compiled under the umbrella term Saami Motif-Cluster, specifically allude, directly or indirectly, to the Saami, or characters portrayed as Saami. Achieved through a systematic analysis of the textual sources, the chapter recognised the commonly accepted notion that descriptions of Saami characters stereotypically, but not exclusively, include features like magic, encompassing shapeshifting, spirit journeys, weather magic, and magical clothing and weapons, as well as supernatural beings; hunting and archery and forest animals like bears, wolves, and reindeer; winter weather and skiing; sometimes fishing; and sinew-bound boats. The chapter also examined whether there were any recognisable features associated with the appearance of Saami characters, grounded in scholarly assumptions based on two derogatory descriptions from *Ketils saga hœngs*, and concluded that no such correlation is traceable in the source material (with the exception of beauty). The chapter established the common association between Saami characters and the dwelling structure *gammi*, but simultaneously recognised the variation in the portrayal of Saami dwelling structures. The chapter also questioned the often-exclusive academic focus on these aspects, particularly magic and notions of "shamanism," and presented some of the problems inherent with overly focusing on these stereotyped images, concluding with the acknowledgement that more conscious readings employing the Saami Motif-Cluster allow for more multifaceted Saami realities to spring off the pages.

Chapter 4 shifted the focus from general Saami portrayals and considered northern Fennoscandian geopolitics and spatial belonging in the medieval period. The chapter discovered how medieval texts dealing with the Saami, particularly the trade with the Saami, reflected the changing political circumstances, both internally and externally, in northeastern contexts. By analysing the varying portrayals of the historical landscape Finnmǫrk, the chapter established a framework for understanding sociocultural borders as fluid and stated that regardless of potential borders, such borders were never clear-cut delineations between cultures and peoples. The prevalence of this spatial fluidity in the sources was emphasised through the analysis of the textual portrayals of other northeastern groups, and how intricate social processes between these other groups and the Saami are visible in medieval texts.

Chapter 5 elaborated on the portrayal of northern Fennoscandian geopolitics and considered how Norse-Saami trading affairs, or *finnkaup*, are presented in the textual material. The chapter argued that the emphasis in saga material on the conflicts associated with this trade are reflective of perceived anxieties contemporaneous with the time of composition of the texts, concerning both internal processes as well as international affairs affecting the trade. In addition, the chapter challenged accepted historical dogmas and offered an alternative explanation for the nature of the *finnskatt*, and also investigated lesser-discussed trading links to Iceland and England.

Chapter 6 again shifted focus and demonstrated the many opportunities for identity negotiation in medieval Fennoscandian societies. This was achieved through the analysis of Norse-Saami personal relationships as they appear across medieval texts, adapting postcolonial frameworks based on existing archaeological interpretations of certain finds as identity expressions of Norse-Saami cultural fluidity. Culturally fluid characters, *i.e.*, characters assigned both Norse and Saami descent in the texts, were examined, and similar descriptions of characters with no assigned cultural affiliation were interpreted as possible portrayals of people with ties to fluid Norse-Saami societies and liminal identities. The chapter also emphasised the significant social standing of people with ties to both societies and demonstrated the possibilities of reading fluid characters as textual reflections of the different identity strategies available in blended social milieux throughout the medieval period.

Chapter 7 continued the framework set forth in chapter 6. The chapter challenged the commonly perceived "exclusive" association between the Saami and the far north by analysing the textual appearance of medieval Saami presence in southern contexts. This was achieved through a comparative analysis of medieval archaeological material in southern contexts interpreted as having Saami identity markers and the appearance and descriptions of Saami characters across medieval texts set in these areas. The chapter also highlighted the historical and contemporaneous conflicts associated with Indigeneity in the area, and so the main objective of the chapter was to deconstruct and decolonise the source material in order to demonstrate that Saami characters were portrayed as belonging to more southerly landscapes in the medieval period. As such, chapter 7 tied together the overall ambitions of the whole book and demonstrated the many possibilities for reading Saami characters when looking beyond established academic traditions.

The present study has advocated the necessity of incorporating new interpretative frameworks in the reading of Saami characters in medieval texts, particularly Norse ones, and by extension, expanding our knowledge and understanding of Saami groups in medieval Fennoscandia and beyond. This interpretative framework is based on postcolonial methodologies emphasising the value in employing decolonising tools in our study of medieval societies, especially within Norse studies, in addition to being grounded in the view that employing such decolonising tools is crucial and should be standardised in Norse studies, particularly when dealing with Saami characters. Such decolonising measures includes acknowledging the inherent majority culture bias of historiography, especially since "history is important for understanding the present and reclaiming history is a critical and essential aspect of decolonisation,"[1] and actively incorporating minority cultures (past or present) in our readings and consequent dissemination of history. This is specifically important as Indigenous historical actors are often, unintentionally or subconsciously but incredibly efficiently, treated as existing outside of history and as static historical actors,[2] which has also been the case with the Saami in Norse studies. Furthermore, one of the main objectives of the study was to highlight and clarify the role colonialism and lingering remnants of colonial thinking have played, and continue to play, in the narration of the Fennoscandian medieval past, which many scholars of Norse studies today rarely address or are simply unaware of. A result of this approach was the aforementioned proposed framework for reading and narrating Saami characters, and by extension, Saami people, in medieval texts, which includes revisiting previously accepted historical dogmas and confronting the assumptions put forth in these dogmas. As mentioned in the introduction, despite the growing awareness of more neutral Saami and Norse interactions, research committed to investigating the multifaceted relationships between the groups has to date remained small-scale. In addressing this gap in research and accepting the challenge that such a dynamic perspective entails, the present work has led to the exploration of newfound aspects of Saami-Norse relations in the medieval period that Neil Price claimed, some twenty years ago, "at present we can only imagine."[3]

---

[1] Linda Tuhiwai Smith, *Decolonizing Methodologies: Research and Indigenous Peoples*, 2nd edition (London: Zed Books, 2012), 29–30.

[2] Adam Miyashiro, "Our Deeper Past: Race, Settler Colonialism, and Medieval Heritage Politics," *Literature Compass* 16 (2019): 1–11 (9).

[3] Neil Price, "Drum-Time and Viking Age: Sámi-Norse Identities in Early Medieval Scandinavia," in *Identities and Cultural Contacts in the Arctic: Proceedings from a Conference at the Danish National Museum Copenhagen, November 30 to December 2 1999*, ed. Martin Appelt, Joel Berglund, and Hans

In creating space for Saami characters and alternative readings of Saami characters in medieval texts, particularly in Norse narration, the abundant medieval source material addressing the variation of Saami peoples and lifestyles has been highlighted. In addition to the textual motifs inherent in the Saami Motif-Cluster, Saami characters are portrayed as active agents in the narrative and as contributors to Norse society, significantly, in contrast to the accepted notion of the peripheral Other or magical outsider in Norse society. Employing the Saami Motif-Cluster to identify Saami characters or potential Saami characters across the sources also clarified that while the motifs associated with Saami characters in these texts are expected, they are rarely exclusive and Saami characters are portrayed as dynamic. Through my analysis of the source material, Saami characters have emerged as dynamic characters that are portrayed as living lives among, besides, and sometimes distant from the Norse, hunting, herding, fishing, building boats, skiing, holding feasts, and drinking beer or sharing mead, fighting, entering high standing personal relationships, teaching magic, and participating in rituals, communicating, solving, or creating problems, offering help, and as having personal and political ambitions. It is through the emphasis on the heterogeneity of the Saami portrayals, that the tendency for homogeneous portrayals of Saami characters in previous scholarship has been challenged and confronted. Rather than repeating the many ways Saami characters reportedly function as symbols of the peripheral Other or the magic outsider across the source material, I chose to examine the other multifaceted realities offered by portrayals of Saami characters across the texts. Through this examination, it became clear that Saami characters are predominantly treated with respect and as high standing members of society and as embodying valuable attributes like prestige associated with ritual performance, trade, and personal relationships. Simultaneously, I examined whether archaeological material from the medieval period consisting of both Norse and Saami identity markers and interpreted as expressions of cultural fluidity was reflected in the texts. The focus on Saami characters as "more than" expressions of the dichotomy of "Us" versus "Them" also enabled the presentation of these Saami characters as dynamic actors in the narrative, again confronting the (often unintentional) assumption of Saami people as static historical actors. Saami characters or people are portrayed in these dynamic ways throughout the medieval period, which in my opinion should be indicative of these expressions being reflections of reality at the time of composition or as perceptions of past realities. The fact that there is a continued tradition of writing about Saami people from the late ninth century

---

Christian Gulløv (Copenhagen: Danish National Museum and Danish Polar Center, 2000), 12–27 (25).

to the late fourteenth century, I would argue, signifies the continued relevance and significance of Saami peoples throughout the medieval period. Strengthened by interpretations of the archaeological material referred to throughout the book, I suggest that the portrayal and inclusion of deep-rooted ties to Saami people in these texts should not be read as simply historiographic accounts of the past, but also as contemporaneous with the time of writing. Similarly, I would argue that the source material emphasises the dynamic presence of Saami people in Norse society, also in southern contexts.

Primarily, this work demonstrates the value in, and expressed need for, employing decolonising tools in our readings of medieval texts and consequently shows the many varied expressions of Saami characters, and by extension medieval Saami people. Emphasising the heterogeneity of medieval Saami societies as well as incorporating more inclusive readings of Saami characters should not be seen as an obstruction to either past or future scholarship, but rather as a way of further expanding the field of Norse studies and to demonstrate the diversity of medieval Fennoscandia. Neil Price, although in my opinion overly emphasising the dichotomy between "us" and "them," summarises the rewards of creating and disseminating more inclusive narratives of Norse societies:

> Clearly, the creation of a Viking Age [or more broadly: medieval period] in which the Saami are not accorded their due prominence, influence and expanded population distribution, is unjust to Saami people today, who are deprived of their heritage. However, it is *also* a misrepresentation of the Nordic people's history, because a Saami-less Viking Age [and medieval period] distorts their past too.[4]

The present study has demonstrated the benefits of deconstructing historical dogmas and emphasising the many ways possible for reading the source material. The investigation of Saami characters as dynamic actors in Norse society is particularly important since it has direct implications for the present, and simultaneously contributes to the active confrontation of the misappropriation of medieval material and scholarship by harmful organisations that perpetuate the myth of a monocultural medieval Fennoscandia. By emphasising the multifaceted portrayal of what can be read as Saami people or people with Saami ties in medieval texts, strengthened by archaeological material from the same period, this study has demonstrated the normalised, longstanding, spatially wide-ranging, varied, and significant presence of Saami people in medieval Fennoscandia.

---

4 Neil Price, *The Viking Way: Magic and Mind in Late Iron Age Scandinavia*, 2nd edition (Oxford: Oxbow Books, 2019), 196. His italics.

List of References

Primary Sources

Adam of Bremen. *History of the Archbishops of Hamburg-Bremen*, trans. Francis Joseph Tschan. New York: Columbia University Press, 2002.
Andersson, Theodore M., and Kari Ellen Gade, eds. *Morkinskinna: The Earliest Icelandic Chronicle of the Norwegian Kings (1030–1157)*. London: Cornell University Press, 2000.
Arnamagnæanske samling. "AM 194 8vo, f. 34v–35v," handrit.is, https://handrit.is/en/manuscript/imaging/da/AM08-0194#page/34v++(87+of+124)/mode/2up [retrieved 15.09.20].
Arnamagnæanske samling. "AM 727 I 4to," handrit.is, https://handrit.is/en/manuscript/view/is/AM04-0727-I [retrieved 01.09.21].
Arnamagnæanske samling. "AM 735 I 4to, f. 1r," handrit.is, https://handrit.is/en/manuscript/imaging/en/AM04-0736-I#page/1r++(1+of+4)/mode/2up [retrieved 27.03.20].
Berggren, J. Lennart, and Alexander Jones, eds. *Ptolemy's Geography: An Annotated Translation of the Theoretical Chapters*. Princeton: Princeton University Press, 2000.
Bertelsen, Henrik, ed. *Þiðreks saga af Bern*. Vol. 2. Copenhagen: S. L. Møllers Bogtrykkeri, 1905–11.
Bjarni Aðalbjarnarson, ed. *Heimskringla 1*, Íslenzk fornrit 26. Reykjavík: Hið íslenzka fornritafélag, 1941.
Bjarni Aðalbjarnarson, ed. *Heimskringla 2*, Íslenzk fornrit 27. Reykjavík: Hið íslenzka fornritafélag, 1945.
Bjarni Aðalbjarnarson, ed. *Heimskringla 3*, Íslenzk fornrit 28. Reykjavík: Hið íslenzka fornritafélag, 1950.
Bjarni Einarsson, ed. *Fagrskinna*, Íslenzk fornrit 29. Reykjavík: Hið íslenzka fornritafélag, 1985.
Björn K. Þórólfsson and Guðni Jónsson, eds. *Vestfirðinga sǫgur*, Íslenzk fornrit 6. Reykjavík: Hið íslenzka fornritafélag, 1943.
Björn Sigfússon, ed. *Ljósvetninga saga*, Íslenzk fornrit 10. Reykjavík: Hið íslenzka fornritafélag, 1940.
Boer, Richard Constant, ed. *Ǫrvar-Odds saga*. Leiden: E.J. Brill, 1888.
Bremensis, Adam. *Gesta Hammaburgensis Ecclesiae Pontificum*, ed. Martin Lappenbergh. Hannover: Impensis Bibliopolii Hahniani, 1876.
Byock, Jesse, ed. *The Saga of King Hrolf kraki*. London: Penguin, 1998.
Clunies Ross, Margaret. "Ǫrvar-Odds saga 79 (Ǫrvar-Oddr, Ævidrápa 9)." In *Poetry in fornaldarsögur*, edited by Margaret Clunies Ross, 894. Skaldic Poetry of the Scandinavian Middle Ages 8. Turnhout: Brepols, 2017.
Dennis, Andrew, Peter Foote, and Richard Perkins, eds. *Laws of Early Iceland: Grágás I*. Vol. 1, University of Manitoba Icelandic Studies 3. Manitoba: University of Manitoba Press, 2012. https://doi.org/10.2307/844616.
Diplomatarium Norvegicum, vol. 6, no. 106, https://www.dokpro.uio.no/cgi-bin/middelalder/diplom_vise_tekst.cgi?b=5857&s=n&str= [retrieved 13.12.19].
Diplomatarium Norvegicum, vol. 8, no. 79, https://www.dokpro.uio.no/cgi-bin/middelalder/diplom_vise_tekst.cgi?b=7439&s=n&str= [retrieved 13.12.19].
Diplomatarium Norvegicum, vol. 17, no. 849, https://www.dokpro.uio.no/cgi- [retrieved 10.02.20].
Diplomatarium Norvegicum, vol. 19, no. 112, https://www.dokpro.uio.no/cgi-bin/middelalder/diplom_vise_tekst.cgi?b=16086&s=n&str= [retrieved 09.12.19].

Driscoll, Matthew James, ed. and trans. *Ágrip: af Nóregskonunga sǫgum*. London: Viking Society for Northern Research, 2008.
Dronke, Ursula, ed. *The Poetic Edda: Mythological Poems*. Oxford: Clarendon Press, 1997. https://doi.org/10.1093/actrade/9780198111818.book.1.
Einar Ól. Sveinsson, ed. *Laxdœla saga*, Íslenzk fornrit 5. Reykjavík: Hið íslenzka fornritafélag, 1934.
Einar Ól. Sveinsson, ed. *Vatnsdœla saga*, Íslenzk fornrit 8. Reykjavík: Hið íslenzka fornritafélag, 1939.
Einar Ól. Sveinsson, ed. *Brennu-Njáls saga*, Íslenzk fornrit 12. Reykjavík: Hið íslenzka fornritafélag, 1954.
Einar Ól. Sveinsson, Matthías Þórðarson, and Ólafur Halldórsson, eds. *Eyrbyggja saga*, Íslenzk fornrit 4. Reykjavík: Hið íslenzka fornritafélag, 1985.
Ekrem, Inger, and Lars Boje Mortensen, eds. Peter Fisher, trans. *Historia Norwegie*. Copenhagen: Museum Tusculanum Press, 2006. https://doi.org/10.26530/oapen_342356.
Finnbogi Guðmundsson, ed. *Orkneyinga saga*, Íslenzk fornrit 34. Reykjavík: Hið íslenzka fornritafélag, 1965.
Fjellström, Pehr. *Kort berättelse om Lapparnas björne-fänge*, ed. Louise Bäckman. Umeå: Två Forläggere, 1981.
Gade, Kari Ellen. "Halldórr skvaldri, *Útfarardrápa* 10." In *Poetry from the Kings' Sagas 2: From c. 1035 to c. 1300*, edited by Kari Ellen Gade, 491. Skaldic Poetry of the Scandinavian Middle Ages 2. Turnhout: Brepols, 2009.
Gade, Kari Ellen. "Sturla Þórðarson, *Hrafnsmál* 1." In *Poetry from the Kings' Sagas 2: From c. 1035 to c. 1300*, edited by Karen Ellen Gade, 728. Skaldic Poetry of the Scandinavian Middle Ages 2. Turnhout: Brepols, 2009.
Godden, Malcolm R., ed. *The Old English History of the World: An Anglo-Saxon Rewriting of Orosius*, Dumbarton Oaks Medieval Library 44. Harvard: Harvard University Press, 2016.
Grammaticus, Saxo. *Gesta Danorum: The History of the Danes*, ed. Karsten Friis-Jensen, trans. Peter Fisher. Vol. 1. Oxford: Oxford University Press, 2015.
Guðbrandr Vigfússon and Carl Richard Unger, eds. *Flateyjarbok: En samling af Norse Konge-Sagaer med inskudte mindre Fortællinger om Begivenheder i og udenfor Norge samt Annaler.* Vol. 1. Christiania: P.T. Mallings Forlagsboghandler, 1860.
Guðbrandr Vigfússon and Carl Richard Unger, eds. *Flateyjarbok: En samling af Norse Konge-Sagaer med inskudte mindre Fortællinger om Begivenheder i og udenfor Norge samt Annaler.* Vol. 3. Christiania: P.T. Mallings Forlagsboghandler, 1868.
Guðni Jónsson, ed. *Grettis saga Ásmundarsonar*, Íslenzk fornrit 7. Reykjavík: Hið íslenzka fornritafélag, 1936.
Hermann Pálsson and Paul Edwards, eds. *The Book of Settlements: Landnámabók*. Manitoba: University of Manitoba Press, 2006.
Hermann Pálsson and Paul Edwards, eds. *Orkneyinga saga: The History of the Earls of Orkney*. London: Penguin Classics, 1981.
Jakob Benediktsson, ed. *Íslendingabók – Landnámabók*, Íslenzk fornrit 1. Reykjavík: Hið íslenzka fornritafélag, 1968.
Jesch, Judith, "Sigvatr Þórðarson, *Erfidrápa Óláfs helga* 16." In *Poetry from the Kings' Sagas 1: From Mythical Times to c. 1035*, edited by Diana Whaley, 663. Skaldic Poetry of the Scandinavian Middle Ages 1. Turnhout: Brepols, 2012.
Jóhannes Halldórsson, ed. *Kjalnesinga saga*, Íslenzk fornrit 14. Reykjavík: Hið íslenzka fornritafélag, 1959.

Jónas Kristjánsson and Vésteinn Ólasson, eds. *Eddukvæði 1*, Íslenzk fornrit 36. Reykjavík: Hið íslenzka fornritafélag, 2014.

Keyser, Rudolf, and Peter Andreas Munch, eds. *Norges Gamle Love: Norges Love ældre end Kong Magnus Haakonssöns Regjerings-Tiltrædelse i 1263*. Vol. 1. Christiania: Chr. Gröndahl, 1836.

Keyser, Rudolf, and Peter Andreas Munch, eds. *Norges Gamle Love: Lovgivningen under Kong Magnus Haakonssöns Regjeringstid fra 1263 til 1280*. Vol. 2. Christiania: Chr. Gröndahl, 1848.

Keyser, Rudolf, and Peter Andreas Munch, eds. *Norges Gamle Love: Lovgivningen efter Kong Magnus Håkonssons Död 1280 indtil 1387*. Vol. 3. Christiania: Chr. Gröndahl, 1849.

Keyser, Rudolf, and Carl Richard Unger, eds. *Olafs saga hins helga: En kort saga om Kong Olav den Hellige fra anden halvdeel af det tolfte aarhundrede*. Christiania: Feilberg and Landmarks Forlag, 1849.

Laula-Renberg, Elsa. *Inför Lif eller Död? Sanningsord i de Lappska förhallandena*. Stockholm: Wilhelmssons Boktryckeri, 1904.

Lunde, Paul, and Caroline Stone, eds. *The Land of Darkness: Arab Travellers in the Far North*. London: Penguin Group, 2012.

Mierow, Charles Christopher, ed. *The Gothic History of Jordanes*. Princeton: Princeton University Press, 1915. https://doi.org/10.2307/4387132.

Munch, Peter Andreas, ed. *Fornmannasögur eptir gömlum handritum*. Vols. 1–2. Copenhagen: Kongelige Nordiske oldsskriftselskab, 1825–26.

Munch, Peter Andreas, ed. *Fornmannasögur eptir gömlum handritum*. Vol. 10. Copenhagen: Kongelige Nordiske oldsskriftselskab, 1835.

Neahttadigisánit. "Čáhci," sanit.oahpha.no, https://sanit.oahpa.no/detail/sme/nob/%C4%8D%C3%A1hci.html?no_compounds=true&lemma_match=true [retrieved 03.01.19].

Nielsen, Yngvar. "Lappernes fremrykning mot syd i Trondhjems stift och Hedmarkens amt." *Det norske geografiske selskaps årbog*. Vol. 1 (1889–90): 18–52.

Oddr Snorrason. *The Saga of Olaf Tryggvason*, trans. Theodore M. Andersson. Ithaca: Cornell University Press, 2000.

Ólafía Einarsdóttir. "Om samtidssagaens kildeværdi belyst ved Hákonar saga Hákonarsonar." *Alvíssmál* 5 (1995): 29–80.

Ólafur Halldórsson, ed. *Færeyinga saga – Óláfs saga Odds*, Íslenzk fornrit 25. Reykjavík: Hið íslenzka fornritafélag, 2006.

Paul the Deacon. *History of the Lombards*, ed. Edward Peters, trans. William Dudley Foulke. Philadelphia: University of Pennsylvania Press, 2003.

Phelpstead, Carl, ed., and Devra Kunin, trans. *A History of Norway & The Passion and Miracles of the Blessed Óláfr*. London: Viking Society for Northern Research, 2001.

Pinder, Moritz, and Gustav Parthey, eds. *Ravennatis anonymi cosmographia*. Berlin, 1860.

Poole, Russell. "Eyvindr skáldaspillir Finnsson, *Lausavísur* 12." In *Poetry from the Kings' Sagas 1: From Mythical Times to c. 1035*, edited by Diana Whaley, 231. Skaldic Poetry of the Scandinavian Middle Ages 1. Turnhout: Brepols, 2012.

Poole, Russel. "(Introduction to) Eyvindr skáldaspíllir Finnson, *Háleygjatal*." In *Poetry from Kings' Sagas 1: From Mythical Times to c. 1035*, edited by Diana Whaley, 195–196. Skaldic Poetry of the Scandinavian Middle Ages 1. Turnhout: Brepols, 2012.

Rafn, Carl Christian, ed. *Fornaldar sögur nordrlanda eptir gömlum handritum*. 3 volumes. Copenhagen: Ennu Poppsku, 1829–30.

Riksarkivet. "SDHK-nr 3558," https://sok.riksarkivet.se/ [retrieved 03.04.20].

Regesta Norvegica, vol. 1, no. 849, https://www.dokpro.uio.no/cgi-bin/middelalder/regest_vise_tekst_ 2020.cgi?b=851&s=n&str= [retrieved 12.12.19].
Schröder, Franz Rolf, ed. *Hálfdanar saga Eysteinssonar*. Tübingen: Max Niemeyer Verlag, 1917.
Scudder, Bernard, trans. "Egil's saga." In *The Complete Sagas of Icelanders including 49 Tales*, edited by Viðar Hreinsson, 33–177. Vol. 1 Reykjavík: Leifur Eiríksson Publishing, 1997.
Sigurður Nordal, ed. *Egils saga Skallagrímssonar*, Íslenzk fornrit 2. Reykjavík: Hið íslenzka fornritafélag, 1933.
Snorri Sturluson. *Edda: Prologue and Gylfaginning*, ed. Anthony Faulkes. London: Viking Society for Northern Research, 1988.
Snorri Sturluson. *Edda: Skáldskaparmál*, ed. Anthony Faulkes. Vol. 1. London: Viking Society for Northern Research, 1998.
Snorri Sturluson. *Heimskringla*, trans. Alison Finlay and Anthony Faulkes. 3 volumes. London: Viking Society for Northern Research, 2014.
Storm, Gustav, ed. *Islandske Annaler indtil 1578*. Kristiania: Grøndahl & Søns Bogtrykkeri, 1888.
Tacitus. *Agricola and Germania*, ed. James Rives, trans. Harold Mattingly. London: Penguin Classics, 2010.
Titlestad, Torgrim, Elizabeth Ashman Rowe, and Bergsveinn Birgisson, eds. Edvard Eikill and Bergsveinn Birgisson, trans. *Flatøybok*. Vol. 1. Hafrsfjord: Sagabok, 2015.
Vidar Hreinsson, ed. *The Complete Sagas of Icelanders Including 49 Tales*. Vol. 1. Reykjavík: Leifur Eiríksson Publishing, 1997.
Viljálmur Finsen, ed. *Grágás 1852: Konungsbók* (Odense: Odense Universitetsforlag, 1974).
Waggoner, Ben, ed. *The Hrafnista Sagas*. New Haven: Troth Publications, 2012.
Wawn, Andrew, ed. "Vatnsdœla saga." In *The Complete Sagas of Icelanders including 49 tales*, 4, edited by Viðar Hreinsson, 1–66. Reykjavík: Leifur Eiríksson Publishing, 1998.
Whaley, Diana. "Þjóðólfr Arnórsson, *Sexstefja* 15." In *Poetry from the Kings' Sagas 2: From c. 1035 to c. 1300*, edited by Kari Ellen Gade, 127–128. Skaldic Poetry of the Scandinavian Middle Ages 2. Turnhout: Brepols, 2009.
Þórður Ingi Guðjónsson, ed. *Morkinskinna 1–2*, Íslenzk fornrit 23–24. Reykjavík: Hið íslenzka fornritafélag, 2011.
Þórhallur Vilmundarson and Bjarni Vilhjálmursson, eds. *Harðar saga*, Íslenzk fornrit 13. Reykjavík: Hið íslenzka fornritafélag, 1991.
Þorleifur Hauksson, ed. *Sverris saga*, Íslenzk fornrit 30. Reykjavík: Hið íslenzka fornritafélag, 2007.
Þorleifur Hauksson, ed. *Hákonar saga 1–2*, Íslenzk fornrit 31–32. Reykjavík: Hið íslenzka fornritafélag, 2013.
Þorleifur Hauksson, ed. *Jómsvíkinga saga*, Íslenzk fornrit 33. Reykjavík: Hið íslenzka fornritafélag, 2018.

Secondary Sources

Aalto, Sirpa. "Alienness in *Heimskringla*: Special Emphasis on the Finnar." In *Scandinavia and Christian Europe in the Middle Ages: Papers of the 12th International Saga Conference, Bonn/Germany, 28th July 2003*, edited by Rudolf Simek and Judith Meurer, 1–7. Bonn: Universität Bonn, 2003.

Aalto, Sirpa. "Encountering 'Otherness' in the Heimskringla." *Ennen ja Nyt* 4 (2004): 1–10.

Aalto, Sirpa. *Categorizing Otherness in the Kings' Sagas*. Dissertations in Social Sciences and Business Studies 10. Joensuu: University of Eastern Finland Publications, 2010.

Aalto, Sirpa. "Finnar in Old Norse Sources." In *Viking Age in Åland: Insight into Identity and Remnants of Culture*, edited by Joonas Ahola, Frog, and Jenni Lucenius, 199–226. Helsinki: Finnish Academy of Science and Letters, 2015.

Aalto, Sirpa. "Finns in the Sagas." In *Footprints in the Snow: The Long History of Arctic Finland*, edited by Maria Lähteenmäki, 24–42. Prime Minister's Office Publications 12. Helsinki: Prime Minister's Office, 2017.

Aalto, Sirpa. "Hyväksikäyttöä vai kumppanuutta? Saamelaisten ja skandinaavien kohtaamiset islantilaisissa saagoissa." In *The Barents and Baltic Sea Region: Contacts, Influences and Social Change*, edited by Kari Alenius and Matti Enbuske, 17–37. Rovaniemi: Pohjois-Suomen Historiallinen Yhdistys, 2017.

Aalto, Sirpa. "Växelverkan mellan samer och skandinaver i medeltiden." In *Uppsala midt i Sápmi – Sábme – Saepmie: En supradisciplinär antologi härrörande från vårsymposium organiserat av Uppsam – Föreningen for samiskrelaterad forskning i Uppsala, Uppsala universitet, 28–29 april 2014*, edited by May-Britt Öhman, Cecilia Hedlund, and Gunilla Larsson, 114–20. Uppsam skriftserie 2. Uppsala: Vulkanmedia, 2017.

Aalto, Sirpa, and Veli-Pekka Lehtola. "The Sami Representations Reflecting the Multi-Ethnic North of the Saga Literature." *Journal of Northern Studies* 11, no. 2 (2017): 7–30.

Acker, Paul, and Carolyne Larrington. *Revisiting the Poetic Edda: Essays on Old Norse Heroic Legend*. London: Routledge, 2013. https://doi.org/10.4324/9780203098608.

Afanasyeva, Anna. *Forced Relocations of the Kola Sámi People: Background and Consequences* (MA diss., University of Tromsø, 2013).

Aikio, Ante. "On Germanic-Saami Contacts and Saami Prehistory." *Suomalais-Ugrilaisen Seuran Aikakauskirja* 91 (2006): 9–55. https://doi.org/10.33340/susa.81944.

Aikio, Ante. "An Essay on Ethnolinguistic Prehistory." In *A Linguistic Map of Northern Europe*, edited by Riho Grünthal and Petri Kallio, 63–117. Vol. 266, *Mémoires de la Société Finno-Ougrienne*. Helsinki: Suomalais-Ugrilainen Seura, 2012.

Amundsen, Hilde Rigmor. "Changing Histories and Ethnicities in a Sámi and Norse Borderland," *Acta Borealia* 34, no. 2 (2017): 178–97. https://doi.org/10.1080/08003831.2017.1398537.

Amundsen, Hilde Rigmor, and Kristin Os. "Funnel-Shaped Reindeer Trapping Systems in Hedmark: Saami or Norse?" In *Currents of Saami Pasts: Recent Advances in Saami Archaeology*, edited by Marte Spangen, Anna-Kaisa Salmi, Tiina Äikäs, and Markus Fjellström, 16–33. Monographs of the Archaeological Society of Finland 9. Helsinki: Archaeological Society of Finland, 2020.

Andreassen, Irene. "Kven og kainu(lainen)," Kainun Instituutti, http://www.kvenskinstitutt.no/kvener/kven-og-kainulainen/ [retrieved 30.03.2020].

Andrews, Tarren. "Indigenous Futures and Medieval Pasts. An Introduction." *English Language Notes* 58, no. 2 (2020): 1–17. https://doi.org/10.1215/00138282-8557777.

Ármann Jakobsson. "The Extreme Emotional Life of Vǫlundr the Elf." *Scandinavian Studies* 78, no. 3 (2006): 227–54.

Ármann Jakobsson. "King Arthur and the Kennedy Assassination: The Allure and Absence of Truth in the Icelandic Sagas." *Scandinavian-Canadian Studies* 22 (2015): 12–22. https://doi.org/10.29173/scancan96.

Ármann Jakobsson. "Introduction." In *The Routledge Research Companion to the Medieval Icelandic Sagas*, edited by Ármann Jakobsson and Sverrir Jakobsson, 1–3. New York: Routledge, 2017. https://doi.org/10.4324/9781315613628-1.

Ármann Jakobsson. *The Troll Inside You: Paranormal Activity in the Medieval North*. Santa Barbara: Punctum Books, 2017. https://doi.org/10.1353/book.66790.

Arnold, Martin. "Hvat er rek nema þat? The Cultural History of the Troll." In *The Shadow-Walkers: Jacob Grimm's Mythology of the Monstrous*, edited by Tom Shippey, 111–55. Tempe: Arizona Centre for Medieval and Renaissance Studies, 2005.

Arnold, Martin. "*Við þik sættumsk ek aldri: Ǫrvar-Odds saga* and the Meanings of Ǫgmundr Eyþjófsbani." In *Making History: Essays on the Fornaldarsögur*, edited by Martin Arnold and Alison Finlay, 85–104. London: Viking Society for Northern Research, 2010.

Arntzen, Johan Eilertsen. "En sen vikingtids våpengrav med østlige rek fra Løding, Bodø k." *Arkeologiske undersøkelser. Tromsø Museum: Universitetsmuseet* (December 2015).

Aronsson, Kjell-Åke. "Research on Human Remains of Indigenous people: Reflections from an Archaeological Perspective (With an Example from Rounala)." In *More than Just Bones: Ethics and Research on Human Remains*, edited by Halvard Fossheim, 65–80. Oslo: Forskningsetiske komiteer, 2012.

Ashby, Stephen, Ashley N. Coutou, and Søren Michael Sindbæk. "Urban Networks and Arctic Outlands: Craft Specialists and Reindeer Antler in Viking Towns." *European Journal of Archaeology* 18, no. 4 (2015): 679–704. https://doi.org/10.1179/1461957115y.0000000003.

Baglo, Cathrine. "The Disappearance of the Sea Sámi as a Cultural Display Category: Assimilation Policies and the Role of Industrial Expositions." *The Journal of Nordic Museology* [special issue: From Lappology to Sámi Museology] 27, no. 3 (2019): 25–44. https://doi.org/10.5617/nm.7725.

Ballovara, Mette. "Bekymret over kunnskapsmangel," NRK Sápmi, 12.02.2020, https://www.nrk.no/sapmi/vanja-reiste-rundt-til-norske-skoler-_-bekymret-over-kunnskapsmangel-1.14865671 [retrieved 14.02.21].

Ballovara, Mette, and Dan Robert Larsen. "Vil forske på samehets," NRK Sápmi, 18.12.2020, https://www.nrk.no/sapmi/likestillings-og-diskrimineringsombud-tar-abid-raja-pa-ordet-_-vil-forske-pa-sa mehets-1.15291942 [retrieved 01.02.21].

Balto, Runar Myrnes. "Organisasjonen EDL sprer farlige konspirasjonsteorier om samer," Utrop, 09.11.2020, https://www.utrop.no/plenum/ytringer/234081/?fbclid=IwAR31b7U4dtiOs3j2a_Hj-OeKZ-KKIJD4E4o5SDF_zgd3WZ5ps_JKw5lNNJs [retrieved 01.02.21].

Bampi, Massimiliano. "Genre." In *The Routledge Research Companion to the Medieval Icelandic Sagas*, edited by Ármann Jakobsson and Sverrir Jakobsson, 4–14. London: Routledge, 2017. https://doi.org/10.4324/9781315613628-2.

Barraclough, Eleanor Rosamund. "Arctic Frontiers: Rethinking Norse-Sámi Relations in the Old Norse Sagas." *Viator* 48, no. 3 (2017): 27–51. https://doi.org/10.1484/j.viator.5.116347.

Berg-Nordlie, Mikkel, "Two Centuries of Russian Sámi Policy: Arrangements for Autonomy and Participation Seen in Light of Imperial, Soviet and Federal Indigenous Minority Policy." *Acta Borealia* 33, no. 1 (2015): 40–67. https://doi.org/10.1080/08003831.2015.1030849.

Bergman, Ingela, and Lars-Erik Edlund. "*Birkarlar* and Sámi: Inter-Cultural Contacts Beyond State Control: Reconsidering the Standing of External Tradesmen (*birkarlar*) in Medieval Sámi Societies." *Acta Borealia* 33, no. 1 (2016): 52–80. https://doi.org/10.1080/08003831.2016.1154676.

Bergman, Ingela, Lars Östlund, Olle Zackrisson, and Lars Liedgren. "Stones in the Snow: A Norse Fur Traders' Road into Sami Country." *Antiquity* 81, no. 312 (2007): 397–408. https://doi.org/10.1017/s0003598x00095260.
Bergsland, Knut. "Om middelalderens Finnmarker." *Historisk tidsskrift* 49, no. 4 (1970): 365–409.
Bergsland, Knut. "Synsvinkler i samisk historie." *Historisk tidsskrift* 53 (1974): 1–36.
Bergstøl, Jostein. *Samer i Østerdalen? En studie av etnisitet i jernalderen og middelalderen i det nordøstre Hedmark.* Acta Humaniora 325. Oslo: Unipub, 2008.
Bergstøl, Jostein. "Hunting Native Reindeer, While Herding Imported Ones? Some Thoughts on the Development of Saami Pastoralism." In *Currents of Saami Pasts: Recent Advances in Saami Archaeology*, ed. Marte Spangen, Anna-Kaisa Salmi, Tiina Äikäs, and Markus Fjellström, 34–45. Monographs of the Archaeological Society of Finland 9. Helsinki: Archaeological Society of Finland, 2020.
Bergstøl, Jostein, and Gaute Reitan. "Samer på Dovrefjell i vikingtiden: et bidrag til debatten omkring samenes sørgrense i forhistorisk tid." *Historisk tidsskrift* 87 (2008): 9–27. https://doi.org/10.18261/issn1504-2944-2008-01-02.
Bierning, Tine Jeanette. "The Concept of Shamanism in Old Norse Religion from a Sociological Perspective." In *Old Norse Religion in Long-Term Perspectives: Origins, Changes and Interactions: An International Conference in Lund, Sweden, June 3–7 2004*, edited by Anders Andrén, Kristina Jennbert, and Catharina Raudvere, 171–78. Vägar till Midgård 8. Lund: Nordic Academic Press, 2006.
Blom, Jon Gunnar. *Mennesker og steder i et nordnorsk landskap: en studie av landskapsforståelse og landskapsbruk fra jernalderen til nyere tid* (MA diss., University of Tromsø, 2012).
Braseth, Leif. *Samer sør for midnattsola: Sørsamenes forhistorie, kultur og levemåte.* Bergen: Fagbokforlaget, 2015.
Brink, Stefan. "How Uniform was the Old Norse Religion?" In *Learning and Understanding in the Old Norse World: Essays in Honour of Margaret Clunies Ross*, edited by Judy Quinn, Kate Heslop, and Tarrin Wills, 105–36. Turnhout: Brepols, 2007. https://doi.org/10.1484/m.tcne-eb.3.4070.
Bruchach, Margaret M. "Decolonization in Archaeological Theory." In *Encyclopedia of Global Archaeology*, 2069–77. New York: Springer, 2014. https://doi.org/10.1007/978-1-4419-0465-2_258.
Bruun, Inga Malene. *Blandede graver: blandede kulturer? En tolkning av gravskikk og etniske forhold i Nord-Norge gjennom jernalder og tidlig middelalder* (MA diss., University of Tromsø, 2007).
Brännström, Malin. The Enhanced Role of Archaeological and Historical Research in Court Proceedings About Saami Land Rights." In *Currents of Saami Pasts: Recent Advances in Saami Archaeology*, edited by Marte Spangen, Anna-Kaisa Salmi, Tiina Äikäs, and Markus Fjellström, 177–88. Monographs of the Archaeological Society of Finland 9. Helsinki: Archaeological Society of Finland, 2020.
Bull, Ida, ed. *Trøndelags Historie.* 3 volumes. Trondheim: Tapir akademiske forlag, 2005.
Bull, Tove. "Samisk påverknad på norsk språk." *NOA* 27, no. 1 (2011): 5–32.
Cardew, Phil. "'Mannfögnuður er oss at smjöri þessu': Representations of the Finns within the Icelandic Sagas." In *Text and Nation: Essays on Post-Colonial Cultural Politics*, edited by Andrew Blake, and Jopi Nyman, 146–58. Joensuu: Joensuun Yliopisto, 2001.
Clunies Ross, Margaret. *A History of Old Norse Poetry and Poetics.* Cambridge: D.S. Brewer, 2005. https://doi.org/10.1017/9781846154010.
Clunies Ross, Margaret. "Royal Ideology in Early Scandinavia: A Theory Versus the Texts." *The Journal of English and Germanic Philology* 113, no. 1 (2014): 18–33. https://doi.org/10.5406/jenglgermphil.113.1.0018.

Cole, Richard. "Racial Thinking in Old Norse Literature." *Saga-Book* 39 (2015): 21–40.
Crocker, Christopher. "What We Talk About When We Talk About Vínland: History, Whiteness, Indigenous Erasure, and the Early Norse Presence in Newfoundland." *Canadian Journal of History/Annales Canadiennes D'Histoire* 55, nos 1–2 (2020): 91–122. https://doi.org/10.3138/cjh-2019-0028.
Damm, Charlotte. "Archaeology, Ethno-history and Oral Traditions: Approaches to the Indigenous Past." *Norwegian Archaeological Review* 38, no. 2 (2005): 73–87. https://doi.org/10.1080/00293650500402357.
DeAngelo, Jeremy. "The North and the Depiction of the 'Finnar' in the Icelandic Sagas." *Scandinavian Studies* 83, no. 3 (2010): 257–86.
Deloria, Jr., Vine. "Indians, Archaeologists and the Future." *American Antiquity* 57, no. 4 (1992): 595–98.
Dictionary of Old Norse Prose. "Almenning," ONP, https://onp.ku.dk/onp/onp.php?o2730 [retrieved 24.05.21].
Dictionary of Old Norse Prose. "Finnskattr," ONP, https://onp.ku.dk/onp/onp.php?o20687 [retrieved 19.05.20]
Dictionary of Old Norse Prose. "HálfdEyst," ONP, https://onp.ku.dk/onp/onp.php?v206 [retrieved 29.04.21].
Dictionary of Old Norse Prose. "StSt," ONP, https://onp.ku.dk/onp/onp.php?v493 [retrieved 29.04.21].
Dommelen, Peter van. "Colonial Matters: Material Culture and Postcolonial Theory in Colonial Situations." In *Handbook of Material Culture*, edited by Chris Tilley, Webb Keane, Susanne Küchler, Mike Rowlands, and Patricia Spyer, 104–25. London: SAGE Publications, 2006. https://doi.org/10.4135/9781848607972.n8.
DuBois, Thomas. *Nordic Religions in the Viking Age*. Pennsylvania: University of Pennsylvania Press, 1999.
DuBois, Thomas. "Ethnomemory: Ethnographic and Culture-Centred Approaches to the Study of Memory." *Scandinavian Studies* 85, no. 3 (2013): 306–31. https://doi.org/10.5406/scanstud.85.3.0306.
DuBois, Thomas. "Encounters: Sámi." In *The Pre-Christian Religions of the North: History and Structures*, edited by Jens Peter Schjødt, John Lindow, and Anders Andrén, 353–72. Turnhout: Brepols, 2020. https://doi.org/10.1484/m.pcrn-eb.5.116944.
Duođaš Sámecielaheami / Dokumenter Samehetsen (Facebook group), https://www.facebook.com/groups/1977174939210038/permalink/2841480316112825 [retrieved 26.01.21].
Duperron, Brenna, and Elizabeth Edwards. "Thinking Indigeneity: A Challenge to Medieval Studies." *Exemplaria* 33, no. 1 (2021): 94–107. https://doi.org/10.1080/10412573.2021.1893095.
Einar Ísaksson. *To Die into the Mountain: A Study of a Northwestern Icelandic Burial Mound and the Sámi Cultural Influences in Viking Age Iceland* (MA Diss., Stockholm University, 2013).
Eira, Nils Johan. *Negative Discourse in Social Medias: An Analysis of Hate Speech in the Saami Context*. Kautokeino: Sámi allaskuvla, 2019.
Gallo, Lorenzo Lozzi. "The Giantess as Foster-Mother in Old Norse Literature." *Scandinavian Studies* 78, no. 1 (2016): 1–20.
Gaski, Harald. "Indigenism and Cosmopolitanism: A Pan-Sami View of the Indigenous Perspective in Sami Culture and Research." *AlterNative: An International Journal of Indigenous Peoples* 3, no. 2 (2013): 113–24. https://doi.org/10.1177/117718011300900201.

Gauslaa, Jon, and Bjørn Bjerkli. "Samisk naturbruk og rettssituasjon fra Hedmark til Troms," Norges Offentlige Utredninger 14, 03.12.2007, https://www.regjeringen.no/no/dokumenter/nou-2007-14/id584312/ [retrieved 25.11.20].

Gjerde, Hege Skalleberg. "Samiske tufter i Hallingdal?" In *Viking*, edited by Ellen Høigård Hofseth and Egil Mikkelsen, 197–210. Norsk arkeologisk årbok, vol. 72. Oslo: Norsk Arkeologisk Selskap, 2009.

Gjerde, Hege Skalleberg. "Tilfeldig? Neppe: Finsk-Ugriske smykker i Sør-Norge." In *Viking*, edited by Britt Solli, Zanette Tsigaridas Gjørstad, and Egil Mikkelsen, 49–60. Norsk arkeologisk årbok, vol. 73. Oslo: Norsk Arkeologisk Selskap, 2010.

Gjerde, Hege Skalleberg. *Sørsamisk eller førsamisk? Arkeologi og sørsamisk forhistorie i Sør-Norge: en kildekritisk analyse* (PhD thesis, University of Oslo, 2015).

Gjerde, Hege Skalleberg. En gjøgler blant guder? Om det samiske i vikingtidsutstillingen." In *Om vikinger og virkninger: Festskrift til Ellen Høigård Hofseths vikingtidsutstilling*, edited by Hege Skalleberg Gjerde and Gro B. Ween, 103–15. Oslo: Primitive Tider, 2016.

Gjerde, Hege Skalleberg. "Common Ground: Saami-Norse Interactions in South Norway During the Late Iron Age and Early Medieval Period." In *Currents of Saami Pasts: Recent Advances in Saami Archaeology*, edited by Marte Spangen, Anna-Kaisa Salmi, Tiina Äikäs, and Markus Fjellström, 149–59. Monographs of the Archaeological Society of Finland 9. Helsinki: Archaeological Society of Finland, 2020.

Gjerde, Hege Skalleberg, and Jostein Bergstøl. "Sámi Vikings?" In *Vikings Across Boundaries*, edited by Hanne Lovise Aannestad, Unn Pedersen, Marianne Moen, Elise Naumann, and Heidi Lund Berg, 166–78. Viking-Age Transformations 2. London: Routledge, 2020. https://doi.org/10.4324/9780429346194-11.

Hakamäki, Ville. "Late Iron Age Transculturalism in the Northern 'Perhiphery': Understanding the Long-Term Prehistoric Occupational Area of Viinivaara E, Finland." *Acta Borealia* 33, no. 1 (2016): 30–51. https://doi.org/10.1080/08003831.2016.1154674.

Halinen, Petri, and Bjørnar Olsen, eds. *In Search of Hearths: A Book in Memory of Sven-Donald Hedman*. Helsinki: The Finnish Antiquarian Society, 2019.

Hansen, Andreas Martin. *Oldtidens Nordmænd: Ophav og Bosætning*. Kristiania: Cammermeyer, 1907.

Hansen, Lars Ivar. "Skal en bare bruke kilder som omtaler samer i rekonstruksjonen av samisk fortid?" In *Viester-Alas: Rapport fra et seminar på Vesterålens bygdemuseum og kultursentrum*, edited by Lars Slettejord and Helge Guttormsen, 140–74. Melbu [n.p], 1984.

Hansen, Lars Ivar. "Om synet på de 'andre': ute og hjemme: Geografi og folkeslag på Nordkalotten i følge Historia Norvegie." In *Olavslegenden og den latinske historieskriving i 1100-tallets Norge*, edited by Lars Boje Mortensen, Karen Skogvaard-Petersen, and Inger Ekrem, 54–87. Copenhagen: Museum Tusculanum Press, 2000.

Hansen, Lars Ivar. "Fra Nöteborgfreden til Lappekodisillen ca. 1300–1751: Folkegrupper og statsdannelse på Nordkalotten med utgangspunkt i Finnmark." In *Grenser og grannelag i Nordens historie*, edited by Steinar Imsen, 362–86. Oslo: Cappelen Damm Akademisk, 2005.

Hansen, Lars Ivar. "Sami Fisheries in the Pre-Modern Era: Household Sustenance and Market Relations." *Acta Borealia* 23, no. 1 (2006): 56–80. https://doi.org/10.1080/08003830600789390.

Hansen, Lars Ivar, and Bjørnar Olsen. *Hunters in Transition: An Outline of Early Sámi History*. The Northern World 63. Leiden: Brill, 2014. https://doi.org/10.1163/9789004252554.

Harlin, Eeva-Kristiina. Sámi Archaeology and the Fear of Political Involvement: Finnish Archaeologists' Perspectives on Ethnicity and the Repatriation of Sámi Cultural Heritage." *Archaeologies* 15 (2019): 254–84. https://doi.org/10.1007/s11759-019-09366-7.

Hedeager, Lotte. *Iron Age Myth and Materiality: An Archaeology of Scandinavia AD 400–1000*. London: Routledge, 2011. https://doi.org/10.4324/9780203829714.

Hedman, Sven-Donald. *Boplatser och offerplatser: Ekonomisk strategi och boplatsmönster bland skogssamer 700–1600 AD*. Studia Archaeologica Universitatis Umensis 17. Umeå: University of Umeå, 2003.

Hedman, Sven Donald, Bjørnar Olsen and Maria Vretemark, "Hunters, Herders and Hearths: Interpreting New Results from Hearth Row Sites in Pasvik, Arctic Norway." *Rangifer* 35, no. 1 (2015): 1–24. https://doi.org/10.7557/2.35.1.3334.

Heggestad, Leif, Finn Hødnebø and Erik Simensen, eds. *Norrøn ordbok*, 5th edition. Oslo: Samlaget, 2012.

Heide, Eldar. *Gand, seid og åndevind* (PhD thesis, University of Bergen, 2006).

Hellesvik, Jarl. "Er samene i Norge urfolk?" Utrop, 11.11.2020, https://www.utrop.no/plenum/ytringer/232630/ [retrieved 01.02.21].

Hemphill, Jennifer. *Weather Magic in the Nordic Middle Ages* (forthcoming PhD thesis, University of Aberdeen).

Henriksen, Jørn Erik. *Kulturmøte og identitet på Finnmarkskysten i tidlig historisk tid: Tolkninger basert på arkeologiske analyser av mangeromstufter* (PhD thesis, University of Tromsø, 2016).

Hermann Pálsson. *Úr landnorðri: Samar og ystu rætur íslenskrar menningar*. Reykjavík: Bókmenntafræðistofnun Háskóla Íslands, 1997. https://doi.org/10.7557/13.2143.

Hermann Pálsson. "Searching for the Sámi in Early Icelandic Sources." *Revision* 21, no. 1 (1998): 40–46.

Hermann Pálsson. "The Sami People in Old Norse Literature." *Nordlit* 5 (1999): 29–53.

Hermann, Pernille. "The Horror of Vínland: Topographies and Otherness in the Vínland Sagas." *Scandinavian Studies* 93, no. 1 (2021): 1–22. https://doi.org/10.5406/scanstud.93.1.0001.

Hermanstrand, Håkon, Asbjørn Kolberg, Trond Risto Nilssen, and Leiv Sem, eds. *The Indigenous Identity of the South Saami: Historical and Political Perspectives on a Minority within a Minority*. New York: Springer, 2019. https://doi.org/10.1007/978-3-030-05029-0.

Horn, Miriam. "Möndull Pattason: A Sami Identity in a Dwarfish Guise." In *Samer som "de andra," samer "om de andra": Identitet och etnicitet i nordiska kulturmöten*, edited by Else Mundal and Håkan Rydving, 146–60. Umeå: Samiske studier, 2010.

Höglund, Johan, and Linda Andersson Burnett. "Introduction: Nordic Colonialisms and Scandinavian Studies." *Scandinavian Studies* [special issue: Nordic Colonialisms] 91, nos 1–2 (2019): 1–12. https://doi.org/10.5406/scanstud.91.1-2.0001.

Hultkrantz, Åke. "A Definition of Shamanism." *Temenos* 9 (1973): 25–37. https://doi.org/10.33356/temenos.6345.

International Labour Organization. "ILO 169: Indigenous and Tribal Peoples Convention, 1989 (NO. 169)," ILO.org, https://www.ilo.org/dyn/normlex/en/f?p=NORMLEXPUB:12100:0::NO::P12100_ILO_CODE:C169 [retrieved 23.03.21].

Jahnsen, Sofie Scheen. *The Social Construction of the Norwegian Viking: An Analysis of the National Identity Discourse in Norwegian Viking Age Research* (MA diss., University of Oslo, 2015).

Jazeel, Tariq. "Postcolonialism." In *The Wiley-Blackwell Companion to Cultural Geography*, edited by Nuala C. Johnson, Richard H. Schein, and Jamie Winders, 41–48. Oxford: Wiley-Blackwell.

Jesch, Judith. "Poetry in the Viking Age." In *The Viking World*, edited by Stefan Brink and Neil Price, 291–98. London: Routledge, 2008. https://doi.org/10.4324/9780203412770-32.

Jesch, Judith. *The Viking Diaspora*. New York: Routledge, 2015. https://doi.org/10.4324/9781315708331.

Johnsen, Astrid Mellem. *Troms som etnisk sammensatt grenseområde ca 600–1600* (forthcoming PhD thesis, University of Tromsø).
Jones, Siân. *The Archaeology of Ethnicity: Constructing Identities in the Past and the Present.* London: Routledge, 1997.
Jón Hnefill Aðalsteinsson. *Under the Cloak: A Pagan Ritual Turning Point in the Conversion of Iceland.* Reykjavík: Háskolautgafan, 1999.
Junka-Aikio, Laura. "Institutionalization, Neo-Politicization and the Politics of Defining Sámi Research." *Acta Borealia* 36, no. 1 (2019): 1–22. https://doi.org/10.1080/08003831.2019.1607074.
Kaikkonen, Konsta Ilari. *Contextualising Descriptions of Noaidevuohta: Saami Ritual Specialists in Texts Written until 1871* (PhD thesis, University of Bergen, 2020).
Keller, Christian. "Furs, Fish and Ivory: Medieval Norsemen at the Arctic Fringe." *Journal of the North Atlantic* 3 (2010): 1–23. https://doi.org/10.3721/037.003.0105.
Keskitalo, Alf Isak. "Research as an Inter-Ethnic Relation." *Dieđut* 7, Arctic Centre Reports 11 (1994): 7–31 [Republished article based on a speech held in Tromsø in 1974; and an article published in 1976].
Knutson, Charina. *Conducting Archaeology in Swedish Sápmi: Policies, Implementations and Challenges in a Postcolonial Context.* Lnu Licentiate 33. Växjö: Linnaeus University Press, 2021.
Kuokkanen, Rauna. "Reconciliation as a Threat or Structural Change? The Truth and Reconciliation Process and Settler Colonial Policy Making in Finland." *Human Rights Review* 21, no. 3 (2020): 293–312. https://doi.org/10.1007/s12142-020-00594-x.
Kusmenko, Jurij. "Jätten Thjazi och det samiska elementet i nordisk mytologi." In *Sápmi Y1K: Livet i samernas bösättningsområde för ett tusen år sedan*, edited by Andrea Amft and Mikael Svonni, 11–28. Umeå: Samiska Studier, 2006.
Kusmenko, Jurij. "Sámi and Scandinavians in the Viking Age." *Scandinavistica Vilnensis* 2 (2009): 65–94. https://doi.org/10.15388/scandinavisticavilnensis.2009.2.5.
Kusmenko, Jurij. "Sámi as Giants and Dwarves in Old Scandinavian Literature." *Scandinavian Philology* 11 (2011): 84–95.
Kølvraa, Christoffer. "Embodying 'the Nordic race': Imaginaries of Viking Heritage in the Online Communications of the Nordic Resistance Movements." *Patterns of Prejudice* 53, no. 3 (2019): 270–84. https://doi.org/10.1080/0031322x.2019.1592304.
Laidoner, Triin. "The Flying *Noaidi* of the North: Sámi Tradition Reflected in the Figure Loki Laufeyjarson in Old Norse Mythology." *Scripta Islandica* 63 (2012): 59–93.
Lapps and Norsemen in Olden Times. Instituttet for Sammenlignende Kulturforskning, Seria A: Forelesninger XXVI. Oslo: Universitetsforlaget, 1967.
Larsen, Dan Robert. "Bruker reinsdyr og joik i markedsføring – men samisk navn vil ikke kommunen ha," NRK Sápmi, 10.10.2020, https://www.nrk.no/sapmi/narvik-kommune-bruker-samiske-elementer-i-markedsforing-av-vm-__vil-ikke-ha-samisk-navn-pa-kommunen-1.15180866 [retrieved 01.02.21].
Larsson, Gunilla. *Ship and Society: Maritime Ideology in Late Iron Age Sweden.* AUN 67 Uppsala: Uppsala Universitet, 2007.
Lassen, Annette, Agneta Ney, and Ármann Jakobsson, eds. *The Legendary Sagas: Origins and Development.* Reykjavík: University of Iceland Press, 2012.
Ledger, Paul M., Linus Girdland-Flink, and Véronique Forbes. "New Horizons at L'Anse aux Meadows." *PANS* 116, no. 31 (2019): 15341–43. https://doi.org/10.1073/pnas.1907986116.
Lehtola, Veli-Pekka. *The Sámi People: Traditions in Transition.* Inari: Kustannus-Puntsi, 2004.

Lewis-Simpson, Shannon. "Vinland Revisited, Again: On 'Theories, Scuttlebutt, Crossed Fingers', and Next Steps." In *Viking Encounters: Proceedings of the Eighteenth Viking Congress*, edited by Anne Pedersen and Søren Michael Sindbæk, 565–83. Aarhus: Aarhus University Press, 2020.

Lexicon of Medieval Nordic Law. "Reksþegn," https://www.dhi.ac.uk/lmnl/nordicheadword/displayPage/4311 [retrieved 24.05.21].

Lincoln, Bruce. *Between History and Myth: Stories of Harald Fairhair and the Founding of the State.* Chicago: The University of Chicago Press, 2014. https://doi.org/10.7208/chicago/9780226141084.001.0001.

Lindkjølen, Hans. *Nordisk saga: Samer i litteraturen.* Oslo: Tyri, 1993.

Lindow, John. "Supernatural Others and Ethnic Others: A Millennium of World View." *Scandinavian Studies* 67, no. 1 (1995): 8–31.

Lindow, John. "Myth Read as History: Odin in Snorri Sturluson's Ynglinga saga." In *Myth: A New Symposium*, edited by Gregory Schrempp and William Hansen, 107–23. Indianapolis: University of Indiana Press, 2002.

Lomuto, Sierra. "Becoming Postmedieval: The Stakes of the Global Middle Ages." *postmedieval: a journal of medieval cultural studies* 11, no. 4 (2020): 503–12. https://doi.org/10.1057/s41280-020-00198-1.

Long, Ann-Marie. *Iceland's Relationship with Norway c.870 – c. 1100: Memory, History and Identity*, The Northern World 81. Leiden: Brill, 2017. https://doi.org/10.1163/9789004336513.

Lähteenmäki, Maria. *Footprints in the Snow: The Long History of Arctic Finland.* Prime Minister's Office Publications 12. Helsinki: Prime Minister's Office, 2017.

Magnell, Ola, and Elisabeth Iregren. "Veitstu hvé blóta skal? The Old Norse *blót* in the Light of Osteological Remains from Frösö Church, Jämtland, Sweden." *Current Swedish Archaeology* 18 (2010): 223–50. https://doi.org/10.37718/csa.2010.14.

McDougall, Ian. "Foreigners and Foreign Languages in Iceland." *Saga-Book* 22 (1986–89): 180–234.

McKinnell, John. "The Context of Vǫlundarkviða." *Saga-Book* 23 (1993): 1–27.

McKinnell, John. *Meeting the Other in Norse Myth and Legend.* Cambridge: D.S. Brewer, 2005.

Melhus, Marita, and Ann Ragnhild Broderstad. *Folkehelseundersøkelsen i Troms og Finnmark: Tilleggsrapport om samisk og kvensk/norskfinsk befolkning.* Tromsø: Senter for samisk helseforskning, 2020.

Mignolo, Walter D. *The Darker Side of Western Modernity: Global Futures, Decolonial Options.* Durham: Duke University Press, 2011. https://doi.org/10.2307/j.ctv125jqbw.

Mitchell, Stephen A. "Scandinavia." In *The Routledge History of Medieval Magic*, edited by Sophie Page and Catherine Rider, 136–50. London: Routledge, 2019. https://doi.org/10.4324/9781315613192-12.

Moos, Dennis. *Finnar á Íslandi: Samiske spor i det islandske arkeologiske materialet fra landnåmstid* (MA diss., University of Tromsø, 2013).

Motz, Lotte. "Supernatural Beings." In *Medieval Scandinavia: An Encyclopedia*, edited by Phillip Pulsiano, 622. Garland reference library of the humanities, vol. 934. London: Garland Publishing, 1993.

Mulk, Inga-Marie. "The Role of the Sámi in Fur-Trading During the Late Iron Age and Nordic Medieval Period in the Light of the Sámi Sacrificial Sites in Lapland." *Acta Borealia* 13, no. 1 (1996): 47–80. https://doi.org/10.1080/08003839608580447.

Mundal, Else. "The Perception of the Saamis and Their Religion in Old Norse Sources." In *Shamanism and Northern Ecology*, edited by Juha Pentikäinen, 97–116. Berlin: De Gruyter, 1996. https://doi.org/10.1515/9783110811674.97.

Mundal, Else. "Kong Harald Hårfagre og samejenta Snøfrid: Samefolket sin plass i den norske rikssamlingsmyten." *Nordica Bergensiana* 14 (1997): 39–53.

Mundal, Else. "Coexistence of Saami and Norse Culture: Reflected in and Interpreted by Old Norse Myths." In *Old Norse Myths, Literature and Society: The Proceedings of the 11th International Saga Conference, 2–7 July 2000, University of Sydney*, edited by Geraldine Barnes and Margaret Clunies Ross, 346–55. Sydney: University of Sydney, 2000.

Mundal, Else. "Kong Håkon Magnussons rettarbot for Hålogaland av 1313 og andre kjelder til kristninga av samene i mellomalderen." In *Sápmi Y1K: Livet i samernas bösättningsområde för ett tusen år sedan*, edited by Andrea Amft and Mikael Svonni, 97–114. Umeå: Samiska Studier, 2006.

Mundal, Else. "Samekvinner i norrøne kjelder." In *Åarjel-saemieh. Samer i sør*, 110–25. Saemien Sijte årbok, vol. 9. Snåsa: Saemien Sijte, 2007.

Mundal, Else. "The Relationship Between Sami and Nordic Peoples Expressed in Terms of Family Associations." *Journal of Northern Studies* 2 (2009): 25–37.

Mundal, Else. "Når den 'rette' teksten er rang: Tolkinga av tilnamnet Sigurd Rise." *Scandinavian Philology* 15 (2017): 248–60.

Mundal, Else. "Sami Sieidis in a Nordic Context?" *Journal of Northern Studies* 12, no. 1 (2018): 11–20.

Munch, Gerd Stamsø. "Funnene fra Eiterjord i Beiarn og Vestvatn i Misvær." In *Viking*, edited by Bjørn Hougen and Arne Skjølsvold, 99–122. Norsk arkeologisk årbok, vol. 31. Oslo: Norsk arkeologisk selskap, 1967.

Miyashiro, Adam. "Our Deeper Past: Race, Settler Colonialism, and Medieval Heritage Politics." *Literature Compass* 16 (2019): 1–11. https://doi.org/10.1111/lic3.12550.

Myhre, Elin. "Sørreisa: en del av jarledømmet Hålogaland og Namdalen?" In *Årbok for Dyrøy og Sørreisa*, edited by Elin Myhre, 13–25. Årbok for Dyrøy og Sørreisa, vol. 18. Lierskogen: Rennessansemedia AS, 2019.

Nakata, Martin. *Disciplining the Savages: Savaging the Disciplines*. Canberra: Aboriginal Studies Press, 2007.

Nayar, Pramod K. *The Postcolonial Studies Dictionary*. Chichester: Wiley Blackwell, 2015. https://doi.org/10.1002/9781119118589.

Nielssen, Alf Ragnar. *Landnåm fra nord: Utvandringa fra det nordlige Norge til Island i vikingtid*. Stamsund: Orkana Akademisk forlag, 2012.

Niemi, Anja Roth. "En båtgrav på Hillesøy ved Tromsø," Norark, 01.03.2018, http://www.norark.no/prosjekter/nodvegen-pa-hillesoy/en-batgrav-fra-yngre-jernalder-pa-hillesoy-ved-tromso/ [retrieved 16.09.19].

Norberg, Erik. "The Meaning of Words and the Power of Silence." In *The Indigenous Identity of the South Saami. Historical and Political Perspectives on a Minority Within a Minority*, edited by Håkon Hermanstrand, Asbjørn Kolberg, Trond Risto Nilssen, and Leiv Sem, 65–89. New York: Springer, 2019. https://doi.org/10.1007/978-3-030-05029-0_5.

Norsk Teknisk Museum. "Bilder fra raseforskning/Images from Race Science," (Youtube video), 14.06.2018, https://www.youtube.com/watch?v=urcIBW2NrHk [retrieved 17.02.20].

Norwegian National Human Rights Institution Reports. "A Human-Rights Based Approach to Sámi Statistics in Norway," NHRI, 26.08.2020, https://www.nhri.no/en/2020/a-human-rights-based-approach-to-sami-statistics-in-norway/ [retrieved 05.09.20].

Núñez, Milton, Tiina Äikäs, Jouni Aspi, Gunilla Eriksson, Matti Heino, Kerstin Lidén, Markku Oinonen, Jari Okkonen, and Anna-Kaisa Salmi. "Animal Remains from Saami Offering Places: Glimpses of Human Animal-Relations from Finnish Lapland AD 1000–1900." In *Currents of Saami Pasts:*

Recent Advances in Saami Archaeology, edited by Marte Spangen, Anna-Kaisa Salmi, Tiina Äikäs, and Markus Fjellström, 61–78. Monographs of the Archaeological Society of Finland 9. Helsinki: Archaeological Society of Finland, 2020.

Nurmi, Risto, Jari-Matti Kuusela, and Ville Hakamäki. "Swedenization of the North: The Early Medieval Swedish Northern Expansion and the Emergence of the Birkarls." *Acta Borealia* 37 (2020): 1–26. https://doi.org/10.1080/08003831.2020.1757275.

O'Connor, Ralph. "History or Fiction? Truth-Claims and Defensive Narrators in Icelandic Romance-Sagas." *Mediaeval Scandinavia* 14 (2005): 1–69.

O'Connor, Ralph. "History and Fiction." In *The Routledge Research Companion to the Medieval Icelandic Sagas*, edited by Ármann Jakobsson and Sverrir Jakobsson, 88–110. New York: Routledge, 2017. https://doi.org/10.4324/9781315613628-8.

Ojala, Carl-Gösta. "Discussion: Colonialism Past and Present: Archaeological Engagements and Entanglements." In *The Sound of Silence: Indigenous Perspectives on the Historical Archaeology of Colonialism*, edited by Tiina Äikäs and Anna-Kaisa Salmi, 182–201. New York: Berghahn Books, 2019. https://doi.org/10.2307/j.ctv1850hr9.12.

Ojala, Carl-Gösta. *Sámi Prehistories: The Politics of Archaeology and Identity in Northernmost Europe*. Occasional Papers in Archaeology 47. Västerås: Edita Västra Aros, 2017.

Ojala, Carl-Gösta, and Jonas Monié Nordin. "Sámi Archaeology in a Global Perspective: Heritage, Indigeneity and Politics." *Fennoscandia arhcaeologica* 34 (2017): 122–26.

Olofsson, Camilla. "Making New Antlers: Depositions of Animal Skulls and Antlers as a Message of Regeneration in South Sámi Grave Contexts." *Norwegian Archaeological Review* 43, no. 2 (2010): 97–114. https://doi.org/10.1080/00293652.2010.531584.

Olsen, Bjørnar. "Belligerent Chieftains and Oppressed Hunters?: Changing Conceptions of Inter-Ethnic Relationships in Northern Norway During the Iron Age and Early Medieval Period." In *Identities and Cultural Contacts in the Arctic: Proceedings from a Conference at the Danish National Museum Copenhagen, November 30 to December 2 1999*, edited by Martin Appelt, Joel Berglund, and Hans Christian Gulløv, 28–42. Copenhagen: Danish National Museum and Danish Polar Center, 2000.

Olsen, Bjørnar. "Samenes fortid som arkeologisk forskningsfelt: virkningshistoriske utfordringer." In *Historisk rätt? Kultur, politik och juridik i norr*, edited by Inga Lundström, 209–224. Stockholm: Riksantikvarieämbetet, 2007.

Olsen, Bjørnar. "Sámi Archaeology, Postcolonial Theory and Criticism." *Fennoscandia archaeologica* 32 (2016): 215–29.

Olsen, Leiv. *Sørsamisk historie i nytt lys*. Senter for samiske studier, skriftserie 17. Tromsø: Senter for samiske studier, 2010.

Olsen, Magnus. "Semsveinar i Vatnsdœla saga: Et sproglig og litteraturhistorisk bidrag." *Maal og Minne* 12 (1920): 46–54.

Opedal, Arnfrid. "A.W Brøgger and the Norwegianisation of the Prehistory of Norway." *Acta Borealia* 13, no. 1 (1996): 36–46. https://doi.org/10.1080/08003839608580446.

Oskal, Nils. "Political Inclusion of the Saami as Indigenous People in Norway." *International Journal on Minority and Group Rights* 8 (2001): 235–61. https://doi.org/10.1163/15718110120908411.

Panagiotakopulu, Eeva, Paul C. Buckland, and Stephen Wickler. "Is There Anybody in There? Entomological Evidence from a Boat Burial at Øksnes in Vesterålen, Northern Norway." *PloS ONE* 13, no. 7 (2018): 1–18. https://doi.org/10.1371/journal.pone.0200545.

Pedersen, Steinar. The Coastal Sámi of Norway and Their Rights to Traditional Marine Livelihood." *Arctic Review on Law and Politics* 3, no. 1 (2012): 51–80.

Pedersen, Steinar. "Opptaket som aldri ble sendt," Nordnorsk debatt, 22.12.2021, https://www.nord norskdebatt.no/opptaket-som-aldri-ble-sendt/o/5-124-157086 [retrieved 22.12.21].

Pentikäinen, Juha. 2007. *Golden King of the Forest: The Lore of the Northern Bear.* Helsinki: Etnika.

Pentikäinen, Juha, ed. *Shamanism and Northern Ecology.* Berlin: De Gruyter, 1996. https://doi.org/10.1515/9783110811674.

Perabo, Lyonel. *Here Be Heathens: The Supernatural Image of Northern Fenno-Scandinavia in Pre-Modern Literature* (MA diss., Háskoli Íslands, 2016).

Piha, Minerva. *Eteläsaamelaiset rautakautisessa Pohjolassa: Kielitieteellis-arkeologinen näkökulma.* Scripta Lingua Fennica Edita 498. Turku: Painosalama, 2020.

Porsanger, Jelena. "The Problematisation of the Dichotomy of Modernity and Tradition in Indigenous and Sámi Contexts." In *Working with Traditional Knowledge: Communities, Institutions, Information Systems, Law and Ethics,* edited by Jelena Porsanger and Gunvor Guttorm, 225–52. Kautokeino: Sámi allaskuvla, 2011.

Porsanger, Jelena, and Irja Seurujärvi-Kari. "*Sámi dutkama máttut:* The forerunners of Sámi Methodological Thinking." In *Indigenous Research Methodologies in Sámi and Global Contexts,* edited by Pirjo Kristiina Virtanen, Pigga Keskitalo, and Torjer Olsen, 33–64. New Research – New Voices 2 (Leiden: Brill, 2021). https://doi.org/10.1163/9789004463097_003.

Price, Basil Arould. "Búi and the *blámaðr:* Comprehending Racial Others in *Kjalnesinga saga.*" *Viator* 11, no. 4 (2020): 442–50. https://doi.org/10.1057/s41280-020-00195-4.

Price, Neil. "Drum-Time and Viking Age: Sámi-Norse Identities in Early Medieval Scandinavia." In *Identities and Cultural Contacts in the Arctic: Proceedings from a Conference at the Danish National Museum Copenhagen, November 30 to December 2 1999,* edited by Martin Appelt, Joel Berglund, and Hans Christian Gulløv, 12–27. Copenhagen: Danish National Museum and Danish Polar Center, 2000.

Price, Neil. *The Viking Way: Magic and Mind in Late Iron Age Scandinavia,* 2nd edition. Oxford: Oxbow Books, 2019. https://doi.org/10.2307/j.ctvhhhgz3.

Quinn, Eilís. "How Not to Promote Arctic Tourism: Why Finland's Indigenous Sami Say Marketing Their Region Needs to Change," Eye on the Arctic, 03.02.2020, https://www.rcinet.ca/eye-on-the-arctic-special-reports/how-not-to-promote-arctic-tourism-why-finlands-Indigenous-sami-say-marketing-their-region-needs-to-change/ [retrieved 20.05.20].

Radzin, Hilda. "Names in the Mythological Lay 'Rigsþula'." *Literary Onomastics Studies* 9 (1982): 177–82.

Rambaran-Olm, Mary, M. Breann Leake, and Mica James Goodrich. "Editor's Introduction. Medieval Studies: The Stakes of the Field." *postmedieval: a journal of medieval cultural studies* 11, no. 4 (2020): 356–70. https://doi.org/10.1057/s41280-020-00205-5.

Ramos, Eduardo. "Confronting Whiteness: Antiracism in Medieval Studies." *postmedieval: a journal of medieval cultural studies* 11, no. 4 (2020): 493–502. https://doi.org/10.1057/s41280-020-00200-w.

Rask, Rasmus. "En Afhandling om Sprogkyndigheden (Lingvistikken), især de finniske Folkeslags Inddeling." In *Ausgewählte Abhandlungen,* edited by Louis Hjelmeslev, 285–320. Vol. 2. Copenhagen: Levin & Munksgaard, 1932–33.

Rasmussen, Siv. "Å skrive om fortidens samiske mennesker." *DIN: Religionsvitenskapelig tidsskrift* 2 (2018): 7–11.

Raudvere, Catharina. "Trolldómr in Early Medieval Scandinavia." In *Witchcraft and Magic in Europe: The Middle Ages,* edited by Bengt Ankarloo and Stuart Clark, 73–171. The Athlone History of Witchcraft and Magic in Europe, vol. 3. London: The Athlone Press, 2002.

Ross, Alan Strode Campbell. *The Terfinnas and Beormas of Ohthere.* London: Viking Society for Northern Research, 1980.

Rosvold, Jørgen, Gitte Hansen, and Knut H. Røed. "From Mountains to Towns: DNA from Ancient Reindeer Antlers as Proxy for Domestic Procurement Networks in Medieval Norway." *Journal of Archaeological Science* 26 (2019): 1–9. https://doi.org/10.1016/j.jasrep.2019.05.025.

Rowe, Elizabeth Ashman. "*Sǫgubrot af fornkonungum:* Mythologised History for Late Thirteenth-Century Iceland." In *Making History: Essays on the Fornaldarsögur,* edited by Martin Arnold and Alison Finlay, 1–16. London: Viking Society for Northern Research, 2010.

Ruiter, Keith. *Mannjafnaðr: A Study of Normativity, Transgression, and Social Pragmatism in Medieval Scandinavia* (PhD thesis, University of Aberdeen, 2018).

Rydving, Håkan. "Shamanistic and Postshamanistic Terminologies in Saami (Lappish)." *Scripta Instituti Donneriani Aboensis* 12 (1987): 185–207. https://doi.org/10.30674/scripta.67162.

Rydving, Håkan. "Scandinavian-Saami Religious Connections in the History of Research." *Scripta Instituti Donneriani Aboensis* 13 (1990): 358–73. https://doi.org/10.30674/scripta.67185.

Rydving, Håkan. *Tracing Sami Traditions: In Search of the Indigenous Religion Among the Western Sami During the 17th and 18th centuries.* Oslo: Novus, 2010.

Ryynänen, Eva. "*Karjalen Kukkiva Puu* (The Flowering Tree of Karelia) and Continuity Uncovered." In *Sacred to the Touch: Nordic and Baltic Religious Wood Carving,* edited by Thomas DuBois. Seattle: University of Washington Press, 2018.

Saemien Sijte (website), https://saemiensijte.no/ [retrieved 25.11.20].

Said, Edward. *Orientalism.* New York: Pantheon Books, 1978.

Salmi, Anna-Kaisa, Mathilde van den Berg, Sirpa Niinimäki, and Maxime Pelletier. "Earliest Archaeological Evidence for Domesticated Reindeer Economy among the Sámi of Northeastern Fennoscandia AD 1300 onwards." *Journal of Anthropological Archaeology* 6 (2021): 1–15. https://doi.org/10.1016/j.jaa.2021.101303.

Salvesen, Helge. "Tendenser i den historiske sameforskning: med særlig vekt på politikk og forskning." *Scandia* 46, no. 1 (1980): 21–52.

Sameblod, directed by Amanda Kernell. Nordisk Film, 2016.

Sámediggi. "Hjertespråket," https://sametinget.no/sprak/hjertespraket-vaajmoegiele-vajmo-giella-vaib mogiella-utredningen/ [retrieved 30.11.21].

Sandberg, Nina. *Offerträdet: Spår av offer, blot och kult under vikingatiden på Frösön, Jämtland* (BA diss., University of Stockholm, 2016).

Sandnes, Jørn. "Om samenes utbredelse mot sør i eldre tid." *Historisk tidsskrift* 52, no. 3 (1972): 113–37.

Sandnes, Jørn. "Sørsamenes eldre historie igjen," *Historisk tidsskrift* 53 (1974): 415–21.

Schanche, Audhild. *Nordnorsk jernalderarkeologi: Et sosialgeografisk perspektiv* (MA diss., University of Tromsø, 1986).

Schanche, Audhild. *Graver i ur og berg: Samisk gravskikk og religion fra forhistorisk til nyere tid.* Karasjok: Davvi Girji, 2000.

Schanche, Audhild, and Bjørnar Olsen. "Var de alle nordmenn? En etnopolitisk kritikk av norsk arkeologi." In *Arkeologi og etnisitet,* edited by Jenny-Rita Næss, 87–99. AmS-Varia 15. Stavanger: Arkeologisk Museum UiS, 1983.

Selberg, Kjersti. *Eldre norske rettskilder: en oversikt.* Juridisk biblioteks skriftserie 20. Oslo: Universitetsbiblioteket, 2013.

STDSK. "Truth and Reconciliation Commission Concerning the Sámi People," SDTSK.fi, https://sdtsk.fi/en/home/ [retrieved 16.06.22].

Sem, Leiv. "Om framstillinga av sørsamar i *Trøndelags historie*." *Heimen* 54, no. 2 (2017): 130–44. https://doi.org/10.18261/issn.1894-3195-2017-02-03.
Shepherd, Nick. "Naming the Indigenous." In *Archaeologies of "Us" and "Them": Debating History, Heritage and Indigeneity*, edited by Charlotta Hillerdal, Anna Karlström, and Carl-Gösta Ojala, 33–37. London: Routledge, 2017. https://doi.org/10.4324/9781315641997-4.
Skandfer, Marianne. "Ethics in the Landscape: Prehistoric Archaeology and Local Sámi Knowledge in Interior Finnmark, Northern Norway." *Arctic Anthropology* 46 (2009): 89–102. https://doi.org/10.1353/arc.0.0029.
Solli, Britt. *Seid. Myter, sjamanisme og kjønn i vikingenes tid*. Oslo: Pax Forlag, 2002.
Somby, Ánde, and Øyvind Ravna. "Problematisk perspektiv om det samiske fra NRK," Khrono, 18.12.2021, https://khrono.no/problematisk-perspektiv-om-det-samiske-fra-nrk/642798 [retrieved 22.12.2021].
Spangen, Marte. "Coast as Meeting Place for Believes [sic] and Traditions: Silver Hoards in North Norway." In *Kystkultur: Aktuel arkæologi i Norden*, edited by Anna Beck, Helle Fredriksen, Lise Harvig, Christian Juel, Kjartan Langsted, Tina Rasmussen, and Gerd Bindesbøl Ravnholt, 85–93. Kontaktstencil 44. Copenhagen, 2004.
Spangen, Marte. "Silver Hoards in Sámi Areas." In *Recent Perspectives on Sámi Archaeology in Fennoscandia and North-West Russia*, edited by Petri Halinen, Mika Lavento, and Mervi Suhonen, 94–106. Helsinki: Finnish Antiquarian Society, 2009).
Spangen, Marte. *Circling Concepts: A Critical Archaeological Analysis of the Notion of Stone Circles as Sami Offering Sites*. Stockholm Studies in Archaeology 70. Malmö: Holmbergs, 2016.
Spangen, Marte. "Sámi Myths and Medieval Heritage." In *Myths and Magic in the Medieval Far North*, edited by Stefan Figenschow, Richard Holt, and Miriam Tveit, 119–42. Turnhout: Brepols, 2020. https://doi.org/10.1484/m.as-eb.5.120522.
Spangen, Marte, Anna-Kaisa Salmi, and Tiina Äikäs. "Sámi Archaeology and Postcolonial Theory: An Introduction." *Arctic Anthropology* 52, no. 2 (2015): 1–5. https://doi.org/10.3368/aa.52.2.1.
Spangen, Marte, Anna-Kaisa Salmi, Tiina Äikäs, and Markus Fjellström, eds. *Currents of Saami Pasts: Recent Advances in Saami Archaeology*. Monographs of the Archaeological Society of Finland 9. Helsinki: Archaeological Society of Finland, 2020.
Spangen, Marte, and Johan Eilertsen Arntzen. "Sticky Structures and Opportunistic Builders: The Construction and Social Role of Longhouses in Northern Norway." In *Re-Imagining Periphery: Archaeology and Text in Northern Europe from Iron Age to Viking and Early Medieval Periods*, edited by Charlotta Hillerdal and Kristin Ilves, 11–32. Oxford: Oxbow Books, 2020. https://doi.org/10.2307/j.ctv138wt08.5.
Steinsland, Gro. *Det hellige bryllup og norrøn kongeideologi: En analyse av Hierogami-myten i Skírnismál, Ynglingatál, Háleygjatál og Hyndluljóð*. Larvik: Solum forlag, 1991.
Stenvik, Lars Fredrik. "Samer og nordmenn: Sett i lys av et uvanlig gravfunn fra Saltenområdet." In *Viking*, edited by Sverre Marstrander and Arne Skjølsvold, 127–39. Norsk arkeologisk årbok, vol. 43. Oslo: Norsk Arkeologisk Selskap, 1980.
Store norske leksikon. "Andor," snl.no, 07.12.2018, https://snl.no/andor [retrieved 27.01.20].
Store norske leksikon. "Borgarting," snl.no, 10.11.2017, https://snl.no/Borgarting [retrieved 08.12.19].
Store norske leksikon. "Egils saga," snl.no, 01.04.2014, https://snl.no/Egils_saga [retrieved 20.04.21].
Store norske leksikon. "Eidsivatingsloven," snl.no, 10.11.2017, https://snl.no/Eidsivatingsloven [retrieved 20.04.21].
Store norske leksikon. "Fagrskinna," snl.no, 26.09.2019, https://snl.no/Fagrskinna [retrieved 20.04.21].

Store norske leksikon. "Finnboga saga ramma," snl.no, 01.04.2019, https://snl.no/Finnboga_saga_ramma [retrieved 07.04.21].
Store norske leksikon. "Frostatingslova," snl.no, 05.05.2019, https://snl.no/Frostatingslova [retrieved 24.05.21].
Store norske leksikon. "Grågås," snl.no, 10.11.2017, https://snl.no/Gr%C3%A5g%C3%A5s [retrieved 18.12.19].
Store norske leksikon. "Gulating," snl.no, 10.11.2017, https://snl.no/Gulating [retrieved 09.12.19].
Store norske leksikon. "Magnus Lagabøters Landslov," snl.no, 11.11.2020, https://snl.no/Magnus_Lagab%C3%B8ters_landslov [retrieved 18.12.19].
Store norske leksikon. "Morkinskinna," snl.no, 04.12.2020, https://snl.no/Morkinskinna [retrieved 20.04.21].
Store norske leksikon. "Orkneyinga saga," snl.no, 04.04.2019, https://snl.no/Orkneyinga_saga [retrieved 26.04.21].
Store norske leksikon. "Samisk," snl.no, 20.12.2020, https://snl.no/samisk [retrieved 29.02.20].
Store norske leksikon. "Sverres saga," snl.no, 04.03.2021, https://snl.no/Sverres_saga [retrieved 07.04.21].
Store norske leksikon. "Tersamisk," snl.no, 25.09.2019, https://snl.no/tersamisk [retrieved 27.03.20].
Store norske leksikon. "Vatnsdœla saga," snl.no, 04.04.2019, https://snl.no/Vatnsd%C5%93la_saga [retrieved 20.04.21].
Store norske leksikon. "Ågrip," snl.no, 20.01.2021, https://snl.no/%C3%85grip [retrieved 20.04.21].
Storfjell, Troy. "The Ambivalence of the Wild: Figuring Sápmi and the Sámi in Pre-Colonial and Colonial Discourse to the Eighteenth Century." In *L'Image du Sápmi*, edited by Kajsa Andersson, 112–47. Volume 2. Humanistica Oerebroensia. Artes et linguae 16. Örebro: Örebro University Press, 2009.
Storli, Inger. "Sami Viking Age Pastoralism: or the Fur Trade Paradigm Reconsidered." *Norwegian Archaeological Review* 26, no. 1 (1993): 1–20. https://doi.org/10.1080/00293652.1993.9965550.
Storli, Inger. *"Stallo"-boplassene: Spor etter de første fjellsamer?* Oslo: Novus, 1994.
Strömbäck, Dag. *Sejd: textstudier i nordisk religionshistoria*. Stockholm: Gebers, 1935.
Suneson, Anders. "Sápmi," Samiskt Informationscentrum, http://www.samer.se/1002 [retrieved 01.03.21].
Svanberg, Fredrik. *Decolonizing the Viking Age*. Acta archaeologica Lundensia 8, 43. Vol. 1. Uppsala: Almqvist & Wiksell, 2006.
Sveriges Domstolar. "Mål: T 853–18, Girjasdomen," Domstol.se, 23.01.2020, https://www.domstol.se/hogsta-domstolen/avgoranden/2020/47294/ [retrieved 01.02.21].
Sverrir Jakobsson. "'Black Men and Malignant-Looking': The Place of the Indigenous Peoples of North America in the Icelandic World-View." In *Approaches to Vínland. A Conference on the Written and Archaeological Sources for the Norse Settlements in the North Atlantic Region and Exploration of America. The Nordic House, Reykjavík 9–11 August 1999*, edited by Andrew Warn and Þórunn Sigurðardóttir, 88–104. Sigurður Nordal Institute Studies 4. Reykjavík, 2001.
Svestad, Asgeir. "Svøpt i myra: Synspunkter på Skjoldehamnfunnets etniske og kulturelle tilknytning." In *Viking*, edited by Herdis Hølleland, Kjetil Loftsgaarden, Astrid Johanne Nyland, and Christian Løchsen Rødsrud, 129–56. Norsk arkeologisk årbok, vol. 80. Oslo: Norsk Arkeologisk Selskap, 2017. https://doi.org/10.5617/viking.5476.
Sørsamisk Digitalt. "Gaavnoes" (website), https://gaavnoes.no/ [retrieved 26.11.20].
Sävborg, Daniel. "Den 'efterklassiska' isländningasagan och dess ålder." *Arkiv för nordisk filologi* 27 (2012): 19–58. https://doi.org/10.1484/m.bbl-eb.5.112962.

Sävborg, Daniel, and Karen Bek-Pedersen, ed. *Supernatural Encounters in Old Norse Literature and Tradition.* Turnhout: Brepols, 2018.
Tolley, Clive. *"Hrólfs saga kraka* and Sámi Bear Rites." *Saga-Book* 31 (2007): 5–21.
Tolley, Clive. *Shamanism in Norse Myth and Magic.* Helsinki: Academia Scientarium Fennica, 2009.
Torfi H. Tulinius. "Sagas of Icelandic Prehistory." In *A Companion to Old-Norse Icelandic Literature and Culture,* edited by Rory McTurk, 447–61. Oxford: Blackwell Publishing, 2005. https://doi.org/10.1002/9780470996867.ch26.
Tuhiwai Smith, Linda. *Decolonizing Methodologies: Research and Indigenous Peoples.* 2nd edition. London: Zed Books, 2012.
Turberfield, Lisa. *Intoxicating Women: Old Norse Drinking Culture and the Role of Women* (PhD thesis, University of Aberdeen, 2016).
UNESCO. "UNESCO Atlas of the World's Languages in Danger," Unesco.org, http://www.unesco.org/languages-atlas/index.php [retrieved 30.11.20].
UiT. Sannhets- og forsoningskommisjonen, https://uit.no/kommisjonen [retrieved 01.02.21].
Vasaru, Merri Koskela. "Bjarmaland and Interaction in the North of Europe from the Viking Age until the Early Middle Ages." *Journal of Northern Studies* 6, 2 (2012): 37–58.
Virtanen, Pirjo Kristiina, Pigga Keskitalo, and Torjer Olsen, eds. *Indigenous Research Methodologies in Sámi and Global Contexts.* New Research – New Voices 2. Leiden: Brill, 2021. https://doi.org/10.1163/9789004463097.
Virtanen, Pirjo Kristiina, Pigga Keskitalo, and Torjer Olsen. "Contemporary Indigenous Research within Sámi and Global Indigenous Studies Contexts." In Pirjo Kristiina Virtanen, Pigga Keskitalo, and Torjer Olsen, eds, *Indigenous Research Methodologies in Sámi and Global Contexts,* 7–32. New Research – New Voices 2. Leiden: Brill, 2021. https://doi.org/10.1163/9789004463097_002.
Wang, Solveig Marie. "Conceptualizing the Multicultural 'North' in the *Íslendingasögur*: Peoples, Places and Phenomena." *Nordlit* 46 (2020): 245–62. https://doi.org/10.7557/13.5480.
Westberg, David. "Research on Procopius of Caesarea in the Scandinavian Languages." *Histos* 9 (2019): 8.1–0.
Wickler, Stephen. "The Centrality of Small Islands in Arctic Norway." *Acta Borealia* 11, no. 2 (2016): 171–94. https://doi.org/10.1080/15564894.2015.1134728.
Wilhelmsson, Caroline. "Crusades, Cities and Castles: Finland as Sweden's Militarised Borderland c. 1150–1300." *Apardjón* 2 (2021): 49–76.
Wills, Tarrin, ed. "Búmaðr." Lexicon Poeticum, https://lexiconpoeticum.org/m.php?p=lemma&i=11761 [retrieved 12.02.21].
Wills, Tarrin, ed. "Finnr." Lexicon Poeticum, https://lexiconpoeticum.org/m.php?p=lemma&i=20183 [retrieved 10.11.20].
Wærdahl, Randi B. *Norges konges rike og hans skattland: Kongemakt og statsutvikling i den norrøne verden i middelalderen* (PhD thesis, Norwegian University of Science and Technology, 2006).
Willson, Kendra. "A Putative Sámi Charm on a 12th c. Icelandic Spade: Runic Reception, Magic and Contact." In *Finno-Ugric Folklore, Myth and Cultural Identity,* edited by Cornelius Hasselblatt and Adriaan Van der Hoeven, 267–81. Groeningen: University of Groeningen, 2011.
Yamamoto, Sara Hagström. *I gränslandet mellan svenskt och samisk: Identitetsdirskurser och förhistorien i Norrland från 1870-tal til 2000-tal.* Occasional Papers in Archaeology 52. Västerås: Edita Västra Aros, 2010.
Ylimaunu, Timo, Sami Lakomaki, Titta Kallio-Seppä, Paul R. Mullins, Risto Nurmi, and Markku Kuorilehto. "Borderlands as Spaces: Creating Third Spaces and Fractured Landscapes in

Medieval Northern Finland." *Journal of Social Archaeology* 14, no. 2 (2014): 244–67. https://doi.org/10.1177/1469605313519316.

Zachariassen, Ketil. "Fornorskningspolitikken overfor samar og kvenar," Norgeshistorie, 02.02.2020, https://www.norgeshistorie.no/industrialisering-og-demokrati/1554-fornorskingspolitikken-over for-samar-og-kvenar.html [retrieved 29.01.21].

Zachariassen, Ketil. "Samisk historie – historiefagets oppgåve og funksjon," Nordnorsk debatt, 21.12.2021, https://www.nordnorskdebatt.no/samisk-historie-historiefagets-oppgave-og-funksjon/o/5-124-156793 [retrieved 22.12.21].

Zachrisson, Inger, ed. *Möten i gränsland: Samer och germaner i Mellanskandinavien.* Monographs 4. Stockholm: Statens Historiska Museum, 1997.

Zachrisson, Inger. "The So-called Scandinavian Cultural Boundary in Northern Sweden in Viking Times: Ethnic or Socio-Economic? A Study Based on the Archaeological Material." *Acta Borealia* 5 (1998): 70–97. https://doi.org/10.1080/08003838808580357.

Zachrisson, Inger. "The Sámi and Their Interactions with Nordic Peoples." In *The Viking World*, edited by Stefan Brink and Neil Price, 32–39. London: Routledge, 2012. https://doi.org/10.4324/9780203412770-13.

Zachrisson, Inger. "Samiska och nordiska kvinnor." In *Kvinner i vikingtid*, edited by Nancy Coleman and Nanna Løkka, 243–68. Oslo: Scandinavian Academic Press, 2014.

Østby, Tore, Hanne Magga, and Sara Kristine Bransfjell. "Hva var rasistisk ved Selbu Utmarksråd sitt møte?" Rørosnytt, 09.06.2019, https://rorosnytt.no/hva-var-rasistisk-ved-selbu-utmarksrad-sitt-mote/?fbclid=IwAR2h7DZVLzqmS6pFsvGkAwlm32TG50UZ67sx96haYC7R2mMLSlZdiabmdqI [retrieved 25.11.20].

Index

á fjáll upp   121, 124, 140, 153 f., 243
accommodation   57, 118, 226
Adam of Bremen   34, 37, 40, 71, 74, 97, 224, 229
Adamvalldá   153–155
Agdenes   77, 114, 237
agency   15, 25, 33, 61, 129, 137, 151, 156, 162, 171, 176
Ágrip   1, 55, 57, 78, 82, 84, 86, 113, 149, 158, 179, 185 f., 234 f.
alliances   1, 7, 45 f., 50, 55, 57, 62, 141, 170, 178, 181, 183, 190, 192 f., 204, 210
ancestry   45–47
animals   6, 35 f., 38, 70, 73, 90, 95, 97, 102, 117 f., 164, 209, 224, 248
Áns saga bogsveigis   59 f.
archaeological record   29, 103, 198, 200, 202–204, 218, 235
archery   6, 45, 60 f., 64, 66 f., 73, 99–101, 106, 118, 152, 184, 235, 243, 248
arctic   212
Arnljótr gellini   242
Átti inn dœlski   100, 242 f.

Bálagarðssíða   143 f., 229
Baltic Sea   22, 100, 144, 202, 229
Bárðar saga Snæfellsáss   50
bears   60 f., 63, 84, 94, 102, 104–107, 153, 157, 164, 200, 224, 235 f.
bilingualism   54, 97, 195 f.
birkarlar   142, 147, 157, 175, 228
Bjálkaland   101
Bjarkarey (Bjarkøy)   115, 123, 159, 162
Bjarmaland   56, 61, 70, 117, 121, 125–127, 135–137, 139, 167
Bjarmar   33, 40, 135–137, 139, 142, 149, 168, 180, 189, 193 f., 200
boats   13, 35 f., 107–109, 141, 248, 251
borderland   131
borders   1, 8, 39, 70, 72, 129, 137, 149, 151, 166, 205, 223, 228, 248
Borgarþingslǫg   8, 41 f., 127, 206, 227, 238
Bufinna   See *búmaðr*
búmaðr   44, 115, 123

búmenn   See *búmaðr*
burial traditions   203, 220
butter   52, 77, 152, 158, 173, 175 f.

Christianisation   10, 21, 39, 223 f., 228
Christianity   38 f., 44, 71, 76 f., 80, 82, 84 f., 89, 95, 130, 132, 134, 206 f., 210
Church   41 f., 68, 71, 224
cloaks   79, 103, 113, 117
clothing   36, 60, 94, 112, 117, 169, 205, 213, 248
co-habitation   116
colonial structures   2, 18, 23, 27, 158, 218, 247
colonialism   15, 27, 31, 111, 119, 215, 247, 250
communication   11, 105, 114, 138, 190 f., 194 f., 197 f., 211, 228
composition   34, 58, 60, 72, 75, 116, 134, 138, 150, 154 f., 171, 176, 183 f., 198, 203, 223, 227, 249, 251
conflict   28, 47, 57, 77, 79, 126, 133, 138, 140, 147, 155, 159–163, 170, 183, 211, 217, 228
conversion   34, 38 f., 71, 80, 83, 85, 95, 125, 132, 134, 206–210, 223 f., 228
conversion narrative   80, 83, 95, 208 f.
cultural affiliation   2, 4, 46, 77, 84 f., 89, 103, 132, 180, 186 f., 234, 237, 249

Dalarna   149, 213
De Bello Gothico   35, 107
decolonisation   4, 18, 27, 31–33, 250
descent   2, 4, 7, 45–47, 50, 55, 60 f., 63 f., 71, 87, 100, 183–185, 187, 189, 196, 211, 230, 237, 239, 244, 249
Diplomatarium Norvegicum   37, 68 f., 170
divination   See magic
Dofri   56, 117, 149, 167, 227, 234, 236
Dovre   56 f., 116, 149, 200, 231, 234 f., 237, 245
dreams   46, 50, 122, 244
dualism   163, 165, 198
dwarves   13, 86

Edda   8, 62–64, 104
Eddic   See *Edda*

Egils saga Skallagrímssonar 50 f., 59 f., 87, 110, 124, 125, 127, 133, 140 f., 144, 147 f., 154 f., 157, 165, 169, 190, 193, 227
Eiðsivaþingslǫg 8, 42, 95, 206, 209, 223, 227, 232
Eiríkr blóðøx 76, 97, 99, 114, 187, 195
England 1, 33, 68, 152, 156, 168, 170, 176, 249
etymology 64
Eyrbyggja saga 50, 87
Eyvindr kinnrifa 56, 80, 130, 188, 207, 211
Eyvindr skáldaspillir 46, 67, 98, 237

Færeyinga saga 235
Fagrskinna 46, 55, 57, 107, 122 f., 188, 191
far north 6, 30, 33, 104, 110, 113, 119, 127, 163, 212 f., 230, 246, 249
Faravið 140 f.
farming 44, 60, 81, 115, 161, 184, 235
Fennoscandia 1 f., 6, 8, 13, 22, 29 f., 32 f., 37 f., 42, 61, 67, 70, 81, 103, 111, 119, 133–135, 139 f., 148–150, 167, 175 f., 196, 199, 202, 213, 217, 226, 228, 241, 250, 252
Finland 1, 6, 8, 16 f., 22, 29, 35, 38, 40, 56, 67, 71, 82, 85, 100, 103, 116, 124, 138, 141, 142–149, 167, 219, 223, 229 f.
fínmarkr 41 f., 127 f., 226 f., 238, 243
finn 6, 50, 230
Finna ein fjǫlkunnig 52, 77
Finnakonungr 46, 59, 61, 69, 71, 78, 86, 102, 113, 179, 181, 188
finnar 6, 13 f., 37 f., 40, 45, 69, 87
Finnboga saga ramma 46, 50 f., 78, 99, 106, 157
Finnbogi 51, 99, 106, 157
finnferð 51, 152–155, 159, 161, 165
finnkaup 51, 67, 87, 128, 133, 151 f., 152, 154 f., 157–163, 165, 168, 170 f., 173, 176 f., 181, 190, 193, 196, 207, 243, 249
Finnlendingar 143
Finnmark 16, 32, 112, 123 f., 127, 129, 134, 146, 158, 171 f., 201, 203, 215, 220
Finnmǫrk 39 f., 42, 45, 51, 55–57, 60 f., 68 f., 76, 79, 84, 97, 99, 102, 104, 106, 110, 114 f., 117, 120, 122–125, 127–130, 136, 140, 144, 146, 149 f., 157, 160, 166, 168, 170 f., 173, 181, 188, 191 f., 215, 223, 226–228, 230, 237 f., 248
Finnr Eyvindarson 229
Finnr litli 100, 111, 192, 196, 239, 245

Finns 13 f., 66, 99, 143, 147 f., 173, 231
finnskatt 51, 66, 151, 155, 157, 159, 161, 163, 165, 171, 191, 249
Fishing 9, 11, 16, 39, 64, 102, 107, 108 f., 109, 124, 126, 128, 132, 137, 248, 251
Flateyjarbók 60, 69, 86, 115
fluid spatial awareness 123, 150, 199, 241
fluidity 1 f., 4, 33, 96, 123, 148, 174, 178, 200, 202, 220, 223–225, 249, 251
Forest-Finns 10, 17
fornaldarsögur 7, 47, 49, 58 f., 61 f., 110, 135, 138, 174
fostering 57, 116, 137, 170, 179, 182, 188 f.
framrykningsteori 29, 214 f.
Frösön 223 f.
Frostaþingslǫg 44, 127, 236
fur-trade 1, 51, 71, 128, 130, 141, 148–152, 156, 158 f., 163, 168–170, 172, 175 f., 190

gammi 61, 113 f., 116 f., 248
Gand 92–94
Gautreks saga 59
Geirsver 125 f.
Geographia 35
Germania 35 f., 106, 112
Gesta Danorum 8, 40 f., 146
Gesta Hammaburgensis 8, 37–39, 74, 131
Getica 35 f.
giants 47, 51 f., 64 f., 86–88, 182 f., 185 f.
Gǫngu-Hrólfs saga 59
goods 51, 61, 126, 145, 152, 154, 156, 158 f., 161, 163, 167, 169–171, 173, 175 f., 211
Grágás 43, 97
Greenland 166, 172
Grettis saga Ásmundarssonar 43, 50, 169
Gríms saga loðinkinna 61, 81, 84
Guðbrandsdalr 83, 95, 149, 209, 227, 244
Gulaþingslǫg 8, 42, 136
Gulf of Bothnia 141, 175
Gull-Ásu-Þórðar þáttur 162 f.
Gull-Þóris saga 50 f.
Gunnhildr konungamóðir 46, 55–57, 76, 82, 97, 99, 114, 188, 191, 195, 206, 211

Haðaland 58, 84, 149, 185–187, 227, 231 f., 234, 238 f., 241, 245
Hadeland 1, 58, 200, 231 f., 239

Hákon Hákonarson   45, 68, 159
Hákon Magnússon   69, 71, 125
Hákonar saga Hákonarsonar   55, 68, 132, 137, 159, 192
hálfbergrisi   51, 87, 155, 165, 184
Hálfdanar saga Eysteinssonar   59, 60, 86, 100, 238f., 241
Hálfdanar þáttr svarta   59f., 85, 234
hálftrǫll   51, 60, 87, 184
Hálogaland   34, 37f., 40, 46, 51f., 56, 67, 69f., 79f., 84, 89, 98, 100, 106, 117, 121–124, 127f., 130–134, 137, 142, 149f., 154f., 159f., 163, 167f., 171, 176, 180, 195, 204, 207f., 215, 223, 236–238, 241
Hälsingland   38, 124, 141, 147, 228, 245
Haralds saga hárfagra   55, 57, 82, 88, 113, 179f., 185, 232, 234, 239
Hárekr ór Þjótta   67, 80, 115, 130, 160, 170, 207
Härjedalen   *See* Herdalar
harrying   56, 82, 100, 121, 135, 143, 167, 229f.
Hauks þáttr hábrókar   59f., 86, 103, 189
healing   74, 86, 88
heathen   34, 38, 69, 76, 80, 109, 197, 208
Hedmark   31, 59, 103, 116, 213, 215, 218f., 221, 223, 245
Heiðmǫrk   149, 227, 235, 244f.
Heimskringla   13f., 44, 55–57, 64, 78–84, 86, 88, 95, 97f., 100, 102f., 107, 123, 125f., 130, 134, 135f., 139, 143–145, 147, 157, 160, 168, 173, 179, 180, 184, 186f., 191f., 229, 232, 234, 237, 239, 242, 244
Helgisaga   55, 75, 77, 79, 103f., 113, 118, 122f., 144, 191, 194
Herdalar   82, 143f., 229
Hildiríðarsynir   156, 190
Hinnøya   123, 159, 191, 193
Historia gentis Langobardorum   36
Historia Norwegie   8, 53, 55, 76, 78, 85, 89, 91f., 95–97, 99, 102, 106, 108, 113, 121, 131, 135, 152, 164f., 190, 227
historicity   13, 16f., 214, 217, 231
historiography   15, 27, 32, 48, 59, 80, 85, 215, 250
Hlaðir   51, 130, 160, 168, 235
hostilities   16, 61, 135f., 141
Hrafnhildr   60f., 87, 110–112, 181, 184
Hrafnista   60, 195

Hrafnistumannasögur   60f.
Hrólfs saga kraka   59f., 84, 98, 101, 104, 181, 235
hunting   6, 9, 11, 13, 16, 18, 35, 39, 45, 63f., 67, 73, 99, 101–104, 106, 117f., 137, 144, 147, 151–153, 158, 163, 165, 200, 216, 218f., 223f., 228, 243, 248, 251

Iceland   1, 33, 42–47, 50, 52, 59, 62, 76, 92, 113, 131, 152, 166, 171f., 176, 181, 197, 208, 249
identity   2, 4, 8, 11, 21, 25, 29, 33, 46, 80, 116, 123, 127, 142, 172, 175, 178, 180, 189, 195f., 198, 202f., 205, 207f., 210f., 213, 217, 220–226, 228, 237, 241, 245f., 249, 251
ILO 169   4f., 29, 236
inbetweeners   198, 199
Indigeneity   5, 16, 24, 27, 29, 31f., 217, 236, 249
Indigenous   1, 4f., 8f., 11, 13, 15–17, 19–25, 27–29, 31, 40, 84, 119, 180, 212f., 216f., 229, 247, 250
Indigenous Turn   31
interface   200, 202, 204, 211, 224, 240
Íslendingasögur   8, 43, 47, 49f., 55, 71, 119, 132

Jämtland   124, 149, 200, 213, 218, 223f., 228, 245
Jordanes   35f., 38, 97
jǫtunn   *See* giant

Karelia   1, 6, 138, 223
kennings   *See* skaldic poetry
Ketils saga hœngs   59f., 81, 86f., 99, 102, 110, 114, 173, 181, 248
King Alfred   34, 36–38, 108, 163, 168
Kirjálaland   124, 135, 138, 141, 144
Kirjálar   138, 140, 142, 149, 168
Kjalnesinga saga   3, 50, 188
Kola peninsula   70
konungasögur   8, 47, 49, 55, 57f., 71
Kven   10, 17, 37, 140–142
Kvenir   140–142, 149, 168
Kvenland   124, 135, 141, 144, 146
Kylfingar   51, 140, 142, 149

Landnámabók   8, 44, 46, 52, 100, 181, 184, 208
landscapes   40f., 119, 125, 145–150, 169, 182, 189, 212, 221, 223, 227f., 230, 238, 240–243, 245f., 249

language 6, 9, 15, 29, 37, 43, 52, 54, 87, 135–138, 174, 186, 194–198, 210 f., 213
Lapp 9, 13, 147
Lappi *See* Lappland
Lappia 40, 68, 146, 148
Lappir 141, 146–149
Lappland 40, 142 f., 146, 148, 158
Lappmarken 146
law 41–43, 71, 227
legal matters 34, 41, 44, 58, 61, 69, 71, 75, 83 f., 86–89, 95, 99, 115, 127 f., 141, 159, 206, 210, 228, 231, 233, 239 f.
Lenvik 123, 126
liminality 2, 4, 126, 150, 178, 198
literary tool 23–25, 225, 232, 246
Ljósvetninga saga 46, 50
Lyngen 70, 129, 149

Magic 1, 5, 7, 22, 32, 40, 42, 46, 52 f., 56 f., 58 f., 59 f., 62 f., 67, 71, 73–76, 78–82, 84 f., 87, 89 f., 90 f., 92, 93, 94–96, 99–101, 106, 112, 118, 126 f., 136, 146, 172, 180 f., 184, 186, 191, 193, 195, 196, 205, 206, 212, 233, 240, 248, 251, 252
Magnus Eriksson 147, 228
Malangen 123
marriage 1, 40, 46, 49, 51, 57, 61 f., 82, 137, 170, 178–180, 182 f., 188, 204, 234
methodologies 2, 4, 27 f., 32 f., 247, 250
middle ground 185, 198
Mjǫll 59, 61, 98
Morkinskinna 55–57, 107, 114 f., 123, 132, 158, 161 f., 170, 172, 191
Mǫttul 46, 57, 113, 188, 206
multi-room houses 171 f.
mythology 45, 63 f., 98, 104, 142, 146, 180, 182

Namdalen 19, 47
ǫndurdís 64, 97
negotiation 33, 136 f., 149, 178, 202, 207, 225, 228, 245 f., 249
Niðarós 39, 79, 234
noaidevuohta 93 f.
noaidi 93 f., 113
non-Christian Other 189
Nordland 29, 156, 203, 213

Norway 1, 5 f., 8 f., 11, 13 f., 16, 18, 28, 30, 32, 34, 38–43, 45, 56–58, 68, 70 f., 86, 95, 100, 103, 105, 107–109, 115 f., 119, 121–124, 126, 128, 130 f., 135, 139, 141 f., 144, 146 f., 149, 151, 153, 160, 166, 168, 170 f., 174, 179, 188, 198–200, 202, 206–208, 214, 219, 223, 225–228, 230 f., 233, 235 f., 238, 242–246
Nöteborg 140, 145
Novgorod 9, 68, 71, 101, 126, 133, 136, 138, 145, 148–150, 158, 161, 163, 166, 169, 175

Oddr Snorrason 56, 77, 79 f., 121
Óðinn 54, 64, 67, 77 f., 80, 180, 237
Ohthere 7, 34, 36–38, 51, 68, 102, 106, 108 f., 130, 135, 137 f., 141, 151–153, 163–165, 168, 174, 176, 194
Óláfr Haraldsson 56, 75, 77 f., 89, 100, 102, 128, 143, 229 f.
Óláfr Tryggvason 77, 79, 81, 130
Óláfs saga helga 82, 100, 102, 135 f., 145, 192, 229, 240, 242
Óláfs saga Tryggvasonar 55, 56, 77, 80 f., 100, 114, 121, 131, 134, 169, 191, 192, 207, 229, 235, 237
Óláfs saga Tryggvasonar en mesta 55, 80, 169, 191, 207, 229, 235
Oppland 41, 58, 66, 149, 227
Orientalism 27
Orkney 141, 166
Orkneyinga saga 55, 141, 146
Oslo 12, 19, 23, 25, 31, 34, 41, 54, 84, 111, 116, 119, 129, 179, 181, 203 f., 206, 213, 219–221, 230, 232, 240, 245 f.
Østerdalen 31, 97, 116, 149, 200, 221, 223, 228, 245
Other 12, 20, 22–24, 26, 62 f., 88 f., 110, 164, 185, 189, 200, 236, 247, 251
othered *See* other
Othering 5, 7, 23–25, 50, 52, 61, 73, 77, 118, 185, 189, 211, 232, 241 f., 246
Otherness 21–24, 73, 77, 80, 88, 225

Passio et miracula beati Olavi 39
Paulus Diaconus 36, 97, 102, 112
periphery 23–25, 122, 129, 182

personal relations 1, 7, 33, 45, 55, 60, 68, 71, 114, 137, 157, 169, 174, 178 f., 189 f., 193, 195, 199 f., 210 f., 228, 249, 251
physical characteristics 110
poetry 34, 46, 62 f., 65–67, 100
postcolonial framework 8
privilege 51, 56, 128, 155, 157, 160, 163, 165, 176, 190, 207
Procopius 35 f., 97, 107
prophesy *See* magic
Ptolemy's 35

Rauðr inn rammi 56, 80, 131, 134, 156, 192, 207
Rauðssynir 244
reindeer 9, 16, 29, 36 f., 67, 78, 92, 97, 102 f., 107, 112, 117, 133, 153, 157, 164 f., 170, 173 f., 200, 204 f., 220, 235, 242, 248
rekspegn 44, 236
religion 31, 69, 71, 84, 94, 101, 187, 210, 224
Rendalen 221
Reykdœla saga ok Víga-Skútu 50, 81
Rímbegla 123, 126
ritual 1, 10, 22, 42, 56, 74, 85, 90–96, 105, 113, 127, 134, 178, 196, 205 f., 208–211, 221–224, 233, 251
ritual performer 92 f., 113, 221
Rounala 84
royal retinue 191
Russia 1, 6, 8, 11, 29, 69 f., 127, 133 f., 138, 172, 200, 202
Ǫrvar-Odds saga 59–62, 76, 81, 99, 101, 106, 110, 137 f., 194, 196, 236

Saami history 4, 16, 23, 27 f., 30 f., 214–217, 225
Saami Motif-Cluster 5, 7, 25, 33 f., 40, 45 f., 50, 55, 59 f., 62–67, 71, 73, 118, 152, 184 f., 187, 192, 226, 236 f., 239, 242–246, 248, 251
Saami „princess" motif 59, 78, 82, 98, 149, 179, 181, 211
Sæmingr 64, 237 f.
Sápmi 1, 3, 8 f., 13, 16, 22, 24, 27, 29, 54, 65, 69, 84, 89, 95, 114, 146, 236
Saxo 38–41, 68, 74, 77 f., 84, 97 f., 112 f., 121, 135–137, 144, 146–149, 151, 164, 179 f., 189, 193
Scandia 30, 35
Scridefinne 37

scritefenni 40
seiðr 85, 90 f., 93, 186, 234
semsveinar 34, 53 f., 78, 92, 96, 173, 237
Semsveinum *See* semsveinar
Senja 126
shamanism 6, 22, 43, 53, 73, 90–93, 96, 136, 152, 228, 248
shamans *See* shamanism
shapeshifting 60, 63, 74, 86, 88 f., 91, 104, 107, 118, 205, 248
shared landscapes 58, 129, 148, 195, 206, 225, 235
Shetland 166
sieidi 95, 208
Sigurðr Hranason 115, 161 f.
Sigurðr slembidjákn 114, 123
silver hoards 202, 208, 224
sinew-bound *See* boats
Skaði 64, 97, 100, 180, 183, 237
skaldic poetry 34, 63, 65–67, 100, 237
skattland 166
skiing 6, 35, 43, 45, 63 f., 67, 73, 96–98, 100, 118, 144, 183, 237, 243, 248, 251
Skjoldehamn 204, 208
skrithifinoi 35
Snæfríðr 57, 78, 82 f., 86 f., 95, 98, 114, 149, 179 f., 182, 184–187, 209 f., 231, 234, 239
Snåsa 21, 217, 237
Snorri Sturluson 55 f., 63 f., 79, 91, 143, 157, 187, 232
Social Darwinism 11 f., 30, 111, 214
social processes 49, 148 f., 249
South Saami area 9 f., 212–218, 220 f., 227, 229 f.
spirit journeys 74, 90 f., 94, 205
Sǫrla saga sterka 59, 86, 101, 192
Stiklastaðir 56, 75, 79, 89, 104
Sturlaugs saga starfsama 59, 85, 98, 240
Svási 57, 82 f., 86, 113, 158, 179, 185 f., 235
Sverrir Sigurðarson 122, 159, 229
Sverris saga 55, 122, 159, 169, 229
Svǫlðr 100, 191, 229
Sweden 6, 8 f., 27, 29 f., 38–40, 56, 58, 71, 84, 93, 105, 108, 121, 124, 128, 140–142, 144–149, 153, 166, 168, 175, 181, 200, 213 f., 218 f., 224–226, 228 f., 237, 243, 245
symbolism 224

sýslumenn 134, 154f., 157, 159f., 163, 165, 170f., 176

Tacitus 35f., 112
Tälje-stadgan decree 142, 147, 228
taxation 33, 44, 55f., 69f., 72, 128, 133, 138, 142, 148f., 151, 155, 161, 163–167, 175f.
Terfinnas *See* Tyrfifinnar
Tjaetsiolmai *See* Þjazi
Þjazi 64, 183
Toftemo *See* Dovre
Tønseberg 240
toponyms 229f., 245
Þorgerðr Hǫlgabrúðr 101
Þórir hundr 56, 75, 78f., 102, 104, 122, 135, 156f., 161, 168, 171, 190, 204, 207
Þorkell Þurrafrost 236
Þórólfr 51, 133, 140f., 154, 156f., 169, 190
trade *See* finnkaup
Þrándheimr 155
Þrøndalǫg 43, 56, 77, 114, 130, 160, 227, 229, 236f., 241
troll 51, 60, 84, 89, 106, 113, 234, 242
Troms 34, 112, 123, 129, 132, 149, 171, 202f., 215
Tromsø 11, 16, 18, 28, 46, 101, 108, 112, 123, 126, 132, 172, 199, 203, 230

Trøndelag 34, 56, 60, 97, 214f., 231, 234, 236, 245f.
Truth and Reconciliation Commission 17
trygðamál 43, 97
Turku 145, 212
Tyrfifinnar 137

Upplǫnd 119, 121, 129, 149f., 187, 195, 227, 230, 234f., 238, 239, 241, 245, *See* Oppland

Värmland 39, 100, 229, 243, 245
Vatnsdœla saga 46, 50, 52, 54, 77, 78, 92, 96, 112, 173f., 194
Vermalandi 100, 243
vietjere 221, 223
Vivallen 218f.
Vǫlundarkviða 63, 66, 104

weather magic 6, 39, 50, 56, 60, 63, 73f., 81f., 88, 90, 94, 96, 98–100, 118, 143, 205, 236, 248
winter 6, 38f., 73, 96–99, 102, 107, 117f., 153f., 191, 233–235, 243, 248
wolves 59

Ynglinga saga 55, 64, 85, 88, 91, 98, 144, 147, 180

www.ingramcontent.com/pod-product-compliance
Lightning Source LLC
Chambersburg PA
CBHW060351190426
43201CB00044B/1986